POLICING CHINESE POLITICS

D1572354

ASIA-PACIFIC   Culture, Politics, Society

SERIES EDITORS: REY CHOW, H. D. HAROOTUNIAN,

AND MASAO MIYOSHI

POLICING

A HISTORY

CHINESE

MICHAEL DUTTON

POLITICS

DUKE UNIVERSITY PRESS   DURHAM & LONDON   2005

Printed in the United States of America on acid-free paper ♾
Designed by Rebecca M. Giménez
Typeset in Quadraat by Tseng Information Systems, Inc.
Library of Congress Cataloging-in-Publication Data
appear on the last page of this book.

Duke University Press gratefully acknowledges the support
of the Australian Academy of the Humanities, which provided
funds toward the production of this book.

CONTENTS

PREFACE

I
N UNDERTAKING RESEARCH, one should never underestimate the power or import of serendipitous moments, and this book lends testimony to that fact. Back in 1993, I sat at my desk in Beijing University trying to figure out how to begin this book. The words did not come easily. More out of frustration than inspiration, my eyes and mind wandered. Moving from the wall to the floor, they finally fixed upon a computer mouse pad that a former student and friend, David Bray, had given me. Called the "Mao Pad," its surface was covered with famous sayings of the late Chairman. One saying, in particular, stood out. For reasons that I could not have known at the time, the phrase "who are our enemies and who are our friends?" lodged in my mind. And, while this mouse pad incident happened over ten years ago, it precipitated a slow transformation of this project. From a linear, narrative history revealing the origins of socialist policing in China, it eventually became an empirical work that, hopefully, also speaks to us about the nature of commitment politics and the passions that drive it. If the Mao pad incident provided the theoretical impetus for this work, it was the Ministry of Public Security that provided the empirical content.

By the mid-nineties, its research units had begun work on an official history of socialist policing in China and, to facilitate this, its Police Studies Association ordered each provincial Public Security Bureau research branch to collect historical materials. They gathered up old records, regulations, and stories of communist policing and social control. They conducted interviews with old comrades, collected diaries and notes, and also asked any surviving participants to write their reminiscences. In the end, a library of material would be produced and this came to form the empirical backbone both for their study and for mine.

In using the socialist police as my tour guide, I learned much about the

Chinese revolution but, more than anything, as the empirical detail around this story of revolutionary policing grew, so too did the import of the friend/enemy dyad and my appreciation of it. What I began to uncover, I believed, was an unconscious political dynamic that helped propel that revolutionary history forward. Despite this initial inkling, it was only after I began to seriously read and engage with the much maligned and neglected German political theorist Carl Schmitt that I began to realize the full import of Mao's friend/enemy divide. Schmitt, in fact, defined politics as being this division. Thus, with this binary increasingly taking center stage in my own work, I began to realize that I was writing a history of Chinese policing that, at the very least, put the political back on center stage. In summary, I found myself rewriting the police tale as a history of the policing of Chinese politics. This, in turn, required even greater attention to detail and further theoretical investigation on my part.

The need for greater empirical detail now stemmed from Schmitt's observation that politics was something that could only be revealed in the concrete. To appreciate the political required an even greater emphasis on the empirical, and this, in turn, demanded even more research and an extensive rewriting and realignment of earlier drafts. This proved a massive task and would simply not have been possible but for the outstanding research capabilities of my assistant, Ms. Shaorong Baggio. Prodded by her insistent attention to detail and her sometimes brutal critiques of my flights of fancy, yet another version of this book began to emerge. As this new, detailed account of revolutionary policing emerged, I experienced little difficulty in differentiating this work not only from earlier drafts but also from my earlier published work on the subject of policing and punishment.

Nevertheless, a theoretical kinship remained and, if I were asked to pinpoint it, I would say it relates to an ongoing interest in the government of the collective subject. Indeed, one might go so far as to suggest that this current work supplements my former understanding of revolutionary governmentality. This form of governmentality stands in stark contrast to neoliberal forms and emanates from what I have called in this text commitment politics.

Regimes that are founded on commitment politics require more than the disciplining of the body; they require its passionate involvement. Disciplinary technologies certainly emerge and play an important role in this tale, but they do so either to tame that passion or to harness it. Indeed, in the case of Mao's revolution, these technologies are deployed to keep passion alive and in the service of the revolution. They would do this through recourse to the technology of the political campaign. In this respect, the cold, hard calculating disciplinary machine of Foucault proves itself as an adjunct rather than an enemy of the passionate embrace of revolution. It is this technology, more than anything, that enabled the revolution of Mao to transform and condense this friend/enemy relation into the raison d'être of state. To show this in sufficient detail to enable these claims to have legs not only took many years of research and thought but left me with a trail of intellectual debts that are, by now, too lengthy to detail in full.

This book speaks much of the ability of commitment to forge a community. In the writing of this book, my commitment to the project drew sustenance from an array of communities and friends, some of whom are in China, some in Australia, some in the United States, and some in Europe. These relationships took years to develop, and some only indirectly feed into this book. Nevertheless, all played a role in some way or another. How could I have maneuvered my way around Shanghai and Beijing without the help of my *gemen*, Zhou Tao and Zhao Fengshan? How would I have moved from the confines of the household register and seen the broader issues of policing had it not been for the help of Zhang Qingwu? If Zhou Tao and Zhao Fengshan made my life in China easier, Zhang Qingwu facilitated my study of policing by hosting me at the Public Security University when it was hard to get in as a foreigner. Later, he would tell me of his own experiences and introduced me to people such as the former Deputy Minister of Public Security, Yu Lei. Yu Lei, whom I had long thought to be the most able and intellectual of the deputy ministers, is also to be thanked for his time and interest. For similar reasons, I wish to thank one of the other famed members of the Chinese police force, Wang Zhongfang. As Luo Ruiqing's political secretary, he could fill in details about the history of the force that the arid and edited books of police history did not cover. Yet meeting him was, like my meeting with Yu Lei, not a chance encounter. I formed part of a community, and friends within that community made it possible. To meet Wang Zhongfang, my friends Sun Xiaoli, then with the Ministry of Justice, and Ma Weigang, of the Ministry of Public Security, hosted dinners. Those meetings, however, make for but a very minor reason for thanking Xiaoli and Weigang.

Ma Weigang honors me with his friendship. Gifted and charming, Weigang has prodded me for years to finish this work and along the way offered enormous help and encouragement. Sun Xiaoli also gave help, guidance, advice, and friendship. Sun Xiaoli was one of a unique and exciting group of young scholars who came out of the China Political Science and Law University in the eighties and went on to prominence in various law-related fields or ministries. It includes one of the new stars of China's legal academy, Professor Xu Zhangrun of Qinghua University, and also another close friend, Li Tianfu. To Zhangrun, with whom I have laughed and fought, and from whom I have learned so much, I want to once again offer thanks. When it comes to setting me straight on the grittier side of Chinese policing, however, it is to Li Tianfu that I owe a special debt. Tianfu was a researcher on this project in its very early days; he introduced me to the crucial debates within policing and to important bodies of literature. He also introduced me to other police experts and to additional facets of everyday Chinese life. I experienced life in a work unit largely through the kindness of his family. Through his family, I also came to hear snippets of history from his father, who was with Mao in Yan'an, and from his mother, who had once been in the Social Section. I came to know some of Tianfu's closest friends in the police. Indeed, his close friend Wang Zhimin, currently a police commissioner, is now also my close friend. Again, I could not mention Zhimin's name without recording a debt. Here is a person of enormous talent without whom much of this work would not have been possible. Somewhere along the way, and largely through the good graces of these friends, I met Professors Guo Xiang of the Juvenile Justice Institute, Dai Yisheng, the former head of research at the Ministry of Public Security, Fang Chongyi and Shao Mingzhen of the Political Science and Law University, and Yang Shiguang, a former senior bureaucrat within the Ministry of Justice. These older cadres and intellectuals told me of their own revolutionary experiences, introduced me to the Red Guard groups in the legal arena, told me of the role of the Soviets in China, helped explain inner Party intrigues, or simply aided me in overcoming difficulties while in China.

Professors Guo and Dai, in particular, I saw much of. Again, through them, as I seem to recall, I was linked back to a group of largely Australian educators, legal scholars, and criminologists interested in China and who had become their friends. Through these Chinese friends, I met the organizational genius Sandy Cook. For many years, Sandy became the linchpin of a group consisting at various times of me, Bob Semmons, Li Tianfu, Dan Curren, Xu Zhangrun, Sarah Biddulph, and Wang Weiping. We organized countless exchanges through Guo Xiang's institute and, for many years, scraped up enough money to produce enough contacts to enable some life-long friendships to be built. Friendships, not conferences, are what matter in such cross-cultural exchanges. Conferences often mask the cultural con-fusions that go on just below the surface. I know this intimately because at just about every conference Sandy and I helped organize, I would translate and help Sandy try to hose down some problem or other that had emerged in the course of events. Our original group has long since splintered into dif-ferent fields of interest, but I benefited from my membership of it and from the broadening of my knowledge of criminology and law. At that time, I had a group of students interested in aspects of policing and, very roughly de-scribed, it could be said to include Elaine Jeffreys, David Bray, David Martin, Adam Driver, Kaz Ross, and, of course, Sarah Biddulph. We may have fought at times, but where would I have been without them? They were there when I needed to figure out various conundrums or offered valuable criticism when it really was needed.

Special thanks should also go to Børge Bakken and Harry Harootunian in this regard. Both have supported me intellectually in a way that I deeply appreciate. I appreciate it because I know, in both cases, that their support was based on a rigorous assessment and genuine appreciation of what I was trying to do in my work. Others have read or heard part of this work and provided insightful commentary. Pitman Potter, Murray Scot Tanner, Sue Travaskis, Bob Weiss, Wes Pue, Harald Bøckman, Jing Wang, and Alf Luedke are some of these people. Then there are the people whose patience I have tested and who still stuck by me. Pip McGuiness and, later, Marigold Acland stand out. My thanks go to the many anonymous readers who with diligence and care offered some fantastic comments and advice. To Reynolds Smith of Duke University Press I offer special thanks. He recognized the under-lying implications of this work, saw it as important, and made sure that it remained a book that spoke to wider issues. Pam Morrison, who came to my rescue with copy editing, also deserves special mention.

In a much less tangible but no less intellectually profound way I can say that this book would definitely not have taken the form it has had it not been for my coeditors on the journal *Postcolonial Studies*. What could I have done without Sanjay Seth and Leela Gandhi? This debt to them extends to the rest of that "family"—Raju, Vanita, Pauline, Michele, Amanda, Jane, and also Jeannette. It is a debt that goes beyond the journal and out to the broader community that is the Institute of Postcolonial Studies. It includes its director, Phillip Darby, members such as John Cash, and sometime members such as Don Miller. It also includes some very old and close friends such as Rob McQueen, who is an encyclopedia on law and legal theory, and an old supervisor, Nick Knight, who doubles as my guru on Mao and Mao Zedong Thought. Other than Nick, this, then, is my community here in Melbourne. It would be an incomplete list, however, without mentioning people like Valentina and David from the band or, most important of all, Deborah and Tavan. Of Deborah and Tavan what is there that I can adequately say? More than any other people on this list, they are the ones who have had to live with my many moods, tantrums, and anxieties. Deborah bore the brunt of this and then read through the countless "final drafts" during these "ten years of chaos."

Another person I must mention is Professor Hu Guotai. As a graduate student I learned much from Hu Guotai and benefited enormously from the help he gave me with my earlier book on policing and punishment in China. I also knew from writing that earlier book that when it came to late dynastic and Republican China he was, intellectually, far better equipped and more accomplished than I could ever hope to be. If I were to write an overall history of policing in China I knew of no one better to collaborate with. It was in this way that this project began with two authors. As I proceeded to research the revolutionary component of this story, however, a large body of new material began to appear from within China itself.

The emergence of a huge body of previously unavailable material did complicate and make unworkable our original plan. Too much empirical source material became available on communist policing to allow us to both do justice to this revolutionary tale yet maintain the vast historic sweep. Instead, a far more limited tale of communist policing would be undertaken and, while Professor Hu Guotai and I would therefore go our separate ways, his contribution to my overall intellectual development will always be remembered and a debt to him remains.

Institutionally, I owe a significant debt to the University of Melbourne and to the Australian Research Council. Both have invested considerable money and faith in me. I hope they regard the fruits of their investment as worthy. They are, however, not the only supporters of my research. The Nordic Institute of Asian Studies (NIAS) in Copenhagen and the Max Planck-Institut in Göttingen, where I spent time writing or rehearsing parts of this work, are especially to be thanked in this regard. Parts of the last chapter of this book have also been previously published. *Social Justice* (27, no. 2, 2000) and Børge Bakken's *Punishment and Policing in China* both carried an earlier, shorter version of the argument and this has enabled me to respond to critics and commentary more broadly.

Nor should I forget those other communities of support, such as the one in London that centers on Babaji, Vivienne, and Pal, or the one in New York within NYU Asian studies, or the one forming in Boston around Jing Wang, or even the one in Hong Kong around Wing-Shing Tang. Despite the fact that the community of the heart is here in Melbourne, all these other interlocking communities matter to me. They are the groups that have made it possible for me to write this book. I want to thank them all.

Finally, I want to say just a few words about the documents used in this volume. While most of the materials used in this study are and remain classified, some remain so highly classified as to be unmentionable. In relation to the unmentionable material, I have designed the term *confidential material*. Readers will simply have to take their own leap of faith about the veracity of this material, for I simply cannot in good faith name these documents. In relation to the naming of this material, I have to think of my own future as well as balance academic responsibility and a responsibility to Chinese friends and colleagues who supplied it. If there is one ethic I hope I can always hold to, it is that friends and colleagues should always come first.

Introduction

A THEORETICAL EXPLANATION

A man in life's grip was obviously dealing
with questions of philosophy as if he were in
a stranglehold. —GEORGE BATAILLE

Map 1. The People's Republic of China

Friend and Enemy: The Bookends of a Revolution

I F YOU WANT to understand the concept of the political, turn to the first line of the first page of the first volume of Mao Zedong's *Selected Works*. There, one finds an article originally written in 1926,[1] that expresses in the form of a question to our (revolutionary) selves the quintessence of politics: "Who are our enemies, who are our friends? That is the question germane to the revolution." This is, of course, more than a question; it names a divide that assumes and leads toward a way of understanding. As the Chinese revolution demonstrates, it also leads to a way of living. Living turns on action and, in making revolution, one's actions are caught firmly in life's grip. The intensity of revolutionary action forces life into a simple binary choice of friend and enemy and imprints that choice upon the mind such that it becomes the only question worth asking. Under these conditions, philosophical questions become a stranglehold because every decision borders upon questions that are, quite literally, matters of life and death. For nigh on fifty years this deadly division between friend and enemy framed revolutionary politics and life in socialist China. This division would take a variety of names (class struggle, contradictions, etc.) and forms (psychic, social, governmental) but it would always remain the central question of the Chinese revolutionary movement. Time and again it would be posed and, in each new situation, propel political action forward, often to the point of excess. It would also come to be, for revolutionary China at least, the final question posed by those who wished to push the revolution to its extreme. It would take fifty years for the question to exhaust itself, but exhaust itself it did.

On June 18, 1976, half way through an important meeting of police chiefs, the most senior remaining radical within the Chinese Public Security Ministry, Vice-Minister Shi Yizhi, called a secret caucus meeting of the radical Left. Gathered together in room 355 of the Qianmen Hotel at 7:50 p.m., this small group of radical followers of the Gang of Four set to work organizing a list of agenda items that needed to be adopted by the meeting of police chiefs scheduled for the following day. Item one on the radicals' agenda was the posing of this now familiar question: who are our enemies and who are our friends? That question, however, would, within months, be turned on them. By October, it was the radicals answering questions, not posing them. Arrested as counter-revolutionaries, they were the last great "enemy within" of a Communist Party that was showing less and less commitment to a politics of binary options. After the demise of the radicals, politics was no longer painted in binary colors but took on a very different and more complex hue.

If the posing of this question of friend and enemy back in 1926 can be said to have given birth to the revolution, then by 1976 we can think of this same question as the revolution's epitaph. Like bookmarks between the pages of Chinese history, these two dates demarcate the chapter conventionally marked out as *revolutionary* in Chinese history. In its revolutionary phase, the nation operated almost entirely on the basis of this binary divide. It was a divide that carved out a revolutionary path and paved that path with endless empirical exemplifications and permutations of this politico-philosophic distinction. Through the figure of public security, this book traces the life cycle of this distinction in China. From its birth in 1926 through to its demise in 1976 and then onto the post-reform story of a society no longer caught in the dichotomy's deadly grip, *Policing Chinese Politics* provides more than a history of public security in China. It offers, in effect, the tale of the political told empirically through the re-telling of the concrete story of Chinese policing. It is the tale of this binary division as it develops and takes on organizational forms. It is the story of what happens when the binary of politics saturates the lifeworld to become its *doxa*—when every facet of life turns on knowing who the enemy is and acting against that figure. It is at that moment that we arrive at the point where society and life itself become fused in politics. It was the friction of this divide that generated the necessary heat to enable such a fusion. The commitment and passion this binary produced enabled the revolution not just to glow but to burn. Life lived only through this binary is always lived in the shadow of excess—revolutionary excess. To police this revolution was to patrol that ever shifting thin red line that separated revolutionary friend from reactionary enemy. Security forces patroled the borderland of excess and, as we shall see, sometimes crossed over that line. This work, therefore, offers an empirical reflection upon a politico-philosophical dilemma. If philosophically, this tale begins with Mao in 1926, empirically, it begins one year later in Shanghai when an act of betrayal by an erstwhile friend decimated the Communist Party. With this act of betrayal the story of revolutionary policing in China begins.

Baptisms of Death

For Chinese communists in 1927, it must have seemed as though the clouds of doom would never lift. In Shanghai, "between April 12 and 15, in just three short days, there were over three hundred communists and revolutionaries killed, over five hundred communists and their supporters locked up in prison and over five thousand people who suddenly disappeared without trace" (Wang Jianhua 1993, 16–17). That was only the beginning of the troubles. In Guangdong province, a similar purge of communists was about to begin. On April 15, the legendary Huangpu Military Academy was closed, two hundred revolutionary organizations banned and two thousand workers and revolutionary youths arrested (Gong'an jianshi). On the sixteenth, purges of communists started throughout Jiangsu province, Zhejiang province and Jiangxi province. A day later, Guangxi and Sichuan provinces followed suit. Nor was it simply the Nationalist Party that had turned on the communists; the northern warlord, Zhang Zuolin, started his own killing spree in Beijing on April 28, his most prominent victim being China's first Marxist and cofounder of the Communist Party, Li Dazhao. Nor was rural China immune from this slaughter. News began to filter back to Party headquarters that twenty thousand pro-Party peasants had been killed in Hunan province alone (Gong'an jianshi). All around, from all quarters, the news was grim as Jiang Jieshi's (Chiang Kai-shek) slogan "better to kill one thousand innocents by mistake than miss one communist" brought forth its bitter harvest in human carnage. These events precipitated the rise of communist policing but for Chinese and Western scholars alike, they did not constitute the main script line of this unfolding story.

Events such as the ones described above caused consternation in the ranks of the Communist Party and Western accounts have traded on this to tell stories of mass betrayal, factionalism, rivalry and endless, unremitting failure.[2] In Communist Party histories of public security, however, these same events provide the platform for an entirely different narrative strategy. Chronicling failure and defeat in no less detail than Western works, they nevertheless employ these events as the wet nurse of organizational rebirth rather than as undertaker. Far from being signposts of despair, or signaling a "loss of innocence," the events depicted function as a technical device to both begin the history of Chinese communist policing and, having done that, unify its organizational development around a pedagogy of struggle.

Dai Wendian's text is emblematic. Early struggles with the Nationalists, Dai suggests, brought forth the first birth pangs of the Chinese communist policing system. "It was not until after the anti-revolutionary, anti-Party coup of 12 May, 1927," he writes, "that the Party came to realize that a specialized type of protection work was essential. Thus, in December 1927, while the Party in Shanghai was in the midst of the white terror, it created its first protection unit—the Central Committee special branch (*zhongyang teke*)" (Dai Wendian 1991b, 93). Leaving aside for the moment, the slight historical inaccuracy of Dai's account,[3] what his book and all the other histories of public security in China rely upon to give birth to their narrative subject and carry it through to victory in 1949, is this association between struggle and invention.[4]

Maoism has long relied upon this connection. Indeed, it was Mao who told us to view setbacks and mistakes as "teachers" (Mao Zedong 1969, 4:422). The written histories of the public security organs in China faithfully reproduce this spirit of the late Chairman, telling tales that evince many history lessons. More than anything, they teach a methodology of struggle through the endless citing of example. Through struggle, as Ci Jiwei puts it, the Party cadre learns to love and hate in equal proportion (Ci Jiwei 1994, 84). "Love the Party and their security forces, hate the enemy and its agents."[5] This, for Ci, was the simple equation that would become the political methodology of revolution. Well, not quite. There can be no "equal proportion" in this revolutionary equation for, as Mao's question makes clear, the enemy always comes first. The preeminence of the enemy in this equation figures not by chance but precisely because "the enemy is our own question as a figure" (Meier 1998, 44).[6] Enemies, therefore, take precedence for they are what define us. Just as a legal trial has meaning only as a result of a breach in the law, or criminal law begins not with a deed but with a criminal misdeed, so too are we defined by our opposite (Meier 1998, 41, 52 n.73, 39).

The preeminence of the enemy in this unequal treaty not only helps explain the reification of class struggle but also the stress placed upon unity, discipline and indebtedness within the camp of the friend. At the same time, we must also recognize that the emphasis upon the enemy also leads to the possibility of deadly excess. To combat an enemy we may be driven to war and it is in this power to drive us to the point of death that the political becomes intense and infectious.

Chinese texts tend to brush aside excess in their depictions of "the struggle" but in highlighting the question of the revolutionary martyr, they return to it in another way. In suggesting that the blood of martyrs is never spilled in vain, these narratives point toward an inevitable economy of retribution within which the only sensible course of revolutionary action leads to a struggle with the enemy ending in death. As in bad detective novels, there is little need to turn to the last page to find out why. One knows where this story line leads: "Fight, fail, fight again, fail again, fight again . . . till there is victory; that is the logic of the people" (Mao Zedong 1969, 4:428), and each and every published text on the history of public security in China seems to reinforce this particular way of seeing and doing.

There is, therefore, a certain rhythm to these Chinese histories of socialist policing that ties these texts to a revolutionary methodology and movement. Through such texts, revolutionary histories are connected to contemporary practices. From these texts, contemporary police are able to attach their own sense of self and self worth to a series of exemplary past events, people and practices. In this respect, contemporary police histories are the *jiapu*, or lineage records, of Party policing and, like these records of old, they come to operate as exemplary ancestors from which contemporary police can learn. The contemporary so-called preventative strategies of the Chinese police, after all, turn on the constant citing of past examples. The cyclical rhythm of "model" police campaigns play on the same rhythm as past Maoist campaigns; stories of exemplary neighbourhood security committees and police stations are collected into handbooks and distributed to other committees and stations for emulation; references to outstanding figures whose practices are to be studied and followed occur constantly. Such, then, is the nature of the narrative chain built up within Chinese policing texts and designed to produce a certain esprit de corp within the force (Bakken 2000).[7] For Chinese police, reading their history becomes part of their training for such texts are essentially "self-referential."[8] They establish links that enable the contemporary Chinese police to appreciate and identify with their own organization's history, thus reducing the gap between contemporary policing in the reform era and policing practices in the Maoist one. The binary nature of this lineage produces a transhistoric identity effect quite unlike equivalent Western narratives of policing. What makes such Chinese historical works so unique is not that they privilege the role of security forces—the Chinese would not be the first police force to have commissioned their own histories essentially for the "glory of the force"—but that they privilege it in a particular way that highlights the political. While Western accounts of the history of their own police forces generally trace the lineage back to community responses to crime or to State attempts to rule, the Chinese begin their historical narrative adventures discussing organizations that essentially do one thing: defend the Communist Party by policing the line between friend and enemy. These accounts tell the story of a police force prior to the invention of the state, and without any community commitment other than the imagined community of the Communist Party.

In effect, these histories tie reader and organization into a larger historical movement. Chinese police cadres, in reading such texts, begin to recognize their organization as a vital part of the revolutionary vanguard. For this policing community, such texts work to produce an historical imagination that "claims kin" with both Party and "people" but not with government and law. Historically, their key task as an organization was not to police the divide between crime and its opposite, but between political loyalty and betrayal. It is this legacy that continues to be remembered and reinvented through the contemporary Party-based police histories. And for this reason all such accounts begin in Shanghai. Here, in 1927, and in the act of betrayal of a former friend, the Communist Party developed its first organizational response to the political question posed one year earlier by Mao.

First, the Party would respond with red terror groups, then through the more professional special branch security organs. Throughout this period, they experimented with organizational forms that would eventually lead to a unique form of socialist policing in China. That the police consciously reference their organizational past back to these "glorious" events rather than telling other stories frames a way in which to appreciate and "refresh the memory" of martyrs' blood spilt and struggles victorious. In this way, contemporary police are reminded of their principle responsibilities and primary loyalties. In a time when the police are being led away from a world dominated by this friend/enemy divide and called upon to professionalize and reform, such "gentle reminders" speak to responsibilities and duties that should never be forgotten. Tracing such a memory of policing's past for me has, of course, a very different purpose. Through this type of history, rather than through the depoliticizing so-called political histories of Western Sinologists—which tend to replace politics with personality—one can at least recognize the possibility of writing political history rather than merely a history of politics. But what is this distinction I am trying to evoke here? What is this thing that I have come to call the political?

In the Name of . . . (the Political)

In raising the specter of the political I am drawn, in the first instance, to Hannah Arendt who writes of politics as something that speaks to the very heart of the human condition. For her, action is political activity par excellence but it is always action shared with others (Arendt 1958, 9, 198). Moreover, it is action based upon a recognition of plurality, which is the condition of all political life (Arendt, 1958, 7). Action that can and does make a distinction between life, instrumental control, and freedom, is, then, the condition of the political (McGowan, 1998, 47). It is in striving for freedom, plurality, and individual identity that one becomes engaged in politics. Other categories such as life and instrumental action, may, sometimes, be drawn into political discourse but not without considerable cost. No revolution, says Arendt, has ever solved the "social question" and each attempt to do so through politics has only led to anguish. Essentially, for Arendt, when the political oversteps itself, when it raises questions not of freedom but of compassion, it starts to raise the specter of terror (McGowan, 1998, 49). "Where do your greatest dangers lie?" Nietzsche once asked himself. "In compassion" was his response (Adorno and Horkheimer, 1979, 119). The danger, then, is that when politics moves beyond the question of freedom and onto compassion, it goes beyond that which sets its limits.

For me, however, it is only when "the political" oversteps the mark in this way and "colonizes" other domains, that one comes to see clearly the types of intensities that would drive one to act beyond oneself in the name of a cause. That is to say, it is only at those moments of intensity that one comes to see the political clearly. At this point, freedom is one clarion call of politics, but only one of them. Politics, in this regard, goes well beyond the singular. Indeed, I would argue that politics is not about freedom per se, but about the production of a particular set of desires and intense feelings based upon the commitment to a cause. To speak "in the name of" something suspends one's own egocentric desires but, simultaneously, leads one to cast aside one's own moral bearings for the pursuit of a greater good. To fight "in the name of . . . (the political)" is to produce and release a series of non-agonal intensities. These are not necessarily reducible to a striving for freedom but they do entail commitments to action that sometimes speak in freedom's name. Only by rephrasing Arendt in this way do we come to capture something of the human condition that is political. And while this may only constitute a minor linguistic modification, it proves a significant theoretical one.

If it is not freedom but commitment that drives one to political action, then the actions undertaken in freedom's name can vary. Hence, a striving for commitment entails recognition of the fact that one strives for a multitude of freedoms (freedom from economic want, from chaos, from oppression) and while this leads one many miles from Arendt's position, it has the virtue of highlighting the centrality of passion and intensity in any political expression. It is this passion that drives one to make distinctions, not between life, instrumentalism or freedom, but, more basically, between friend and enemy. This, of course, brings us back to the political, not in Arendt's name, but in the name of a darker figure, Hitler's onetime "crown jurist," Carl Schmitt. It is in his rendition of the political as a binary distinction between friend and enemy that we come to recognize not only the frictions that produce the intensities (passions?) of politics but also the grounded, theoretical power of Mao. It is, therefore, with this rather bizarre theoretical shift from one German to another that I am led back to the empirical and back to China. It is Mao's opening remark and its effect upon the unfolding history of socialist policing as a history of the policing of the political that is of interest to me.

Yet one must never forget Arendt. In pointing to politics as action, as a striving for something, Arendt enables us to recognize that within the political, commitment is central. In this respect, and almost despite herself,

Arendt helps us focus upon something that is absent from Schmitt. She allows us to recognize — even though she herself does not recognize this because she, too, is enthralled by her own commitments (to freedom) — that any political action is a form of striving based not on innate, animal behavior but on the basis of some sense of (moral) commitment. It is this type of commitment, be it deemed for good or bad, that sets us apart as human. Human, oh, too human! Such is the lesson learned from this Chinese passion play of policing.

This book is not about to explore these issues in any theoretical depth as it is, essentially, an empirical work. Surprisingly, however, in its very empiricism, this work speaks to just about every facet of this theoretical problem. It speaks about it, depending upon one's predilection, in either exquisite or tedious detail. It describes endlessly the commitments and passions fueled by this friend/enemy distinction. It goes through each of the major Chinese political campaigns and speaks of them as though they were factories producing the passion and commitment that would lead to revolutionary action and, sometimes, to excess. It tells of a social life in which friend and enemy moved from being a state of mind to a state of nation. This political history of socialist policing is, therefore, political in a double sense. It is, first and foremost, a history of one political institution, the Chinese public security force. It tells the force's story, some of which has never been publicly revealed before, in great empirical detail, so that one can walk away from this book with some understanding of the historic forces that have shaped and propelled that organization. It is, therefore, at a manifest level, a political tale told historically. Yet it is also political in a more latent sense. In writing a political history, I have almost entirely focused upon expressions of, responses to, attempts to place limits upon, and techniques to promote — indeed I discuss almost every conceivable aspect of — this friend/enemy dichotomy. Ultimately, and through the police, I want to go further. I want to show how the Chinese reform-era state has successfully eaten away at the marrow of these old-style political commitments, and, through this, learn something of the way it has tamed, if perhaps only temporarily, the beast that is politics.

This history is not only the first (non-Chinese) history of public security, but quite possibly the first decidedly empirical exploration of that theoretical rendition of the political offered by Schmitt. That is to say, it employs a concept of the political that gives primacy to the friend/enemy distinction. It is, in part, the story of how China came to live the friend/enemy binary through the Communist Party. By 1978, the Communist Party developed an altogether different trajectory. It had devised a way to tame and turn the beast that Mao's words and Schmitt's theory would feed. This is not to suggest that the beast has died, but surely its temporary docility in a land where the political once reigned utterly supreme should be of interest to those political theorists who have long struggled to explain the Schmittian riddle of how to overcome the friend/enemy divide? Economic reform, therefore, shows the way. So while this book will speak only intermittently of Schmitt and only occasionally remit a theoretical remark, it is, from beginning to end, organized around this theme and, ultimately, interested in this question.

Rather than concerning itself with momentary political explosions or expressions of a return to the political in the post-Mao era (June 4, 1989, the struggle against Falun Gong, etc.) the latter part of this work is more interested in describing how economic reform has tamed politics. In the final chapter of this book, therefore, I trace the fate of the friend/enemy binary as it falls from view. Once again, I offer an empirical tale that shows the repression of the binary of politics by pointing to the de-politicization of the various devices, organs, and expressions of friend/enemy generation. In particular, I will look at the spread and transformative power of this political urge within the police—and by implication within society generally. In this sense, it is a book pivoted by political theory into a concrete tale of socialist policing. This has meant breaking with a Sinological writing tradition that would claim to offer a full account (of the police). *Policing Chinese Politics* provides a much more selective tale organized to excavate that empirical nugget of gold, the political, and to trace its fate. I do this through the police who are, however, more than bit players in its promotion to center stage. They are the political actors around whom this tale is woven. Their fate is the fate of the political. I am interested, and only interested, in this aspect of their being. What groups they chase and how they do this has import only in this regard. When actions fall outside of this, I may cover them only in a perfunctory manner. As a result, this work may appear narrow, but without such a tight focus, I cannot shine a spotlight upon the political.

It is for this reason that, in framing this history, I have not followed the conventional Chinese accounts and begun this tale in 1927 when the first security organ of the Party was formed. In focusing upon this binary relationship of politics, I am principally interested in how it operates when its proponents transform it into a mentality of government. Hence, the first three chapters of this book are concerned with the government of the binary in the base camps and, after 1949, across the entire country. Historically, it is a tale that begins in the remote Jiangxi Soviet region, moves with the Long March to the distant northwest (around the city of Yan'an), and then finally arrives, along with the Red Army, in Beijing and the founding of the People's Republic. If this is the concrete historical account of the revolution that is being told, the story one can read between these lines is somewhat different. In this other register, it is a story in which Jiangxi illustrates the dangers of an unalloyed use of the simple and violent rendition of the friend/enemy distinction; it is a tale in which Yan'an tells a story of governmental moderation and finally it is an account of how, after the establishment of the People's Republic, the binary of politics is turned into the touchstone of a new form of revolutionary governmentality.

In this account, Jiangxi is our starting point; the Jiangxi Soviet becomes the site of an obsession with the "enemy within." At a time when the liberated zones in Jiangxi were surrounded and under attack from the Nationalist army of Chiang Kai-shek (Jiang Jieshi), the Party's paranoid security forces began a massive purge designed to eliminate this invisible enemy. Haunted by the specter of an enemy within, the communists, quite literally, began to devour their own. What becomes truly revealing when one examines the concrete unfolding of the suppression of this enemy across the disparate and isolated communist base camps, is just how similar the dynamics were in all areas. Disparate events I discuss later in the book—such as the Futian Incident in the Central Soviet, the war against social democracy in the Minxi base camp, the waves of repression in Xiang-E'xi, and the White Sparrow Garden Incident in E-Yu-Wan—foreground the way in which this theme of terror is simply too widespread to be laid at the feet of any one person or any single Party leadership group. Moreover, the base camps were so isolated and the campaign so ferocious that it would be inconceivable to reduce these events to mere factional struggles. What becomes clear is that in each of these camps, killings were fuelled by a profound sense of betrayal that built upon a very real sense of imminent death due to the enemy's proximity. As suspects were brought in for interrogation, the security forces were filled with a sense that the answers they extracted could save the Party and the base camps from extermination. With so much at stake, they resorted to torture. Torture, in turn, brought on more confessions, leading to further arrests and more torture. As these events snowballed into a full-scale disaster, the Party imagination would become scarred forever.

In many ways, the tale of policing and politics that follows provides little more than an outline of the various attempts by the Party to continue to promote and harness the intensity of commitment that flowed from the political binary while simultaneously putting in place mechanisms to ensure that the excesses produced by that dyadic structure became a thing of the past. Certainly, that is the way I have read the various efforts at reform visited upon the security forces and the Party during their time in Yan'an. The Yan'an spirit, as it became known, was one in which reforms were visited upon the Party and its security forces under the direction of the newly emerging Party leader, Mao Zedong. It was at this time that he would designate Party committees and the mass-line[9] as the two pillars upon which the Party in general and socialist policing in particular should be built. It was at this time also that he devised a less violent form of campaigning that he and the Party thought would bring forth ideological unity rather than physical violence and excess. This style of campaigning would be called rectification and it would come to define this era. Indeed, one could say that with rectification, Mao brought forth a transformation in the way political power functioned within the Communist Party. While I have not developed this in the body of the book, it is an appreciation of this point that undergirds my understanding. Let me explain.

Binary political forms are little more than a variant upon the either/or question of sovereign power. They are forms in which one must decide to either obey or risk death. The suppression campaign of the Jiangxi Soviet era had posed the revolutionary question in just this way. Yan'an, however, was different. Here, a new form of power, which Michel Foucault has famously labeled disciplinary, began to prevail. Unlike the either/or question of sovereign power, disciplinary power operated as a subtle means of remolding the population so that they could be reeducated and redeployed for useful ends. While the either/or question of sovereign power would always remain as the ultimate test of revolutionary virtue, it was now increasingly accompanied by, and the dangers of the enemy it faced understood through, a disciplinary campaign. Rectification become the Trojan horse of this newly fused form of power. It was one of the key techniques by which the communists attempted to discipline and rechannel the excesses of passion generated by binary, sovereign forms of political power. Thus, while standard accounts of the Yan'an era either laud it as the *dao* (or way) of revolution or, more recently, revisionist accounts speak of its darker side, I have another tale to tell. That "other" tale renders Yan'an as the site of the first explicit attempt to develop this new form of power. It was a form of power that attempted to both discipline the Party and limit the excesses caused by political intensity without racheting down the class-based conflict emanating from the sovereign and political-based friend/enemy distinction. While rectification proved a key technique in this process it was not the only one. No less important was the redefinition of the enemy.

In the Yan'an era, the principal contradiction, as Mao came to call it, was neither the "enemy within" nor the Nationalists. Instead, the principle contradiction existed between the Japanese invader and the Chinese people. By externalizing the enemy, Mao hoped to both limit internal purging and, at the same time, consolidate internal unity. Herein lay the power and importance of Mao's text "On Contradiction," for it offered a variegated notion of contradictions that enabled the national question to take precedence without one's revolutionary commitment being queried. In this respect, Yan'an not only offered a radical model of socialist transformation but also came to offer an example of revolutionary moderation. It was this latter tradition that would eventually lead Mao, in the late fifties, to differentiate between antagonistic and non-antagonistic contradictions and attempt to insert into the friend/enemy dyad the ternary element of an adversary. It was this same question of how to control the excesses of the binary that would lead the Party, in the sixties with the Shanghai Commune and again in the seventies with a notion of an "all-round dictatorship of the proletariat," into new conceptions of the state.

In other words, this question of how to tame and harness the political distinction was to haunt the communists long after their victory. As we follow the Party through its revolution and on to government in the third chapter, we come to see just how much this question played upon the communists as they established the People's Republic. Indeed, I argue in chapter 3 that virtually the entire edifice of state, and all its institutions and its whole structure, were either consequences of or ways of addressing this struggle between friend and enemy. Faced with huge numbers of counter-revolutionaries and a vast array of social problems in the immediate aftermath of revolution, is it any wonder that friend and enemy would come to be the prism through which the Chinese Communist Party would see the world? Because of the centrality of this simple notion, the Chinese revolutionary state developed an array of institutions and ways of thinking that proved to be quite distinct. In this respect, it was not practice alone that carved its name on the Party and police. What becomes absolutely apparent as this history unfolds is that for both the Party and its security forces, good and bad could not be read outside of a politics of friend and enemy. Moreover, the organizational structures the Party built to promote this particular type of dyadic politics would, quite deliberately, end up producing intensities of their own. During this period, virtually every significant problem in China became the basis of a new political campaign predicated on finding a new version of the enemy.

Campaigns sutured into considerations of daily life the friend/enemy distinction. This fusion radicalized the populace and offered a prelude to the types of politics to come. I deal with this radicalization of politics in chapter 4. Here, the Great Leap Forward and the Cultural Revolution are rendered as concrete examples of a renewal and extension of the political intensities and passions unleashed by the friend/enemy distinction. With radicalization, the Party was no longer concerned with finding a way to limit the intensity of the political. Now, both Party and Mao had an interest in rekindling and harnessing political intensity. If Yan'an and the early days of the Peoples' Republic had been haunted by past excess and as a consequence, largely concerned with the question of limit, the radical period that followed was different. State formation and a central plan necessitated a certain degree of bureaucratization and, over time, this raised the specter of complacency, backsliding, and ultimately, revisionism. As revolutionary zeal gave way to normative bureaucratic behavior, moderating excess became less of a problem than keeping the revolutionary spirit alive. To address this question, two almost opposite tendencies emerged.

On the one hand, there would no longer be theoretical or even practical restraints placed upon outbursts of populist political intensity. Instead, one political campaign would follow another in a formulation Mao would come to call continuous revolution. In effect, disciplinary campaigns were being used repeatedly to pose the sovereign question of "us or them." Yet when this extreme populism moderated, it gave birth to an unusually reconciliatory sovereign form that took the name "mass dictatorship." This more moderate tendency gained concrete expression in the tiny town of Fengqiao where mass democracy became synonymous with the ideas of self-policing and local self-government. While Fengqiao attempted to correct error through reintegrative shaming rather than the elimination of the enemy, the continuous revolution that swirled around it ended up pushing the political question in a more radical direction. Fengqiao quickly fell victim to this trend and as this partial but moderate model fell into disfavor, a new more radicalized and comprehensive form of mass democracy grew in its place. Known as the Shanghai Commune, this too would last but a short while. Nevertheless, between the moderation of Fengqiao and the radicalism of Shanghai, one can recognize a shared concern. Both offered a window onto the various attempts, moderate and radical, from within binary politics to devise a new type of politics and a new rendition of state power. By the time of the Shanghai Commune, however, the hopes of mass democracy had all but collapsed into the chaos of Cultural Revolution. In effect, the anarchistic promise of the commune became little more than the chaos of state as the entire civil apparatus of government was struggled against. In this climate not even the security forces that had run all past revolutionary campaigns could feel safe.

Seventeen years of betrayal was how the new and radical Minister of Public Security described past police actions during the Cultural Revolution. Accused of doing the bidding of the "black hands" in the Party, the security forces would become one of the new "enemies" invented in the course of the Cultural Revolution. Their transformation from friend into enemy led to virtually all police being attacked and nearly every official in the Ministry of Public Security being banished to the far north. As the military took over the responsibilities of the Ministry of Public Security, rectification appeared to have given way to revanchism. The result was that the friend/enemy distinction reached new heights of intensity. In the Party's determination to stoke the fires of revolution and keep alive their radical plans, new enemies were constantly being invented. Yet as flames began to lick at the heels of erstwhile comrades, the problem of the radicals' strategy became clear: their almost total concentration on enemies, coupled with a growing weariness of the mobilized, led to increasingly authoritarian and narrow renditions of dictatorship. Culminating in 1975 in the idea of an all-round dictatorship, this radical period of rule would eventually kill off any remaining radicalism among the populace. Weary of endless campaigning, the people became lethargic and it was only with the birth of economic reform that they once again became active. Activism in this period of economic reform, however, was of a very different order from that of the past. For the police, this new era of reform brought forth a major shift in their role and attitude. It is this that is explored in the final chapter of this book.

Where deployment of the single binary of friend and enemy had demanded a constant mobilization against so-called enemies, economic reform transformed the single political question of friend and enemy into a multitude of discrete and largely non- or even de-politicizing questions. Despite such new plurality, what slowly came to undergird all these disparate questions of the reform era was the single issue of profit and loss. The new consumer ethos that grew in this era required a new form of policing that was not political in the same way as it had been in the past. Economic development, it was argued, required stability and it was the task of the police to ensure this. Policing stability, not the revolutionary line, became the new order of the day. Unfortunately, many of the economic reform policies exacerbated social tensions, producing a situation that was anything but stable. Faced with this crisis, the police had little choice other than to rely upon their old politicized mass-line support structures. Unfortunately for the police, the logic of profit promoted in the reform era effectively robbed mass-line policing of its raison d'être. Mass-line organs were a product of the era of political intensity. They had been generated out of political campaigns and were designed to harness political passion for revolutionary ends. In the era of reform, money increasingly replaced political capital. The police responded to this debilitating problem by attempting reform and professionalization wherever possible. Hence, new forms of policing strategies and techniques drawn from foreign countries were slowly introduced. With neither the money, the structure, nor the will to have a root-and-branch reform, however, this policy would always have its limits. On the whole, police were still ideologically committed to a limited and de-politicized version of the Maoist mass-line policing model. More than anything, however, they were tied to the mass-line even more firmly by the sheer pragmatic necessity of maintaining their mass-line support structures at a time when their support was desperately needed to carry out the daily mundane work of social control.

The diminutive size of the police force, coupled with the urgency of dealing with immediate problems, more or less forced the maintenance of the mass-line. Yet these mass-line structures had, within just a few short years of the economic reform program being introduced, begun to fade. To revive them the police would be forced to do something, but with politics no longer inspirational, the problem was always going to be, what? In the end, economic reform offered its own unique answer. With productive performance now the criteria and financial reward the means to achieve it, the police and their mass-line were simply put on financial contracts. Yet this modification of the mass-line pointed to the end of the Maoist mass-line in all but name. Effectively, it signaled a transition out of an era of political distinction and into one of economic distinctions.

So it was that the friend/enemy binary, which had completely dominated Party thinking from 1927 onward, began to fade after 1978 as other distinctions emerged. For policing work, this change in dominant forms of distinction resulted in a major re-focus. The political notion of friend and enemy gave way to a social dynamic based on profit and loss. In terms of policing, this resulted in a diminution of political crimes and greater attention to economic ones. Thus, while political distinctions never fully disappeared, from the perspective of police strategies and structures, they became much less important than they had been in the past. Indeed, a clear sign of the demise of the political lay in the fact that the police themselves were forced into using financial contracts to halt the decline of their own, once politicized, mass-line structures. Therefore, rather than continue to tell the tale of policing in relation to the ever-declining realm of the political, the focus of my final chapter shifts, along with the principle social dynamic, toward an analysis of the demise of this political distinction. To have continued with the political tale of policing in the era of economic reform would have led to an account of public security focusing on the suppression of the democracy wall movement in 1979, then moving on to the Tian'anmen Square massacre in 1989, and finally reaching the contemporary moment by examining events such as the suppression of Falun Gong. To continue in this way would have made for a popular but ultimately misleading account of the dynamics of policing and Chinese society in general. It is not the students of Tian'anmen Square or the practitioners of Falun Gong who hold responsibility for the transformation of contemporary police structures and social thinking; it is the money-based economy.

What these political suppressions do point to, however, is the limited nature of this transition out of politics in the reform era. To fully appreciate where these limits come from and how they operate, requires not an event-based account of political suppression in the contemporary era but a careful examination of the political history of socialist policing. From this, one begins to realize that the contemporary Chinese police are still weighed down by a history that is utterly political. From organizational structures through to mental strictures, the history of the force as a Party organ has placed limits upon any transition induced by the dynamics of economic reform. The changes taking place within policing work off an inherited structural and mental base that still relies on the mass-line and still partially thinks in terms of friends and enemies. Yet it is also true that the old Maoist political way of doing things has diminished significantly in the reform era. To understand the dynamics underpinning this diminution of the political distinction means traveling a very different road to those Western accounts that offer political critiques of current events and, therefore, (unconsciously) read the political distinction as still paramount. Instead, I want to highlight not so much the concrete actions of the security forces as they repress rival political movements, but the structural changes to the police organization as the security forces move away from being an organ enforcing political commitment to something that is beginning to resemble a police force. Just as the mass-line has been reborn as a contractual arrangement, so, too, the friend/enemy dichotomy is being slowly turned into a series of economic and legal distinctions. These distinctions have all had structural consequences for the police force. It is these consequences brought on by a crucial transition away from the political that an event-based description of major political actions would occlude. In the longer term, it is this transition and the structural consequences it brings in its wake that will help determine the nature of policing and politics in China. Just how revolutionary this transition is, can be gleaned from this history of struggle, and it is with this idea of political struggle that I want to begin. And what better place to start than in Jiangxi!

1 Friends and Enemies

THE WAR WITHIN

TIMELINE 1921–1934

Date	Politics	Police
1921	**July:** Chinese Communist Party (CCP) established in Shanghai	
1924	First United Front formed between the Nationalist Party (Guomindang) and the CCP	
1925	**May:** Industrial action led by CCP activists results in workers' strikes and pickets; culminates in the "May 30 Incident," in which the Guomindang clashes with the CCP	Secret picket teams (later called dog-beater brigades) organized by the CCP to deal with scabs and traitors during their industrial action
1926		Gu Shunzhang sent to USSR to study methods of the Soviet secret police (GPU)
1927	**April:** First United Front ends; Guomindang massacres communists **May:** CCP HQ forced to flee to Wuhan **August 1:** CCP organize Nanchang uprising **August 7:** Party HQ moves back to Shanghai **September–November:** CCP organizes Autumn Harvest Rising	**August:** Revolutionary Committee Political Protection Section formed within the revolutionary army **September:** Rural base camps establish Chinese *Cheka* (Committees for the Elimination of Counter-Revolutionaries) **November:** Central Committee special branch (*teke*) established

Date	Politics	Police
1930	**January:** Wang Ming made party leader **October–December:** Guomindang first military encirclement campaign of rural communist base camps	In first half year, Ganxinan base camp starts anti-A-B League campaign; it reaches its peak in the second half of the year **December:** Futian Incident
1931	**April–May:** Guomindang second encirclement campaign **July–September:** Guomindang third encirclement campaign **November:** Central Soviet government established by CCP; Party power grows in rural regions	**January:** Anti-Social Democrat Party Campaign begins in Minxi base camp Elimination of Reformist Faction Campaign in Xiang-E'xi base camps Anti-A-B League and Reformist Faction Campaign in E-Yu-Wan base camp **April 24:** Gu Shunzhang arrested **November:** Soviet State Political Protection Bureau formed
1933	**February–March:** Guomindang fourth encirclement campaign **May:** Guomindang fifth encirclement campaign starts; it ends in October 1934	**Spring:** Temporary Central Party Political Bureau moves from Shanghai to Soviet base camp capital, Ruijin; special branch's role changes, mostly concerned with military intelligence
1934	**October 10:** Long March begins; base camps evacuated; end of Jiangxi Soviet period	

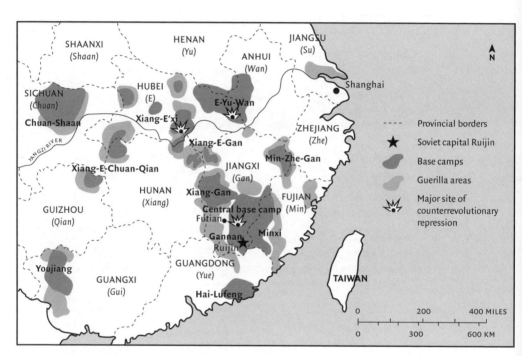

Map 2. Communist Base Camps: The Jiangxi period, 1928–31

I T WAS SHANGHAI, at the beginning of the 1920s, that saw the birth of the Communist Party. And it was the Shanghai massacre, at the end of the twenties, that almost signed its death warrant. But this chapter offers no obituary. Instead, it deals with birth; the birth of the political. The "political" would lead to the rebirth of the Communist Party as a rural force in China, and to the birth of Chinese socialist policing as little other than the policing of the political.

All of this would flow from what the Comintern in Moscow would insist was a moment of "clarification" for the Chinese Communist Party (CCP). At a very general and empirical level, what was clarified was that which was already known. The Nationalists' massacre of communists in Shanghai provided a bloody clarification of the reactionary class nature of the communists' erstwhile ally. The once powerful United Front they had formed together to bring about the unification of China would end in 1927, not with victory, but with the spilling of communist blood. For the Nationalist Party, the Shanghai massacre was meant to be a coup de grâce. Through this one blow, the Nationalists hoped to rid China of the scourge of communism. They almost succeeded. After the massacre, only a very small leadership group would remain underground within the divided city of Shanghai. While this leadership remained hidden within the city, the majority of Communist Party members were forced to flee to the isolated rural hinterland. In Shanghai, the leadership was constantly under threat, and only the strictest security measures would ensure its survival. It was under these conditions that the Party first turned its mind to security and protection. It was at this time that the first Chinese communist security organ, the teke, or special branch, came into being — and this is where histories of socialist policing in China all begin. This is not, however, my starting point. Instead, along with the remnants of the CCP fleeing Shanghai and trying to rebuild their lives in the remote Soviet base camps of Jiangxi, I want to begin in a place where the policing of socialism meant more than the protection of the leadership group.

For a Party of the proletariat, removal to the remote rural border regions of Jiangxi must have felt like banishment. Its members desperately desired a return to the cities, but their strategies of return would all end in failure. In the end, there was but one way to survive, namely, to "rustify" their own class questions. Class questions for the Chinese communists, therefore, would become little more than questions of peasants and property. Class struggle would obtain an almost single-minded concentration upon land and the landlord-gentry problem. That narrowing of perspective not only focused the mind of the communists but also provided the platform for their future political revival. It did not look that way at the time.

Even in the inhospitable, remote sanctuaries to which they fled, the communists never found complete safety. Surrounded by and under siege from Nationalist armies, they lived under the constant threat of death. Far from making them hide their politics, however, such pressure made them live it to the full. If anything, this constant threat of death would lead the Party to push the logic of class struggle to extremes. Only class struggle could save the Party, for only class struggle could liberate the peasant masses materially and spiritually and, only then, would they join with the Party and "make revolution." To survive, therefore, involved fighting on two fronts. On the porous borders of the small Soviet base camps, the communists' newly formed Red Army would fight the ever larger troop concentrations that Jiang Jieshi's (Chiang Kai-shek) Nationalist government would throw at them. On the home front, within the base camps, they would begin a land revolution against landlords and gentry in order to garner peasant support. The wealth and property generated by these attacks on the class enemies of the revolution would be redistributed to the newly liberated poor peasant "friends" of the CCP. The poor peasants would, therefore, gain a material investment in the revolution and become its backbone and foot soldiers. It was for this reason that peasants joined the Red Army, swelling its numbers and stabilizing the battlefront. For nigh on seven years, the Red Army successfully repelled the far superior Nationalist armies and, through its many victories, would demoralize the enemy and recruit a great many of its troops.

Paradoxically, it was this type of success that would also point to the reasons for its ultimate failure.

The possibility of infiltration made for an ever-present fear brought back to the base camps by each Nationalist defection. This fear had a name, betrayal, and one of its constant "forms" was the defecting Nationalist soldier. When such fears of betrayal became wed to a populist exuberance released in the course of an ongoing, violent, and intense class struggle, a potent combination was released into the base camps, one that would fuel the ebullience of revolution, but would also transform each betrayal into a reason for zealous expressions of excess. In relying upon exuberance, commitment politics, by definition, go beyond the pragmatic and the rational. In order to attract hearts and minds, such politics of commitment employs a language and logic that speaks to both but which, in fact, provide only a means by which the pragmatic begins to fade into the poetic.

For the Communist Party, the war and the land revolution were but two facets of a single question. This was the question Mao had posed back in 1926, the question of friend and enemy. When posing this question empirically, reason appears to prevail and to limit any possibility of excess. After all, whether on the battlefront or in the expropriation of rich peasant land, the question of the enemy could always be "objectively" addressed. On the battlefield, one could objectively determine enemy soldiers by their uniform, just as one could objectively identify rich peasants by their property holdings. One's attitude toward the war and toward property relations were, therefore, by extension, the defining questions of the revolution. They would, therefore, become the twin poles around which political commitment was to be judged. Yet when judgments have to be made about attitude, consciousness, or commitment, things become different. Here, no uniform or landholding marks out the enemy. These questions, therefore, can never be addressed objectively, for they all concern internal, subjective thoughts. While the battlefield defines the uniformed soldier and land the propertied class, what existential marker defines attitude and commitment? Under these subjective circumstances, one looks instead for telltale signs of difference. But what stops difference from being read as deviation? What stops deviation, then, from being read as betrayal? In a political climate like Jiangxi, in which, in fact, betrayal was sometimes expressed in telltale signs of difference, the answer was clearly "nothing."

Like a semiotic Midas, everything the Communist Party touched seemed to be transformed into a sign of an "enemy within." The examples are legion: Whistling or hitting bamboo on rocks would connote secret communications with the enemy; brotherhood and sisterhood societies were deemed fronts for counter-revolutionary superstitious organizations; and morally suspect or even apolitical research organs, such as the love research unit or the food-tasting association, were interpreted as examples of reactionary conspiracies (Outline of Public Security 1997, 53; Gao Hua 2000, 43). In such a climate, what chance did the defecting Nationalist army soldier have? What place was left for pragmatism? In this way and with unerring regularity, advantages became transformed into suspicions, and suspicions into paranoia. On this unsteady ground, the basis of survival also laid the grounds for excess. Once purges began, they built upon their own momentum. Through torture and forced confession, others became drawn into the folds of this question of the enemy. Before too long, a climate of fear and paranoid suspicion prevailed.

The Party's best-trained military tacticians would suffer because of this situation. Trained alongside senior Nationalist army officers in the days of the United Front, key military figures of the CCP increasingly fell under clouds of suspicion, and, as a consequence, military tactics were transformed into moments of political tension and signs of betrayal. Every action, every word, every person now fell subject to the same unremitting question—who is an enemy? Beyond the battlefield, it was this question that would begin to define life just as it would determine death. If the battlefield produced a military version of the question, it was the land revolution that produced one for the peasant and the Party.

Violent and extreme, the land revolution became both a motor of excess and a litmus test of loyalty. Few leaders within the Communist Party dared oppose its excess, though few would fail to note its deleterious effects. The silence of Party leaders was as deafening as it was understandable. Like military tacticians, they had become tainted by association and could easily fall victim to charges of treachery should they oppose the land revolution. Quite apart from past associations with the nationalists, most CCP leaders themselves hailed from "impure" class backgrounds. They were therefore open to the charge of defending their own class interests should they call for moderation. Yet even those who, because of class background, were in a position to fight extremism and excess were forced to remain silent. Poor local peasants, for example, would be left "speechless" by the fact that few were entirely able to extricate themselves from the accusation that intimate and finely woven kinship, lineage, and friendship relations tied them back to a class enemy. In a time when the air itself seemed divided and the possibilities of betrayal palpable, both leaders and the led were left with little room to maneuver. An extreme stance was but an extreme indication of one's commitment to the Party. It proved that nothing would override class commitment.

As questions of commitment took center stage, the Chinese communists' world became dominated by signs and symbols of reactionary politics. Under these circumstances, political passions become intense. That was what happened in the communist base camps of Jiangxi in the 1930s, and that is why this time and place constitutes a paradigmatic example of the power of the political divide separating friend from enemy. Jiangxi became the concrete empirical articulation of that theoretical divide and, as such, it may serve as the perfect site to scrutinize the effects of a pure, unmediated friend/enemy dyad upon a program of political action. Jiangxi offers a moment by which to illustrate the effects of the spread of this political dyad across a social landscape. Working on political intensities, the Communist Party was propelled forward but also propelled into excess. Here in Jiangxi, passions were not just harnessed; they were also made electric, and signs of betrayal formed the key alchemic ingredient that transformed intensity into excessive political action. The revolution was, quite literally, being defined by its enemy. While the battlefield established the geographic contours of this early socialist state's domain, it was the ideas of an enemy within that defined the nature of the revolution taking place within the boundaries of each camp. It is for this reason that the focus of this chapter is on the campaign to purge counter-revolutionaries from communist ranks.

Most accounts of this period, indeed most accounts of Chinese political history, tell this tale of the political differently. They narrate the story of communism in disarray. They speak of excess, but principally in terms of localism, factional disputation, and personal bids for power (Zheng Xuejia 1976). Such an approach reminds us of the complexity of politics at a concrete, empirical level but, in tying everything back to reason and utility, these kinds of studies fail to adequately register the enormous power and perverse effects of political intensities. Without an appreciation of the power of passion, excess is read as an immoral move designed to secure advantage within some localized power play. I would argue the reverse of this position: passionate or intense political actions are not immoral, but exemplify the moral in action. Violent excessive political acts are invariably built upon a deep sense of commitment. The willingness of a collectivity to go beyond its social moral code and become excessive, violent, and extreme constitutes, in fact, an empirical sign of the depth of their commitment to the higher moral calling of the Communist Party. It is this higher moral calling that enables them to go beyond ordinary morality, and, in so doing, to go beyond themselves. It is the same code that leads one to kill without hate in the name of God, queen, or country and still live with oneself in good faith. That is to say, it leads one to kill without the opprobrium or psychological weight that the charge of murder would bring. It is, in other words, the most extreme moment of politics, for it is the most extreme example of one's willingness to kill without (individual or personal) hate and live without guilt. To read these struggles as mere personal power struggles, therefore, elides this particular power of the political, a power that turns precisely upon that unique ability politics has to lead one to go beyond oneself. To speak only of the pragmatic downgrades manifestations of this political dyad to mere backdrops or smoke screens disguising the *real* (realpolitik) nature of struggle. While never denying the fact of leadership contests or personal investments and pathologies in the play of politics, it is to this larger existential question of the political that I will turn.

In Jiangxi, it was the concept of class struggle that would become the vehicle through which this abstract political question of friend and enemy was transformed into a series of specific, empirical, and existential targets and, through these, was made electric. For Chinese communists then, Mao's political question was never theoretical. It was a visceral, existential, and lived question of intensity. The communists therefore responded to it from the heart, not from the mind. It was a passion imported from Shanghai and from the spilling of communist blood in an act of betrayal. But if betrayal in Shanghai filled the communists' hearts with hatred, it was the concrete fear of internal betrayal in Jiangxi that established the existential targets. To appreciate why particular targets that became the points of intensity in Jiangxi were chosen, however, requires a brief detour via the Soviet Union.

From Russia with Love: The Campaign to Eliminate Counter-Revolutionaries

In the late twenties, a series of political revelations about an enemy within would rock the Soviet Union. Reactionary Shakhtyite wreckers,[1] Kulak hoarders, and right-wing deviationists from within the Soviet Communist Party all played a part in the production of a political intensity that would quickly lead to excess. These anthropomorphic categories became the new enemies for whom the expression *class war* meant physical extermination (Medvedev 1971, 71–109). Of all these reactionary acts, it was the issue of political betrayal that would focus and harden the hearts of Russian communists most and, simultaneously, make them single-minded in their determination to exterminate their enemy within. This extremist position would soon find voice in other communist parties.

Four times the Comintern would write to their Chinese comrades stressing the need for them to combat such "right deviations" (*Outline of Public Security* 1997, 45). Ultimately, in four different sites of excess (the Ganxinan, Minxi, Xiang-E'xi, and E-Yu-Wan base camps), their Chinese comrades would take up this clarion call. So it came to pass that in the isolated backwaters of rural China, where the Communist Party clung to power in tiny base camps by a thread, equivalents to Russian class enemies became the occasion and the obsession around which they, too, would launch themselves into excess.

Under the rubric of a "Campaign to Eliminate Counter-Revolutionaries" (*sufan*), grain-hoarding Kulaks found worthy equivalents in landlord and gentry resistance to the Chinese communists' land revolution, while Shakhtyite wreckers and Soviet Party deviationists dovetailed into the intense concerns the Communist Party felt about internal betrayal. At exactly the same time as the leadership in the Soviet Union was declaring class war, shooting Shakhtyite wreckers, eliminating an entire class of people (the Kulaks), and uncovering obscure counter-revolutionary groups within their own ranks, the Chinese communists, in their own diminutive way, instituted a Soviet-style elimination campaign of their own. Built on a foundation of forced confessions, the brick and mortar of a collective paranoia about an enemy within became the occasion for the first communist political policing campaign and—the first example of collective party excess. As the sufan campaign blurred into a Party purge, the major threat to internal security was increasingly perceived to come not from visible and objective class enemies such as bandits, the gentry, landlords, or merchants, but from those who stood in their shadows. Moreover, as this fear of these shadowy figures grew, it appeared as though these figures stood behind every act of sabotage. Despite the extreme factionalism within party ranks at this time, all seemed to have shared the view that just about every calamity that befell their Party and base camp was the result of, or was coordinated by, that most dangerous of enemies, the enemy within (Zhang Xibo and Han Yanlong 1987, 1:316). This translated into a paranoia about organized penetration of the Communist Party and, because of this, the violence would focus upon Party members and the covert organizations that recruited and organized them into counter-revolutionary activities.

That Party cadres were at the core of concerns seems beyond doubt. As one veteran Red Army soldier who was in the Xiang-E'xi base camp at the time of the purges would later recall: "We soldiers would look around and ask who was really being targeted as (enemies) here? And we all came to the same conclusion. It was the Party cadres. Naturally, we began to think, 'who would want to be an official, who'd want to join the Party, it was simply too dangerous'" (PSHM 1987, V3, 124). It was the Party's fears of annihilation at the hands of the treacherous that would arouse the most intense of political passions and lead to the greatest examples of excess. Under such conditions, torture became commonplace and, through the use of torture, came the revelation that the treacherous cadres did not act alone. The "discovery" of a range of counter-revolutionary organizations directing the espionage activities of traitors only deepened the anxiety and made the purging process even more intense. Attention would come to be directed principally at three organizations.[2] These were the A-B League, the Social Democratic Party, and the Nationalists' so-called Reformist Faction. Of these, the A-B League clearly emerged as the most significant.

The league had originally been established as an instrument of the left Nationalist Party faction led by Wang Jinwei. Formed in Wuhan at the end of 1926, it had initially been called the A-B League Reformist Faction and was often referred to as the Nationalist Party Reformist Faction. It was under this name that it would be pursued in the base camps of Xiang-E'xi and E-Yu-Wan.[3] After a series of splits, however, former league members became the backbone elements in a series of other organizations. Many of the more liberal league members grew disillusioned with the authoritarianism of Jiang Jieshi's Nationalist Party and established a third party influenced by European social democratic ideals. Hence this organization became known as the Social Democratic Party. This party became the target of major communist repression in the Minxi base camp. Meanwhile, league members who supported Jiang Jieshi formed another organization that became known as Jiang Jieshi's A-B League or the Nanjing A-B League. Even Communist Party splinter groups were known as A-B Leagues. When Trotsky's expulsion from the Soviet Communist Party and Chen Duxiu's dismissal from the Chinese one precipitated a split within the CCP, those who left the Communist Party to join the Trotskyite group were all known within Communist Party circles as A-B Elimination League members. With so many different uses of these letters, little wonder that this organization appeared an omnipotent threat.[4] All such threats, however, proved little more than a fictive effect of employing torture to extract confessions from suspects and then acting on the admission.

The Nationalist Party Reformist Faction and the Social Democrats, in fact, did not even exist when the elimination campaign began. As for the A-B League, it is quite clear that by the time of the communist elimination campaign, it no longer posed any serious threat to any of the base camps (Huang Jinlin 1988, 74–78; PSHM 1990:2, VI6, 93). These organizations, in other words, were mostly ghosts and phantoms haunting a terrified Communist Party. Indeed, it was precisely because this fear of an internal enemy was largely a fear of the unknown that feelings about them would grow so intense. The dynamic of the internal elimination campaign, therefore, followed a script line straight out of a children's storybook—monsters that one could never clearly or fully see frightened the most.

Surrounded by a formidable enemy army and cut off and isolated in a rugged, inhospitable region, the Party launched a vigorous campaign against an internal enemy it feared but could never actually see. While this fear was not entirely without justification,[5] it would quickly take on all the hallmarks of a dangerous obsession. Indeed, even the Nationalist army's military encirclement did little to dampen this need to purge. Despite the immanence of military defeat at the hands of a far superior army, the Chinese communists continued to believe that their greatest threat came from the enemy within. Indeed, just as Jiang Jieshi would later speak of the communists as a disease of the heart, while the Japanese invaders were a disease of the skin, so, too, the communists would think of their enemy within as being at the heart of their problems. It was the veteran revolutionary Fang Zhimin who pointed out that the fear of internal betrayal overrode all other considerations, including those of war preparation.[6] Such an excessive position was clearly not pragmatic, but it did have roots in what could be called revolutionary pragmatism. Such pragmatism would always flirt with excess, for it was based upon attempts to seduce, and then channel, political intensity into revolutionary commitment. In other words, the intense political power that propelled the purges also produced the passion that would drive the revolution.

Without such forms of political intensity, there could be no revolution. The rebirth of the Communist Party in rural areas after 1927 was entirely based upon the Party's ability to produce, and then harness, peasant political intensity. Without such political intensity, there would be no peasant activism and no mass base by which to regenerate the CCP. It was, therefore, quite central to the success of the Party that it generated intensity around its political program. The land revolution the communists instituted did precisely that. Poor local peasants were encouraged to take the lead in what Lenin once famously called "expropriating from the expropriators" (Lenin 1965, 27:246, 307). Backed by the Party, local peasants seized landlord and gentry property, which was then redistributed. This redistribution ensured that the peasants had a material stake in the revolution, as well as a newfound sense of their own collective power. The collective sense of empowerment would then be organized by the Party to promote, consolidate, and extend its revolutionary rule.

The violent and excessive nature of the land revolution, however, did more than liberate land and fill peasants with a sense of their own power. It also ruptured the traditional bonds of loyalty that tethered peasants to a conservative rural value system. Once destroyed, the Party could promote a proletarian morality under which the collective power of the peasants would be channeled into a myriad of mass-line organizations that could then be used to colonize the everyday lifeworld of the rural base camps. Communist Youth League branches, sections of the Women's Federation, and even Children's Corps were all formed at this time, and together they would weave an intricate and intimate network of control that would cover each and every village (Wang Qiuxia 1994, 59). These mass organs then extended the question of revolutionary morality beyond the issue of land and economy and into those domains where proletarian morality was found wanting. Moreover, this spread of the political into the peasant lifeworld ensured that the revolution in Jiangxi did not constitute a revolution from above.

Through such mass-based practices, the Party recruited its cadre force, which was therefore increasingly peasant-based. The populist inclinations of the Party seemed to join with certain pragmatic considerations to push the communists in this direction, even in relation to the sensitive issue of security. Here, the Party would call upon its organizations to tether their practices as closely as possible to the rural masses. Document after document repeated the same line: "The masses, at a glance, know who is local and who is not and therefore [the security forces should] base their work on their local knowledge and come to grips with the main tendencies among the despotic gentry, landlords, rich peasants, and capitalist groups within any area" (PSHM 1990:2, v16, 66). As the Campaign to Eliminate Counter-Revolutionaries extended and deepened, the populist enthusiasm of the peasant masses would be harnessed even more directly. By December 1932, the government of the Central Soviet was already arguing for the "utilization of mass power to strictly supervise the activities of all local tyrants, evil gentry families, and rich peasants" (qtd. in Wang Qiuxia 1994, 60). In base camps as remote as the Chuan-Shaan (Sichuan and Shaanxi) camp, that task was already being incorporated into the civic responsibilities of every revolutionary peasant:

> Irrespective of gender or age, everyone was on the alert for the wrecking activity of the local tyrants and evil gentry in the base camps. Quite a number of women and young people formed "listening brigades" to keep an eye and ear open for the activities of the local tyrants and evil gentry. On some nights they would lie low, surrounding their homes, and listening and keeping an eye on the so-called half household—that is, those households where the father had fled but the women and children remained. (Wang Qiuxia 1994, 59)

According to Wang Qiuxia, such enthusiastic responses to the Party mobilization call became particularly evident after the land revolution. The

Party, in turn, would then use the support it generated through the land revolution to push the peasant activists into acts of "red terror." This kind of terror would envelop the base camps from 1927 onward and give birth to the "Campaign to Eliminate Counter-Revolutionaries" that ran from 1929 until the evacuation of the base camps in 1934 (Li Jinping 1993, 62).[7] Such populist peasant terror would be organized and directed by so-called Committees for the Elimination of Counter-Revolutionaries (*sufan weiyuanhui*) or, as they were known in Russian, *Cheka*.

From Chinese Cheka to the GPU

Formed in November 1927, the elimination committees would receive inordinate powers and would dispense such powers with their own form of rough populist revolutionary justice. Laws would be ignored or simply overruled, torture and forced confessions would become commonplace and, with the acquiescence of the elimination committees, all revolutionary organs, be they Party, youth league, or some other mass organization, were "given the freedom to carry out the elimination of counter-revolutionaries" (Zhang Xibo and Han Yanlong 1987, 1:316; see also Huang Jinlin 1988, 78). In this populist environment, the elimination committees became ringmasters. They were the investigators, prosecutors, judges, juries, and goalkeepers. They even organized their own armed enforcement wings using former Red Army soldiers and reformed bandits (*Summary History* 1989, 32).[8] From November 1927 onward, these armed wings—known as red protection teams—began to spring up in virtually every base camp (Wang Qiuxia 1994, 58). Augmented by local ad hoc organs such as the "worker-peasant insurrection teams,"[9] these teams and the elimination committees that ran them were responsible for some of the earliest displays of organized revolutionary violence as they spearheaded the drive to confiscate landlord and gentry property in the land revolution (PSHM 1990:2, v16, 10).[10] With these armed wings behind them, the elimination committees quickly moved beyond their role of protecting and promoting the land revolution and began to effectively silence any critic of the fledgling Chinese Soviet regime. But as their role extended, the limits of their use also became evident.

By the early 1930s, the party center and the rural Soviet government began to emphasize the temporary status of the elimination committees and the limited role they should play in policing the revolution. They were necessary, the Party noted, in the initial stages of base camp development, for they would enthuse the peasants to forge the land revolution. But even in new base camps, they should operate for no more than six months and, once a base camp had become firmly established and the land revolution was complete, they should be dissolved. While populist committees could incite the masses to attack the propertied rich, they lacked the necessary skills or structure to tackle the increasingly complex problem of a hidden enemy within. Such a task required a professional force that could tease out a hidden enemy by piecing together the true meaning of the few telltale signs of betrayal that were available. In other words, the Party now required an elite cadre force that, through training and specialist skills, would have infallible political judgment. Organizationally, it required a disciplined professional and relatively independent organ not hamstrung by legal limits or the considerations of lower-level and increasingly suspect local Party branches.

What the Party required came into being in November 1931. Called the Political Protection Bureau (*zhengzhi baoweiju*), it would be led by the trusted party veteran Deng Fa and modeled upon the tightly disciplined and independent Soviet secret police force, the GPU (Wang Qiuxia 1994, 59; Zhang Xibo and Han Yanlong 1987, 393).[11] While the bureau, like the elimination committees before it, had extraordinary powers of detention and investigation, it would operate in an almost diametrically opposite way. Where the elimination committees had relied upon mass-based populism, the bureau relied upon its elite cadre force of special agents (*tepaiyuan*).[12] Where the elimination committees had been under the control of local Party committees, the bureau's special agents enjoyed freedom from any such constraint.

Invested with the "absolute power of the center," the bureau was, in fact, only answerable to the Central Committee (interview 1997). At a local level, therefore, they were neither answerable to the local government or the army unit, nor could these local governmental and military structures use their authority to countermand or block any orders that came from the bureau (PSHM 1987, v3, 14; Huang Jinlin 1988, 78). As later documents would attest, the bureau quickly became a "super dictatorship" that ran "well in excess of the powers of both Party and Government" (CCA 1991, doc. 8, 21).[13] While the bureau therefore appears to be little more than a slavish Chinese adoption of the elitist Soviet GPU security structure, I would suggest other-

wise. Irrespective of where the organizational design came from, it was necessarily structured in this way because the nature of the local class struggle
within the base camps demanded it thus.

The new key enemy emerging in the base camps was no longer the objective, visible target. Increasingly, it was the shadowy figure of an enemy
within that appeared to stalk the Party at all levels. To root out professionalized spies required a professionalized security force. Moreover, it required
a bureau independent of all local Party allegiance, for it was to become the
inquisitor of those local Party and government bodies. With such power
came a fearsome reputation, captured admirably in an oft-used colloquial
expression from that time: "I don't fear heaven, I don't fear hell, my only
fear is being called in for a chat with a special agent" (qtd. in Huang Jinlin
1988, 77).

When Deng Fa later reflected on the errors of the bureau and the campaign, he inadvertently revealed the reason why such "chats" with a bureau
special agent evoked widespread fear. The "rhythm of prosecution" used in
political cases, he observed, went something like this: "First, you listened
to a confession, then you heard a second and began to believe it, then you
extracted a third and acted accordingly" (qtd. in Huang Jinlin 1988, 76). It
was left to another witness from that period, Zhang Pinghua, to expand on
Deng's description:[14]

> Executions . . . were all based upon confessions that were forced but
> still believed. Nobody went out to check, nobody stressed the need for
> evidence. Once they were caught, suspects were beaten into confession,
> and once the confession was forced out of them, their accounts were be-
> lieved. So you would end up with a situation where the first one rats on
> the second, the third rats on the fourth. They would tell you anything and
> incriminate anybody. They incriminated many good comrades, so many
> very good comrades were falsely accused and executed. . . . In fact, forced
> confessions at that time were the stock in trade of the workers involved
> in political protection. (qtd. in Huang Jinlin 1988, 76)[15]

What Deng and Zhang are referring to here are the deleterious effects of a
once ubiquitous interrogation technique employed by the bureau, which became known in Chinese communist circles as bi-gong-xin.[16] Time and again,
the results of this forced confession technique, bi-gong-xin, were to lead

the Party into excess: "Investigators would threaten, beat, and secretly torture spies and suspects. They would do this until those under investigation would say anything, malign anybody, including good people. The result was that those under investigation would say anything to the investigators, so their confessions were always unreliable" (qtd. in CCA 1992, doc. 14, 90). Such unreliable evidence was believed because it fed into an existing paranoid view that the enemy within was everywhere. Moreover, the struggle against this enemy was thought too important to be restrained by any legal considerations, and the intermittent attempts to rail in some of the worst excesses of the campaign had the perverse effect of actually authorizing them. When one interrogation manual from the period argued that "forced confessions should only be used as a final measure," it was, as one later commentator would accurately point out, actually giving torture "a green light" (*Gong'an Jianshi*). Given the campaigns' increasing reliance upon bi-gong-xin to both verify the political crimes of suspects and link their particular crimes into various organized conspiracies, the bureau was constantly generating new suspects out of the confessions of the old. It was in this way that the Campaign to Eliminate Counter-Revolutionaries, aimed at consolidating Party leadership and control over the base camps, actually ended up producing a collective sense of weakness. Moreover, the harder the security forces pushed to cleanse Party ranks, the more they employed bi-gong-xin, and the more they did that, the more the enemy within appeared numerically strong, unified, and well organized. Campaign-style politics as a technique offered the Party an almost magical means by which to reduce life to a series of binary oppositions, and thereby to produce enthusiasm. At the same time, it did this by magnifying the threat of and creating the environment for excess. Campaigns were, in Jiangxi at least, technologies of political excess produced out of narratives of political fiction.

Even the Party leadership would eventually and tentatively arrive at this conclusion. Speaking of the A-B League, for example, Zhou Enlai would somewhat hesitantly note that in the campaign to eliminate counter-revolution, it had become little more than "a peg [upon which] . . . to hang charges" (1981, 244). And hang them they did. Nowhere was this peg more in evidence than in the small village of Futian in the Central Soviet region. Here, in an event that would eventually become known as the Futian Incident, the first major example of excess in the base camps was recorded. Indeed, if one Taiwanese source is to be believed, the Futian Incident was the site of a massacre of almost unbelievable proportions. That source estimates that over 14,000 people may have been executed as the incident unfolded (Sima Lu 1981, 55). While exaggerated, the high death toll at Futian was one reason for the notoriety of this incident, but it was far from being the main one. The principal reason history comes to remember Futian rests on the fact that the key figure responsible for this purge was the future leader of the Communist Party, Mao Zedong. In this respect, Futian was to the Chinese revolution what Kronstadt had become to the Soviet one. Both became litmus tests of failed revolutionary virtue, both stand as signs of murderous revolutionary intent.[17]

Far from being signs of failed revolutionary virtue, however, I'd suggest these two events were signs of revolutionary virtue being tempted by moderation, yet not succumbing. With this understanding, the Futian Incident can be read as the first significant site of political excess flowing from the Party's adoption of a dyadic view of politics. Viewed in this light, Futian is not about the purity of leadership, or the evil and ruthless ways of Mao Zedong. Viewed through the politics of friend and enemy, Futian becomes a symptom of the "virtuous excess" so easily generated by binary political mappings. To shine this particular light upon Futian, however, requires more detail.

Tales of Terror I: The Central Soviet and the Futian Incident

The Futian Incident began in November or early December 1930, after a revolt by sections of the First Front Army against Mao Zedong's leadership of the Central Soviet government.[18] While the specific causes that precipitated this revolt remain something of a mystery, we do know from one veteran of the Central Soviet campaign, Zhu Kaiquan, that it began over differences within the Party and army relating to the land revolution. This, in turn, led to accusations of A-B League membership (PSHM 1990:2, V16, 190). One recent study suggests that the incident grew out of the escalating tension between the newly established but "foreign" leader of the Central Soviet base camp, Mao Zedong, and the Party and army "locals" from the Ganxinan (southwestern Jiangxi) region (Gao Hua 2000, 11). According to Gao, the radical nature of the land revolution Mao called for in the Central Soviet caused

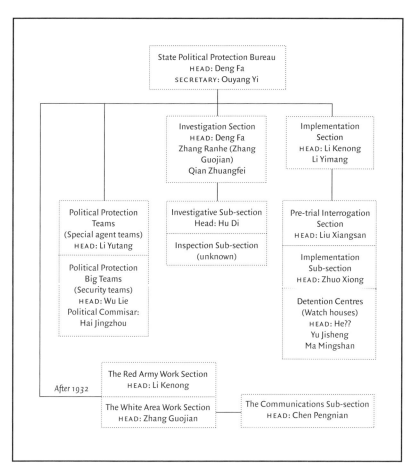

Figure 1. Key Organs and Personnel within the State Political Protection Bureau
Source: Based on materials in PSHM 1990:2, v16, 17.

disquiet among those who had relatives and kinship linkages in this area.
Where Mao wanted land confiscated from rich peasants, local officers and
cadres only wanted the land of local "tyrants and landlords" taken (Gao Hua
2000, 9). These differences of opinion would explode into a major political
dispute in February 1930, at a joint meeting of the Front Committee of the
First Red Army, the Army Committee of the Fifth and Sixth Red Armies, and
the Special Committee of Ganxi (western Jiangxi). The leaders Mao had dispatched to the area to implement his line had encountered significant local

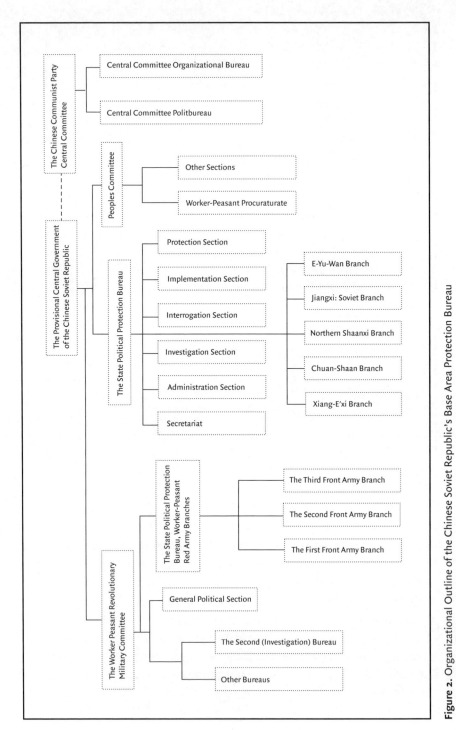

Figure 2. Organizational Outline of the Chinese Soviet Republic's Base Area Protection Bureau

Source: Based on a chart in *Activities of the Chinese Communist Party's Special Agents* 1983, 279.

resistance, and these differences of opinion quickly escalated into a major political dispute. Politicized in this way, Mao raised the stakes. He accused the locals who resisted his line of opportunism and of taking the side of the rich peasants.

Here opportunism was used as a political code for Trotskyism, and this line of argument would find expression in the "number one circular" that launched the Central Soviet's class war to eliminate landlords and rich peasants. As becomes obvious from this document, however, it also constituted the opening gambit in a second front being developed against an enemy within:

> There is a serious crisis within the Party of Ganxinan. The problem is that the landlords and rich-peasants have taken up leading positions within the Party organization at every level there. The Party's policy, therefore, has become an absolutely opportunistic one. If these elements are not eliminated immediately, not only will the Party fail to fulfill its great political tasks but the essence of the revolution itself will be lost. This joint meeting calls for revolutionary comrades to eradicate the political leadership of the opportunists, throw the landlords and rich peasants out of the Party, and Bolshevize the Party immediately. (Mao Zedong 1984, 84–85)

One key question facing the Maoist leadership which adopted this line of thinking, however, was how the claim of opportunism could be tied back into the issue of the so-called rich peasant line. Trotskyist opportunism was, in itself, an unconvincing ideological peg upon which to hang such charges since Trotsky was, theoretically, no friend of the peasants, much less the rich ones. If the linkage seemed unworkable ideologically, it proved more promising on the ground. Here, Mao would link the two through a politics of blood (Dai Xiangqing and Luo Huilan 1994, 82).

In the case of the leadership of Ganxinan, a politics based on blood was easy to argue, for the vast majority of the local leaders came from rich-peasant and landlord-class backgrounds. In establishing the link between their class background and their "opportunistic" political positions, Mao effectively read their political position as a telltale sign of their reactionary class background: "To not actively divide up the land (of the rich), to drag one's feet on the formation of political power, to fail to arm the worker peasants (Red Protection Teams), these are all the most potent signs of opportunism and a consequence of the landlord and rich peasant's ideology that wants to suppress the masses within the Party," he claimed (SHMCBC 1983, 3:646). Yet such "tell-tale signs" alone were insufficient to prove the case. Only when combined with class background did they prove to be irrefutable. Leading Party figures and followers of the "opportunistic line" were designated reactionary class members, and their class backgrounds as children of landlords or rich peasants was offered as proof that their "opportunist" stance was not based on error or poor judgment, but constituted a sign of their reactionary class thinking. They could never, therefore, be trusted, and the only truly revolutionary choice would be how to eliminate them. The Communist Party held an unequivocal stance. For the real Party of revolution, personal difficulties in policing the binary divide were becoming a test of political commitment. For the real revolutionary, there could be no "soft option" when dealing with this enemy.

It was this particular concrete rendition of the binary logic of the political that issued forth the case against so-called opportunism, and it was this same logic that would drive security organs into excess. Precisely because they were the most moral and pure, they were also the most ruthless in the defense of the revolution. No effort would be spared to keep Party ranks pure, and the use of physical torture would become commonplace. As one Party document from the time noted:

> A-B League members are all very cunning and stubborn. If you don't apply the harshest forms of corporal punishment, they simply won't confess. We must use all sorts of methods, both hard and soft when interrogating them. We must continuously apply harsh corporal punishment in our investigations. Get them to confess, discover any clues, and then, on the basis of evidence derived in this way, track down more of them. The main goal here is to force these people to confess to being A-B League members and to wipe out that organization. (SHMCBC 1983, 3:646)

Once membership in the A-B League was "proven" by forced confession, then the evidence would be used to further politicize the masses. And it was in the ritualization of their own deaths that the bodies of the A-B League members would finally be of use to the revolution. In the act of execution, the political passions of the masses were intensified as they joined in the struggle to physically eliminate the threat of contamination: "Concerning the leadership [of the A-B League], naturally they should be handled extremely harshly, but there is one thing to note here in this regard. They should be put to death by the masses at mass meetings. . . . Kill without mercy any A-B League member with a rich peasant, petty bourgeois, or hooligan background. . . . Kill without mercy workers and peasants who joined the league and attained positions of rank or are highly active" (SHMCBC 1983, 3:648–49).

With a purge of the Communist Party in Ganxinan (southern and western parts of Jiangxi) now under way, Party ranks in the region were decimated. By October, 1930, well over one thousand Party members from that region had been expelled because of their landlord or rich-peasant class background, and well over one thousand A-B League members had been exposed and executed. Indeed, something like 25 percent of all those who worked for the Soviet government in Ganxinan were accused of being A-B League members and, in the vast majority of cases, they would end up being shot (Gao Hua 2000, 16). By October 1930, disputes about the land revolution were joined by tensions within the army. Disputes over military strategy erupted in that month after Mao Zedong withdrew troops from the recently conquered town of Ji'an. Complaints from within the army, and particularly from within the ranks of the local officers and soldiers, followed, and Mao responded by ordering a rapid rectification of the army. Once again, the rectification posed the simple class question of friend and enemy and, once again, officers who had a family background in the landlord or rich peasant class became targets. Within a month, over 4,400 of them were eliminated (Mao Zedong 1984, 184). It was in the process of this army rectification that a number of local soldiers in the towns of Futian and Huangpi faced accusations of being A-B League members, and it was their arrest that precipitated the Futian Incident.[19]

Included among those accused was an influential local officer named Xie Hanchang, head of the political section of the Twentieth Red Army. Under torture, he and other soldiers confessed to a range of crimes that actually widened the circle of suspicion. Of particular concern was the fact that these confessions had resulted in a number of leading members of the Jiangxi Provincial Implementation Committee and a number of senior army officials falling under a cloud of suspicion. Not only was the problem now moving beyond the confines of the Ganxinan region to cover the whole base area but it was also increasing the degree of political intensity being generated. The enemy, it seemed, was far more organized and integrated into the Party than had at first been suspected. Forced confessions "revealed" that senior Party and army leaders had secretly formed a branch of the A-B League within the Central Soviet base camp and were using that to promote and coordinate their counter-revolutionary activities. As revelations grew, fear turned to paranoia.

By December 7, Mao Zedong was convinced that "opportunists" dominated significant sections of the Party and the Red Army, and he dispatched the security official Li Shaojiu and a company of troops to Ganxinan to "help" the Jiangxi Provincial Action Committee further their investigations. In penning the letter that authorized Li's elimination work, Mao would write that at each level of the county and region one would find rich peasants, hoodlums, and wavering elements who should, for the most part, be executed. It was, however, his final remarks that proved most chilling: "Whichever region doesn't arrest or execute, then it is clear that the Party and government of that area must all be A-B League" (Dai Xiangqing and Luo Huilan 1994, 98).

In such a poisoned atmosphere, it did not take Li long to act. Almost immediately upon his arrival in the area, the killings began. By December 12, more than 120 people had been arrested, and 50 of these were immediately executed. What concerned the Party leadership most was not the number of executions taking place, but the fact that some of those arrested as A-B League members held important Red Army and Soviet government posts. Four of the arrested, in particular, caused considerable concern. Apart from the aforementioned Xie Hanchang, the other three key figures named were the Provincial Implementation Committee member Duan Liangbi and two senior government officials, Li Baifang and Jin Wanbang (PSHM 1990:2, v16, 99; PSHM 1987, v3, 43–44).

Li Shaojiu felt so concerned about the power that this group could wield locally that he decided to carry out further investigations in a more secure setting. Taking Xie Hanchang with him under guard, Li retreated to the headquarters of the "loyal" section of the Twentieth Red Army in nearby Donggu. There, Li continued his investigations, which included an interview with the political commissar of the 147th regiment, Liu Di. During this interview, he accused Liu of being a league member but, for some inexplicable reason, refrained from arresting him.[20] Liu, however, was well aware of what this "chat" with Li meant. Seeing the writing on the wall, Liu acted in a manner that would, for those who believed in his guilt, come to constitute the group's first open act of counter-revolutionary betrayal. Gathering together a battalion of rebel troops drawn from the Twentieth Red Army, Liu encircled the army headquarters and forced the release of Xie Hanchang at gunpoint. With a serious military rebellion now brewing, Li fled for his life.

After this initial act of mutiny, there could be no going back. Pushing on to the town of Futian where Duan Liangbi was being held, the rebel soldiers encircled the Provincial Implementation Committee headquarters and forced guards loyal to the Soviet government to hand over their weapons. Once they had secured the town, they rescued Duan. From Futian, the rebels crossed the Rubicon, striking out from the communist-controlled area and setting up a separate base camp on the western side of the river Gan. Despite their disillusionment with the Party leadership of the Central Soviet, the rebels attempted to prove their loyalty to the revolutionary cause by continuing to fight the Nationalist army, yet doing so independently of any Party control.

At first, the rebels thought they would gain the support of a number of disaffected Party and army leaders from within the Central Soviet. Concerns over the radical nature of the land revolution and the military strategies of Mao had not been confined to locals. Many others within the Party shared their concerns about the way Mao was handling these issues, and this, coupled with endemic factionalism within the Party and the army at the time, provided fertile ground for an anti-Maoist coalition (Zheng Xuejia 1976; Gao Hua 2000). In particular, the rebels thought that support for their cause might be forthcoming from those Party and army leaders whom they knew to be estranged from the Maoist leadership of the Central Soviet. Peng Dehuai, Zhu De, and Huang Gonglüe stood out as the most likely candidates in this regard.

"Leaking" a forged letter ostensibly written by Mao to his comrade Gu Bo (Qin Bangxian), the rebels hoped that the denunciation of Peng, Zhu, and Huang as A-B League members within its pages might lead this group into their proposed coalition (Gao Hua 2000, 22; Dai Xiangqing and Luo Huilan 1994, 129; Zeng Fanzheng 1998, 1:6). Far from helping, however, the letter became another nail in their coffin. Quickly exposed as a fake, this forged letter became simply another piece of evidence indicating their counter-revolutionary and conspiratorial ways. Moreover, with this hoax revealed, the hoped-for allies became the rebels' most ferocious critics. Peng, Zhu, and Huang would pen a letter of their own: "Duan Liangbi, Liu Di, Li Bai-fang, Xie Hanchang, Jin Wanbang etc. have all been in the league for a long time. . . . The Futian Incident is a major outbreak of counter-revolutionary activity organized by the A-B League Elimination Faction" (qtd. in Sima Lu 1981, 57, 58).

Having failed spectacularly to gain any support from local army and Party leaders, the rebels tried their luck in Shanghai with the Central Committee. Communication between the Central Committee leadership and the base camps was very poor at this time, and so it was decided to send Duan Liangbi to Shanghai to explain the rebel position.[21] Duan was duly sent to Shanghai to lobby for Mao Zedong's expulsion from the Party and for a reversal of his and his companions' verdicts. The Central Committee, however, remained unconvinced. It ordered Duan to rescind his call for Mao's expulsion, some-thing he dutifully acceded to. This back down did little to assuage Mao Ze-dong. From the very beginning, Mao and the General Front Line Commit-tee he organized to investigate this incident were convinced that the rebels had more sinister motives on their minds than his ousting.[22] These were not the actions of a disgruntled group of communists, they would suggest, but a major outbreak of counter-revolutionary sabotage organized and led by the A-B Elimination League (Mao Zedong 1984, 183). In other words, it was not something one could or should compromise on. The rebels' actions did not constitute a contradiction among comrades, but the actions of "the enemy." Under these circumstances, compromise equaled a betrayal of the revolution.

It was after the sixth plenum of the Third Central Committee that the party established the Soviet Central Bureau. It was this bureau, under its sec-retary Xiang Ying that would carry out all the multifarious tasks of the Cen-tral Committee at the local Soviet level. But in January 1931 in the Central Soviet there was, of course, one overriding task—to clear up the Futian Inci-dent. With the bureau now undertaking an investigation into this incident, there was no longer a role for the General Front Line Committee, which, as a consequence, was eliminated. With its elimination went Mao's crucial role as committee secretary, and, while he was made a bureau member, Xiang Ying effectively took over his old role. It was Xiang who would release the bureau's findings, and while on most matters the bureau concurred with the assessment of the incident given by Mao's General Front Line Committee, it did rebuke the local leadership on a number of important matters (PSHM 1987, v3, 45). Overall, the bureau came to the same conclusion as the General Front Line Committee and its January report reflected that fact. It concluded that the incident was "absolutely anti-communist and counter-revolutionary." By February, the bureau had slightly modified its position. It began to suggest that, "objectively," while the Futian Incident helped the A-B League, it did not, in fact, constitute an A-B League conspiracy. The bureau concluded that there was absolutely no basis, in fact, for this claim (PSHM 1987, v3, 47; Zeng Fanzheng 1998, 1:10). Indeed, one of the reasons why this incident had become a major case was because of the way the General Front Line Committee had presented the rebels as A-B League members.

By February 1931, the Central Committee Bureau under Xiang Ying was calling for a "peaceful resolution" of the incident and for the rebels to return to the Party fold (Zeng Fanzheng 1998, 1:12–13). The Central Committee Bureau sought a compromise and designated the rebels' error not one committed by counter-revolutionary enemies, but one that had resulted from internal Party contradictions (Party document 11, Feb. 19, 1931, qtd. in *Gong'an Jianshi*). The bureau said that apart from Duan Liangbi and four other rebel leaders, all others should be allowed back into the Party once they had admitted their errors and promised that, henceforth, they would submit to Party discipline. With this compromise in hand, the rebel elements of the Twentieth Red Army moved back to the western side of the Gan river, and back into the Central Soviet base area. The current of compromise that carried them into the base camp in February then, was made possible by the redesignation of the rebels from "enemies" to "adversaries." That softening of the designation would again change in March. In an event that could all too easily be interpreted as cynical betrayal, a wave of repression replaced the current of compromise. Rather than reading this volte-face as betrayal, however, it is probably more accurate to relate it to a change in political perception accompanying yet another leadership change back in the Shanghai Central Committee.

In January 1931, a new Party leader emerged from the cadre training schools of Moscow. Wang Ming and his Soviet-trained supporters, known as the twenty-eight Bolsheviks, were installed in leadership positions at the fourth plenum of the Sixth Central Committee. Having trained in Moscow at a time when the name Trotsky stood for traitor, they were keen to revisit the Futian Incident and examine its alleged connections to the Trotskyist movement. The findings they made, given their agenda, were predictable enough: Futian had indeed constituted an A-B Elimination League conspiracy, and the previous report of Xiang Ying's bureau had been far too lenient. In April, the new Central Committee leadership dispatched a team of three to the Central Soviet to communicate this new assessment to the Soviet government in Jiangxi. Made up of Ren Bishi, Wang Jiaxiang, and Gu Zuolin, this three-person team effectively replaced the more moderate Xiang Ying as the voice of the Central Committee. Xiang Ying, meanwhile, faced criticism for the error of leniency. He was, the team concluded, "totally mistaken" in his views and had "completely confused the counter-revolutionary nature of the Futian Incident" (Zeng Fanzheng 1998, 1:17). Again, however, Xiang Ying's error had been one of judgment rather than politics, and no long-term consequences would flow from this mistake. For the rebels, however, it was a different story.

At a mass meeting in April, the counter-revolutionary nature of this rebel group was "revealed" when the three-person committee's assessment was relayed to the base camp as a whole. In this new radical climate, Mao would make a comeback. In May, he would officially replace Xiang Ying as the acting Central Committee representative in the base camp. With this (re)turn to Mao Zedong and to the position on the rebels originally advanced by his General Front Line Committee, the arrests and killings would begin once again (PSHM 1987, v3, 48–49). It was, in fact, in the period between May and July that the Campaign to Eliminate Counter-Revolutionaries would reach a new peak.

During this period Liu Di, Xie Hanchang, and Duan Liangbi were all re-arrested and executed. It was in this period also that the entire leadership of the Twentieth Red Army, from deputy platoon leaders upward, were all proclaimed A-B League backbone elements. These newly discovered enemies were all arrested and, in the vast majority of cases, shot. Indeed, well over seven hundred soldiers would end up executed at this time (PSHM 1987, v3, 49; Li Jinping 1993, 65; Dai Xiangqing and Luo Huilan 1994, 152). These deaths killed off more than the Twentieth Red Army's leadership; the entire army was now regarded as suspect and quickly dismantled. As the Central Soviet descended into a killing field once again, the Party Central Committee was forced to intervene. This time, they would return to a mood of compromise and moderation.

Very soon after this, the powerful figure of Zhou Enlai would arrive on the scene. More by chance than design, he had been forced to leave Shanghai for the Central Soviet because of the defection in April of one of the veterans of the communist security structure, Gu Shunzhang. Gu served as the Party's "wet work" specialist in Shanghai, and he, along with Zhou, had set up the first Party security organ. Gu's knowledge of Party security, coupled with his intimate knowledge of the Party leadership, made his defection a disaster for the Shanghai Party and a death sentence for Zhou Enlai, should he remain in that city. With no other choices available, Zhou would flee Shanghai for the rural base camps.

By December 1931, Zhou had arrived at the Minxi base camp where he viewed firsthand the poisoned climate caused by the excessive killings. He reacted with disbelief when told that a "tail" remained to be dealt with. This tail amounted to over six thousand suspects still needing to be eliminated. After seeing the excesses in Minxi, Zhou realized that one of his key tasks when he arrived at the Central Soviet would be to revisit the Futian Incident and bring the matter to a definitive conclusion. By January 1932, he issued yet another verdict on the incident. The Central Committee's conclusion was that while it remained necessary to continue to fight the A-B League, that fight must, at all costs, avoid excess. The A-B League had indeed instigated the Futian Incident, Zhou claimed, but the method the Party had used in response had been too vicious and had led to people being killed "as though life were a game" (CCA 1991, doc. 8, 21).

From the Party's perspective, this would be the final twist. Yet while it clearly turned on a complex mix of factional and personal differences, it was, in fact, energized by the political intensities produced through the friend/enemy divide. In this respect, the Futian Incident did not concern the moral (or otherwise) turpitude of individual leaders such as Mao or Zhou. What separated these two leaders was nothing other than their ideological perceptions of these events. Zhou was no less ruthless than Mao when he believed the occasion demanded it.[23] Indeed, were it to be otherwise, one would begin to doubt his degree of commitment. The Futian struggle was waged only because of this power of commitment to drive one beyond everyday morality into the killing fields. In this regard, Futian would have many equivalents. But it has equivalents not as a tale of individual leaders and their immoral character, but as a tale that highlights the power of political commitment to transform ordinary people into political activists willing to commit acts that, in other circumstances, they themselves would denounce as barbaric. No one emerges as an innocent in this process of politicization, for every act speaks of a passion play of obsession, fear, and excess. The expression of this power of political commitment and the obsessions it produces, however, only becomes apparent in context. As we move away from the Central Soviet and on to other tales of excess in other base camps, this point becomes clearer.

Tales of Terror II: The Minxi (Western Fujian) Base Camp and the War against the Social Democratic Party

If Futian demanded the annihilation of a Trotskyite enemy who betrayed because of an adherence to the program of the Fourth International, the Minxi base camp purge spoke of combating an enemy within who was equally committed to the agenda of the Second International. In January 1931, this base camp would launch a campaign against social democrats that could be thought of as a surrealist comedy but for the fact that the communists used real bullets. The events' tragicomic opening moments best captured their surrealist quality.

This campaign began as a result of an incident that occurred at a meeting called to critique the revisionism of the Second International by the Twelfth Division of the Fourth Red Army of Fujian in 1931. What this meeting purportedly revealed, however, were rats within the (army) ranks.[24] This revelation unfolded in the course of a mass meeting when a local peasant soldier named Wu Zhuozai misheard the chant of "long live the Third International." Unsure of the differences between the Second and Third Internationals, Wu inadvertently began to chant, "endorse the Second International" and "long live the Social Democratic Party." He would be joined by seven other similarly confused soldiers who sat beside him. When nearby soldiers overheard this "row of revisionists" chanting their slogans, they reported it to the divisional political commissar, Lin Meiting. Lin, however, simply dismissed it as unimportant (*Gong'an Jianshi*; Zeng Fanzheng 1998, 1:24).[25] Others, however, would take the occurrence far more seriously.

When the matter was brought to the attention of Lin Yizhu, the head of the Minxi committee for the elimination of counter-revolutionaries, he called for further investigations. Wu and his soldier friends, as well as Lin Meiting, were all brought in for interrogation. Under torture, they revealed what Lin Yizhu suspected, namely, that they formed part of a social democratic conspiracy to undermine the Communist Party. During the next two months, over sixty other "social democrats" were arrested on information gained by the torture of Wu, Lin, and the other soldiers. In the end, even Fu Bocui, the former commander in chief of the Fourth Division of the Fourth Red Army and the proposed finance minister of the base camp, was implicated (PSHM 1990:2, VI6, 103–5; Zeng Fanzheng 1998, 1:24).

Fu Bocui would, in this way, join the ever lengthening list of the condemned. Wrongly accused of being the special committee secretary of the Social Democratic Party, Fu and his "covert activities" were regarded as so central to that organization that he could not have undertaken them without the complicity of his hometown. A purge of that town began after it was labeled the home of the Social Democratic Party. With his back to the wall, Fu, like the Futian rebels before him, gathered his troops. Attempting a last-ditch stand in his hometown, he, in fact, could not sustain the rebellion. For his insubordination, Fu would never live to see his rehabilitation, despite the fact that he was cleared of all the substantive charges against him.[26] Fu could never live to see his rehabilitation for he had committed a sin at least as grave as that of counter-revolution. When faced with the choice between Party and home, even under these extenuating circumstances, he chose home, thus proving himself committed to a more earthy morality than that expected of a good Party member. Judged unfit for the title of Communist Party member, he was expelled from its ranks (PSHM 1990:2, VI6, 104).

Very young peasant soldiers yelling erroneous slogans at esoteric commemorative meetings through lack of knowledge of the international communist movement hardly warranted the type of response that this event elicited from the authorities. Nevertheless, already convinced that the base camp was full of enemy agents, and buoyed by Comintern advice that the principle threat to international communism now lay with "right opportunism" and factionalism within Party ranks, the western Fujian Soviet launched a major campaign to root out and suppress the Social Democratic Party.[27] The result was a campaign of terror that would sweep across the entire base camp (PSHM 1990:2, v16, 105). By the end of the campaign, it gathered up over 6,500 people falsely accused of membership in the Social Democratic Party, all of whom were either arrested or executed (Huang Jinlin 1988, 2:77). As Mao Zedong would later, rather wryly, comment to the head of the Minxi base camp, Zhang Dingcheng: "If this continues, there will be no need for enemy attacks, we'll have cut our own throats."[28]

No investigations by the Party or the security organs were ever undertaken to determine the veracity of the charges that began the purge. Yet as is now clear, the whole campaign was generated on the sole basis of forced confessions from one group of soldiers who, under torture, implicated others. This, in turn, led to further arrests and further forced confessions. The fate of the original eight serves as a pitiful footnote to the whole event. Charged with a ridiculously large number of counter-revolutionary crimes, they were, of course, executed. While on death row, it is said that all eight once again began chanting slogans. This time, however, they chanted "endorse the Communist Party" and "endorse the Soviets." This time, however, no one was listening. When the new chant finally came to the attention of Lin Yizhu,[29] the prosecutor of the campaign would remark, "This is the last five minutes of deceit we will hear from them" (qtd. in Huang Jinlin 1988, 2:75).

The difference in the treatment of the two chants—the reactionary one at the beginning of the campaign which was believed, the revolutionary one at the end of the chanters' life which was not—highlights the effects of symptomatic reading strategies borne of the friend/enemy dyad. Once the political intensity transforms every word into a telltale sign of a political inclination, a dynamic is released that contaminates the entire lifeworld. Life itself is compressed into the tiny space of politics, and everything, including mistakes, becomes merely telltale signs connoting a particular political stance. Once that is set, so, too, are the ways of reading statements. For an enemy in this climate, denial is useless because the enemy is regarded as the absolute inversion of the good communist. Denial, therefore, is but a cunning ploy, while confessions that require force—precisely because they do require force—come to stand as revealed truth. Indeed, the degree of force employed to extract the confession becomes a calibrated index of the enemies' depth of commitment to their cause. In what was to become a regular feature of this confessional logic, the enemy was, for the committed communist, a mirror of his or her own question of commitment. In this respect, the enemy became the communist's own question in the figure of the other.

Tales of Terror III: Xiang-E'xi (Hunan and western Hubei) Base Camp and the Four High Tides of Repression

On the borderlands of Hunan and Hubei provinces, another major communist base camp existed known as Xiang-E'xi, and this, too, became a site where questions of commitment would lead to violence and excess. While this base camp purge would feature no major event such as the Futian Incident, nor any significant "spark" like the Minxi meeting, that did not stop the killings. Excess in Xiang-E'xi would come in waves that constituted the most zealous moments of campaigning. When these waves came crashing in, arrests and killings followed and, in the Xiang-E'xi region, four such moments of tidal proportions occurred.

The first of these would sweep through the Honghu region (diqu) in May 1932, after communist troops successfully captured Tianhan county from the local Nationalist army garrison. Not only did the communists capture the town but they also persuaded the nationalist company commander, Zhang Xihou, to defect to the communist cause. It was after this initial success that the killings would begin.

Convinced that the ease of the conversion of Zhang Xihou was a sign of its fraudulent nature, the Political Protection Bureau of the base camp ordered his arrest.[30] Brought in for interrogation by bureau agents, Zhang would endure beatings and torture. Eventually, like everybody else in the bureau's custody, he confessed. Yes, he was an enemy agent, and, yes, as the bureau had suspected, he did not work alone. His accomplice, he claimed, was the Party military chief of Tianhan county, Yang Guomao. With this "evidence," the inquisition moved on. After a "session" with Yang, he, too, would admit guilt and implicate others in a plot allegedly designed to get the entire Third Red Army to rebel and join the Nationalists. The bureau now felt it had a major case on its hands and, as it proceeded, the whole of the Third Red Army fell under suspicion (Zeng Fanzheng 1998, 1:36–37). Needless to say, the list of suspects not only expanded dramatically but other areas of Xiang-E'xi were also drawn into the maelstrom. At the very time the base camp needed high morale among its troops in order to fight the war against the nationalists, the main army force was being accused of treachery. But not only morale was suffering through these investigations. The fighting strength of the Red Army was also being sapped.

Knowing the bureau's fearsome reputation and the fact that it was now turning its attention to the military, many soldiers decided against waiting for their final verdict. Thus, by the beginning of June 1932, sections of the Red Army began to desert. In the E-Yu border region, for example, the cadres of the provincial committee and government, as well as their troops, were all that remained in the face of bureau investigations. But even then, fighting strength in this area was reduced to a paltry 170 troops (PSHM 1987, V3, 110). In this period, between May and September 1932, the first phase of the elimination campaign reached its zenith. But as one veteran cadre, Xia Xi, made clear, this first phase really only exposed the dominant position of the Nationalist Reformist Faction within army ranks, but did not eliminate it. The first high tide was, therefore, to be but the opening salvo.

Xia Xi was in a good position to make such comments. As chair of the military committee of this base camp, he was in overall charge of the local elimination campaign. His report to the Central Committee, in September 1932, on the so-called first phase illustrated both the scale of the campaign under way and the way this Party branch's elimination organs were dealing with suspicious elements. "Arrests ran into the thousands, executions, well into the hundreds," Xia Xi would write in his report (PSHM 1987, V3, 109). The Central Committee responded to this report by fully endorsing Xia Xi's "accurate line." This made for just the type of fulsome support he would need to extend his investigations even more deeply into army affairs (PSHM 1987, V3, 111). Local political zealousness seemed to have dovetailed with Central Committee concerns to give this purge renewed life, but this is not how some scholars read these events.

Insisting that Xia Xi was driven not by political zealousness but by pragmatic factional considerations, Zeng Fanzheng's work, for example, highlights the factional links between Xia Xi and Wang Ming's twenty-eight Bolsheviks who ran the Central Committee. In Zeng's book, these factional allegiances explained both the targets and the degree of excess. Xia Xi, like Mao in the Futian Incident, would purge the base camps of so-called impure elements who also happened to be his factional rivals. These rivalries, not political passions, would drive Xia Xi into excess. This is why the target of these purges, he asserted, were always the local base camp Party leaders (Zeng Fanzheng 1998, 1:37).

This argument proves compelling precisely because factional struggles did come to play a key role in the prosecution of base camp elimination. My quarrel is not with that line of reasoning per se, but with the way factional struggles are interpreted as being bereft of any real ideological content. If factions were mere vehicles to attain power, one would then need to ask whether factionalism alone offers an adequate means to account for the violent combustion that would drive these bloody events. After all, factional rivalries hardly make for a solid enough basis upon which to bring forth the type of passionate commitment needed to enable one to kill one's own comrades.[31] To kill without personal hate, and kill on a grand scale, requires a moral basis upon which to legitimate one's actions. Such actions, therefore, need to be underpinned by loftier feelings than merely those of personal hatred of one's rivals. To achieve collective hatred, it needs to be public, not private and personal. In summary, it needs to be political.

Overriding any question of factional difference, therefore, is the issue of political difference. In particular, this issue requires a framework of understanding that not only politicizes rival factional claims but then also views such claims as telltale signs of enemy activities. Once read in this particular symptomatic way, purges no longer constitute moments of cynicism and immorality, but examples of the highest morality borne of idealism. In other words, under these conditions, one kills not for selfish egoistic or pragmatic ends, but because one is convinced, rightly or wrongly, that the reasons for the suppression are political and nonagonal. To convince oneself to kill, and kill en masse, is to participate in a political event taking one beyond the squalid concerns of the everyday and into a higher moral realm that must (self-)authorize such killing as legitimate and necessary. In Xiang-E'xi, it was just this type of moral realm that played a part in authorizing the mass killing, and it is here that one begins to witness this phenomenon as the Campaign to Eliminate Counter-Revolutionaries unfolds.

Between August and October 1932, a second wave of repression swept through the base camps. This phase began at the very time the Nationalists' military was beginning its fourth so-called surround and exterminate campaign.[32] Purged of its leaders during the first phase of the campaign, the rudderless Red Army of Xiang-E'xi proved no match for the well-equipped Nationalist army. Leaderless and in imminent danger of defeat, morale plummeted, and soldiers began to desert en masse. The elimination campaign was moving on to victory at the cost of the war. This was not, however, how Xia Xi or the Political Protection Bureau assessed the situation.

For Xia Xi, desertions gave simply another example of political defections and one further sign, if such a sign was needed, of the power of the Reformist Faction to turn politically weak elements within the Red Army into committed reactionaries. Only by smashing the Reformist Faction, and thus halting the defeatism and wrecking that this enemy organization promoted, Xia Xi believed, could the war against the Nationalists be won. Hence, while the open battles against the Nationalist Party continued on the front lines, there was an equally vicious secret and dirty war being prosecuted against spies and enemy agents behind communist lines. As the second wave of repression unfolded, the arrests and executions not only continued but actually increased. All this at a time the CCP was warding off an intense attack from the Nationalists.

Morale dropped to an all-time low as fatigue from fighting set in. This, coupled with a lack of food and a perception among ordinary soldiers that the Campaign to Eliminate Counter-Revolutionaries targeted them, produced a despondent attitude, which cadres within the Protection Bureau then interpreted as counter-revolutionary defeatism. As troops began to flee, the Red Army was forced to draw upon cadets from the local military academy that Xia Xi believed propagated Reformist Faction thinking. The increasingly close attention now being paid to the military would produce its own grim dividends. By the end of the second phase of this elimination campaign, a total of 241 army personnel had been arrested and executed as enemy agents (Zeng Fanzheng 1998, 1:42). With attention now focused upon the military, everything it did was read through the grid of friend and enemy.

The military reversals that began to hit the Xiang-E'xi base camp and forced the communists to dissolve the camp and move to Badong in March 1933 should not have come unexpectedly given this climate of fear. Nevertheless, these reversals were not attributed to the declining morale of troops, but as indications of the strength of the enemy "fifth columnists" sowing the seeds of defeatism within Red Army ranks. This would constitute the spark that fired the third phase of the campaign. Time and again, it seems, the communists thought that in order to win the war, the battle against the internal enemy needed to be won first. It is on the basis of this type of logic, rather than the effects of a cynical factional power struggle, that the spark that ignited the third and fourth phases of this campaign can be understood.

Under siege and facing imminent defeat, the Third Red Army arrived in the Xiang-E (Hunan and Hubei) border region, but looked pessimistically upon their military position. These Third Red Army soldiers had been drafted from the flatlands of Honghu and were quite unused to the mountainous and harsh terrain of this particular border region. With limited experience fighting in such terrain, they suffered significant losses, and ordinary soldiers began to complain. As defeats mounted, the Red Army company commander Duan Dechang suggested that a tactical withdrawal was necessary. He advanced the idea that the best way forward for the Red Army was to break through the White stranglehold and fight its way back to Honghu. Xia Xi regarded Duan's plan as defeatist and as yet another thinly veiled attempt to desert the revolution. Yet again Xia Xi jumped to the conclusion that this plan was a plot and Duan a Reformist Faction mole. Duan was duly arrested and, in May 1933, executed. He would not die alone. According to a report penned by the Xiang-E'xi branch of the Central Committee, 41 other soldiers would die with him and a further 236 would be arrested. Yet again, the figures were a gross underestimation. In Zeng Fanzheng's book it is suggested that the real number of soldiers killed in this affair was substantially higher but that the Xiang-E'xi Party branch of the Central Committee suppressed those figures for fear that they would cause alarm (Zeng Fanzheng 1998, 1:46). They certainly caused alarm within the ranks of the security forces. Indeed, once evidence from the third phase of this elimination campaign suggested large-scale enemy infiltration, Xia Xi swung into action. Up until this point the elimination campaign in Xiang-E'xi had been largely restricted to investigations of senior officials or regimental officers and above. The security forces under Xia Xi now called for a root-and-branch purge of the Party that would run alongside a Party membership re-registration drive. This drive took place alongside the final phase of the elimination campaign that opened in May 1933 and ran through the summer of 1934. The results of this particular phase were utterly devastating.

By April 1934, the strength of the total Third Red Army had fallen from ten thousand soldiers to just over three thousand (Zeng Fanzheng 1998, 1:50). While fighting would account for many of these deaths, it could not explain all of them. Zhang De, a veteran of the Xiang-E'xi campaign, would later recall what was going on within Red Army ranks at this time: "Some companies went through six or seven company heads. Such leadership changes were the result of endless purging. Everyone appointed to a leadership position ended up dead, leaving the troops without officers and with more guns than men." It got so bad, another of these veteran soldiers said, that no one in the army was willing to take responsibility anymore: "I can still remember one soldier whom they wanted to promote to a squadron leader; he went down to headquarters and cried his eyes out" (PSHM 1987, V3,124). This was not, however, how Xia Xi would report upon the situation to the Central Committee. He grossly underestimated the number of arrests and deaths, suggesting that in all three stages of this campaign only four thousand people were involved. Yet as He Long would later recall, in the first phase of the elimination campaign in the Honghu area alone, over ten thousand people were executed (PSHM 1987, V3, 117). Indeed, on the basis of estimates from the Nationalist Party, the communists had been just as successful at eliminating communists as their army had been in open warfare. Guo Hualun suggests that the Nationalists exterminated 50,000 communists either by arrest, execution, or by turning them into agents. He then estimates that the CCP eliminated the same number in the course of their Campaign to Eliminate Counter-Revolutionaries (Guo Hualun 1969, 260). It was the constant fear of betrayal that would shift the focus of the Campaign to Eliminate Counter-Revolutionaries toward Party and army figures, and, in this respect, the purges in Xiang-E'xi were far from abnormal.

Tales of Terror IV: The A-B League in the E-Yu-Wan (Hubei-Hunan-Anhui) Base Camp

The fear of betrayal also fueled the purges in the other big base camp of the Soviet region, E-Yu-Wan. The elimination campaign in E-Yu-Wan began later than most. Indeed, it was only really with the accession of Wang Ming to Party leadership in January 1931 that it started in earnest. By that time, rumors of betrayal in E-Yu-Wan, which dated back to October 1930, reached the Central Committee leadership in Shanghai. In particular, they were informed that intelligence leaks had caused a series of significant military defeats and deaths in the Seventh Red Army. It was these rumors that led to Central Committee intervention. In May 1931, Wang Ming sent Zhang Guotao, Shen Zemin, and Chen Changhao to E-Yu-Wan to establish a Central Committee branch there and to investigate rumors of hidden counterrevolutionary activities. By August, the Central Committee branch found what they sought. Three separate investigations brought to light a number of minor examples of betrayal that, when tied together, appeared to the Central Committee branch as a major problem requiring a fully blown elimination campaign. The three events were the General Hospital Reformist A-B League Case, the plot to encourage Xu Jishen to defect and the White Sparrow Garden Incident.

The General Hospital Reformist A-B League Case began in early August 1931, when a number of injured nationalist soldiers were captured, taken to hospital and, while in recovery, engaged in a number of light duties that included food preparation. After a bout of food poisoning in the hospital, suspicions were raised. Accused of deliberately poisoning the food, they were arrested and tortured. Under torture, they "revealed" that a local pharmacist had supplied them with the poison. Even more worrying was the fact that the pharmacist they accused of helping them was in fact the wife of a local Red Army regimental commander (tuanzhang). Interrogators no longer thought of this incident as either accidental or even an opportunistic crime by a small group of enemy soldiers. They now began to suspect a much larger conspiracy.

With the discovery of the general hospital case, the long-held fears of betrayal seemed to have evidence behind them. After that, other "hard" evidence of enemy activities began to emerge. In August, a conspiracy to bribe the local commander of the Twelfth Division of the Fourth Red Army, Xu Jishen, to defect with his troops was uncovered (E-Yu-Wan 1989, 4:502).[33] While Xu would reject the offer and blow the whistle on the conspirators, this did not suffice to fully prove his allegiance. By November, he was dead. Accused of being a counter-revolutionary for communicating with the enemy, he would die in a sweep that enveloped the base camp and led to the execution of over 2,500 Red Army soldiers in its first three months of operation. Indeed, in E-Yu-Wan, something like 60–70 percent of all regimental cadres and above were either arrested or killed as a result of this particular purge (E-Yu-Wan 1989, v4, 506). Suspicion mainly fell on Xu because this was not the only "conspiracy" he had been involved in. Barely had the plot to seduce him been revealed, when another prairie fire involving him erupted. This third incident, again in August, began as a simple tactical dispute. Given the overall political climate in the wake of recent revelations, however, even considerations of military tactics became threshold political questions involving issues of commitment.

The event, which would eventually become known as the White Sparrow Garden (Baiqueyuan) Incident began innocently enough. Xu Jishen had led his Fourth Red Army troops to victory in Yingshan. The mood was buoyant, and when news of the victory was communicated back to the base camp, so, too, was the base camp leader Zhang Guotao. On behalf of the Central Committee branch he congratulated Xu and then ordered him to continue north and invade the Nationalists' capital, Nanjing. Xu refused. He regarded Zhang's order as adventurist and militarily ill-informed. Instead of heading north to Nanjing, he moved his forces south. Flaunting the orders of the Central Committee branch would prove a costly decision. Zhang would read it as an act of open rebellion from an already suspect commander. Putting this "rebellion" together with the general hospital incident and the conspiracy to turn Xu Jishen, Zhang began to see connections (PSHM 1989, v4, 141). Together, Zhang thought, these three incidents were signs that the internal enemy was not only active but actively planning a much more significant rebellion.

No doubt Zhang's thoughts on these matters were much influenced by the fact that the arrests, interrogations, and torturing that followed the general hospital incident had begun to yield intelligence dividends that pointed in this direction. Under torture, both the pharmacist accused of supplying the enemy soldiers with poison and the army's chief of staff, Li Ronggui, had both separately admitted to the existence of a counter-revolutionary military committee operative within the ranks of the Fourth Red Army. This, coupled with the attempted seduction of the Fourth Red Army and Xu's insubordination at the head of it, focused Party attention. Interrogations into the activities of the perceived counter-revolutionary military committee began in earnest almost immediately after these revelations. The Party set up a special interrogation center in White Sparrow Garden and then began investigations and interrogations at each and every level of the Fourth Red Army. With bi-gong-xin in operation, confessions followed, leading to the deaths of twenty important Red Army leaders. In total, eight hundred people were arrested for membership in the Reformist Faction, the Social Democratic Party, or the A-B League. As mentioned earlier, the White Sparrow Garden Incident would end with the deaths of over 2,500 people (PSHM 1989:4, v14, 140–43). On November 25, Zhang Guotao wrote a report on the incident to the Central Committee in which he boasted that the experience of prosecuting this counter-revolution campaign had Party-wide significance: "The experiences we can draw from this counter-revolutionary elimination campaign are far greater than those that can be drawn from the Futian Incident and offer lessons for the whole Party" (qtd. in PSHM 1989:4, v14, 143). Zhang was lucky to have been able to write such a report. Many others could not. They were prevented from doing so by the fact that the Campaign to Eliminate Counter-Revolutionaries had targeted so many Party intellectuals that not enough literate people remained in this Party branch to do the work. This was revealed in a provincial government report from September 1932, in which senior officials bemoaned the fact that report writing was proving arduous after purging because it had left too few literate people alive. Indeed, intellectuals were now so few in number that even Party secretaries were forced to write up their own reports (Gong'an Jianshi). None of this was lost on the local populace.

Paralyzed by fear, the people began to speak of the "five unwillings." After the winds of the campaign had swept through their villages, the peasants said they were unwilling to become Party members, were highly reluctant to join the Red Army, did not want to become cadres, would refrain from encouraging their children to get an education, and would not allow their offspring to become intellectuals. In fact, they would not even allow their daughters to marry Party cadres because they did not want them to return as young widows (PSHM 1989:4, v14, 154). One old cadre who recalled his visit to a small town in E-Yu-Wan at this time summed up the general feeling: "Xinji was a small town with over 3,000 people in it, but during the elimination campaign, no one dared move at night and, during the day, no one was game to walk the streets. I went to E-Yu-Wan with six cadres; Zhang Guotao killed three of them" (PSHM 1989:4, v14, 154). Another cadre would recall how: "A number of cadres who had made real contributions to the opening up of the base camp area died, not by the sword of Jiang Jieshi's Nationalists, but by the dagger of Zhang Guotao and his Campaign to Suppress Counter-Revolutionaries" (PSHM 1989:4, VI4, 152).

To reduce these purges to the errors or evils of Zhang Guotao, while understandable, is nevertheless to seriously underestimate the collective dynamic harnessed by these campaigns and their almost inevitable descent into excess. Zhang Guotao, Xia Xi, and Mao Zedong would never have succeeded in their excess but for the power of the campaign to transform everything and anything into an intensity that could be assessed politically. The cost of this binary logic would prove enormous.

From February 1931 to February 1932, Party numbers dropped from around eight thousand people to less than five thousand (PSHM 1990:2, VI6, 106). Indeed, by the early thirties, in just three base camps (Xiang-E'xi, E-Yu-Wan and Xiang-E-Gan), it has been estimated that something like forty-six thousand people were falsely arrested or lost their lives in the course of this campaign (Huang Jinlin 1988, 77). These figures do not include the arrests and executions in the Central Soviet, much less other smaller base camps. In southwestern Jiangxi province, for example, from the time of the "discovery" of the A-B League through until the Futian Incident, over four thousand people were said to have been wrongly executed (Huang Jinlin 1988, 77). As the number of deaths and arrests mounted, one thing became increasingly clear. Had it not been for the final success of Jiang Jieshi's fifth extermination campaign forcing the evacuation of the base camps and a reevaluation of Party policy, Mao's wry comments to Zhang Dingcheng about "cutting our own throats" may well have been prophetic.

Ironically, the military disaster that led to the collapse of the base camps and the forced end to this campaign probably ended up saving the lives of many notable Communist Party leaders. People such as He Long, Guan Xiangying, and Lu Dongsheng, it is said, were next on the elimination campaign "hit list" (Li Jinping 1993, 65). Ironically, then, just as Jiang's actions in Shanghai seemed to spell the end of the communists but ended up leading them in the direction of their peasant-based future, his actions in the extermination campaign ended up saving them from themselves and opening up a future that, through the Long March, would become legendary. If the recovery after Shanghai made for a wonder to behold, after Jiangxi, the recovery was nothing short of a miracle. It set in stone the image of an indomitable communist fighting spirit that would gain clearest definition in Yan'an. This, ironically enough, would be the legacy of Jiang's persistence. The legacy of the elimination campaign, however, was to be very different. Bloody campaigns, like the sufan, could not be repeated. This campaign had offered bloody proof that even though revolutionaries required passion, they also needed to devise ways to limit it. Yan'an would be the first attempt to limit excess while remaining within the politics of a friend/enemy dyad.

Conclusion

In 1925 or thereabouts,[34] Mao Zedong posed a simple question that would mark a moment of theoretical and practical clarity in the unfolding revolutionary process of China. The posing of this question not only established the language of revolution but also created the very basis of its conceptual framework. "Who are our enemies, and who are friends?" Mao asked. "This," he continued, "is a question germane to the revolution."

With characteristic simplicity and eloquence, Mao posed a question of such profundity that it would not only haunt each and every turn in his own thought—from his richly complex expression of dialectics in "On Contradiction" through to his more bellicose declarations of class war that marked the beginnings of his two-line struggle theory of history—but would become the basis upon which the entire revolutionary process in China would unfold. Moreover, in establishing the discursive terrain of revolution, Mao transformed the world into a series of political questions.

This chapter has explored, in a profoundly empirical way, how this theoretical line between friend and enemy operated as the material and concrete "thin red line" patrolled by the Chinese Communist Party's security organs. It is this patrol work against the enemy that more than any other single cause or duty, defined not only the issue of security but the entire politics of the Communist Party. While Mao's simple question would, in the end, cradle a revolution, it is in recognizing and focusing upon this question that one begins to notice the degree to which the story of policing in China is, in truth, the tale of the Party in miniature. In effect, policing the base camps was the policing of the political.

A myriad of police histories from other nations exist, covering countless police forces across the globe. What ties these stories together (as police histories), what establishes their kinship in that Wittgensteinian sense of the word, would be the ways, the almost inexhaustible multiplicity of ways, in which they relate to the government of life, labor, or community. They would all, in their very different ways, as Charles Reith somewhat idiosyncratically pointed out, either lead to stories of community or tales of military government (1952, 13–21). In the prehistories of English policing, for example, the tales all too often begin with the semimythical origins of community policing in the tithing, work their way through the so-called hue and cry, examine the establishment of the parish constabulary system, and then move on to the tale of modern policing (see, e.g., Critchley 1967). In stories of the continental gendarmerie, in contrast, the focus lies upon military separation, the universalizing, all-embracing conception of a government of life giving rise to the policing of happiness in a corporatist or even authoritarian form (see, e.g., Luedtke 1989 and Oestreich 1982). Even the tale of socialist policing only began when the first socialist state came into being and the Soviet Party established Cheka as its security wing (see, e.g., Conquest 1968; Barghoorn 1971; Leggett 1981; and Hingley 1970).

In contrast, Chinese policing, as told by Chinese police historians, is a tale that begins prior to the formation of the Chinese socialist state and only vaguely relates to either state or community. Instead, police accounts focus almost exclusively upon the policing of the Party and the revolution. Policing expressions of dissent in the embryonic socialist state was not simply to patrol the divide between friend and enemy but to define it. Police work was held together by this very thin thread of understanding. Empirically, the thread becomes the path along which the border patrols of the police walk. Chinese police patrolled the line separating friend from enemy to ensure no ambiguity and no "tails." It is a world in which clarity is necessary and, as we have seen, it is gained through the intense and violent struggle against the enemy.

Looking back over this period of history many years later, the Communist Party would recognize that it had sometimes fallen into error and "confused the line." All such errors, however, are never analyzed as an effect of the binary but instead sheeted home to individuals. The Party, it seems, never fails. The Party (and the people) suffered as a result of the defeatism of Chen Duxiu, the errors of Qu Qiubai, the line of Li Lisan, or the ultraleftism of Wang Ming. These were not individuals as much as code names that stood in for a single word: *deviation*. They were to materialism what sins are to the believer, and, in its own materialist way, the Party proved itself "saintly" by recognizing this and attempting correction. It is, therefore, more than Party history being told here. It is the pilgrim's progress and, like Bunyan's tale of old, it is a story told through symbols, through the tyranny of symbols. In this mindset, factions and even individuals stand in for "lines," defeats offer the didactic tools of victory, treachery means "clarification," and excess constitutes the wet nurse of correction. In this tyranny of the symbolic realm, it was the campaign that would loom the largest.

The symbolic excess of campaign-style politics was only paralleled by its physical excess. The tyranny of the sign required the obliteration of the body. The logic of the campaign constituted a semiotics of destruction. Yet all too often, one finds both Western and Chinese accounts refusing to accept this, opting instead for a process of cynical, shallow demonization. Here, the Futian Incident becomes little other than Mao's cynical treachery against his rivals (Faligot and Kauffer 1989), while the deep purges in E-Yu-Wan are explicable as Zhang Guotao's treacherous means of dealing with recalcitrants (PSHM 1989:4, V14, 140–55). Such pragmatic smoke-screen theories block out too much of the story. The dynamic of the campaign never becomes obscured from view by an ideological smoke screen; it *is* the smoke screen. The smoke screen of intense belief is precisely what drives the campaign forward. Hence the excesses are, in the main, not the result of nonbelief—the cynical deployment of smoke screens to hide true egoistic intentions which usually relate to the gaining or maintaining of power—but are produced as an effect of believing in the cause too much. In this way moral zealousness expresses itself in a semiotics of tyranny.

The Party had little choice for, other than ideas and symbols, it had little to offer. Through these ideas and symbols the CCP was able to harness the passionate commitment to politics and thereby find the strength to build its remote base camps. Relying upon the masses required their politicization, and that largely took place through the land revolution. Such political intensity, however, was not restricted to the pragmatic considerations surrounding recruitment. Indeed, under the conditions of war, the political enveloped everything such that everything became a question of friend and enemy. Just as money homologizes everything into the commodity form, politics would transform everything and anything into a question of friend and enemy. Contrary to Party thinking at the time, it was neither the populism of the elimination committees nor the elitism of the Political Protection Bureau that caused campaign excess. Rather, the problem was one much more central to the Party and the revolution. It was an unmediated and pure form of binary politics being unleashed on the Jiangxi Soviet region. And when this mixed with the growing sense of paranoia about defeat and betrayal, a potent combination leading to excess emerged.

By 1934, the endless process of campaigning and purging had taken its toll. The campaigns that had initially ignited revolutionary enthusiasm and commitment had, by this time, sapped the base camps of their strength. Finally defeated by Jiang Jieshi's Nationalist army, the CCP was forced to flee Jiangxi. This would put an end to the elimination campaign, but not entirely to the campaign mentality. As Mao was later to say, the Campaign to Eliminate Counter-Revolutionaries was excessive, but equally, it was necessary (*Gong'an Jianshi*). From that moment on, however, the Party was at least aware of the deleterious effects of excessive zeal. This was something it would need to come to terms with if the revolution was not to be lost. And it was to be in the yellow lands around Yan'an that the first attempts to tame this political beast were put in place. It is therefore to Yan'an that we will travel next in order to continue this concrete tale of the political.

2 From Class to Nation

LIMITING THE EXCESS IN YAN'AN

TIMELINE 1935–1945

Date	Politics	Police
1935	**January:** Zunyi meeting **October:** Long March ends; Central Committee Northwestern Bureau established	Shaan-Gan-Ning Provincial Political Protection Bureau dismantled, replaced by Northwest Political Protection Bureau
1936	**December:** Xi'an Incident; second United Front begins	
1937	**March:** Party HQ moves to Yan'an, the Communist administration of the Shaan-Gan-Ning border region, and renamed the government of a "special region of the Republic of China." **July 7:** Marco Polo bridge incident; Sino-Japanese war begins	**July:** Elimination work turns away from counter-revolutionaries to focus on traitors **September:** The Northwest Political Protection Bureau becomes the Shaan-Gan-Ning Border Region Security Division **December:** Army General Office starts to train protection workers; mass elimination of traitors organs formed in Jin-Cha-Ji, Jin-Ji-Lu-Yu, Jin-Sui, Shangdong, and Huazhong (central China) base camps
1938	**October:** CCP sixth plenum of the Sixth Central Committee meeting	

Date	Politics	Police
1939		**February 18:** Central Social Section established
		August–October: Mass-line elimination work strengthened and Party committee's leadership over security announced
		September: Huxi Incident
1940	**January:** Mao's *On New Democracy* published	
	March: Wang Jinwei sets up puppet Japanese government in Nanjing	
1941	**February 20:** CCP leadership decision on the errors of Huxi Incident	**August 1:** Central Intelligence Department established in Yan'an
		September: Jin-Cha-Ji follows Yan'an's lead
1942	**February 1:** Mao gives lecture on the rectification of party work style, signaling the beginning of the rectification campaign in Yan'an	**April:** Wang Shiwei affair begins
		November: Red Flag Party case begins
		December 6: Campaign to Check on Cadres (*shengan yundong*) begins

Date	Politics	Police
1943	**May 21:** Central Committee turns its attention to problem of *bi-gong-xin* and issues the Six Point Policy **July:** Guomindang initiates anti-CCP campaign **October:** Mao coins slogan: "Don't execute a single one, and arrest only a few"	**April 9–12:** Frank admissions campaign begins Kang Sheng initiates rescue campaign **August:** Mao releases "Nine-Point Policy" **December:** Rehabilitations begin
1944	Efforts made to curb the left tendency	

I N OCTOBER 1934, some 90,000 communists, facing certain defeat in the Jiangxi Central Soviet, chose the uncertainty of the road.[1] Breaking out of the Nationalist army's blockade, they struck west for what must have appeared, at the time, to be certain oblivion. It was, however, their finest hour; the legend of the Long March had begun. By January 1935, a new leader was emerging from within the ranks of the Communist Party and, in a tale of almost biblical proportions, he would lead the communists out of the wilderness and onto the center of history's stage.

"We Communists are made of special stuff," Joseph Stalin once remarked. It was Mao Zedong in China who would demonstrate this. In an epic journey that would see the main force of the Red Army crossing six thousand miles of territory, scaling eighteen mountain ranges, and fording twenty-seven rivers in eleven different provinces, the communists proved that they were indeed made of "special stuff." They would fight and recruit along the way, join up with other Red Army units fleeing their own base camp extermination campaigns, and finally, after a lengthy period in the wilderness, reappear in the remote, northwestern region of Shaanbei to begin a journey back to the center of Chinese politics. Few would survive. From a peak of around 300,000 in Jiangxi to just "a few ten thousands" in Shaanbei, from a range of base camps throughout the country to just one north of Yan'an, the communists appeared, initially at least, a spent force (Meisner 1986, 36).

"Are we now stronger or weaker?" Mao would ask his troops soon after they arrived in the northwest. "Stronger," he himself replied, "because those who survived are like gold" (interview, 1997). The Long March truly was, as Mao himself would later write, a Party "manifesto" (Mao 1975, 1:160). Despite the physical inhospitality of the yellow earth of Shaanbei, the legend

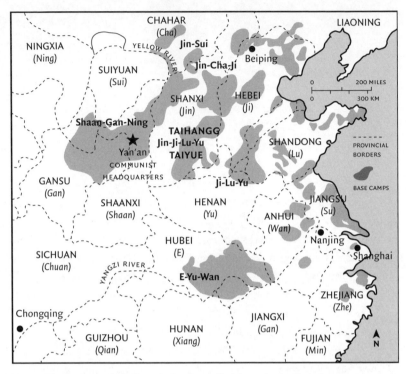

Map 3. The Yan'an Period: Communist-Controlled Areas in the Early Forties

of Mao, the Party, and Yan'an would take root and flourish in these harsh climes, embodying, in the end, what the leading Western scholar of this period once described as "the Yan'an way" (Selden 1972).

How Yan'an became molded into what appeared to be "a single discourse community" around the figure of Mao is a tale that has been told before (Apter and Saich 1994, 26). It is a story in which the Long March formed the bedrock upon which the myth of Mao, the Party, and Yan'an would be built on the basis of complex narrative wizardry. It is a story of a single place, Yan'an, a single figure, Mao Zedong, and finally, after "rectification," a single line—the Party line. Yan'an became the furnace in which, under the aegis of Mao, the many competing Party narratives were cast into one. It was this task, undertaken by the Party as a whole, it is claimed, that enabled the real lived community of Yan'an to be fused with the "imagined community" of communist legend. Yan'an may well have operated as a furnace to mold views but, for me, what is far more important than what it created was what this furnace of Yan'an burned away.

With the Japanese invasion, a new political intensity exploded like a bombshell upon China. Intense hatred was now being generated around the figure of Japan and, as these feelings grew and infected communist rhetoric, the old class codings that had been rusted onto the Jiangxi revolution began to drop away. While class would never be forgotten, there now existed a more pressing and immediate enemy for the nation as a whole to fight. In this changed political climate, the old class dogmatism of Jiangxi was no longer sustainable. Dressed in the garb of revolution, the dogmatism of class politics had frozen every relation in Jiangxi into the form of an either/or choice. The fixity with which class issues were approached not only contributed greatly to the purges but also led to an underestimation of the power of nonclass factors in producing political passions. Such passions, like the political itself, would always exist, but they would gain a different expression in different periods. The principal tension or contradiction of any given period could, therefore, neither be known in advance nor in the abstract. Only concrete analysis could draw it out and Mao's "On Contradiction" became central to any understanding of this phenomenon.

From "On Contradiction" it is clear that the task of the Party was to recognize and work to highlight the principal contradictions of any given moment.[2] While doing this, however, it must never lose sight of the hidden, underlying class dimensions of all contradictions. For the Chinese communists, a call to arms in defense of nation therefore, still ultimately, amounted to a class question, but one spoken through the trope of nation. Indeed, the Japanese invasion underlined the power and correctness of a Marxist class analysis for it highlighted the global nature of capitalism and the link between the Japanese invasion of China and the development of fascism. The road from Jiangxi to Yan'an proved a complex and winding one. Nevertheless, it was one that led from the binary political coding of class to one in which that binary was now mapped onto nation. Nation emerged as the (momentary) site of the principal contradiction and, as such, the key to defining the principal enemy. The thread that tied narratives of class to the discourse of nation in Chinese communist thought, however, was still the friend/enemy weave of politics.

Even though the transition from class to nation produced quite radical changes within the community of communists, the binary motif of the political remained intact. While this binary might appear gossamer-like at times, it is important to note that often the thinnest of threads weave the strongest of fabrics. The discourse of friend and enemy, when transformed into a question of nation, would weave a cloth as strong as it was enduring. Like Jiangxi, Yan'an would become a place where the dichotomous discourse would take on a spatial form. Where Yan'an differed, and differed radically, was that the intensity produced there did not inevitably lead to self-mutilation.

Class struggle had defined Jiangxi and given existential weight to a pure, unmediated expression of the political dyad, resulting in an endless spiral into excess. Yan'an was different. Configured largely under the sign of national salvation, the political binary worked to ensure an expanded category of friendship that included anyone who could be united with in the fight against Japan. The expansion of the circle of friendship produced an equivalent diminution of the category enemy. This diminution enabled that category to become smaller, clearer, and more objective. Of equal significance, however, was the fact that with the exception of the traitor, the category of the enemy no longer signified someone within Party ranks. The principal enemy was now the Japanese who could be known objectively because of their cultural, linguistic, and physiological differences. Moreover, since the enemy was now largely rendered external, the intensity that once surrounded the question of the enemy within diminished. Paradoxically, then, the release of intense political passions against Japan had the effect of diminishing internal excess. What the Chinese communists had almost inadvertently stumbled upon was a way of negotiating dyadic tensions. Indeed, Yan'an offers an exemplary case study of how an ethics of limit was instituted from *within* the framework of binary political distinctions. It does this by rechanneling political intensities away from the opaque and internal, such that one can learn to live with contradictions rather than be consumed by them. The shift from class to nation as the central organizing "contradiction" in communist discourse was, therefore, crucial in this transition and led to a range of other changes and reforms.

The shift would produce the need to rectify the ideas of Party cadres, to modify the CCP's organizational structures, and to moderate its program of land revolution. Despite all these moderations, however, commitment politics, by its very nature, never fully overcomes the possibility of the reappearance of intensity and, in this regard, Yan'an was no exception. Particularly in the period when the United Front began to fray, the question of an enemy within once again began to stalk the communists and threaten their carefully crafted calls for moderation. Under these pressures, the rectification campaign took an altogether different trajectory. Instead of moderating ideas, rectification led to cadre checking, which, in turn, resulted in the infamous and excessive "rescue campaign." While this campaign would be far less murderous than the elimination campaign of the Jiangxi period, it did illustrate the way in which Yan'an offered no lasting answer to the question of excess. Even the most cautious and essentially sympathetic of revisionist Western critics tend to treat Yan'an not as a site of moderation, but as a moment of revolutionary and nationalist fervor. In this guise, Yan'an stood as an omen of a future punctuated by "Great Leap Forwards" and "Cultural Revolutions" (Apter and Saich 1994, 25).

Linkages such as these, however, are no less a part of the Yan'an legacy than the moderation it attempted. Far from being a single-discourse community, Yan'an was, at best, an ambivalent state of affairs pointing to possibilities that were both moderate and radical. Yet what is perhaps most remarkable about the Yan'an period was not that excesses occurred, but that they looked like minor events when compared to past horrors. The moderate Yan'an was not the Yan'an of rectification, checking, and then rescue. Rather, it was the Yan'an of rectification, education, and then correction. It was a Yan'an of structural change put in place as a result of the United Front by the new Maoist leadership bent on ensuring that the wanton excesses of the past would never again be revisited. It was this side of Yan'an that gained expression not only in the generalized United Front policy and the moderate program of land reform but also in the important structural transformations undertaken in all areas and, in particular, in the realm of security.

Two innovations undertaken in relation to security work during this period were of the greatest import. They were instituted to ensure that security work would never again seem "mysterious" to the masses, or be conducted in a manner that would override Party directives (Wang Qiuxia 1994, 59). One was to make the security organs subject to local Party committee authority, rather than have them being an authority unto themselves. The other was to weave security work into the mass line. While these two innovations would have significant consequences, both ultimately proved failures. Neither addressed the basic problem of radicalization borne of the inherently unstable character of the political. At best, these Maoist innovations laid trip wires to slow down this process of radicalization and excess. Ultimately, it was the concrete situation that would determine the communist mind-set, and when that changed, so, too, did the degree of moderation. Once the concrete situation changed, such that United Front friends became suspect allies, the enemy within once again became the focus of attention. As this category of suspect grew, the category of friend began to diminish. As the category of enemy grew, it once again began to lose the limitations imposed upon it by concrete circumstances and Maoist innovation. Where Japanese had been an objective and external enemy, the enemy within was not. When the basic stabilizing dichotomy upon which Yan'an was founded began to slide into subjectivism, the mass-line fell into populism, and a combination of panic and passion produced the now familiar dynamic that had fueled past excesses.

The persecution of the literary dissident Wang Shiwei—not to mention the short-lived purge of Trotskyites or, somewhat later, the equally short-lived but even more vicious rescue campaign of Kang Sheng—were all, in their own way, effects of this dyadic process of framing politics. Moreover, when such contingencies began to operate alongside a populist policing system, the result would prove, quite literally, lethal. Aided by mass-line policing, the simplicity of the friend/enemy formula was wed to the populism of the crowd. The lowest-common-denominator politics of Yan'an, which had given rise to moderation ("unite with all those who can be united with"), could just as easily be turned on its head. Suddenly, another Yan'an appeared—the radicalized "other" of the moderate anti-Japanese base camp. The mixed messages emerging at this time indicated, then, the limits of the Party's ability to institute parameters.

Yan'an would build its discursive community on this fault line. It was a fault line that had a demonstrable propensity to excess, but also a lesson in how that could be partially and momentarily corralled. From this Yan'an, one can draw some broad lessons. The United Front policy demonstrated how the beast of excess could be momentarily tamed by the transference of intensity to another, external domain. Particularly in the early years, the constant pragmatic demand for unity in the face of a powerful enemy produced a nuanced and calibrated appreciation of "differences within," captured brilliantly in Mao's famous analysis, "On Contradiction." The constant re-iteration of unity discourse, coupled with the later compromises entailed in the three-thirds system (sansanzhi) of government,[3] produced a rhetoric and reality of national unity. This type of class inclusion limited the scope of internal campaigning to counter-espionage work.

As the United Front crumbled, the war became more pressing, and the Party larger and less reliable, class struggle once again began to intensify. As it did, the concept of friend was transformed into comrade, while enemy was read as a code word not just for the Japanese but also for deviationalists. Out of these temporal, pragmatic, contingent, and disparate sets of concerns emerged a number of rarefied models that would later be compressed into a single legacy that the postliberation Party would then try to celebrate. It is, however, important to recall the specific detailed and pragmatic nature of these events and organizations in order to demonstrate how they could be as much a part of the pragmatic, moderate, and reformist tradition the Party recalled as they were its radical leftist "other." It is for this reason that Yan'an looms large in any version of postliberation China, and the reason why we will now turn to it for lessons about the political.

Setting the Agenda

Sometime in October 1935, as the Long Marchers stopped for a toilet break, the reactionary newspapers they used to wipe themselves revealed more than what had been on the revolutionary menu the night before.[4] From these enemy newspapers the Party leadership learned of the purge of Liu Zhidan. Liu had been the creator of a liberated base camp in the northwest, but he had subsequently fallen foul of the politics of the Jiangxi-style elimination campaign conducted there.[5] While the Central Committee thereby became aware of Liu's fate, the unwitting communists who had usurped leadership of the Shaanbei base camp remained unaware of theirs.[6] A new, more moderate Party line was adopted after the Long March halted at the town of Zunyi and convened a meeting in January 1935. Mao, while not yet leader, had begun his ascent, becoming the preeminent Party voice. In Zunyi, both the leftism of Wang Ming and his military ineptitude were roundly condemned.[7] What emerged was a new and more pragmatic brand of politics that vowed never to return to the excesses of Jiangxi. All attention was now turned to the increasingly aggressive Japanese invasion. If the communists had earlier wished to save the Chinese masses from the oppressive classes, they now realized that they must first save all Chinese from the Japanese invaders. The result was a Party platform almost wholly consumed by the Japanese invasion and pitched almost entirely at developing a popular front against it. This not only put pressure on the Nationalist Party to alter its anticommunist stance but, as time wore on, it increasingly enabled the communists to wear the mantle of nationalism and, on this basis, reinvent themselves as a much more moderate nationalist force. This more moderate stance was summarized in the simple slogan: "unite with all those who could be united with" but it began as a concrete message from Mao to the far-off Party branch in the northwest: "Stop the killing, stop arresting" (*daoxia liuren, tingzhi buren*) (Wang Shoudao 1983, 25; PSHM 1992:3, V25, 18; *Gansu Provincial Gazetteer* 1995, 13).

The events in the northeast that precipitated Mao's orders were, in general, familiar enough. Forced confessions, more arrests, more confessions —until most of the top local leaders had fallen.[8] In the end, more than two hundred Communist Party members, and possibly many more (Apter and Saich 1994, 50), had been wrongly executed in this, the last of the major base camp elimination of counter-revolutionary campaigns (PSHM 1992:3, V25, 18). While the Long March had seen the complete disintegration of the organization that ran the campaign in Jiangxi, in the northwest, the Shaan-Gan-Jin Political Protection Bureau still operated as though the sun had never set on Jiangxi (*A Summary History* 1989, 33). Like the Jiangxi purges, those in the northwest were also complicated by vicious and protracted local leadership struggles. For the new national leadership, a demonstration of the current unity discourse was to begin with the imposition of unity upon its own people.

Thus when the Long March veterans finally began arriving at the Shaan-Gan base camp in October 1935, they immediately began a complete restructuring of the CCP and the governmental leadership of the base camp.[9] The Shaan-Gan-Jin provincial committee was wound up. In its place, the Party established the Central Committee Northwestern Bureau to cover Party matters and a northwestern office of the worker-peasant democratic government to administer the base camp (PSHM 1992:3, V25, 18). A similar reorganization, but one involving a more significant leadership purge, was undertaken in the area of security.

On October 30, the Shaan-Gan-Jin Political Protection Bureau was dismantled and its director, Dai Jiying, dismissed for excesses in the prosecution of the elimination campaign.[10] Protection work would henceforth be undertaken by the Shaan-Gan-Jin Political Protection Bureau under the leadership of Wang Shoudao. This new arrangement, coupled with the changes in practice it foreshadowed, were conveyed to local protection branches in two ways: First, a meeting of all cadres of the newly reorganized Northwest Political Protection Bureau was held at which they were told that the focus of work had shifted to "consolidating the Soviet, the Red Army, and the great majority of the nationalities into a united front."[11] Second, a team, headed by Wang himself, was dispatched with a brief to investigate all allegations of excess in the Shaanbei elimination campaign. Wang proceeded by sending his people into all local detention centers and initiating checks on all the political cases they found. Wang's teams did this so swiftly that the local cadres could do little to cover their tracks. Hence, "after a few tense days of work," the teams reached a unanimous verdict: those purged had no case to answer (PSHM 1992:3, V25, 19).[12] Given the politics of the moment, this was an inevitable outcome.

Mao had earlier insisted that "cutting off heads isn't like cutting up chives. Chives regrow, heads don't. If we kill the wrong people, if we execute revolutionary comrades, then we are the ones committing the crime. Everyone should remember this point, do things very carefully, and make sure that the research work has been done properly" (qtd. in Wang Shoudao 1983, 25). Wang obviously remembered this, for his report would reflect that logic when it announced that all charges against the local leadership had been completely erroneous (*Outline of Public Security* 1997, 65; Wang Shoudao 1983, 29). With the purge of the bureau complete, Wang would return to the front line in February 1936, leaving Zhou Xing in charge.

Ironically, then, the protection bureau which had begun life in Jiangxi as the vehicle by which to purge counter-revolutionaries had become, under this new Party leadership and line, the instrument of mass rehabilitation and overall restraint. Yet this did not result from any structural changes undertaken at the time, nor did it come about due to any change in the bureau's function. Indeed, it functioned, as it had always done, as a willing tool of the Party. What had changed was Party policy. In the new climate of United Frontism, as one source put it, the logic of the Jiangxi "Campaign to Eliminate Counter-Revolutionaries" no longer made sense (PSHM 1989:4, V14, 22). The theory of focusing upon the principal enemy, when translated into the language of United Frontism, meant "uniting with the many against the few," and, under this banner, the public security units took on a twin role of not only attacking the enemy but also ensuring that any attack undertaken did not confuse enemy with friend (PSHM 1989:4, V14, 22). It was because of this new role of limiting excess, while still pursuing "Japanese imperialists, Chinese traitors, Japanese supporters, and the Trotskyite faction," that it was thought necessary to inaugurate a comprehensive reorganization of all security forces (Mao Zedong 1975, 1:269, 273). This, it was hoped, would qualitatively transform protection units such that they would become structurally unable to fall back into Jiangxi-style excess. Transforming the structures of the security forces so that they maintained peace and operated with moderation therefore became a crucial and concrete expression of the Communist Party's overall desire to hold on to a dyadic political framework but work within its folds. In other words, this was to be the first concrete attempt to tame the beast of politics, rather than unleash it. In part, it constituted an inevitable consequence of a union with the Nationalist Party.

After the Xi'an Incident,[13] all significant Nationalist Party opposition to the formation of a United Front with the communists evaporated, and in July 1937,[14] the two parties became formal allies in the war against Japan. In the months that followed, the governmental structures of the communist bases were formally incorporated into the national government structure. In August, the Red Army, while maintaining its independent structure, was formally incorporated into the national army of China and redesignated the Eighth Route Army. In September, the communist administration of the Shaan-Gan-Ning border region (Yan'an) was renamed the government of a "special region of the Republic of China."[15] Along with these changes, the security organs of the Communist Party were redesignated governmental organs. Hence the Party's Northwest Political Protection Bureau was renamed the Shaan-Gan-Ning Border Region Security Division (bao'anchu) in September 1939 and fell under government control (PSHM 1992:3, V25, 23; Outline of Public Security 1997, 74; Questions and Answers 1994, 22; A Summary History 1989, 51).[16]

This redesignation of the Party's security wing as a division of government only increased the paralysis of a force already demoralized. Political considerations dictated that the communists "governmentalize" their Party security apparatus, just as the later three-thirds system of government necessitated the inclusion of non-Party officials in the government of the base camps. These two things alone meant that the Nationalists, in theory at least, would have some access to the highly sensitive security apparatus of the Communist Party. This restructuring of security, therefore, added to existing woes.

Dogged, on the one hand, by continued criticism of their past excesses, the security forces were criticized on the other by "some people" (Wang Ming's faction) for existing at all. What use was internal protection during the United Front period, these critics would ask? After all, former key targets of the revolution, such as the landlords and rich peasants, were no longer having their lands confiscated and their families watched. The transformation of the notion of the enemy, from being an actual class of people (that is, a struggle against landlords and rich peasants) into an abstract concept (that is, fighting the idea of feudal exploitation), made sure of that. Through this move, rich peasants as individuals, or even as a class, were now deemed acceptable coalition partners in the struggle against the principal enemy, Japan (Selden 1995, 78).

While such abstraction may have helped facilitate a major policy shift, all it did for security personnel was introduce a greater degree of confusion and uncertainty into their work. As morale within the security and intelligence apparatus plummeted, it began to have a deleterious effect upon the communists' war effort and directly resulted in the sixth plenum of the Sixth Central Committee in 1938 resolving to "strengthen the elimination of traitors' work."[17] To strengthen protection work, the CCP needed to ensure that the public security forces were under its control, rather than under the United Front government. To ensure that the most sensitive aspects of security work remained under the armed forces, the Red Army had established its own security and protection wing. Indeed, since departing from Jiangxi, the Red Army had more or less come to monopolize all work relating to security. While the Jiangxi-based Political Protection Bureau had disintegrated during the Long March, the army security wing had not. When the Party leadership arrived in the northwest, therefore, it was this army security wing that quickly took charge. In conditions of war, their heavy involvement in security matters made sense. Beneath such common sense, however, was a political maneuver. By transferring the most sensitive types of security work to the communist military, the Party not only maintained its control over key aspects of security but simultaneously ensured that all security cadres would learn from the revolutionary spirit of the Red Army.

Army tutelage enabled the Party to maintain its control over security despite the United Front forms of government coming into vogue and threatening that monopoly. In 1939, the Jin-Cha-Ji base camp was already experimenting with power sharing under the newly devised three-thirds system of government. In this system, one third of the government's elected positions were allocated to communists, another third to left progressives, and the last third to "intermediate sections who are neither left or right" (Mao Zedong 1975, 2:418). The Party summarized the experiences of Jin-Cha-Ji and adopted them as a model for the government of all base camps in March 1940 (Apter and Saich 1994, 211). While this system of power sharing may have strengthened the Party's credibility as a United Front partner and constituted a means of overturning local village-level elites (Dorris 1976, 697–719), it nevertheless eroded Party power. While the three-thirds system limited Party power at a governmental level, the Communist Party maintained its direct control over the army. Burnt by the betrayal of the Nationalist Party in their earlier United Front arrangement, the Communist Party was not about to give up its guns. The Party was, therefore, careful to ensure that unlike other government-based organs, the Red Army, when incorporated into the national army, involved no diminution of Communist Party control. Thus while overall Party control of government in base camps appeared to diminish somewhat as it broadened its leadership to incorporate noncommunists, no such decrease of Party power occurred within the army. The Party could exempt the army from the liberalization process by insisting upon the need for strong, clear lines of military command in what was a wartime setting. It could then use this command structure to maintain Party control over its armed force. By placing public security work within the purview of the army therefore meant that the CCP maintained its control over all security issues. Moreover, it could justify this army control of security matters on purely pragmatic grounds and, in this way, cover its own political machinations.

Strengthening Protection I: The Army Takes Control

The Communist Party could readily allocate security matters to the army because it had a history of working in this domain. In fact, the only organ that could have run protection work properly in the early Yan'an period was the army. Ever since the Party leadership arrived in Shaanxi, the task of eliminating traitors had largely fallen on its shoulders. It was the army that set up most of the base camps, developed the governmental structures within these camps, and began the task of uncovering enemies through their Elimination of Traitors Bureau (chujianbu) (interview, 1996). While in the smaller and less stable base camps the army ran everything (PSHM 1993:4, V30, 27), in the more developed camps, it shared power with the CCP and government in "three-in-one combinations" that would become the leitmotif of governance in the later years of the Cultural Revolution (CCA 1991, doc. 12, 183).[18] The significant role the military played in governing base camps was, in part, explicable by the nature of the times.

Most of the base camps were behind enemy lines, which led to life itself, not to mention security concerns, becoming military matters. With the constant threat of invasion and the regular changing of base camp boundaries, regular policing became impossible. Nevertheless, the strong army role in protection work was irreducible to such temporal considerations. Increasingly, the army became viewed as the virtuous model around which new styles of policing to replace the derivative Soviet model could begin to take shape. By September 1937, the role of the army in security work became formalized with the establishment within the Eighth Route Army's General Political Department of a Section for the Elimination of Traitors and Political Protection. Operating under the leadership of Yang Qiqing, some indication of its importance can be discerned from the fact that the five-person protection committee overseeing its work was made up of some of the Party's foremost generals, including Luo Ruiqing who would go on to become the first and most important Minister of Public Security in the People's Republic (PSHM 1993:4, V30, 2).[19] Hence even when the communists actually inherited an existing civilian police service, it was the army's protection units that played the pivotal role in reforming it and ensuring it was "red."

The takeover of existing police stations occurred as a result of the near collapse of the Shanxi warlord regime of Yan Xishan. Faced with ever-increasing attacks from the Japanese, Yan was forced into an alliance with the Communist Party that allowed the Party to take over all those areas that Yan had controlled, but which his forces could no longer protect. As the Japanese attacked, Yan's forces retreated, and eventually he was reduced to controlling but a small area in southwestern Shanxi. As Yan's influence waned, that of the communists grew. They would eventually incorporate much of his territory into three of their base camps—Jin-Cha-Ji, Jin-Sui, and later the Jin-Ji-Lu-Yu base camp.[20] The latter base camp would incorporate the two important areas of Taihang and Taiyue, which is where the police station structure of Yan was still operating. The incorporation of these two areas occurred after a series of ongoing Japanese attacks paralyzed Yan's forces and their hold on power began to slip. Even his county leadership and the chief of police were forced to flee in the face of Japanese attacks. In desperation, Yan turned to the communists. He would conclude a deal with two local patriotic association chiefs, Bo Yibo and Rong Wusheng,[21] who were using these associations as communist front organizations. Yan agreed to allow them to reform his government and security services in the area in exchange for military support. Bo and Rong began their "reforms" by selecting a number of trusted communists from within their patriotic societies.[22] These communists then began transforming the old government structure, taking over most leadership positions in Taihang and Taiyue, including the key posts of county chief and police chief.[23] After these reforms, Taihang and Taiyue became little more than communist territories, and the old police bureaus' little more than communist elimination of traitors organizations (PSHM 1987, v6, 14–15).

As if to confirm this, in November 1937, the 129th division of the Eighth Route Army entered Taihang and, along with local Party cadres, began to tighten security operations in the area.[24] They sent out investigative teams who set up protection units in each county. This, it has been subsequently argued, was the real beginning of public security work in the area (PSHM 1993:4, v30, 2–4). In effect, real public security work began only after the 129th division takeover. It was the 129th that took overall control of each of the "elimination of traitors" departments established by so-called patriotic organizations. When, in December 1939, a governmental police force was finally established in the Taihang region,[25] it was the head of the 129th's Political Bureau's elimination of traitors section, Liu Minghui, who was put in charge (PSHM 1993:4, V30, 7; PSHM 1992:3, V25, 26). While the prominent role of the army in establishing elimination of traitors' units in these areas could no doubt be explained as a wartime exigency, its role in training security officers generally suggests that the army's influence was far more central to the constitution of the new socialist policing ethos than one might at first think.

The Eighth Route Army became involved in training the security forces quite early on. In the late thirties, they established the first police academy in Liao county, Shanxi. By November 1938, it also began a system of training security teams. In both cases, the ethos of police training was decidedly military and Maoist. Cadres were trained to become, in the language of the Party, both "red and expert." Courses given to cadets combined political training with work and study. The courses focused practical and theoretical attention on the work of investigating and cracking cases and maintaining social order, and, while no overall statistics on the number of graduates exist, it is known that between 1937 and 1941, over five hundred cadres underwent training in these army-based teams and academies. After training, these cadres then went back to their own protection units and became "backbone elements" in public security work (PSHM 1993:4, V30, 3). What they learned through their army-based study was how policing could, in fact, become more Party and mass based.

In central Ji, for example, training courses that ran between February 1940 and February 1943 were all based upon the army model of being red and expert. This meant that there was "studying, on the one hand and 'doing' on the other." After two months of study, cadres would be sent out to the counties to carry out social survey work, look into files, and propagate the Party line (PSHM 1993:2, V28, 34). Throughout this training program, one finds a social science version of those wandering Party-army cultural workers who were sent out to learn the dances, songs, and habits of the local people and then infuse these with the Party message. In effect, the concept of the mass-line being proffered by the army meant that protection workers, too, were involved in much the same sort of work as the cultural workers, but they were doing it in relation to security. In place of song, the police cadres collected local grievances. Like the local songs, however, these grievances were transformed into a means by which the people would be shown that salvation could only come through the Communist Party. In this respect, the

Yan'an tradition was part bibliographic, part transformative, and yet also part performative.

Performance was yet another element of the mass-line policing practices the army taught the security forces. In the prosecution of the Elimination of Traitors Campaign in Shaan-Gan-Ning from mid-1937 to the end of 1939 alone, one thousand propaganda meetings were held, more than ten articles on the topic published in *New China*, and forty issues of *Public Security Half Monthly* distributed. In addition, over the same time period, eighty plays and musicals about protection work were performed and five comic and song books released.

Political theater in the Yan'an period also had a darker side. At the same time as these plays and musicals were being staged, 129 public show trials took place. Such mass trials formed part of an economy of equivalencies between right and wrong, friend and enemy, wherein both positive and negative models were put on display. In relation to the former, public meetings would be held to praise the positive heroes of the Elimination of Traitors Campaign, while, in relation to the latter, "typical cases" featuring negative role models would be selected and then given a show trial before being publicly executed (*Outline of Public Security* 1997, 86). Whether in literature, in social survey work, or in carrying out public executions, all acts demonstrated the value and correctness of the Communist Party's line. The army again showed the way. The idea of mass-line practices under the leadership of the CCP proved central to the army's philosophy, and now, with the help of the army, it would be translated into a practical program for security workers.

Peng Zhen summed up this new ethos when he spoke to a cadre training school in Fuping county, Jin-Cha-Ji, in May 1939. Security work, he said, had to be carried out under Party leadership, but always with mass support (PSHM 1993:2, v28, 32). The two were inseparable, he noted, but the former would always take precedence. To make sure of this, the new policing model would once again follow army practice. Like the army, protection units would establish Party cells at each and every level of their organization to offer grassroots leadership over their work. In that way, and at every level, policing would always be Party policing. Peng Zhen was, in effect, telling these police cadets their future. The records of attendance at this inaugural Fuping county training school at which Peng Zhen spoke said it all: forty-odd security cadres in attendance and "basically, all of them were Party"

(PSHM 1993:2, V28, 32). More Party security cadres in leadership positions and a Party committee leadership structure would help maintain Party control, but it was still not enough. To ensure Party control, the Communist Party needed its own security organization, and it was this that would be covertly established and charged with the task of coordinating all protection and security work. If the object of this exercise was to enable the Party to secretly gain control over all aspects of policing, then these communist security cadres were to be the policy's shock troops. The name of this clandestine organization that would operate as the Party's Trojan horse in relation to security matters was to be the Social Section.

Strengthening Protection II:
The Formation of the Social Section

> To each Central Committee Bureau Secretary, Zhu De, and Peng Dehuai,
>
> At the current time, the Japanese bandits, Chinese traitors, and other anti-revolution hard-liners are sending their secret agents into our camps by various means; they are plotting a conspiracy that will damage us. In order to consolidate and protect Party organs, the Central Committee has decided to establish the Social Section [shehuibu] within the upper echelons of the Party organization.[26]

So begins the document of February 18, 1939, that announced the birth of the most significant pre-liberation security organization in Chinese communist history (Li Jinping 1993, 124).[27] Contrary to the practices of the much-vaunted mass-line in policing, however, this organ was not born in the full light of public scrutiny. Indeed, the very existence of this organization, and even the document that announced its birth, were to be kept top secret. Even lower-level Party organs were to be kept in the dark about its existence.[28] One reason for this secrecy may well lie in the agency's role in counter-espionage. After all, according to one influential mainland source, "the decision [to appoint Kang Sheng as head of the Social Section] more or less tells us that its key role was counter-espionage work" (A Summary History 1989, 52).[29] At one level, this is undeniably true. However, while counter-espionage was one key element of the overall brief of the Social Section, it was not the only one.[30] Indeed, as even its founding document made clear, it was in charge of all protection, intelligence, and counter-intelligence work throughout the liberated zones. Why, then, the secrecy?

Given that policing was, technically, a government, not a Party matter, the leadership role given to the Social Section in relation to security questions proved, from the perspective of the United Front government, highly provocative. It threatened to make the moderate and nonpartisan appearance of government appear to be little more than window dressing. Yet how could the Party possibly allow a United Front government to control base camp security when the threat to security in the communist zones increasingly came from its United Front allies? The threat was too great to be left to chance, and the Party therefore needed its own means of controlling security.

How the Communist Party would maintain its control was explicitly addressed at the third meeting of county- and bureau-level security chiefs of the Jin-Cha-Ji border region in June 1940. The meeting concluded that Party control over security would be guaranteed not simply by getting Party cadres to occupy the leadership positions in protection agencies but by "seeding" communists throughout the organization at all levels. This so-called seeding process, however, required Party security chiefs to promote the surreptitious Party takeover of base camp security. When it came to internal protection, it seems, the United Front was not on the agenda. As point 6 of the Jin-Cha-Ji security chiefs resolution made clear: "The Public Security Bureau is not a United Front organization. This means that stress is laid on the fact that their personnel structure is not based on the 'three-thirds system of government,' but needs to guarantee that, organizationally, it is absolutely of one color" (PSHM 1993:2, v28, 36).

That "one color" was, of course, red, and it was this coloration that ensured that security organs in the base camps were absolutely different from the policing organs of the Nationalists (PSHM 1993:2, v28, 33). Yet public security organs in the base camps were still United Front government organs. To transform them into Party organs while still enabling them to have the appearance of being governmental was never going to be easy. For that reason, this effort needed organization. It also required a loyal, dedicated group of elite communists who could be trusted to hold their tongues and carry out their secret duty. Indeed, in February 1939, communist base camp leaders were told that if cadres of such high caliber could not be found among their own area or county committees, they should "temporarily refrain" from forming Social Sections and establish, instead, a training program for candidates (qtd. in PSHM 1987, v6, 3).[31]

If the Central Committee Social Section was something of an elite recruitment and training ground for future police leaders, organizationally, it became a model for all future protection work. The concrete details of how it spread into various base camps need not detain us, but the way it spread, by taking over and then disappearing into the bowels of every public security unit so that it became virtually indistinguishable from them, was one way it could hide its presence. As one source noted:

> After the establishment of the Central Committee Social Section, every level of Party Committee also established "Social Sections." In quite a number of areas, the "Social Section" and the Public Security Bureau occupied the same space and, although there were two names on the building, there was in actuality only one job being done. Classified work was simply described as being "social section work," while public work was defined as public security work. In actuality, all such work was carried out under the one unified leadership of the Party Committee. (*A Summary History* 1989, 53)

More than simply an intelligence or counter-espionage agency, the Social Section's principal function was that of Trojan horse. It was the means through which the Party could unobtrusively regain complete control over security matters, despite the civilian environment and the strictures of the United Front three-thirds system of government in the base camps. The Social Section offered the Party a means to project its agenda onto local policing agendas and scrutinize every level of the security and intelligence apparatus. The Social Section became the vehicle through which the Party made itself central to police work. It was the mechanism by which the platitudes about overcoming the "vertical leadership and independent system model of the GPU" (Dai Wendian 1991a, 13) would be translated into action. At the same time, the Social Section would maintain, if not increase, tight Party control over policing by promoting the leadership role of the local Party committees. It was with the formation of this local Party committee system that we discover Communist Party control and the promotion of the mass-line—the two pillars upon which postliberation policing would be built—beginning to operate in tandem (interview, 1993). As one source states:

> At this time, the mistakes of the land-revolution war period [i.e., the Jiangxi period], which involved the excesses of the Campaign to Eliminate Counter-Revolutionaries, had been restrained and corrected. Nevertheless, a systematic assessment and summary of the experiences and lessons to be learned had yet to be made. In order to successfully develop the "elimination of traitor" work under the new social conditions, the Central Committee of the Party deemed that the strengthening of Party leadership over the "elimination of traitors" work and the opposition expressed to the vertical structured command system [of the past] were utterly necessary. To mobilize and rely on the masses for elimination of traitors work would prevent this work becoming mysterious. It was after the sixth session of the Sixth Central Committee and the establishment of the Central Committee Social Section that great stress was laid on the "Elimination of Traitors" Campaign. (*Outline of Public Security* 1997, 80)

The excesses of Jiangxi, it was thought, could be avoided by reliance upon these twin pillars of the mass-line and strong local Communist Party committee leadership. It was hoped that this new structure would make the errors of excess visited upon Jiangxi a thing of the past. The weakest link in this chain, however, was always going to be the local Party cadres. The problem of cadre "purity" was far from new. Indeed, knowing the genuine political positions of local Party members in leadership positions had always been a concern of communist parties around the world, but in China, with real power now invested in these local Party committees and in the mass-line, it became an even more pressing concern. Lenin once proposed constant checking of cadres to ensure no deviation,[32] but Mao would focus more on education and rectification. In either case, however, what both Lenin and Mao sought was cadre loyalty. In Yan'an in 1940, with the enemy at the gate and "friends" increasingly ready to betray, it is easy to understand how loyalty could become such a key virtue. It is also easy to understand how the fear of internal betrayal that starts to blur the line between friend and enemy could easily transform education into checking and checking into accusation. As the United Front began to fray and as the war with Japan grew

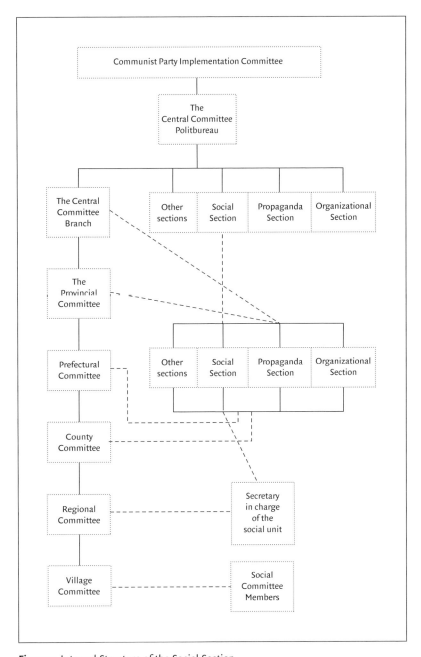

Figure 3. Internal Structure of the Social Section

Source: *Activities of the Chinese Communist Party's Special Agents* 1983, 267.

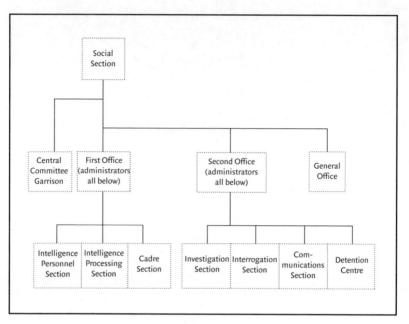

Figure 4. The Communist Party's Social Section Structure
Source: *Activities of the Chinese Communist Party's Special Agents* 1983, 266.

more desperate, mass-line protection work gave way to intelligence work, and much of that would be taken up vetting local communist cadres. One part of this program would be the public checking of them in the process of rectification. Another, less visible side involved an elaborate reconstruction of an internal surveillance network designed to monitor cadre behavior for telltale signs of deceit.

Refocusing on Intelligence Work

From the late 1940s onward, conditions in quite a number of base camps deteriorated rapidly. Increased Japanese military attacks on a number of base camps, along with the discovery of a number of enemy infiltrations, refocused Party attention (PSHM 1993:2, v28, 67–69; PSHM 1987, v6, 25–26). Counter-intelligence work took on a new urgency as evidence emerged that Japanese espionage organizations were increasingly active within camps such as Huainan and because of the increasing espionage work undertaken by the communists' United Front "friends," the Nationalists. What made the situation in Huainan particularly difficult was the strength of the right-wing Nationalist "CC faction" in the area.[33] They were thought responsible for carrying out assassinations, spreading rumors, using "left" slogans to undermine the Party, instigating rebellions against the communists, and even sending in drugs and "pretty women" to seduce communist soldiers and cadres (PSHM 1989:4, V14, 18–20). As signs of this Nationalist betrayal grew, the United Front deteriorated and, as it did, the cycle of suspicion turned into covert action on both sides. The Nationalists and communists both began jockeying for position as the cover of friendship began to disintegrate and reveal the depths of animosity that lay between these two parties.

As the communists' counter-intelligence work began to uncover more and more signs of Nationalist espionage, the category of the enemy began to extend beyond the Japanese and their local recruits to include another group beginning to fall into that frame—the "reactionary backbone and stubborn elements of the Nationalist Party" (PSHM 1989:4, V14, 23). To counter these three enemies, three communist intelligence positions were brought back into service: the detective, the networker, and the inspector. All three positions had seen extensive use in the Jiangxi period, but they had fallen into abeyance since the Party's arrival in the northeast. It was now thought time for their return.

The detective was to carry out covert surveillance of Party and government agencies in order to eliminate any traitors within. Every village was to have at least one or two detectives (PSHM 1989:4, V14, 25), and every season they would undertake comprehensive checks of all work unit and departmental cadres. In these seasons of surveillance, detectives would open every cadre file. They would search within them for those telltale signs of betrayal that lay buried but unrecognized in the cadre's narrative of revolutionary conversion and work. The detective could also employ the services of a local secret "work networker" (*gongzuo wangyuan*) to further any inquiry. Recruiting local communist backbone elements, the Party would use these networkers in their home county. They were instructed to use their original jobs as covers and keep their real role and identity secret (PSHM 1989:4, V14, 26, 27). Networkers, like detectives, were positions resurrected from the bad old days of Jiangxi. Indeed, even their name was initially maintained

Table 1. Detectives in Some Counties of Southern Huai

County	Number	INCOMPLETE ESTIMATES OF COUNTY POPULATION	
		1939	1944
Tianchang	20	231,615	231,615
Liuhe	11		
Lai'an	12	127,894	127,894
Other (unnamed) county	8		

Source: Figures on detectives in some counties of Southern Huai from PSHM 1984, v14, 27. Population figures drawn from the *Provincial Gazetteer of Anhui* (population volume) 1995, 37–38.

(*Outline of Public Security* 1997, 87).[34] The final security position resurrected at this time was that of the inspector. Inspectors held responsibility for border security checks on all incoming and outgoing mail and for checking on any passport issuances.

In addition, some base camps also introduced other Jiangxi-style positions into their security work. Prominent among these were the "detective instructors" (*zhidaotan*), who trained personnel and offered leadership in counter-espionage work; the "sleeper" or stationary detective (*zuotan*), who was a deep cover agent operative within enemy territory or within enemy organizations; and the "activity detective" (*xingdongtan*), who was basically a "wet work" specialist or assassin (PSHM 1989:4, v14, 26). While there are no statistics available on the overall numbers of these agents, the August 1941 figures from southern Huai, covering a range of counties, does give some indication of their density on the ground and the degree of effort that had gone into redeveloping this grassroots intelligence network.

What is interesting about all these revivals is that they placed security work on a new footing. The Communist Party now demanded that even its lowliest-level informants display a strong commitment to the Party cause. The differences between the Yan'an and Jiangxi version of the networker sum this up. In Yan'an, only those who displayed "the strongest commitment and competence" and the "greatest love of the Party" seemed acceptable, whereas in Jiangxi, networkers could be recruited from anywhere, for it was elite special agents who were the key, not the networkers (PSHM 1989:4, v14, 26). In Yan'an, the mass-line ensured that this degree of trust and power

Table 2. Activity Detectives, Sleepers or Stationary Detectives, and Detective Instructors in Some Counties of Southern Huai

	COUNTIES					
	Lai'an	Jiashan	Liuhe	Yizheng	Tianchang	Total
Activity detectives	2	6	5	2	17	32
Sleepers	3	13	2	1	29	48
Detective instructors	3		1		5	9

Source: PSHM 1989, V14, 27.

would never be given to an officer from an elite professional security force. With the reformed work styles of the security forces now centering upon a mass-line style of work under the leadership of the local Party committee, the burden of commitment, purity, and trust became a burden for all. No longer was it sufficient to demand this level of commitment only of an elite force. From now on, everyone in the Party needed to be utterly committed, pure and trustworthy. Perhaps it was because the whole Party was now being structured around this ethos of local mass-based leadership that the Party center felt secure in reviving structures that had once directly contributed to the excesses of Jiangxi? Perhaps the revival of these Jiangxi-style security positions suggests a certain confidence in the new Party-organizational ethos of Mao? If so, such faith proved misplaced.

Indeed, it is much more likely that this resurrection of Jiangxi-style policing positions was less a sign of confidence than of desperation. If so, then this revival gives us some indication of the unusual degree of fear and anxiety abroad at this time because of the reemergence of that troubling character, the treacherous friend. That this fear of betrayal would force the Party to test the strength of its new structures by reviving aspects of Jiangxi gives some indication of the power this figure of the enemy within had in setting both Party and security agendas. In this new regime, much would be made of the need for local, mass-orientated, reliable, and pure communist cadres to uncover impurities within Party ranks. But what happens even here when suspicions of impurity relate not to overt evidence, but to intangible, and quite often subjective, assessments of cadre motives? What happens when telltale signs are thought to say more than they actually do? It is at this point

Table 3. Work Networkers in Some Counties of Southern Huai

| County | Number | INCOMPLETE ESTIMATES OF COUNTY POPULATION | |
		1939	1944
Jiashan	75	115,906	115,906
Yutai	46	296,800	296,800
Tianchang	37	231,615	231,615
Lai'an	17	127,894	127,894
Liuhe	17		
Huaibao	11		
Gaoyou	36		
Banta	39		

Sources: Figures on work networkers from PSHM 1989, v14, 27. Figures on population drawn from the *Provincial Gazetteer of Anhui* (population volume) 1995, 37–38.

that the specter of excess begins to reappear, despite the existence of the mass-line and the power of the local Party committee. Under such circumstances, local Party control and mass-line orientation actually contribute to the dynamic by adding the specter of populism to the mix. It was just this sort of situation that came to frame the first major case of campaign excess registered in these "Yan'an years" — the so-called Trotskyite campaign that developed around the little-known West Lake or Huxi Incident.

The Huxi (West Lake) Incident

Trotskyism might seem an unlikely catalyst for the first large-scale campaign in post-Jiangxi China. After all, barely had the Trotskyist movement begun in China in 1931 when its leaders, including the ex-leader of the CCP, Chen Duxiu, were arrested by the Nationalists and sentenced to long years of imprisonment. Moreover, even when they formed a united Trotskyist organization, called the Leninist Left Opposition Faction, it had no more than 360 members (*Outline of Public Security* 1997, 195). Yet Trotskyism played a key role in the iconography of the Communist Party. It had become part of a narrative string that added up to a way of saying "enemy." In the endless series of documents listing the enemy, one always finds Trotskyism mentioned.

It featured in the October 1939 "Resolution," just as it appeared in Mao's writings and speeches.[35] Its appearance partly demonstrates the continuing influence of Soviet discourse among Chinese communists, but, more importantly, it indicates a mind-set wherein a danger so minor could appear so great. How could that be?

Liu Shaoqi once remarked that the elimination of traitors work involved two types of struggle—one open and armed, the other secret and constituting a struggle of the mind. Whoever ignored this latter struggle, he went on to say, would be lost (Guo Hualun 1969, 2:228). The Japanese were numerically strong, but visible. The Nationalists were, likewise, a physical force to be reckoned with, but morally, they were thought to be bankrupt. Trotskyism, on the other hand, dreamed the communist dream. It was the "disease" that appeared to Party cadres as the great temptation. In the struggle over hearts and minds, a battle that was always central to communist thinking, Trotskyism was no chimera.

Like any disease, Trotskyism proved infectious. Like any temptation, its allure was great. What Trotskyism threatened was the core narrative arithmetic of the Communist Party. Friend and enemy were no longer clearly marked. Rendered internationally as "the great betrayal," Trotskyism became the organizational manifestation of all Party fears and doubts about itself and its cadre force. The Chinese case was illustrative of this. After all, how could ordinary cadres be relied upon when even an ex-leader of the Party, Chen Duxiu, had been tempted? How could the ordinary cadres be relied upon to remain true, when the Soviet purges demonstrated that Trotskyism had spread even to the furthest branches of that Party? In the USSR, an identically structured Party to the CCP had produced this "deviant" tendency that proved so virulent that the struggle against it was described as being a matter of life and death. The Soviet anti-Trotskyite campaigns stood as both remedy and sign of the disease communist parties feared. The infection was severe and the cure drastic. Here is a logic that the Chinese Party inherited and believed. It would stay with them long after the problem of Trotskyism was gone. It would reappear, decades later, to frame the narrative structures around which Party fears of another form of "revisionism" would find cure in the ideas of Cultural Revolution, and its reappearance would, once again, find voice through Kang Sheng's rhetoric. In 1939, however, revisionism appeared not as revisionist Soviet betrayal but as Trotsky's.

Kang Sheng, the Communist Party security czar, returned to China from the Soviet Union in November 1937 and brought with him a set of Soviet concerns about internal struggle that were quickly to become Chinese dilemmas.[36] As the Chinese communists in Yan'an took up the Soviet agenda, Trotskyism became a major concern from 1937 onward (*Outline of Public Security* 1997, 96). In January 1938, Kang would publish a long article denouncing Trotskyism and calling for greater vigilance (Lin Qingshan 1988, 62). The Central Committee did not take long to respond. In February, it refocused the Elimination of Traitors Campaign onto the question of "Trotskyite bandits." At the same time, however, the Central Committee issued instructions which were highly contradictory. "Don't miss one single enemy agent," security cadres were advised, "but don't deal erroneously with a single good person," they were warned; "don't let one enemy agent through the net," they were told, "but don't manufacture enemies"; "don't let one spy from within escape," they were cautioned, "but don't falsely accuse comrades" (Social Section Directive, PSHM 1987, v6, 8–10).[37]

These slogans repeated the need to police the line between friend and enemy carefully, but left open the crucial question of where stress should be laid. Earlier, security organizations had been charged with excess. Now they were being accused of inaction. As the pendulum swung back to action, cadres responded. As Trotskyism was the target, Trotskyite traitors would be found. Given the almost infinitesimal number of Trotskyites in China, plus the lack of clarity as to what exactly constituted a Trotskyist, any momentary dispute could therefore become the grounds upon which to present this particular accusation. So begins the story of how West Lake or Huxi became infamous as the site of the so-called Huxi Incident.

In June and July 1939, a small group of Pei county students from the Hubian (lakeside) Prefectural Committee's cadres school had just graduated. As was standard practice under the socialist system, graduation meant job allocation in places where the Party required cadres. The Pei county students, however, refused to accept their job allocations and asked instead to be returned to their home county, where they thought they would be most useful. They were supported in their demands by a teacher at the college, Wei Dingyuan, who had previously worked in Pei county. The trouble was that Wei was deeply unpopular with the college leadership, who regarded him with some suspicion. "It is not so simple as some people having strong ties to their home town," argued the Hubian Prefectural Committee leader, "the cadre institute is a place where we produce cadres for our Party and our army; we cannot let enemy spies make chaos in our college." As for Wei Dingyuan, the school described him as a person who "harbored evil intentions" and was "a troublemaker and the organizer of the whole affair" (PSHM 1988:3, v9, 145). Wei was arrested, and the head of the organization department of the prefectural committee, Wang Xuren, was called in to handle his interrogation. Wang believed Wei was more than just a troublemaker; he was a Trotskyite, and Wang was prepared to use force if necessary to get Wei to admit this. Under torture, Wei confessed and began to offer details of other Trotskyite activities in the Hubian area. He admitted to being "the Su-Lu-Yu Border Area Special Committee Secretary" of the Trotskyist organization and then named a range of other ranking Party members as other Trotskyites (PSHM 1988:3, v9, 145–50). Acting on this information, Wang started arresting others, forcing confessions and then carrying out more arrests on the basis of these forced confessions.

Within two months, the Pei county student case had spread from being a concern about the purity of the Huxi Prefectural Committee (*diwei*) to one which enveloped the entire Regional Committee (*quwei*). By the end of the purge, only Wang Xuren remained on the Huxi Prefectural Committee; all the rest were shot (Dai Wendian 1991a, 15). The Regional Party Committee suffered a similar purge, and only Wang's main supporter on that committee, Bai Ziming, remained. The Su-Lu-Yu base camp branch political commissar for the Eighth Route Army, Wang Hongming, also joined in the purge and extended the struggle into army ranks, "unmasking" over five hundred enemies there. In the end, three hundred of those unmasked in the army were executed and over two hundred (forcibly) gathered together for further "collective training" (*jixun*).

After Huxi, other places began to discover that they, too, had Trotskyites in their ranks. In the Shandong base camp area alone, Ludongnan (southeast Shandong), Luxinan (southwest Shandong), Jiaodong, Taishan, and Qinghe all followed Huxi's lead. In Taishan, in August 1940, the anti-Trotskyite campaign led to the arrest of thirty people and to ten executions. Like Huxi, the Taishan campaign was also based upon forced confessions. Following Taishan, similar campaigns opened in Boshan, Tailaibian, and Xueshan. More wrongful arrests, more executions, more suspects. The campaign in Shandong even began to spread to other provincial base camps. There is some evidence of persecutions taking place even as far afield as Huazhong (central China) (*Outline of Public Security* 1997, 93).

It was not until November that the arrests and killings stopped, when the scale of the Huxi campaign began to alarm more senior cadres (*A Summary History* 1989, 63).[38] An investigation into the affair by the Shandong branch of the Party followed. In June 1940,[39] it concluded that Wang Xuren (who had by this time committed suicide)[40] was, in fact, an alien-class element, while Bai Ziming and Wang Hongming had both been responsible for organizational and political errors. While this report continued to label Wei Dingyuan and six other people Trotskyites, the other suspects, it said, had confessed under torture and were, in fact, innocent of the charges. While innocent of the substantive charges, the report concluded that these people had nevertheless "betrayed themselves and the revolution" by falsely confessing under torture. In a remarkable move, the report demanded that these people now be punished for their weakness. In cracking under torture, the report concluded, these people had shown themselves unworthy of the name Communist Party member and therefore should be "removed from Party ranks forever" (*Outline of Public Security* 1997, 93; PSHM 1988:3, V9, 162).

The Central Committee in Yan'an was dissatisfied with this report and commissioned their own. A five-person investigation team led by Chen Yun, and including Peng Zhen, Li Fuchun, Kang Sheng, and Tao Zhu, was then dispatched to investigate, and on February 20, 1941, they handed down their verdict. They reported that the campaign "lacked correct knowledge of the counter-revolutionary nature of the Chinese Trotskyite faction and subjectively overstated the strength of the Trotskyite faction." They pointed out that although the incident was now over, work in the region had not recovered and the masses still lived in fear. Moreover, a number of innocent people still had not had their names cleared, while the punishment of Wang Hongming and Bai Ziming still had not taken place (qtd. in PSHM 1988:3, V9, 163).

As a result of this report, new action was initiated. For instigating the excess, Wang Hongming was court-martialed, removed from all posts, and stripped of his Party membership. Bai Ziming was said to have been a follower who participated under pressure from Wang Hongming. He was demoted and his Party membership made provisional. Of the accused, the report continued with the argument that Wei Dingyuan and six others were Trotskyites, but in relation to those who confessed under torture, it redesignated them as "good comrades" (*Outline of Public Security*, 1997, 94–95).[41] The report concluded with six recommendations designed to ensure that no repeat of this sort of excess would occur. In the light of subsequent events, one of these holds particular interest.

In order to prevent future errors, the "Central Committees Report" concluded that a check of all cadres should be undertaken alongside the purging of all traitors. This, it was hoped, would ensure that minor mistakes in political life, in work, or in private affairs would never again be mistaken for signs of counter-revolutionary or traitorous intentions (*Gong'an jianshi*). In this respect, the report put legs on the 1940 Social Section document to security cadres that stated, "Don't let one enemy agent through the net, but don't manufacture enemies." In the Central Committee's Huxi Incident report, however, the new two-pronged approach to the problem of deviation and its rectification was weighted in favor of education and rectification, not repression. This approach dovetailed with growing preparations for a Maoist campaign that would educate the cadres but repress deviants. This process of rectification would begin with a call for a more careful screening of evidence in relation to charging people with counter-revolutionary crimes. This demand was raised in two notices that appeared in April and August, respectively. The first concerned the need for a resolution of a number of pending cases involving suspected counter-revolutionaries. While these cases were still under investigation by "some military-political protection organs," the cadres concerned "hadn't been checked out," and those who were suspects and those already convicted were simply being lumped together in prison. Security cadres, it insisted, needed to differentiate between error and enemy.

The second notice came out in August 1941. Summarizing the actions taken in the security cleanup in Yan'an, it found that all too often, people were being labeled suspected counter-revolutionaries simply because of inadequacies in the investigation process. It found cases of internal Party problems and complex social relations being confused for counter-revolutionary attitudes. It found that in some cases, the protection units had confused those who raised genuine complaints with those who spread vicious rumors, and it thought that the security organs sometimes confused honest but critical opinion with malicious rumor (*Gong'an jianshi*).[42] To ensure that cadres could differentiate between these different types of problems, further political education was needed. Moreover, as these constituted errors in demarcation between friend and enemy, they were problems that pointed to an issue of central concern to the revolution. The Party was increasingly finding that it was impossible for cadres to differentiate friend from enemy because they knew so little about class analysis and Marxism. Clearly, one of the things this process of checking revealed was the need for greater political education and, by February 1942, this received a name: that name was the rectification campaign and, under this title, it entered into Chinese communist folklore.

From Checking to Rectification and Back Again

It is little wonder that the Party found its cadre force inadequately trained by the 1940s. The war years had seen an enormous growth in both the base camps and in Party membership. Between 1937 and 1940, Party membership had grown by over 90 percent, from only 40,000 odd people in 1937 to around 800,000 in 1940 (Li Jinping 1993, 129). The growth was so rapid that by 1939, the Politburo called for a suspension of the "storm membership drives." The order of the day in 1940 was consolidation, but numbers continued to increase. Since the United Front was signed in 1937, the Party had grown by over 700,000 people (CCA 1992, doc. 14, 29). The problem was that something like 90 percent of these new Party recruits were of petty bourgeois origin, with the great majority coming from an intellectual or peasant background (Harrison 1972, 323). Ninety percent was also the figure given for the existing Party cadres who had not attended any Party schools and who were, by and large, without training in Party principles or theory (Apter and Saich 1994, 282). With an endless string of "90 percent problems," the Party decided to act. Unity and discipline in Party ranks proved an absolute necessity if the CCP was to overcome the increasing array of problems it faced.

A lack of unity would offer even more opportunities for a Japanese army that had, since late 1941, turned its attention to, and weapons upon, the communist base camps. The "three mop-ups campaign" or *sanguang* policy of "burn all, kill all, loot all" was creating havoc in the base camps and forcing major retreats or, at best, base camp boundary realignments.[43] These base camp attacks, however, were also a sign of the growing importance of the communists as a force to be reckoned with, and this point was not lost on the communists' long-term rivals, the Nationalist Party. As if crystallizing this point of view, Jiang Jieshi would at this time speak of the state of the Chinese nation as a medical condition. The Japanese, he insisted, were "a disease of the skin," while the communists, he pointedly stated, were one "of the heart" (Clubb 1972, 238). The continued growth in communist numbers did little to dissuade the Nationalists of this viewpoint. Rather than supporting the growth of an ally, the Nationalists tried, instead, to limit the growth of a rival ideology, communism. They began to blockade the base camps and use the storm membership drives to infiltrate the Communist Party. The communist fear of an enemy within was, therefore, never without foundation.

This cluster of problems demanded attention, and the rectification campaign constituted one means of shoring up internal Party unity and creating a sense of shared purpose.[44] A massive Marxist educational program designed to popularize Communist Party ideology and raise the basic standards of Party work and political literacy ensued (Li Jinping 1993, 129–30). It was an education program designed to provide the conceptual tools that enabled the differentiation not only of friend and enemy but also of enemy and error. Rectification would, therefore, help the Party work out who was a genuine recruit and who was not. In providing the means to separate error from enemy, it helped rectify past Party practices that had resulted in excess. If Yan'an generally can be thought of as the first Maoist attempt to reform the (Schmittian) political, then rectification was to be one of its key technologies. In the language of Michel Foucault, we might think of this moment as an attempt to augment the simplicity of the either/or choice of sovereign power with a complex pedagogy based largely upon the disciplining of the cadre.

It was through rectification that the Party attempted to balance the necessity of the either/or choice of sovereign power (friend/enemy) with the techniques of disciplinary power, and while the sovereign question would always remain supreme, it was no longer the only one. It would prove a difficult balancing act. It was, nevertheless, absolutely necessary to avoid a descent into the hell that was Jiangxi-style excess. Why the need for this balance? The Party needed the binary of friend and enemy to inject revolutionary passion into the people. But if such passions turned to populism, then past experiences demonstrated that passions aroused could easily spiral into excess. Rectification constituted an attempt to balance these two sets of interests by reforming the dyadic structure of the political without loosing the intensity necessary to propel the revolution forward. It did not aim to overcome the binary, but to work within its folds and harness it to its own ends. The sovereign question was never abandoned, only supplemented, and the discipline imposed during rectification was the way to do this.

The rectification campaign would take place in three stages, and this was to become the metronome of virtually all future campaigns in China. Rectification began with a "preparatory" stage (December 1940) that then moved into a mass organizational stage (January 1942) and finally ended with the "cleanup of tails" stage (October 1943).[45] Ideologically, rectification also established Mao Zedong's thought as the new basis for Party unity. In terms of content, it was built around the idea of "uniting with all those who could be united with." Politically, it invented the means—unity-criticism-unity—for dealing with internal contradictions nonantagonistically. In this respect, rectification appeared to offer a set of techniques by which to limit the intensity of the dyadic structure of the political by building upon the recognition of a calibrated understanding of contradictions and difference. Difference no longer constituted a telltale sign of the enemy, but could simply signal an "adversary." Just as the United Front policy had made friendship a much broader category, rectification now offered a subtle and sophisticated means of diminishing the category of the enemy by recognizing that difference did not always mean deviance.

Such a "rectification" of the political, however, presupposed its continued operation within the logic of the dyadic frame. The category of error within the rectification framework opened a space to read difference that did not signal death. Death remained for those who continued to be deemed the enemy, for rectification always included more than a hint of a draconian solution. Nevertheless, the attempts to introduce the category of error cannot be dismissed out of hand. All one can say is that this attempt to reform the dyadic political structure to make it more liberal ultimately failed. After all, every error deemed serious was still read symptomatically as a sign of a dubious political affiliation that could potentially spiral into more dramatic claims. Curing the Party of these serious problems therefore always had the potential to drive rectification off course. In cases that necessitated more than simply criticism-unity-criticism, rectification attempted to limit excess by speaking of them as medical problems.

"Learn from past mistakes to avoid future ones," went the slogan, "cure the sickness to save the patient" (*chengqian bihou, zhibing jiuren*), came the couplet. Here, in the language of cure, hid another face of rectification. Education plus cure, training plus discipline, encouragement plus the possibility of punishment: these make for the two-sided dialectic of the Yan'an experience. One side of the Yan'an way tries to resolve contradictions internally, maintain the United Front, and build upon the logic of the new distinctions between enemy and error. The other side of the dialectic was devoted to the cure of serious error, the elimination of deviation, and the destruction of the enemy. These two faces of Yan'an provide us with a glimpse of two potential political futures for China.

The Yan'an experience of moderation enabled the United Front to survive and grow, just as the educational side of rectification offered the Party a set of techniques that could later play a role in framing the strategy to ensure the peaceful rectification of China's cities. At the same time, however, Yan'an also came to inform a postliberation Chinese future that would be punctuated by terror and this, too, had a history that was tied back to Yan'an. In relation to the first of these two possible futures, the Party's United Front policy and the stress on education within the rectification campaign offered a means of work and training that would eventually enable peasant cadres to come to an understanding of the historical and practical need for revolution, but simultaneously to an appreciation of the revolutionary stages of human history. It enabled the peasant cadres to come to an understanding of the limits imposed by different historical stages and different geographic modalities. It educated them so that they could in the future read these in relation to their own concrete political tasks such as taking over and transforming the cities.

Rectification, however, also played a part in radicalizing Yan'an. The rectification campaign provided evidence of a very powerful "enemy within." This evidence propelled Yan'an into excess. The fear that gripped the communists in Yan'an enveloped the space of moderation and once again saturated the communist camp in the dyadic colors of the political. The fear that followed the rectification campaign's discovery of an "enemy within" momentarily overwhelmed Yan'an. Clouds of doom and betrayal began to gather and as these clouds gathered, a reign of terror followed. Yet as the city takeovers would show, terror was not the inevitable or only possibility opened up by the Yan'an way.

The Janus Face of Yan'an I: The City Takeovers

By the late forties, the liberal potential of Yan'an and rectification would metamorphose into a programmatic series of techniques designed to peacefully rectify the Chinese cities after years of Nationalist rule. If the United Front model of Yan'an established the general mood of the takeovers, it was the original rectification campaign that established both the three-tiered rhythm of the process and the stress upon educating and training the cadre force prior to each city takeover. Taken together, Yan'an and rectification offered a template for the training of revolutionaries in moderation.

The battle for the cities, therefore, constituted more than a struggle over territory; it was a fight over hearts, minds, and productive potentials. For two decades, the Communist Party had been forced to live outside the city. In those years, it had renewed itself in a way that accentuated its difference from city life-forms. This Party renewal process was, by necessity at first, built on a peasant mass base within a series of rural base camps. Later, with Maoism, necessity turned to virtue as Maoist-Marxism developed dreams bordering on romantic pastoralism.[46] The "dark satanic mills" of the Chinese cities were far removed from the yellow plains and "feudal traditions" struggled against in Yan'an. Moreover, cities always seemed to be in enemy hands. For two decades, being sent into enemy territory meant being sent into the cities (A Summary History 1989, 67). This left an indelible, if unconscious, mark upon rural communist cadres' attitudes toward city life and its people. Unremarkably, given the strength of their dyadic understanding of life and all its forms, cities in the abstract, were coded by many ordinary communist cadres as alien and enemy.

With this attitude prevailing, it is little wonder that when the communists finally did get to take over their first city (Harbin), Party plans were disrupted because of unprecedented degrees of insubordination and illegal activities committed by communist troops who regarded the city as "war booty."[47] Unsurprisingly, given that it was a peasant-based army, the ordinary communist cadre sent into the city seemed, initially at least, unable to appreciate the value of the finely grained historical differences Marxist theory established between the reactionary rural landlord classes and the progressive city-based capitalists. Yet an understanding of such differences was central to Marxism, for it was this that separated the science of Marxism from idealism. Moreover, it established the basis of the claim that socialism required a high level of development of the productive forces in order to function. The development of these productive forces meant recognizing that differences among the various elements of the ruling class were important. When the productive forces remained underdeveloped, it meant that the city-based capitalist class was "objectively" a progressive force, and, even by Maoist pastoralist standards, this Marxist theoretical understanding was still absolutely fundamental to their appreciation of politics. For the rural-based Chinese Communist Party, the city takeovers offered a salutary reminder of what it was that differentiated Marxist socialism from its utopian cousins. The ordinary communist cadre, however, needed to learn such differences.

The communist cadre would come to an understanding of this via a unilinear reading of history. It was, after all, this reading of history that helped the Chinese communists frame their own understanding of where their nation lay on this chart of historico-economic development. China, they concluded, was economically and industrially backward,[48] and this meant that national liberation would not lead to socialism, but only to the bourgeois democratic stage of the revolution. That, in turn, would necessitate an alliance with the national bourgeoisie for, without them, the productive forces would never develop to the point whereby the material possibilities of socialism could be realized. Mao Zedong's claim, voiced in "On New Democracy," that Party policy was not "to abolish private property but to protect it" (Mao Zedong 2:339–84), was, therefore, not simply a hollow, pragmatic, and realpolitik ploy to allay the fears and suspicions of city dwellers and the national bourgeoisie. It was a heartfelt and theoretically informed promise borne of the necessities of the transition process.

Before convincing city folk of this, however, Mao and the Party needed to persuade their own cadre force. Education and training made for the only ways forward, and rectification constituted the only mass-scale model of reeducation available to the Party. Thus while rectification and the city takeovers were in many ways completely different, they at least shared a common pedagogical understanding reliant upon mass reeducation through the institution of a Maoist revolutionary praxis. Instituting a mass education program also ensured a certain order of appearance of events. As a result, even the three phases of the rectification campaign appear to have become the template for the three phases of the city takeovers.

The first phase of the campaign, which was always a preparatory stage, involved organizing small but concentrated training courses for ordinary cadres involved in the city takeovers. The second phase, always mass-based, involved physically taking over the cities and becoming involved in struggles, while the third phase, which was always coercive, turned on weeding out those hidden reactionary tails that the initial two phases had missed. This combination of education and action was all designed to teach cadres the value of revolutionary moderation. In other words, this way of approaching the issue was designed not to radicalize cadres, but to ensure that they understood that the actual takeover of the cities should be viewed in the same way as they had formally come to understand the Party's moderate United Front program.[49] In order to illustrate how moderation should be achieved, a series of "model takeovers" were advanced, and the most widely used of these examples was the takeover of Shenyang in October 1948.

Studied intensely in the preparatory stage before every city takeover, Shenyang highlighted the importance of detailed knowledge of city conditions prior to action being taken. The preparatory stage of the city takeover, like the preparatory stage of rectification, worked on the idea that knowledge was power. To make cadres powerful, they needed to be taught. While the first stage of training differed from rectification in that it involved no autobiographical work, it shared with rectification a commitment to gathering research materials that were both of a theoretical and a practical nature. This combination of material was then used in classes organized for all the future city cadres involved in the takeover. Practical material had a range of sources, but one key component came from a series of detailed social surveys that the Party's underground city workers had conducted. By October 1948, the idea of compiling social survey material into collections for cadre training had itself become something of a model followed in future takeovers.[50] By 1949, social survey work had become so detailed that when it came to a city like Wuhan, Party cadres were even issued with local road maps and telephone books (PSHM 1990:4, V18, 145–59). In the earlier takeover of Nanjing and Shanghai, the material collected ran to fifty-three volumes (*juan*), thirty of which were devoted solely to Shanghai (PSHM 1989:2, v12, 242–43).[51] While detailed and voluminous, this was not the only material used in cadre training.

In the takeover of Beiping, for example, four types of texts were collected and used to train cadres. Theoretical works outlining such things as the general principles of the People's Liberation Army's moral doctrine would be examined alongside the work of Mao Zedong. Added to this were the writings of local communist leaders or specialized sections of the Party. In Beiping, this meant that Peng Zhen's writings on Party and government matters were widely consulted, as were the writings of Ye Jianying on the military and of Li Kenong on policing and security (PSHM 1987, v3, 158). Apart from such theoretical writings, cadres were also directed to read of past Party experiences in city takeovers. These past experiences were summarized into a series of models that could then be read alongside the survey work underground Party members had undertaken.

Under a Party regime demanding moderation and care, the "unity discourse" of Yan'an was revived. To ensure that this was turned into action, the Party would rework the pedagogic techniques of Yan'an generally, and of rectification in particular. Through these techniques, the Party learned how to train its cadre force so that it understood the theoretical basis of the Party's calls for moderation. The CCP did this while simultaneously supplying cadres with an array of practical examples that highlighted past impediments to this policy and gave them a taste of the type of issues they may face in implementing the Party's new form of United Front. But before lauding the United Front policy and rectification as a means by which the dragon of excess was slain, one must recognize that these were techniques and, as such, were not restricted to a singular usage or meaning. Techniques cannot offer any a priori guarantee of moderation. Indeed, under different sets of political conditions, they will operate differently. Hence, as a set of techniques, rectification and the Yan'an spirit could just as easily radicalize as moderate political demands. Indeed, once any of the research undertaken or collected began to point to an enemy within, as it did in the early forties in Yan'an itself, the moderate and liberal forms of rectification almost inevitably gave way to much harsher pronouncements. Under such conditions the dyadic colors of politics began, once again, to shine through. And as these colors began to glow, the compromises possible under the sign of liberal moderation evaporated. If city takeovers illustrated the potential for rectification and the Yan'an way to induce a moderate path, the radical potential of rectification became visible in embryonic form in the later Yan'an period itself.

The Janus Face of Yan'an II: The Other Side of Moderation

It was in November 1942 that the first signs of this darker side of Yan'an came to the fore. This version of Yan'an did not interpret rectification simply as clarifying the line between proletarian and non-proletarian ideology and thought; it was, as Mao pointed out, establishing who was a revolutionary and who was not. That is to say, it was a return to the question of friend and enemy. For this reason, Mao insisted, Party members needed to remember that not every error could be rectified. Some things constituted not errors but deliberate acts of sabotage. For people who committed this type of act, there could be no rectification or redemption (CCA 1992, doc. 14, 92). A key task of rectification was establishing this line between error and enemy. Here, then, was the point of slippage between the educational side of rectification and its more coercive side. Here was the point at which the leader of the revolution, Mao Zedong, handed things on to his security chief, Kang Sheng. Kang was in charge of both the Social Section and the Intelligence Bureau, but, during rectification, he would also act as Mao's deputy on the Central Committee's General Study Committee (zhongyang zongxuewei). This committee would oversee all study undertaken during the rectification campaign (Apter and Saich 1994, 283; Zhong 1982, 83, 349–50),[52] and Kang's role seems to have asked him to focus upon those cases in which wrong ideas appeared to reflect "bad intentions."

Looking for the divide between error and intent, Kang began by examining various expressions of liberal sentiment within the base camps. In April 1942, the liberal wall newspaper Light Cavalry (Qingqidui) came to his attention, and he would speak of it in scathing terms: "The Nationalist special agents are praising Light Cavalry as the only audible voice under the Yan'an dictatorship," he said (qtd. in Outline of Public Security 1997, 115). By midyear, attention was beginning to turn to the field of art and literature. In June 1942, Liu Xuewei, an art columnist for Liberation Daily (Jiefang Ribao), was criticized for publishing an article on revolutionary literature that described it as "coarse, dull, and inferior." Another columnist, Ding Ling, was attacked for pointing to the gender inequality extant in Yan'an (Apter and Cheek 1994, xxiii). It was, however, Wang Shiwei and his story *Wild Lily* that brought matters to a head. In this novella, Wang, a researcher in the Research Center for the Arts in Yan'an, lambasted the Party for the hierarchized nature of life in Yan'an and for continuing to accept inequalities.[53] The moral duty of the artist, Wang said, was to act as social critic. Attacking Mao's taste for beautiful women, he offered a critique of Mao's new wife, Jiang Qing, by comparing her with a true revolutionary woman he had once known (Apter and Saich 1994, 61–62). The Nationalists used this short story as propaganda against the communists and, because of this, it also became an important political issue, with Wang becoming increasingly regarded as a dubious friend (Xu Linxiang and Zhu Yu 1996, 150).

Criticism of Wang began more or less from the time this work was published. At first, critiques of Wang were limited to newspaper attacks and focused on his alleged "petty bourgeois mentality" (Apter and Saich 1994, 62). Unlike other criticized writers, however, Wang refused to concede any error and, as a result, from the end of May on, both the tempo and temperature of criticism about him began to change (Xu Linxiang and Zhu Yu 1996, 150). By May 2, 1942, Mao Zedong was laying down the law on the nature of "true art." The political divide now began to infect the world of the artist. True revolutionary literature, Mao said, had to be both proletarian and mass-based. Good literature was politically committed literature, and he deemed the idea of art for art's sake unacceptable (Mao Zedong 1975, 2:69–98). Wang's radical style and content was clearly out of step with this dyadic aesthetic assessment, yet he seemed to revel in this difference rather than cower before it. Contrary to Mao's Leninist position, which essentially homologized all facets of life into politics, Wang argued, in "Politicians and Artists," that these realms of human activity differed intrinsically. The politician's life, suggested Wang, was dominated by pragmatic concerns focusing upon revolutionary tactics and strategies. In contrast, artists, he said, were "engineers of the soul," and their task was not pragmatic but to encourage human cultivation (qtd. in Xu Linxiang and Zhu Yu 1996, 149).

In line with the new pragmatic and political climate, the Central Research Institute found Wang's words objectionable. He became the subject of a struggle-and-criticism session, in the course of which he admitted to having contacts with Trotskyites. From that time onward, he found himself thus labeled (Xu Linxiang and Zhu Yu 1996, 151).[54] Trotskyism once again functioned as the communist's mark of Cain. It required no further explanation, only condemnation. For this reason it would reappear, time and again, to designate those who were the target of attack and expulsion from the revolutionary ranks. Nevertheless, art and literature were but one expression of this more general program of repressing dissent underway in Yan'an at this time. Indeed, art and literature inhabited a minor domain when compared with the time and energy expended on unearthing the moles within Party ranks.[55]

By year's end, Kang Sheng had become concerned with the negative effects of gossip in Yan'an. On December 6, 1942, under the auspices of the Central Committee's General Study Committee, he issued a document highlighting the extreme dangers of gossip. Those who gossiped often revealed Party secrets, propagated rumors, and made up things injurious to the Party. Those who spread such gossip were to be checked and their ideological standpoint assessed (CCA 1991, doc. 13, 460–71). At a time when the base camp social security division (bao' anchu) began discovering a range of cases involving Nationalist espionage agents at work in Yan'an, it is little wonder that gossip was becoming a big issue.

According to Party sources, the Nationalists' military had set up a special station in the northwest to train agents in the art of infiltration. Known as the Northwest Special Agents' Station, its sole aim was to infiltrate the Communist Party base camps. Its main target was the Shaan-Gan-Ning base camp, but it also dispatched agents to Taihang, the E-Yu-Wan (Hubei-Henan-Anhui) base camp, and communist base camps in Shandong. Running twenty-nine small espionage groups active across thirteen provinces, the station was said to have successfully sent over eighty agents into communist-controlled areas. The vast majority of these agents would end up in Shaan-Gan-Ning and, in a number of instances, ended up in important positions within government and Party departments (Dai Wendian 1991a, 16–17).

Faced with this growing problem, it was Mao who first set the ball rolling back to a friend/enemy dyad when, on March 16, 1943, he said that the Party not only had to combat petty bourgeois thinking but also had to address the question of counter-revolutionaries (Hu Qiaomu, 1994, 276). With new and disturbing information about Nationalist spies, and with Mao's apparent approval, Kang Sheng called upon the Politburo on March 20, 1943, to make the checking of cadres the focal point of work for 1943 (Xu Linxiang and Zhu Yu 1996, 134). In the eyes of Kang Sheng, if not of the whole Party, the final phase of rectification was simply the beginning of a new, more coercive program of checking that would become known as the Campaign to Check on Cadres, or *shengan* campaign. This was to mark the beginning of a slippery road leading back into binary excess.

From Checking to Rescuing

The veteran communist, Tao Jian, tells the story of this slide into excess in miniature when he recounts his own role in the shengan campaign. Along with two other comrades from the Party committee school in Taihang, Tao was pulled from his "rectification classes" and sent back to his local public security bureau because it was said to be in the hands of the Nationalists and in need of checking. Following a blueprint set out in the rectification campaign itself, these three cadres returned home and convened a large meeting of all twenty cadres in the bureau's headquarters. They then split this group into rectification classes and spent the next ten days locked away with them, studying documents on rectification that came from the Central Committee. Being forced to read Central Committee documents might well be regarded as torture enough but, in this case, it was simply the beginning. It would start a trajectory captured admirably in the arithmetic of Kang Sheng. "Rectification = cadre checking = the elimination of counter-revolutionaries," Kang would say (Lin Qingshan 1988, 103). This, then, was the formula about to be tested by the three young cadres from Taihang. Tao Jian's words offer us a firsthand account of the dynamics that would lead this formula into terror. It would begin as a normal process of rectification and then slowly move on to personal histories. But these personal historical recollections were no ordinary reminiscences. The "key thing" for the three cadres was to unlock how it came to pass that these security cadres "came to be active in the revolution." Nor was this question to be the stuff of vague generalities ("We got them to tell us in quite concrete terms"). The three cadres sought quite precise details "about how [the security cadres] physically got into the Taihang base camp." Once they got this information, the three interrogators would return to the issue repeatedly. First, an oral account of the journeys of those under interrogation was given. Then, the same tale was repeated, but this time it was written down. The opening shot on this road to terror was, it seems, nothing more sinister than the cross-checking of the oral and written accounts.

Kang Sheng had highlighted to his security cadres the value of such cross-checks when he spoke of the role of autobiography in the interrogation process:

> When the person first arrives in Yan'an, they must write of their own, personal journey. When rectification is underway, they must write about their lives. When they are undergoing checking within the organization, they must write of their own introspective thoughts. All these three components of their autobiography are then compared so as to bring out the many contradictions. Some people are a bit scared about getting into trouble, so they just write a very general outline, beginning with various versions of their personal history, according to the general guidelines. These hardly have any contradictions in them. Then, if you ask them to write in front of you, they will. Then you get them to write at home. It is at this point that many contradictions can be found. (qtd. in Shi Zhe 1992, 202)

Signs of doubt arose when suspicious circumstances seemed to surround a cadre's move into the base camp. Similarly, doubt may have followed the discovery of a small contradiction in the account given when oral and written versions were compared. Contradictions would raise little suspicions, and little suspicions would grow wings if it were found that the cadre had "been a member of the Nationalist Party or Nationalist Party student organization leader while they were at college." Alternatively, if they were found to have reactionary relatives, then this, too, served as further proof of their suspicious character. The three interrogating cadres would dwell on these types of things when talking to a suspect. But they dwelt on such things only for a short time. After a while, dwelling turned to action, and when that moment came, these three good communists were not found lacking in their resolve to get to the bottom of the counter-revolutionary activity. Despite their cautious words, if one remembers Jiangxi, one knows exactly what these cadres are saying when they admit to sometimes having to "press" suspects for information: "It was only when we really pressed them, when we forced them, that was when they began to make confessions and, of course, when they confessed, we believed them. So the whole thing relied upon bi-gong-xin, and the net result was that over 90 percent of all the cadres in the Public Security headquarters ended up being accused of being CC faction special agents" (PSHM 1993:4, V30, 198).

Kang Sheng's arithmetic began to yield dividends as the three cadres moved from rectification to checking and, from there, to bi-gong-xin. The final part of Kang's formula, the part where cadre checking equals the elimination of counter-revolutionaries, was proving to be true, for bi-gong-xin was making it so. Such "truth" did not simply come from Taihang. Across the lands where communists held sway, public security units everywhere were engaged in similar exercises and beginning to uncover Japanese bandits and Nationalist spies within their own local Party branches. Rectification did not just turn into checking; it turned in upon itself. In this climate, rectification would almost inevitably turn into checking and, as Tao Jian's words reveal, that always required a bit of force. For a Party already hardened by Jiangxi, the consequences of using such force must have been all too apparent. But then again, so, too, were the dangers to the Party if force were not applied.

Alarming revelations now began to emerge about enemy penetrations. This forced the hand of the Party center that then authorized the initial transition from "soft" rectification to "hard" checking. This, in turn, seems to have reinforced a climate within which bi-gong-xin seemed a necessary measure. To refuse to commit bi-gong-xin was to refuse to fully commit oneself to the Party cause. The methods used to extract information seemed far less important than the information gained. Hence security cadres readily used sleep-depravation techniques, round-the-clock interrogations, and physical torture to force the accused to confess. People were drawn and quartered, starved, and psychologically tortured by false executions; all this in the name of the revolution (Gao Hua 2000, 504–5). As long as the rats within Party ranks were found and neutralized, the question of method was inevitably a secondary concern. Perhaps this is why Kang Sheng would tell cadres in almost humorous tones of the best techniques he knew of for uncovering enemies. "Think of it as rat catching," Kang would say and then proceeded to elaborate:

The first thing that needs to be done is to catch a really big male rat. Once you've got it, stick a soy bean up its arse, and then stitch the bugger up. After a couple of days the bloody thing will be huge. This will drive it crazy, and it'll go from one rat hole to the next biting its comrades to death. After it has taken care of all the others, it, too, will die. This is how we should be running things in the course of the Elimination of Traitors Campaign! (qtd. in Lin Qingshan 1988, 115)

Kang Sheng's "rat campaign" began in March, but it did not become official until October 1942. At this time, the campaign received an official imprimatur by the Central Committee that decided to name it the "Campaign to Check on Cadres" (Li Jinping 1993, 133). It constituted a reluctant but nonetheless official recognition of the link Kang was making between rectification and checking. At first this campaign remained confined to Yan'an. There, after all, was where the secrets were. Apart from educational institutions, it would involve checks upon Central Committee branch and department cadres (Li Jinping 1993, 132–33). By March 1943, however, Kang thought the results warranted a more extensive set of checks. The experiences in Yan'an, he suggested, should be "communicated" to all base camps (Outline of Public Security 1997, 116). Fearing the consequences of any such extension, the Central Committee balked. They needed to be sure that an extension of checking did not simply mean that the security forces were chasing phantoms. To convince them that this was not the case, Kang needed to detail the possibility of serious threats that would be missed if such an extension was not granted. The opportunity to demonstrate this would unfold at this very point in time in the form of the Gansu Red Flag Party case.

From Red Flag to Rescue

The Gansu Red Flag Party case centered upon a nineteen-year-old communist activist from Lanzhou by the name of Zhang Keqin (Dai Wendian 1991b, 17).[56] Zhang had been an underground Party member in Lanzhou until 1939. In that year, the reactionary local authorities began to investigate his revolutionary activities. Fearing his arrest, the local Party organization gave him permission to depart for Yan'an. After he arrived in Yan'an, he received word from the Gansu provincial capital, Lanzhou, that both his father and his wife had been arrested. Under pressure, both had turned against the Party. Suspicion once again fell on Zhang. This time, however, it was the Communist Party that became suspicious of him. They feared he was, in fact, an enemy agent who had "turned" prior to his arrival in Yan'an and had been sent to the communist capital as a spy. Nothing other than the betrayal of his family members supported such suspicions. In a climate where the fear of betrayal was palpable, however, that was enough. In December 1942, Kang Sheng personally ordered that Zhang be brought in for more detailed questioning (interview, 1997; Byron and Pack 1992, 176).

He was arrested and subjected to round-the-clock interrogation for three days by a team of people including Wang Dongxing and Wu De (confidential material 1988). They used threats, enticements, and force to make him admit to being a spy (Li Jinping 1993, 133). Confused and fearful, the nineteen-year-old cracked. Fed information by his interrogators, Zhang Keqin admitted that he and the Gansu underground Party branch he was associated with were secretly part of an organization known as the Red Flag Party (Xu Linxiang and Zhu Yu1996, 137).[57] Despite the dubious nature of the confession, Kang was convinced that the Red Flag Party, like Trotskyism, constituted a major threat to Communist Party security because of the way they "waved the red flag to oppose the red flag." At the same time, in order to encourage others to follow Zhang's lead, he made the young man into a confessional role model. On April 10, 1943, on the back of a horse festooned with red flowers, Zhang was paraded around Yan'an to advertise the fact that frank confessions brought forth leniency and that all must attend a confessional mass meeting that would launch his infamous rescue campaign. Zhang's ride, it has subsequently been claimed, was the reason for the huge attendance at Kang's meeting (Wang Suyuan 1991, 212).

In May, Kang would again use the Zhang Keqin case to illustrate his point about the need for vigilance at a grouping of shengan campaign cadres held in the Dabiangou Eighth Route Army lecture hall. At this meeting, Kang directed all security cadres to study Zhang's case. It served as an exemplary confessional model of how they could get those who had taken the wrong road to repent and confess, he said. He later added that all of those who "had lost their footing" needed to be made to confess, and he began to personally mark out a list of suspects who needed "help." This group was then detained for further investigation (Dai Wendian 1991a, 17–18). But it was not just the Yan'an branch of the Party that had lessons to learn from the Red Flag Party case. Indeed, in the light of revelations about betrayals in the Gansu Party branch, Kang believed it to be high time for the spotlight to be turned on all underground Party branches (Li Jinping 1993, 133). As further confessions produced ever greater degrees of doubt, the entire underground Party branch in Gansu was put under investigation. Investigations also extended into other branches, and "quite a few" underground Party members in Gansu, Henan, and Sichuan were identified as Red Flag Party members and arrested. From then on, all Communist Party members from these areas who ventured to Yan'an were immediately treated with suspicion and often investigated as traitors or spies (Xu Linxiang and Zhu Yu 1996, 137–38; A *Summary History* 1989, 58; Li Jinping 1993, 134). So suspicious of Party members from so-called white areas did Kang Sheng become that he started to refer to them as "radishes": red on the outside and white on the inside. They professed a belief in the Communist Party, he said, but in reality, they were Nationalists (Dai Wendian 1991a, 17).[58]

White area communists were not the only ones under suspicion. What the Red Flag Party case highlighted was the need for vigilance in relation to anyone who had close links with the Nationalists. This became all too apparent on April 1, 1943, when the Nationalist general responsible for blockading Yan'an, Hu Zongnan, arranged for a delegation, led by his senior staff officer Hu Gongmian, to be sent to negotiate with the communists in Yan'an. Hu Gongmian was, in fact, a former communist with an extensive friendship network among Communist Party members in Yan'an. His presence in Yan'an made the communist leadership very nervous. They believed that there would undoubtedly have been Nationalist espionage agents within his delegation. To prevent these agents from connecting with their local operatives and contacts, Kang Sheng drew up a list of suspect residents of Yan'an and ordered them all arrested before any contact with the delegation could be made. On the night of April 1, security forces carried out a series of raids on suspects and, by the next morning, over two hundred people were in custody in Yan'an city alone (Wang Suyuan 1991, 211).[59] If one were also to include the border regions around Yan'an, the number of arrests jumps to well over four hundred people (Shi Zhe 1992, 6; Hu Qiaomu 1994, 276).

With the number of telltale signs of betrayal increasing, the Central Committee acted to bring this matter to the fore. On April 3, 1943, they issued a decision that extended cadre checking beyond Yan'an to all base areas. This decision pointed out that rectification meant more than resolving ideological problems; it involved eliminating the enemy within. Checking cadres, therefore, was not just about checking their level of ideological commitment but also necessitated "checks into their history and their political appearance so as to discover and eliminate any hidden spies among them" (CCA 1992, doc. 14, 30). The April 3 decision not only extended the campaign, therefore, but also deepened it.

It was Mao Zedong who would make the shift explicit. On April 5, Mao chaired a meeting of the Party secretariat at which the call for traitors and spies to come forward and confess was issued. With this logic now informing rectification, moderation disappeared. The Campaign to Check on Cadres "went mad, hurtling itself forward without restraint" and transforming itself into the infamous rescue campaign (Xu Linxiang and Zhu Yu 1996, 135). The dynamics fueling the expansion and deepening of this campaign are familiar enough. They are ominously similar to those that propelled the earlier sufan campaign in Jiangxi into excess. Nevertheless, given the deteriorating military and political situation at this time, the refocusing of rectification so as to enable the security forces to check for enemy agents hardly seems surprising or unwarranted.

Due to the secretariat decision of April 5 a series of meetings were convened in Yan'an between the ninth and twelfth of that month. At these meetings, those cadres with problems were told to step forward and frankly admit their shortcomings and errors. Something like 20,000 cadres attended these meetings and, from this, the campaign to check on them was transformed into a mass campaign focusing on opposing spies (*Outline of Public Security* 1997, 117). The result was that so-called frank confessors would go to the central auditorium in Yan'an and confess. At the same time, each unit organized its own meetings where people were called upon to confess. If a suspect failed to confess, it led to further investigations and struggle sessions. Increasingly, "frank admissions" were requiring a little force and, in some cases, the result was a confession that was palpably untrue (*Outline of Public Security* 1997, 117). Again, the snowball was beginning to roll, and, as it turned and gathered momentum, shengan or cadre checking became "rescue." One can date the rescue campaign, or, more correctly, "the campaign to help those who had lost their footing" (*jiangjiu shizuzhe yundong*), from around this time.[60]

The rescue meetings reaped a bitter harvest. By their end, over two thousand cadres had been accused of being either spies or traitors (Li Jinping 1993, 134). In the Yan'an border region's government units alone, about one hundred of the three hundred or four hundred staff would receive "help" (Dai Wendian 1991a, 18). The scale of this movement, while dwarfed in comparison to the Jiangxi purges, still proved quite significant and illustrated the way Maoism's famous answer to excess—the mass-line and local Party control—provided no answer at all. In this respect, the campaign emerges as more than a sign of Kang Sheng's mistakes or his evilness. Instead, we could view rescue as one more example of the way dyadic politics, pushed to extremes, has no where else to go but into excess. Naturally, the excesses related to the way Kang conducted his work, but the key point to remember is that this movement into excess grew out of a dyadic framing of the political which everyone shared. In this respect, the rescue campaign was simply the multiplier effect of events that fed on each other and, when integrated into the overarching binary understanding of the political, produced a sense of danger around every corner. It fed on a belief of Nationalist Party omnipotence, Japanese power, and internal political treachery. It made for a powerful political diet that nourished the healthy paranoia already in play. In Yan'an, however, the binary of politics had history to contend with. The looming specter of a return to Jiangxi-style excess would always cause alarm bells to ring, and they began to ring loudly as the rescue campaign unfolded. The Party center grew alarmed at both the speed at which the campaign developed and the methods it used to extract confessions.[61] The Party leadership began to institute checks and controls of its own in an attempt to rein in the possibility of excess. On May 21, the Central Committee issued a document establishing six points governing all counter-espionage work that was clearly aimed at curbing some of the excesses of the political campaign (*Outline of Public Security* 1997, 118; Dai Wendian 1991a, 18).[62] These six points in effect constituted a not-so-subtle hint of general disquiet within the Party leadership about the way things were proceeding. As the campaign moved from being an internal Party campaign to one that touched the broader community, the Central Committee followed these six points with a resolution on methods of leadership on June 1. This resolution again reiterated the basic principle of close ties between the Party leadership and the masses in any decision (Dai Wendian 1991a, 18).

In terms of wayward methods, the Party began making clearer statements. On June 18, the Central Committee issued detailed regulations demanding that abuses in the interrogation procedures come to an end. The Basic Regulation Governing the Central Committee Social Sections' Interrogation Work was "no ordinary regulation but clearly set forth concrete regulations that were pointedly aimed at the then current practice of forcing people to confess" (*Outline of Public Security* 1997, 118). In outlining those practices it wished to curtail, the Central Committee listed a litany of abuses that painted a dark picture of the way people received "help" during this campaign.

As if these regulations and notices did not constitute a clear enough warning that the campaign had gone off the rails, Mao Zedong personally weighed in, writing a letter to Kang Sheng on July 1, a missive subsequently published and now known as the "Nine Point Policy."[63] In this letter, Mao said,

> The accurate [method of checking] is: leaders taking [overall] responsibility, individuals taking personal responsibility for their own actions, and backbone leadership elements uniting with the masses. Generally, this means slogans and concrete directions are as one, research and checking is undertaken, and a clear line is drawn between light and heavy offenders. One tries to win back those who have slipped along the way, one trains cadres and educates the masses. The erroneous line is to torture, to force confessions, and to believe what is divulged under torture. (Mao Zedong 1996, 35).[64]

While the campaign's methods received behind-the-scenes criticism, the actual attempts to halt what Kang thought was the specter of an imminent Nationalist invasion of Yan'an seemed to demand that they continue. With fears of an imminent invasion ignited, the campaign was momentarily revived with a series of mass meetings. This attempt to transform the internally oriented rescue campaign into a mass movement was wed to an equally unsuccessful attempt to present it in a positive light.

On July 15, Kang rather pointedly described the campaign as one propelled by the broad and lenient policy of the Party. It was under this rubric of leniency that he encouraged all those who still harbored secret "errors" to come forward and confess because, as he said, "our broad policy has its limits, and on this point, we will pay very strict attention" (qtd. in Dai Wendian 1991a, 18).[65] After a series of big rescue meetings in Yan'an throughout July, the revival of the campaign came to the attention of the Central Committee leadership who, once again, began to put limits on it (*Gong'an Jianshi*). On August 15, 1943, the Central Committee issued a document effectively banning bi-gong-xin. Hot on the heels of that came the publication of Mao's now famously moderate "Nine Point Policy" (Dai Wendian 1991a, 19; Li Jinpin 1993, 133; PSHM 1992:3, V25, 34).[66] Collectively, these two things seem to have killed off the tail end of this campaign, and it is again Tao Jian's recollections of events that we can turn to in this regard. Tao alerts us to the sudden turnaround as it played itself out locally within the Taihang area police headquarters.

Tao Jian's story begins where we left off—with the purging of over 90 percent of the public security personnel after they were accused of being counter-revolutionaries. He continues his recollection of how this led to Central Committee and Northern Bureau intervention. Ordered "to put a brake" on the campaign, the three purging cadres were replaced by the local Party area committee that began investigations into the charges of betrayal the three had made against the local security forces. In the vast majority of cases, the purged were rehabilitated. Those with questions to answer were now the three purging cadres. Tao Jian was now forced to show contrition:

> In the struggle against spies, we had implemented the erroneous "bi-gong-xin" method and, through this method, the struggle had just kept on growing, leading to many fine comrades being forced to wear the label of a Nationalist spy. Then [we] read Mao's Nine Point Policy and, after that, and with some excruciating re-examination of our own work practices, we were able to get our public security work back onto the right path, the path that led back to the mass-line. (PSHM 1993:4, V30, 198)

The "Nine Point Policy" and some soul-searching may have led Tao Jian to reappraise his work style, but others were not so easily charmed. Despite the death of the purging dog, the tail of the campaign still appeared to be wagging in some places. In early September, in the town of Panlong in Yan'an county, a meeting of over five thousand people saw twenty-three of them admitting to spying for the enemy and being rescued. Why did they confess to what later turned out to be ridiculous charges? *Liberation Daily* of September 21, 1943, had the answer: "If one admitted things then it was no big deal, but it is impermissible not to admit" (qtd. in *Outline of Public Security* 1997, 120). While *Liberation Daily* offered soothing words to would-be confessors, events elsewhere suggest that sometimes admissions did, in fact, become a really "big deal" for those who made them.

In September 1943, at the northern Zhun middle school which had been turned into a training center for cadres, a student stole some money. The theft was linked to allegations of a conspiracy to steal, rob, and develop an armed insurrection. The school authorities listened to these preposterous suggestions and started to "out" various people as spies. Forced confessions followed, with people admitting to being spies and to carrying out all sorts of counter-revolutionary acts. One student, Hu Jian, was forced to confess to the theft and subsequently beaten to death. Before he died, however, he linked his own "espionage" activities to fifty-six teachers and forty-eight people outside the school. More purges followed before the authorities discovered that the whole thing had been a fabrication (*A Summary History* 1989, 64).

A similarly ridiculous purge played itself out at Suide Teachers College, where 160 youths were rescued at a mass meeting. The vast majority of the youths brought before the meeting confessed. Many of them were only in their teens. One fourteen-year-old girl accused of being a spy was said to be "only as tall as a table." Her diminutive size, however, would not save her. For nine days, these youthful counter-revolutionaries were struggled against, resulting in a further 230 students, or 73 percent of the entire student body, being denounced as spies (*Liberation Daily*, September 22, 1943; Wang Suyuan 1991, 219). Even more ridiculous was the case involving a sixteen-year-old boy who admitted to being the head of a Yan'an-based counter-revolutionary organization. This organization was known as the Rock Head Group because its main counter-revolutionary activity consisted of throwing rocks at communist troops and trying to hit them on the head and kill them (Lin Qingshan 1988, 110–11).

Mao read these reports of continuing purges and grew alarmed. On October 5, he coined the slogan, "Don't execute a single one, and arrest only a few" (*yigebusha, dadoubuzhua*). With these simple written instructions transmitted to all base camps, the campaign came to an end by December 1943. The reexamination process that Tao Jian discussed began immediately after this. It started in the heart of communist power, Yan'an, and from there spread to other camps. As Li Weihan would later put it, there were to be "no tails" left behind in this campaign, so all cases had to be cleared up (Li Weihan 1986, 513). From this so-called clarification came a report issued in the spring of 1945 that drew conclusions in relation to 2,475 cases of purge victims. The report discovered that the security forces had relied upon voluntary confessions in only 10 percent of cases. In 30 percent of all cases, harsh verdicts were found to have been completely erroneous. In most cases, inner Party conflicts or external political problems had been mistakenly treated as struggles between the Party and the enemy. Of those cases where error was detected, the report found that in 40 percent of them the problem was one of internal Party error and, in a further 26 percent of these cases, the charges laid were baseless. In only 4 percent of the remaining cases was a verdict still to be determined. In these cases, Mao offered a less than appealing verdict.

"Let these people all go to work in the northeast," he said, "for this is where they can exonerate themselves through hard work." That is exactly what happened (Wang Suyuan 1991, 228).[67] In a strangely halfhearted yet self-critical manner—a manner almost identical to the one the Chairman would adopt some fifty years later during the Cultural Revolution[68]—Mao, on February 15, 1945, concluded his views on rectification with an apology. Errors about people, frame-ups, false accusations, and wrongful arrests had taken place during the rescue campaign, he noted, and he would be the first to raise his hand to salute the victims. But he would only do so, he said, if he knew that the rest of the Central Committee was going to express their own opinions on the matter in an equally frank fashion (Mao Zedong 1996, 3:262–63).

Spoken so shortly after the rescue campaign had "helped" so many "frank confessors," this call by Mao for comradely frankness may well have been genuine. On the other hand, and with the benefit of historical hindsight, it may not have been. Wasn't the One Hundred Flowers Campaign of the late fifties a similar call to critique? Didn't that simply turn out to be a ruse to reveal the "rightist" poisonous weeds that were buried within the ranks of the people and needed to be campaigned against? Wasn't a similar sentiment expressed in the Cultural Revolution toward old cadres? Was it quite so easy to believe that the tag of *enemy* would not reappear and be attached to those who raised criticisms?

Conclusion

"A single spark can light a prairie fire," Mao Zedong once wrote, but who would have thought that "a single line" could spawn such divergent options as Jiangxi and Yan'an? As the complexities of life and friendship blurred the simplicity and clarity of class war that was Jiangxi, an elaborate set of shaded lines began to emerge. In Yan'an, life was no longer quite as simple as the purity of the friend/enemy dichotomy would lead one to believe. Instead, suspicious friends and temporary allies would join in a common fight against an obvious enemy. If Jiangxi was defined purely by reference to Mao's revolutionary question, which was, of course, the question of the political, Yan'an could perhaps best be summed up by reference to another Mao text, "On Contradiction." This is because Yan'an itself was a living contradiction.

Caught between a dyadic class analysis and a nationalist political program, Yan'an lived on a knife's edge. Struggling against the constant threat of excess, it moved toward a loose and liberal notion of unity that would, in turn, come to threaten the cohesion of the Communist Party. The notion of public unity, therefore, framed a political program that attempted to avoid the excesses of a dyadic political structure while remaining committed to an internal Party unity itself built upon the friend/enemy framing of the political. In this respect, Yan'an can be thought of as the first structured and serious attempt to limit the excesses that flow from dyadic political intensities, while still remaining true to that way of framing politics. The road from Jiangxi to Yan'an was, therefore, not a departure from the binary logic of friend and enemy, but only an attempt to limit the effects of this logic by reinforcing commitment to the Party's nationalist program. The path from Jiangxi to Yan'an was, in fact, one that led from the binary of class to a binary of nation.

This shift to nation greatly broadened the scope of friendships possible. It reintroduced an "objective" element into the rendition of the enemy. During this period, the enemy would largely remain restricted to the externalizing and limiting category of the Japanese. Physiologically, culturally, and linguistically distinct from Chinese friends, the enemy no longer lived within;

it was no longer a treacherous brother. Instead, the enemy was now a visible form of difference. The moderation induced by this nationalist troping of the revolution was further reinforced by a conscious Party program aimed at moderation.

If the United Front policy brought forth national unity, rectification in 1942 would achieve the same thing in relation to the Party. Moreover, it would do this through education. The reforms to the Party's organizational structure, examined in this chapter through the lens of the reform of security agencies, reified the mass-line and brought to prominence local Party committee leadership. The transformation of the land revolution into land reform constituted another attempt at instituting limits. In Yan'an, the excesses of the Jiangxi land revolution would be avoided, it was thought, both by moderating the land reform and by transferring the source of enmity from a concrete existential class enemy (the rich peasant, landlord, and gentry) who could be purged to an abstract theoretical concept of the enemy as feudal exploitation that could not.

In this respect, moderation was attempted by increasing the education that Party cadres would be given. This education promoted an increased degree of individual commitment to the Party. Intense commitment to the Communist Party's nationalist agenda, to its moderate land reform, indeed, even to its mass-line and local Party committee leadership system could, however, offer only temporary relief. None of these policies addressed the heart of the problem of the political, for this question remained buried in the very binary quality of the politics the CCP demanded a commitment to. Indeed, it is precisely this type of intense commitment, a commitment felt so strongly that one is compelled to undertake any form of action, including radical excess and moderate compromise, that was thought to be essential to the Party's cause. Intense commitment can momentarily produce moderation, but when needs dictate otherwise, terror will follow. Terror arises not as a result of a lack of cadre morality, but largely because of it. Maoism's answer to excess, therefore, failed to address the destructive power of binary politics and invested instead in structural changes and a tactical modification to the Party's policy. This is not to say the moderate policies of the Party at this time were not heartfelt.

The Party was indeed shell-shocked by the revelations that had emerged about the excesses in Jiangxi and realized that they would need to be corrected if the Party was to survive. It is for this reason that the initial role of the Yan'an security agencies was rehabilitation, rather than retribution. Moderation became the new order of the day, and as this new creed was established, the ethos of the past, wherein the protection agencies wielded enormous power because of their duty to protect the purity of the Party, began to fade. The lines of friendship expanded as Yan'an moved from being a communist base camp to the hope of the nation. But as these lines of friendship extended to embrace the many, the fears of the chosen few were aroused. Liberalism, they feared, would pollute the purity of Party ranks. Just as the fear of past excesses would, in part, evoke the liberal tradition of Yan'an, the fear of impurity and betrayal would lead to calls for greater vigilance. When the United Front began to crumble, when the war intensified, and when the specter of betrayal cast a shadow over the very possibility of the revolution, the time had come for intense action. In such moments of intensity, the enemy emerged once more as a partly visible but highly charged symbol. As the objectivity surrounding the earlier definition of the enemy gave way to a more opaque figure, the limitations imposed by the moderate Party program began to erode. Nowhere was this partial rehabilitation of past actions more clearly foregrounded than in the words of Kang Sheng who tied the Yan'an tradition of rectification back to the Jiangxi campaign to eliminate counter-revolutionaries by speaking of rectification, checking, and the elimination of reactionaries as being a three-in-one (*sanweiyiti*) process (Lin Qingshan 1988, 103).

As Yan'an grew in importance and size, so, too, did the contradiction between these liberal and illiberal tendencies. The slogans of the day best captured the dilemma: "Don't miss one enemy agent, but don't deal erroneously with a single good person"; "Don't let one enemy agent through the net, but don't manufacture enemies"; "Don't let one spy from within escape, but don't falsely accuse comrades" (PSHM 1987, v6, 8–10). The overriding question never asked was which of these many don'ts would prevail. As the Party's security cordon weaved its way through an endless series of don'ts, an image of Yan'an begins to emerge. Like wrinkles on an aging face, the crisscrossing lines that emerged in between these don'ts tell of a variety of revolutionary experiences and potential futures. Good and bad, big and small, left and right—they all potentially form part of a greater story and lengthier inheritance. In hybridic and metamorphosed forms, many of these small stories would find their place in postliberation discourse.

Clairvoyance, in hindsight, is the art of history. Lines that appeared weak or ill defined in Yan'an grew bolder and became more developed as the revolution developed. Contradictions that were potent but held at bay in Yan'an became lines of irreconcilable difference later on. Such then, is the contradictory legacy of Yan'an. The lines of this story offer many potential futures, many possibilities, many ways forward after victory. Yan'an, in particular, is less a dress rehearsal for postrevolutionary governance than the embryonic form of a tug of these various traditions. There were at least two imagined communities living side by side in Yan'an, and both were fueled by fear. One feared the errors of the past, while the other lived in mortal fear of the enemy. Here were two imagined communities bordering each other, divided only by a line as thin and as blurred as that which separated the United Front friend from the "real," unambiguous enemy.

The traffic between these two communities crossed a bridge built and patrolled by the security forces. They were both literally and figuratively living on this crossing point. Reconfigured to ensure that the Jiangxi excesses would never be revisited, they were the agency through which its return in miniature was made inevitable. The fear of betrayal was the border pass that led from New Democracy to Cultural Revolution. Yet it was a tendency held in check for decades by another slogan and another potential tradition. At the end of the rescue campaign, and reading of its excess, it was Mao Zedong who articulated the key slogan: "Don't execute a single one, and arrest only a few." No doubt with thoughts reaching back to Jiangxi, he would add: "How many people have to die in this type of struggle before we recognize the importance of these eight words?" Looking back on these words from contemporary times, after so many campaigns and so many deaths, one might well want to ask Mao this very same question.

3 The Government of Struggle

INSTITUTIONS OF THE BINARY

Those who recognise *only* the class struggle are not yet Marxists; they may be found to be within the bounds of bourgeois thinking and bourgeois politics. To confine Marxism to the theory of class struggle means curtailing Marxism, distorting it, reducing it to something acceptable to the bourgeoisie. Only he is a Marxist who *extends* the recognition of the class struggle to the recognition of the *dictatorship of the proletariat.* —VLADIMIR LENIN

TIMELINE 1949–1956

Date	Politics	Police
1949	**October:** People's Republic of China established	First National Public Security Conference
		Central Committee's Military Commission becomes Ministry of Public Security; Luo Ruiqing is made Minister of Public Security
		November: Anti-prostitution campaign starts in Beijing
1950	**October 10:** "Double Ten" instructions issued, launching the Campaign to Suppress Counter-Revolutionaries (*zhenfan*)	**February:** Anti-drug campaign starts
		Campaign to Suppress Counter-Revolutionaries starts
1951		**February:** The government enacts the "Regulations Regarding the Punishment of Counterrevolutionaries in the PRC"
	December: Three Antis Campaign begins	Three Antis Campaign in public security

Date	Politics	Police
1952	**January:** Five Antis Campaign begins **October:** Three Antis and Five Antis Campaigns end	**June:** Ministry of Public Security convenes First National Reform Criminals through Labor Work Conference **July:** Ministry of Public Security issues "Temporary Methods Used to Put Counter-Revolutionaries under Surveillance and Control" **August:** Ministry of Public Security issues the "Organizational Regulations of Resident and Work Unit Security Committees"
1953	**July:** Announcement of first five-year plan	Temporary national household registration laws enacted Campaign to Suppress Counter-Revolutionaries ends
1954	**February:** Seventh plenum of the fourth session of CCP Anti Gao-Rao campaign	
1955	**July:** Campaign to Suppress Internal Counter-Revolutionaries (*nebu sufan yundong*)	**April:** Pan Hannian and Yang Fan arrested
1956		Second suppression campaign ended

O NLY HE IS A MARXIST who *extends* the recognition of the class struggle to the recognition of the *dictatorship of the proletariat*" says Lenin. Mao obviously agreed. The entire postliberation Chinese state was to become a condensation of class-related weapons designed to prepare the revolutionary state for the class battles ahead. In other words, the entire structure of mass-line government put in place after 1949 constituted a weapon of struggle predicated upon a drive toward communism and propelled by the friend/enemy dyad. The mass-line friend formed one part of a dialectic, while the counter-revolutionary enemy made up the other. This dialectic proved central to the constitution of the state structure set up under the new rubric of the People's Republic. This is the tale of how this state came to be structured on the basis of such concerns.

The Language of Revolution

In 1951, the new government of China undertook a massive reform of the Chinese language. They simplified Chinese characters, standardized pronunciation, and introduced the pinyin system of romanization. The result was *putonghua*, or the common (people's) language. With this top-down reform, the revolution left a lasting mark on Chinese language. Below, at street level, the common language was making its own mark through a series of reforms of a slightly different order. A new revolutionary metaphoricity hit town as the communists hit the city streets. As the cities became "rustified" by the arrival of the rural-based communists, so, too, did the language of everyday life (Dutton and Li 2002). Rural metaphors came into vogue. Young, hardworking revolutionaries were increasingly referred to as "straight-rooted red seedlings"; those who passed on revolutionary experiences became known as "irrigation channels, heart and soul." Rustification of the vernacular was but one linguistic effect of the communists' takeover; the militarization of language was another.

A new range of colloquial expressions pointed not just to the militarization of language but to the militarization of life itself. As the friend/enemy distinction became a way of life, people started to speak of daily events through the metaphors of revolution and war. "Repulse the savage offensive of the right," "open fire on the anti-Party and anti-socialist black line," and "charge the enemy lines to promote the revolutionary line" were but a few of the expressions employed that signified this dyadic way of thinking. As city folk began to speak like country bumpkins and military generals, what Yang Dongping terms a "semantic trap" developed and revealed a semiotic intent of its own (Yang Dongping 1994, 266). The connotative effect of this type of expression suggested that life itself was increasingly undergoing rustification and militarization. In other words, buried in the new words of the communist revolution was a new worldview that coded everything either as friend or enemy. So soon after the revolution such language hardly seems surprising. Strangely, however, it was not the language of the revolutionary government.

The symbolism of October 1949 was not that of October 1917. In 1949, Mao talked of new democracy, not of state and revolution. When Mao stood atop the Tian'anmen gate facing away from the old dynastic edifice of the Imperial Palace, he may have looked out longingly toward a socialism that remained on the distant horizon, but he focused squarely on the immediate tasks of national reconstruction. A new democratic government of the people, not a dictatorship of the proletariat, was the order of the day, and this required new and, by communist standards, quite moderate sets of social policies to govern the country. Thus while the masses on the street responded to the communist victory by shouting loudly in the language of revolution, the dialect of the revolutionary party was being toned down for its new role as the government. Direct Party and military controls were quickly relinquished to make way for the appearance of civilian rule. City Military Control Committees (shi junshi guanzhi weiyuanhui) gave way to civilian local governments just as the Party's Social Section and military public defense units gave way to the new, government-run Ministry of Public Security.

Despite cosmetic appearances, neither the Party nor the army ever really left the matter of security entirely to government. Rather, they remained (not so) hidden beneath the cloak of the new governmental order. Thus, in October 1949, when the Central People's Government Organizational Law authorized the formation of a governmental policing authority, they decided that the policing functions of the old Ministry of Public Security of the Central Committee's Military Commission (*zhongyang junwei gong'anbu*) would be handed over to the new Ministry of Public Security (*gong'an bu*). They also decided that the head and deputy head of the Military Commission, namely Luo Ruiqing and Yang Qiqing, would become the new Minister and Deputy Minister of Public Security. In addition, key staff for this new ministry would be drawn from the recently dismantled Central Committee Social Section and the North China Social Section (Tao Siju 1996, 5; PSHM 1993:1, V27, 49, 63).[1] Long after the establishment of this government ministry, Luo Ruiqing was to describe it in words that betrayed the fact that its master was the Party and its model, the army: "The public security detachments are also under our Party's leadership. Their system, discipline, tradition, work style, and our national defense forces are one and the same. The public security forces, are, in fact, a part of the People's Liberation Army" (qtd. in Tao Siju 1996, 161).

The Party and military not only stamped their authority over this new organ but also set about to infuse it with the same mass-line ideology as the army. As Luo Ruiqing put it in June 1950, "Among the public security forces we must strengthen the ideological education work that comes from the people and is for the people" (qtd. in Tao Siju 1996, 184). This process of education was further bolstered by the leadership role given to the Party committees operating at each level of the ministry. After 1952, these committees had political workers in every branch of the public security organization, ensuring that the entire public security apparatus was, like its Social Section predecessor, "100 percent Party."[2] When it came to policing, Mao Zedong was insistent that the only authority was Party authority. Even the country's fraternal big brother, the Soviet Union, had its advisors frozen out.[3] As noted earlier, however, things appeared otherwise.

As the communists mopped up the remaining opposition to their revolution—Guangzhou in October, Guilin in November, Nanning in December, Hainan Island in April 1950, and Tibet in October—the nation appeared to consolidate behind the Communist Party. By 1950, only the tiny colonial out-posts of Hong Kong and Macau, as well as the renegade province of Taiwan, remained to be "liberated." In an otherwise moderate climate, the only talk of "struggle" took place in relation to enemy agents and remnants. It was upon this rather small pool of historic enemies that police attention would focus. Enemy agents, landlords, former enemy soldiers, and bandits joined beggars, drug addicts, and prostitutes as the targets of policing actions in the newly liberated cities. Stability would, henceforth, be ensured through the registration of such elements.

Yet the moderate tone of these early drives to eradicate the historic enemy would not remain. Externally, cold winds were beginning to blow this agenda off course, and foreign threats magnified the danger of internal historic enemies. Chinese communists had good cause to feel besieged. The United States entry into the Korean civil war in June 1950 was read in Beijing as being more than simply another sign of U.S. belligerence toward communism. This time, it was an attack that the Chinese thought was directed at them. The fact that the United States used the war as an excuse to declare the Taiwan Straits neutral—which facilitated Guomindang raids on mainland China—only further "clarified" this point. When U.S. forces in Korea reached the banks of the Yalu river and directly threatened China in November 1950, the Chinese communist celebrations of their own civil war victory gave way to a new call to arms. The campaign to "Resist America and Aid Korea" further hardened a government agenda that was already moving to the left. As the government agenda moved to the left, it bumped into the masses who seemed to have already devised a populist revolutionary agenda of their own.

They had picked up on the new common language of communism not only to celebrate the Party victory but to highlight their dissatisfaction with the initially moderate stance the communists had taken. Mass dissatisfaction took the form of mimicry, spitting back the officially authorized slogans given to them by those above with a little bit of popular sentiment from below. While the Party sought to stabilize society through moderate and lenient policies, activists thought that the only thing stabilized by moderation was enemy power. What was needed, they insisted, was more revolutionary action. "There is no order under heaven," went one mimicked Party slogan, "only limitless leniency." "Why is the situation like this?" came another questioning chant, "because the government sleeps" came the reply (*Campaign to Suppress* 1992, 17; Yu Lei 1992, 3).

What the government was sleeping through, so these people thought, was a range of atrocities committed against both the Party and the people. Under such conditions, the communists did not proclaim leniency for long. After all, they were far from committed to it. For them, leniency and moderation were but the tactics of the moment. Indeed, almost from day one, the Party had publicly proclaimed leniency, while behind the scenes it prepared to implement a far more radical program. The myriad of problems the Communist Party faced in the transition to government, however, left it with few resources to turn radical from day one. While it readied itself for more radical action, the Party bought time by implementing its moderate leniency policy. On the day of the "Double Tens" (October 10, 1950) the Party was ready for (revolutionary) action.

On that day, the Central Committee announced the first large-scale politico-policing campaign of the new era, the Campaign to Suppress Counter-Revolutionaries (*zhenfan*). The leniency policy adopted toward historic enemies in the first year of communist rule was, by the second, being labeled a rightist deviation. Driven by external events, its own internal agenda, and by its own constituency, the Party entered into a war on two fronts: one in Korea, the other at home. Campaign-style politics would now take hold within the country as it prepared for a military campaign in a foreign land. The military campaign in Korea would run in tandem with a military-style policing operation at home. What this war at home unleashed was not simply a purge of the politically suspect—although it certainly did that—but a whole new way of thinking about government. It was through this that the mass-line formally became an organizational form of government. In this first politico-policing campaign of the new era, the newly formed public security forces would learn to adapt the military-derived strategies they had employed as temporary exigencies during the war years to fight against the new enemies they encountered in the post-liberation era. These strategies would, with repeated use, compact into institutions of government. Perhaps more importantly, however, they would solidify into a way of thinking that came to inform an entirely new way of life. Underlying all this thinking, of course, was the friend/enemy distinction.

It was this new way of thinking that unconsciously habituated the populace into a new mentality and methodology of struggle and of government. More than at any other time, it was in this first campaign of the new era that politics as a style of thought was transformed into an institutional form. The institutional forms produced under the shadow of this friend/enemy distinction constituted localized and highly politicized street-level forms of government. While the mass-line organs that emerged under this form of politics were both nongovernmental and voluntary, they nonetheless served as crucial conveyor belts for the government to transmit the revolutionary ethos to the masses. Because of this, many within the Party would come to think of these mass-line organs as crucial component parts of a new style of revolutionary government that would one day come to dominate the whole country. Many others within the CCP, however, viewed these organs as little more than transitory forms born of necessity and temporary in nature.

The head of the Politics and Law Committee of the Administrative Council, Dong Biwu, most clearly articulated this latter position. He suggested that the politico-policing campaign was, in fact, a technology from a bygone era that would be replaced by law once the constitution was enacted (qtd. in Rice 1972, 126). In hindsight, it is easy to say that Dong underestimated the power of campaign-style political struggle to mark the minds and mentalities of those who participated. Nevertheless, his remarks do help us appreciate just how fluid, tentative, and temporary many of these structures and strategies were. There was no grand model nor any over-riding vision being put into effect at this time. Rather, there was only a remorseless series of problems that constantly needed addressing and a wellspring of dyadic thinking that constantly returned to the mass-line and the masses as the answer. Through constant use, the campaign and the mass-line became, not just a means of doing things, but a way of seeing.

What Dong and possibly other legal advocates within the Communist Party had not taken into account in their claim that the rule of law was imminent, was the lasting effects of the repeated use of campaign technology upon the practical politics of police and the Party.[4] To be sure, when the security forces first employed campaign-style policing, they did so because it offered a politically correct way of helping them carry out their tasks while their own forces remained numerically weak and politically mixed. The crisis of numbers and politics would partly be overcome by reallocating army troops and by training new politically sound recruits. More than anything, however, it was the development of mass-line policing organs based on voluntary neighborhood committee and work unit activists that helped solve the problem. As it was solved in this way, China became wedded to the mass-line.

Because of this, campaign-style policing would never diminish. Indeed, if anything, campaigns grew. The training, predilection, and background of the new public security recruits ensured that. For all of these people, campaigns were not so much a tactic to overcome momentary weakness as much as they gave concrete expression to their own politics. The problem with this approach, however, was that the campaign never became theoretically linked to this revolutionary ethos. Its shadowy form evolved out of a dialectic between concrete pragmatic political demands and socialist political dreaming. This would produce a unique mentality of governance that came together more as a set of family resemblances than as a clearly defined form. Because of the fluid nature of the times, the flexibility offered by campaign-style politics proved far more potent than the legal enactments or constraints advanced by people like Dong Biwu. Moreover, it was for just this reason that campaigns and the mass-line structure of government would become key means by which China would be policed throughout this era. This chapter is the story of how that process began.

Cleansing the Ranks

At the first Ministry of Public Security meeting held in Beijing from October to November 1949, Luo Ruiqing had to admit that the police force he was creating was, for a range of reasons, organizationally and politically unreliable, lacking in the technical skills of policing, and desperately short of officers. That such problems needed to be addressed was obvious for, as Luo concluded in his speech to the meeting, "If the Ministry of Public Security doesn't complete its tasks, then we could well lose political power" (Luo Ruiqing 1994, 3). Yet the completion of tasks required a thoroughly transformed police force, and that, he added, would take one and a half to two years to complete (Tao Siju 1996, 8). Even then, it would require Herculean efforts. The force was, after all, underresourced, dominated by unreliable remnant police from the old regime, and had a small hard-core communist police corps that was, according to one source, still "dizzy with success." This ministry faced the task of policing a fractured society still unsure about what shape socialism would take and still offering a range of capitalist-style inducements to the unwary and the corrupt (*A Summary History* 1989, 93).

Of these problems, the one most obviously in need of urgent address was the shortage of staff. Police statistics from 1950 reveal a force with only 72,684 officers, and, of these, a mere 1,636 were members of the Communist Party cadre corps (confidential material 1986).[5] The problem for the force, then, was not only that it faced a serious shortage of personnel but also that it was numerically dominated by politically suspect "remnant elements."[6] This was a serious problem for a force that was, as Luo Ruiqing pointed out, predominantly involved in tasks of a political nature (Tao Siju 1996, 165). Party leadership within the police was essential, and a series of decisions taken in the early 1950s pointed to the way this would be ensured.

The first move in this regard was to disband the social sections in most places and transfer these cadres into Ministry of Public Security leadership positions (*A Summary History* 1989, 87).[7] Luo Ruiqing pointed out that with the Central Committee's abolition of the Party's Social Sections, all responsible security cadres were to become both Party committee members or standing committee members, as well as joining the various government and Party organizations (Tao Siju 1996, 9). Such transfers were therefore designed to help stabilize Party control over the various levels of leadership of the force. This was a crucial point for Mao Zedong. He was far less concerned with the numerical strength of the force than with its political color. In March 1950, he made his views clear when he said that "in terms of public security numbers, we really don't want too many, but what we do want are officers of good quality" (qtd. in Tao Siju 1996, 159). The idea of a diminutive police force was one thing, but there was a clear problem of numerical weakness, and this had to be addressed even before work could proceed. Yet the citing of police numbers fails to explain the extent of the crisis. Indeed, these numbers prove misleading for, in the majority of cases, most police were of a dubious political nature.

In terms of police numbers, it was claimed that the police would require a further 4,000 middle-ranking cadres, 19,000 base-level cadres, and 40,000 ordinary-level cadres if the force was to reach its authorized strength of 190,000 officers (*Outline of Public Security* 1997, 247).[8] Appeals from Luo for more police officers led the Central Committee to authorize troop transfers in September 1950. These soldiers then formed the basis of the armed public security detachments that were the precursors to the contemporary People's Armed Police (Tao Siju 1996, 158).[9] This force was initially made up of twenty army corps transferred in November. They maintained a quasi-military organizational structure and an independent chain of command that led, via Luo Ruiqing, back to the Central Military Affairs Committee rather than to the central government. In the main, these troops would be used in the first few years of the regime in rural China against bandits and "heretical religious sects." By October 1950, the combined actions of police, armed police, and the army led to over 1 million of these bandits and sect members being either eliminated or giving up (*Outline of Public Security* 1997, 251). November 1950 was also an important month for the (unarmed) People's Police. It was at this time that the Central Committee authorized the transfer of cadres from Northern, Eastern, and Central Committee units into the Ministry of Public Security. At the same time, a virtual embargo on transfers out of the ministry ensured that numbers were not depleted (*A Summary History* 1989, 89–90).

Army and governmental transfers helped relieve some of the problems of inadequately low personnel numbers. It also helped shape their socialist ideology, but it did little to solve the problem of communist inexperience in the specialized work of policing. As long as this problem persisted, the new police force would remain reliant upon the remnant police officers from the former regime (Luo Ruiqing 1994, 13). Remnant elements from the old force, therefore, remained within the new police force, but found themselves increasingly governed by an internal regime of control and surveillance. Politics alone would have dictated this policy, but it was not the only factor. Corruption and other illegalities within police ranks were constantly being discovered in these early days. Research undertaken in Beijing in December 1951 indicated a significant number of officers exploiting their positions for corrupt purposes, using police powers for their own benefit, taking things from criminals while not disclosing this fact, and receiving bribes (*A Summary History* 1989, 93). In addition, checks revealed that quite a number of "serious counter-revolutionaries" had managed to evade checks and take up positions within the Ministry of Public Security itself. Indeed, in a number of newly liberated areas, it was even suggested that counter-revolutionaries had managed to gain control over the public security units and were using them for counter-revolutionary ends (Hu Zhiguang 1986, 55).

Serious flaws in the character of the police officer corps, coupled with clear indications that the old corrupt police ways were prevailing despite the new unitary structure of the police ministry, led to calls for reform which, at this time, meant redoubling efforts to strengthen Party leadership over the force (Hu Zhiguang, 1986 55). Luo Ruiqing was quick to act. Setting forth the Ministry of Public Security contribution to the Three Antis Campaign (*sanfan*) against waste, corruption, and bureaucratization, he issued the scathing "Report Concerning the Promotion of the Struggle against Corruption, Laziness, and Bureaucratism within the Central Ministry of Public Security and the Whole of the Public Security Apparatus" in December 1951. In this, he attacked the criminal, illegal, and immoral practices that, he said, still existed within the force. To respond to this, he called for greater discipline. To ensure that this call for greater discipline did not become a "dead letter," he set in place a "strict leadership" regime that brought forth much greater levels of Party vigilance and control over the force (A *Summary History* 1989, 93).

The necessity of such a call for strict leadership at this time appears somewhat surprising. After all, the Party had demanded this of the Ministry of Public Security from the very beginning. Indeed, it had put in place a structure unitary in nature and shadowed, at every level, by an all-powerful Party committee structure that offered local governmental organs leadership and supervision.[10] Part of the problem for these Party committees, however, was that they offered leadership only to unit-level leaders but had little direct influence on the ordinary officers on the street. It was important to inculcate these ordinary officers with Party spirit so that they would check on colleagues and on their own work style. As a leadership organ, the Party committee was not in a position to do this, so a specialized ideological policing unit was set up.

The personnel bureau within the ministry began operations in November 1949 as one of the original five bureaus and one department within the ministry structure (Tao Siju 1996, 5). As the Party leadership expressed increasing concern about the political character of the force, the personnel bureau's powers were greatly strengthened. This occurred after its first work conference in June 1950.[11] As its role became more important, its educational program for police became more Maoist and military. The Maoist-inspired politico-ideological programs operative within the army became the model upon which this bureau built its own programs and after which it structured its own affairs. Like the army, the Public Security Personnel Bureau established a work department for cadre management, a Party work section, and a propaganda and education unit. Under the leadership of the Party committee, its political education tasks were twofold: First, the bureau had to carry out security checks on all police and clean out any "bad elements." Second, it was to select and recruit the first wave of new "revolutionary police." Skilled young revolutionary cadres and peasant and worker activists were brought into the force after they had undertaken short training courses mounted by the personnel section. These new "revolutionary police" would finally enable the communists to begin replacing remnant police officers still working within the force (Hu Zhiguang 1986, 55). This attempt to transform "red" into "expert" involved a massive educational program that saw some thirty-five police academies built in the first few years of the new regime and the introduction of specialized short-term courses that would last for three to four months. By the end of 1952, these courses had pushed through around 80,000 young communist graduates. These young officers then took up positions at police stations throughout the country (Yu Lei 1992, 433; Tao Siju 1996, 204). Despite the addition of these graduates, police numbers did not rise significantly. New communist police recruits, it seems, were merely replacing the remnant forces and not adding to overall police numbers.

Every city told the same story. Revolutionary cadres had taken control of policing, but they could do little without the support of personnel from the old system. Under these circumstances, more cadres were needed in the force, and an emphasis was placed on training them (PSHM 1990:4, VI8, 141). As remnants were replaced, the nature of the police force began to change. Transferred army officers, wartime Party veterans, and younger, newly trained recruits started to modify the way the police functioned. By November 1952, such a modification seemed appropriate in the light of the scandalous revelations of police corruption that came out as a result of the Three Antis Campaign and Five Antis Campaign (wufan). But quite apart from corruption, there was also the more mundane problem of high-handed police attitudes to be countered.

This appeared particularly worrying for communist police seemed to share this attitude with their "remnant" colleagues. Indeed, so worrying had this situation become that a central part of police rectification brought on as a result of the Three Antis Campaign was an educational program to stop police acting like the old police and to halt their arrogant and self-serving ways (Tao Siju 1996, 184–85). This, in turn, involved the introduction of more direct political controls over police activities. The personnel section with its numerous duties was no longer specialized enough to carry out the important task of political work. Hence a new, more specialized unit made up of highly politicized officers from the personnel bureau came into being. It became known as the political work unit.

In March 1953, the Central Committee approved a resolution from the Fifth Public Security Work Meeting of October 1952 to establish political work units. These units were directly modeled on political units operative within the army (Hu Zhiguang 1986, 57).[12] Indeed, this work meeting demanded that these new political units adopt the so-called 1929 Gutian decision as their own.[13] This decision, attributed to Mao, ensured that the Red Army would always remain a Party vehicle, rather than an independent or semi-independent "kingdom." By focusing on politico-ideological work within army ranks, the Party ensured that soldiers were red first and army second. It was this focus on political education within the Red Army that would find its way into the training programs of the security forces (Hu Zhiguang 1986, 57–58). This new Ministry of Public Security political unit was to be staffed by cadres "of rank" and to operate from central units all the way down to county-level ones (*Questions and Answers* 1994, 139). The ongoing process of strengthening politico-ideological work flowed from a belief that armed organs of the state, more than any other, must be "Party first." Mao made this clear in 1950 in relation to economic protection work when he said, "In [social] protection work, we must especially stress the role of Party leadership and, in actual fact, directly draw leadership from the Party committees, for to do otherwise would be very dangerous" (qtd. in Luo Ruiqing 1994, 34). This, however, left aside the whole question of police numbers and the continuing need for remnants to remain in the force because of their professional expertise.

Even after the massive draftings and short-term training programs, there were still only 330,175 public security personnel in 1953 and, of these, only 79,871 were designated as People's Police (confidential material 1986). Census figures for this year indicate a population of just under 588 million people (Kane 1987, 63), meaning that policing levels remained ridiculously low, running at about one Ministry of Public Security member for every 1,781 people and one people's police officer for every 7,361 people. Clearly, and even with the addition of the remnants, if the Ministry of Public Security relied only on its own resources, policing would be impossible. Luckily for the ministry, it was not solely reliant on its own numbers.

Additional personnel were available to the police, and these would greatly increase their numerical strength and effectiveness. This supplementary force, however, did not come from within the policing agencies themselves, but from the myriad of mass organizations that flanked the lower branches of the communist party structure. These organizations would enable police to penetrate every small laneway and every work unit. As this solution to the problem became more and more apparent, there emerged a need to formalize and clarify the nature of the linkage between the formal and the informal structures. Eventually, this form of policing would take a name— the mass-line in policing. It is, however, important to remember that this particular mass-line form came about not simply because of a preexisting vision about how China should be governed but because of a range of pragmatic responses to social pressures that pushed the regime to rely upon the masses, and political pressures that constantly encouraged them to do so. In the immediate aftermath of revolution, to have done otherwise may have proven fatal.

Cleansing the City

Despite the appearance of being in full control, the situation the Party faced immediately after the revolution proved quite daunting. Estimates presented to the first national meeting of public security workers in October– November 1949 painted a grim picture (*Questions and Answers* 1994, 66). Police sources estimated that there were still some 2 million armed bandits, 600,000 spies, and 600,000 Nationalist backbone elements at large (PSHM 1992:3, V25, 71). Apart from remnants, there was also the problem of addressing the active and violent opponents of the regime. A wave of politically motivated assassinations swept the country, and prominent communists and their allies found themselves targeted. Leading figures such as Ye

Jianying, Tan Zhengwen, Yang Jie, Li Jishen, Cheng Qian, and Chen Mingren all became targets. In addition, detailed assassination plans aimed at eliminating Peng Dehuai, He Long, Chen Yi, and Pan Hannian were uncovered.[14] There were even claims that a hit squad had been dispatched from Taiwan to assassinate Mao Zedong, Zhu De, and other Central Committee leaders.[15] But senior leaders of the Party and government were not the only assassination targets. Internal Chinese police reports revealed a concerted attempt by the Nationalists to make the new Chinese state unworkable by what was little more than a large-scale terrorist program. Between the spring and autumn of 1950, close to 40,000 communist cadres and activists were assassinated in this way (Yu Lei 1993, 38; *Campaign to Suppress* 1992, 11).

As if political assassinations by counter-revolutionaries did not constitute a big enough problem to have to cope with, the situation with regard to law and order generally was in a dire state. In what has subsequently been described as the first high tide of common crime in contemporary China, the year 1950 witnessed 513,461 criminal cases opened against what were, in the main, hardened bandits and thieves (Yu Lei 1993, 38). Between these two sets of concerns arose the notion of "two plenties," that is, plenty of counter-revolutionary criminals and plenty of criminal remnants from the old society (Yu Lei 1993, 38–39). In the city of Shanghai alone, 33,000 people were tracked down on various types of criminal charges between 1950 and 1953. Of these, 0.68 percent were said to be fleeing landlords; 1.45 percent remnants of the old army, police, or government forces; 4.3 percent unlawful capitalists; 8.77 percent hardened thieves or bandits; and 18.26 percent local riffraff or hooligans (Yu Lei 1993, 38). Aside from the problem of common and counter-revolutionary crime, there also existed a host of crime related to social problems that needed addressing urgently. Once again, it seemed that the cities emerged as the site of most of the Party's ongoing problems. Foremost among these issues were the problems of prostitution, drug taking, and vagrancy.

These three social ills would become the targeted concerns of the new era, picked on not simply because they gave evidence of past moral turpitude but, more pragmatically, because they created the type of environment that would make the two plenties even more plentiful. Drug addicts, prostitutes, and vagrants not only added to instability but in many cases provided hideouts, funding, and alibis for escapee landlords, bandits, spies, and traitors.

In terms of vagrancy alone, it was found that between 1950 and the spring of 1951, some 37,700 of those registered and taken in as vagrants were also tied into secret societies (*A Summary History* 1989, 121). Faced with these type of sociopolitical problems, the weakness of the new socialist police force became all too apparent. Indeed, such was the weakness of the Ministry of Public Security at this time that if one were to regard the state of the nation as perilous, then one would have to add that the state of the police force was even worse. The only option in these early days was to operate pragmatically. In rural regions, this meant targeting social-order problems such as banditry that impinged upon the Party's ability to deliver on key and popular policies such as land reform. In the cities, it meant treading much more carefully. Social problems had to be addressed, but they would be dealt with by a slow, moderate, and pragmatic program of reform rather than by harsher instant measures. Nowhere was this pragmatic, realist program more in evidence than in relation to prostitution.

Prostitution

Prostitution was an issue on which communist views appeared clear cut. Since the first International Women's Day Convention in Guangzhou, in March 1924, communists had come out in support of the convention's key goal of "eliminating the system of prostitution." The expectation, therefore, was that once the communists achieved power, brothels would be closed and prostitution outlawed. The reality turned out to be quite different. The sheer size of the problem in many places simply proved too daunting for the new state.

Before 1949, an estimated 10,000 brothels existed throughout China. Shanghai alone was said to have more than 800, while Tianjin was estimated to have more than 500, and Xi'an no fewer than 375 (Ma Weigang 1993, 7, 9).[16] In such places, the ratio of prostitutes to the rest of the population ran somewhere in the vicinity of 1 to 150–200 people (*Questions and Answers* 1994, 78). Faced with such huge numbers, the immediate closure of brothels in some areas would have had dramatic and quite negative multiplier effects on other industries. Moreover, the lack of police resources to effect such a closure meant that many public security bureaus decided to make haste slowly. A dual policy was put in place that promised immediate closures in sensitive or relatively small cities where the problems could be dealt with effectively and a slower, more calibrated approach in more difficult cities.

Brothels immediately faced closure in those cities with greater police resources or those places deemed politically sensitive. Beijing, the new capital, was the most visible example of a city that closed its brothels immediately. Yet even here, preparatory work was undertaken for quite some time prior to the actual event. Liberated in late January 1949, the city's government had designated brothels a "special business" (tezhong hangye) by March that year.[17] Under this rubric, police were granted extensive powers to scrutinize, check, and control the operation of brothels. All brothels were ordered to update their client lists after each evening. This would state the name, age, and occupation of every client. The brothel operator would then present this list to the police at 10 a.m. every morning. Secret reports were to be filled out on any plain-clothes police, spies, armed criminals, vagrants, deserters, government officials, or leading members of organizations who frequented prostitutes. Wherever possible, these people were to be detained in the brothels until police arrived on the scene. In addition, any person from the army, or with military equipment or bombs, was to be immediately reported (Li Runshan and Mao Dianliang 1993, 81). Police also instituted measures to ensure that the women had not been not mistreated or tricked into prostitution. They also ensured that none had STDs or were under age. With controls such as these bringing the brothels to heel, by November 1949 the government felt it was in a position to undertake more decisive action.

On November 12, 1949, the Beijing City Second People's Congress issued "The Regulation Concerning the Closure of Brothels." This, in turn, authorized the city mayor, Nie Rongzhen, to use the public security forces, the civil authorities, the health department, and the Women's Federation to close all brothels and detain every madam, owner, and pimp on November 21 (Han Feng 1993, 51). Across the city, 2,400 community police officers and cadres set to work closing all the city's 224 brothels in just one night. Some 1,288 prostitutes were taken into custody before being dispatched to eight Women's Production, Education, and Fostering Institutes (funü shengchan jiaoyangyuan). Medical checks undertaken at the institutes revealed that 96.6 percent of the detainees were diseased and, in the vast majority of cases, these were sexually transmitted diseases (Questions and Answers 1994, 78).[18]

As their title suggests, these institutes also arranged work and education.

After a period of time, if the detainees had families, they were released and sent home. If they had no home or were orphans, they were organized into study groups, learned crafts, and then sent to production units. Police also arranged suitors for many of the women. Prostitutes were not criminalized but treated as victims and, in an array of "meetings to recall past sufferings" (*yikuhui*) and "accusation meetings" (*kongsuhui*), this viewpoint was underlined. Moreover, these meetings would furnish the Party with further evidence to propagate the communist line against the madams, owners, and pimps (Ma Weigang 1993, 11). From April 1950 onward, those who ran the brothels in Beijing were dealt with in three sets of trials which resulted in 2 people receiving the death sentence and 333 serving fixed-term imprisonment (*Questions and Answers* 1994, 80). Nevertheless, even the treatment of this group was, on the whole, rather lenient. In summing up the Beijing operation, *People's Daily* wrote that it was "an important measure in the liberation of women," which was also of "historic significance." With such high praise, little wonder that Beijing became the template for all future city brothel closures (*Outline of Public Security* 1997, 254–55). Not all cities, however, were to close their brothels.

Another model, adopted in large cities such as Tianjin, Shanghai, and Wuhan, allowed brothels to continue to operate under very tight controls. This second policy, known as the "tight control within limits" (*yujin yuxian*) policy, was adopted for those cities in which brothel numbers were too large, state resources too limited, or where large numbers of people depended upon the brothels to earn their living. If closures were undertaken too rapidly in these cities, the livelihoods of rickshaw drivers, gatekeepers, and various peddlers would be endangered, which, in turn, could lead to social unrest and instability at the very time the new state could least afford it. There was also the added problem of what to do with the prostitutes. With severely strained budgets, many places simply could not afford the retraining schemes put in place in cities such as Beijing. Thus, while this slow method ensured that prostitution did not expand, it did not lead to a closure of brothels, nor to an immediate end of prostitution.

This more limited measure was first suggested for the city of Taiyuan in March 1949, but was formally adopted in Shanghai on September 9, then in Tianjin on September 24, and finally in Wuhan in early 1950 (Ma Weigang 1993, 8). Like the early policies in Beijing, the "tight control within limits" policy turned on tight control through the registration of virtually all facets of brothel life. The background of the brothel owner, as well as the brothel's architecture, hygiene facilities, and equipment all underwent registration. Limits were placed on the number of prostitutes in each brothel, and owners could no longer freely recruit new "girls" or advertise their services. Every brothel received a special license, while each prostitute was issued a permit that had her photograph affixed. Girls under the age of eighteen, those with contagious diseases, those more than four months pregnant, and those who had given birth in the last three months no longer had permission to work. Military personnel, public servants, youth under the age of twenty, and those "without a clear status" were to be refused entry to brothels. A strict regime of regular medical checks was introduced and entertainment and gambling within the premises banned. Any brothel found to be harboring bandits would face immediate closure, and those responsible arrested. Any mistreatment of the prostitutes by customers was severely dealt with, as was the use of drugs by prostitutes or customers. Prostitutes were no longer free to leave the brothel, but had to seek written permission to do so from their local police station.

These internal management measures also had an external component that turned on discouraging custom. Police did this by "taking drastic measures" and "giving customers hell." If the daily register of johns revealed the names of public service employees or students, police would contact their work units or educational institutes. The clients would then be disciplined and educated. In addition to this, militia patrols were sent into the red light districts each night to carry out checks and ask visitors their business (*Questions and Answers* 1994, 79). Sometimes such patrols would even write on a visitor's documentation, or even on his clothes, "discovered to be a john in a brothel" (Li Runshan and Mao Dianliang 1993, 82). With the noose tightening around their necks, many brothels simply shut up shop, enabling the policy of eventual closure to come that little bit closer to fruition. Even in that most complex of cities, Shanghai, this policy was taking its toll upon the sex industry. By January 1950, the Public Security Bureau was able to announce that the number of brothels had dropped from 500 to just 209 and, by May, there were said to be only 158 brothels left operating in the entire city (Henriot 1995, 471). By 1951, that number had dropped again. In November, only 180 licensed prostitutes in 72 brothels were reported. There were, of course, far more prostitutes than that. As Gail Hershatter notes, the number of women with licenses constituted only a very small fraction of all prostitutes in the city (1997, 308–9). Nevertheless, this reduction in licensed prostitutes does give some indication of the general trend underway and the intentions of the communists with regards to prostitution.

Between 1951 and 1953, the yujin yuxian policy of tight control gave way to closure and, by 1954, all brothels in China were said to have been closed. Indeed, by 1956, the year China proclaimed itself socialist, the last former prostitute graduated from the Women's Production, Education, and Fostering Institute (*Questions and Answers* 1994, 80).[19] The birth of socialism, it seems, was the death of prostitution.[20]

Drugs

Socialism also signaled the death of another historically constructed social scourge, drugs. Like prostitution, drug addiction was considered a thorny social problem, and so the communists adopted a tolerant and careful attitude toward its eradication. Addicts, like prostitutes, were victims not criminals, and, as such, they required cures not punishments. Harsher measures were adopted toward dealers and smugglers, but no more so than those metered out to madams, brothel owners, and pimps. This, at least, was the prevailing attitude up until late 1950. From late 1950 onward, however, evidence began to mount that the illegal drug industry was linked to counterrevolutionary activity, and as this link became clearer, official attitudes hardened (*Questions and Answers* 1994, 81; Ma Weigang 1993, 4). What had long been dealt with as a social problem was becoming a political one. This hardening of attitudes was reinforced by investigations undertaken during the Three and Five Antis Campaigns in 1952, which revealed that drugs were also a source of police and government corruption (*A Summary History* 1989, 94). The social war on drugs thus became a political campaign. It was increasingly viewed as a struggle against reactionaries and against corruption within Party and government ranks. As the characterization of the war changed, so, too, did official attitudes.

At first, the war on drugs clearly formed part of an ameliorist social strategy. The first volley in this crusade came in February 1950, in the form of the "Circular Concerning the Prohibition of Opiates" from the Government Administrative Council (*zhengwuyuan*) (*Questions and Answers* 1994, 80). This was then followed in November by a methods paper from the Supreme People's Court and, while this latter document called for harsher penalties, it still remained quite moderate in tone, advocating fines and medical treatment for addicts rather than their imprisonment. Together, these various documents established the parameters of a campaign that was, by Chinese communist standards, tentative in nature and moderate in tone. Guiding documents not only offered local area governments considerable autonomy in pursuing this campaign but even gave them a say in determining when, and if, the campaign should be launched. Moreover, these documents noted the importance of showing due regard for, and sensitivity toward, local minority customs which may include some drug use.

It was during this liberal time and organizational frame that the "Circular" and methods paper called on all levels of government to establish elimination of drug smoking and trading committees. Made up of cadres from the Ministry of Public Security and other related agencies, the first of these committees was established in May 1950 by the South-Central Military Control Committee (*zhongnan junzheng weiyuanhui*). This was followed by the formation of one in the southwest in July, one in eastern China in September, and one in the northeast in October 1951. While these offered local areas considerable independence of action, all regions appeared to follow an almost identical path. Indeed, the campaigns undertaken in all areas seemed almost formulaic in the way they proceeded—first register, then cure.

Addicts were to go to their local police station or government offices to register and then, within a set time period, surrender all drugs and drug-related instruments. National-level statistics from the latter half of 1952 showed that 360,000 addicts registered, while a further 36,000 people were arrested on more serious drug-related charges (Yu Lei 1993, 39; Yu Lei 1992, 7). For the vast majority, the registration drive was more ameliorist than punitive. Nevertheless there was a coercive element. Addicts would be cured by forcible enrollment in the newly established anti–drug smoking clinics (*jieyansuo*). During this period of treatment, addicts would be given pensions, and all their medical expenses subsidized. At the same time, police checks were carried out to source their suppliers and harsher penalties put in place for all who transported or sold drugs (Ma Weigang 1993, 3). If the story line was supposed to run in this way, financial constraints and other political concerns meant that it increasingly deviated from this script. Nanjing, cited on July 28, 1952, by Xu Zirong, then Deputy Minister of Public Security, as "one of the earliest and most successful places to carry out this work," offers an example of the way this campaign, hamstrung by finances and increasingly politicized, did not always run according to plan (PSHM 1990:1, VI5, 124).

In Nanjing, the war on drugs began soon after liberation when the Military Control Committee ordered military police pillboxes established at each of the ten city gates. Their main duty was to check for drugs. By September 1949, military police had successfully stopped the importation of drugs into the city, seizing 5,647 liang (or 282.35 kilograms) of drugs and seven drug-related implements. With the communists having demonstrated their ability to reduce the flow of drugs into the city to a trickle, they then moved the campaign into town. In May 1949, the Military Control Committee handed power over to the city government, which, in turn, established a special drug squad within the newly formed city Public Security Bureau. Working with the city household registration police, who were themselves engaged in a registration drive in July 1949, the drug squad established a users and dealers register that became part of the so-called special household register (tezhong hukou dengji). Like the special business register under which brothels were dealt with, this special household register gave police unique powers. These powers facilitated investigations that resulted in 1,569 drug-related cases being cracked and 472 people arrested between May and December. With the tolerant attitude still guiding action, however, penalties were light. Only 26 people were given criminal trials and sent to prison, and even then, sentences stretched from a mere six months to a maximum of two years. Of the remaining people, 205 were given short periods of administrative detention, 215 were "educated" and then released, and 26 people were sent back to their original places of abode (PSHM 1990:1, VI5, 113–14).

Like many places, however, Nanjing in 1950 was unable to finance an anti–drug smoking clinic or subsidize a medical scheme that could supply the much-needed preventative drugs. Their focus, therefore, turned away from curative treatment and toward coercion. With their curative program stalled through lack of funds, police focused most of their efforts on tracing the major dealers. As part of this drive, they issued a document on February 24, 1950, demanding that anyone who sold, produced, or transported opiates, heroin, or narcotics register immediately. Users were exempt. The object of this second registration drive was to get information on major drug sources. A number of factors worked in favor of the drive to register dealers. First, policy still focused on leniency, and this was especially the case in relation to all who "sincerely confessed." Second, unregistered dealers knew that the special population register contained the names of many addicts and other dealers. They also knew that these people had been interrogated and told to reveal all their contacts. Many feared that their names may already have been supplied to the authorities. In these circumstances, opting for the leniency policy seemed preferable to facing the possibility of arrest and harsh punishment. Finally, to help these unregistered dealers decide, police began a series of arrests. By deliberately releasing figures from these raids, the police hoped to instill fear in those who had not registered. By the end of August, the police announced, 360 people had been charged with various drug crimes. Particularly chilling for those still in hiding were the newspaper reports indicating that these arrests constituted but the tip of an iceberg. These 360 arrests, the newspapers announced, made up only 14 percent of all those who had actually been brought in to "help police with inquiries." The circle around the unregistered was tightening, and most of them took this opportunity to cooperate in the hope of leniency. But the time for cooperation and leniency was quickly drawing to an end.

By early September 1950, the police determined that those who would come forward voluntarily already had. It was now time to use the stick. Criminals who had not been "open and frank" were now to be shown no mercy. In the politically charged atmosphere that was leading inevitably toward the October 10 Central Committee decision to launch an all-out war on counter-revolutionaries, this new no-mercy policy also extended to "counter-revolutionary habitual criminals." In all, 350 people immediately fell into this category and were dealt with accordingly (PSHM 1990:1, V15, 126). From October 1950 on, the wind that blew this campaign to the left grew particularly frosty. Checks on anti-Party elements undertaken as part of the newly launched elimination of counter-revolutionaries campaign revealed that money from the drug industry not only financed many counter-revolutionary activities but was also being used as a device by many landlords and local gentry to maintain or garner peasant loyalties (PSHM 1990:1, V15, 116).[21] From that time onward the die was caste.

Links between drugs and counter-revolution were now being highlighted in police and Party propaganda and, as they were, the campaign became more mass-oriented. On September 3, 1950, the Nanjing Public Security Bureau organized a large-scale denunciation meeting where an estimated 150,000 people gathered to hear the verdict of death announced in relation to a number of major drug dealers. This meeting brought to the podium a range of official speakers, but it also included a number of witnesses who had suffered as a result of the actions of these dealers. For the Communist Party, transforming the trial into theater was an old but highly successful act. The confessions and speeches of dealers and victims became the stuff of street broadcasts and local neighborhood blackboard newspaper reports. As victim after victim spoke, "the media," it was said, "caught the anger of the people" (PSHM 1990:1, V15, 126). So, too, did the communists. The mass trial of September would serve as the template for a series of mass-judgment trials in seven other parts of the city. Police then pressed home this advantage by organizing 8,530 follow-up meetings of residents, which, in turn, led to a new high tide of denunciations in the course of which 58,300 denunciation letters were received and 3,411 people came forward with accusations. Even children joined in, with one coming forward to denounce his father with the words, "It isn't strange that my dad has been taken in, he did some bad things and should have been nabbed for them" (PSHM 1990:1, V15, 127).[22]

By the early fifties, politics was increasingly in command, and this trend was further reinforced by discoveries in the Three and Five Antis Campaigns of a further 263 major criminal cases that tied the drug trade to counter-revolutionary activity. Some of these cases sent police back to their old records, where they discovered evidence to help cement the link they were making between drugs and counter-revolution. From 1949 to June 1952, 4,441 major drug dealers had been arrested in Nanjing, and of these, 151 were spies, 109 "backbone elements" in counter-revolutionary organizations, 132 reactionary army officers, 156 civil officials of the Nationalist government, 280 heads of triad gangs, and 47 heads of illegal religious sects. A further 50 were "evil despotic landlords," 55 Nationalist army "riffraff," 28 members of counter-revolutionary families, and 5 bandits. In total, 1,014 or 22.83 percent of all those arrested on drug-related charges were also tied into counter-revolutionary activities or held reactionary viewpoints. The conclusion the police drew may appear circumstantial, but it was enough for them to link their crusade against drugs to the increasingly important Party Campaign to Suppress Counter-Revolutionaries. They concluded that "the drug trade is one type of counter-revolutionary wrecking activity undertaken by the Nationalist spying organs and a way by which the remnant counter-revolutionary forces could keep control of those elements who were social outcasts" (PSHM 1990:1, VI5, 119–20).

A confluence of circumstances began to lead toward a high level of politicization of the anti-drug campaign and its merging into an all-out attack upon counter-revolutionaries. Police began moving in on very large dealers at about the same time as popular opinion was hardening toward the Party's leniency policy. But drugs were not the only thing driving this change. Between January and the October launch of the Campaign to Suppress Counter-Revolutionaries, something like 816 so-called counter-revolutionary violent incidents had occurred, and many of these attacks were thought directly attributable to the government's policy of leniency. In Bobei county, Guangxi province, for example, a village peasant association head captured one bandit leader only to see the authorities release him as part of an act of reconciliation. Shortly afterward, he returned to the village and murdered the village head along with his entire family. In Jianning county in Fujian province, a group of bandits were likewise released under the leniency policy and once again immediately took to robbery and murder.[23] When families of some of the victims finally managed to capture one of these bandits for a second time, rather than handing him over to the authorities, they killed him and then hung his corpse at the entrance of the local country government office in protest (*Campaign to Suppress* 1992, 17). That was but one of the many protests the Party faced for creating a situation in which, according to Wang Zhongfang, leniency in the cities allowed "reactionaries" "enormous sway" and, in the countryside, kept the ordinary people firmly under the heel of the landlords (1992, 2).

"We don't fear heaven, we don't fear hell," went the old slogan from the Jangxi days, "our only fear is when the Communist Party proclaims leniency," came the new twist added by the masses of the fifties. It was a twist that would end up bending Party policy. And it was well reflected in the call by the Minister of Public Security at around this time for his police force to limit the leniency policy (*Campaign to Suppress* 1992, 20). To move away from the leniency policy, however, meant greater reliance upon mass-line organs and upon popular political action. By relying on these organs police would simultaneously shake off the problem of low numbers, deal with the issue of politically dubious colleagues, and heed the minister's call. The result would be a new type of mass-line experience, one in which police and population alike would be drawn further to the left and back into a dyadic framing of politics. As police numbers grew and younger communist police cadets took the place of the remnant elements, the consequences of a public security training program that leaned to the left became clear. For the Communist Party, this slow policy was beginning to show dividends, and, sometimes, it showed them in unexpected ways.

Short of numbers and resources, police were turning to the masses in a whole host of ways, producing, as they did, a new generation of mass-line policing experiences. The importance of these cannot be overestimated. This new extension of the mass-line style of policing enabled a degree of comprehensiveness in social control that would be the envy of any police force. In effect, the public security forces were becoming the key nodal points in a system that ultimately relied upon neighborhoods and work units to do the leg work. More than anything else, the development of this system effectively signaled the end of both organized prostitution and drug dealing in China for, with this system in place, dealers, addicts, pimps, and prostitutes had nowhere to hide and nowhere to go (Henriot 1995, 475; Zhou Yongming 1999, 108). Yet even apart from these stunning successes, this system was remarkable for it showed a uniquely Chinese form of popular policing as unparalleled as it was unrecognized.

The Campaign to Suppress Counter-Revolutionaries, 1950–1953: Soviet or Maoist?

In the early postrevolution days, writes Susanne Ogden, "the Chinese reliance on the Soviet model was so complete that the Chinese copied the Soviets in almost every major area" (1989, 38). For Franz Schurmann, this included the terror of the early Campaign to Suppress Counter-Revolutionaries (1968, 312).[24] Yet this campaign, far from being based on Soviet advice as some seem to suggest (Chesneaux 1979, 41), possibly constitutes the earliest and clearest example of Mao's postliberation China breaking the mold. Moreover, it was in this campaign that the public security forces began to lay down the foundations of a distinctly Maoist model of social control that would come to frame a way of life. Both because of their ubiquitous character and their dyadic nature, these new structures of the mass-line helped politicize the society and offer that politicization as a structural form. In this respect, far from being derivative of Soviet practices, this campaign and the institutions it constructed were consummate Mao.

"In the early 1950s," claims Laszlo Ladany, "the Russians were everywhere" (1992, 64). Maybe so, but as Wang Zhongfang notes, it did not stop the Chinese from teaching their "big brother" some important lessons:

> There is also one other lesson that needs to be explained and that is that the Campaign to Suppress Counter-Revolutionaries also broke with practices adopted by the Soviet public security forces. For a very long time, our security work showed the influence of the Soviet Union. After we entered the cities, the Soviets began to send advisors. When we began the Campaign to Suppress Counter-Revolutionaries, the Soviet experts didn't understand what we were up to and didn't agree to it. But under the leadership of Chairman Mao, we were not restrained by them and, on the basis of Chinese characteristics, we created a form of operation that was suitable for us. As the campaign developed, it also taught the Soviet experts a thing or two and, afterwards, they were convinced. (qtd. in *Campaign to Suppress* 1992, 4)

This Campaign to Suppress Counter-Revolutionaries signaled the beginnings of a new tactic of socialist governance as military-style campaigning was mimicked and redeployed in the realms of politics and policing. Arguably, it could be said that this had all been seen and done before. Whether it was in Stalinist purges of counter-revolutionaries or in the Chinese campaigns to check and rescue cadres, the idea of a campaign against counter-revolutionaries was far from new. What *was* new in 1950 was not so much the content of the campaign as its form.

In the long period of struggle to gain power, the Communist Party had constantly reenergized itself by relying upon a dyadic, mass-based political line to intensify activist commitment. After it took power, the Party was no less dependent upon this form of politics. It would lead to campaigns themselves throwing up institutions that could organize the participation of the masses and also intensify their commitment. These institutions of the (political) binary, which Maoism would come to call mass-line organs, would end up profoundly altering virtually every facet of Chinese social life. In the end, and partly through these mass-line organs, Maoism produced more than a set of social institutions. What these institutions represented was a style of work and quite habitual political posture that would reinforce the dyadic framing of the political. The friend/enemy binary reordered as a question of class would become the motor of every campaign. And it was the populist forms these campaigns took, coupled with the overheated political intensity they produced and relied upon to politicize, that so concerned the Soviets.

For Soviet advisors, the methods employed in this campaign appeared troubling, if not downright heretical. Any program that involved mass, populist politicization that was ongoing and intense would inevitably worry Soviet advisors who had not seen such actions since the days of their own first five-year plan. Moreover, not since the time of the disgraced Evgeny Pashukanis had notions of legal flexibility been so much in evidence. Even for that onetime doyen of Soviet jurisprudence, the "withering away of law" had never meant that mass actions would be allowed to generate legal forms. Yet this is precisely what was taking place in China. As one Chinese scholar put it, "in the 1950s, law didn't come prior to campaigns, but out of them. Editorials from *People's Daily*, speeches from the Party leadership, and the necessities and consequences of mass campaigns all played a part in framing all legal and quasi-legal formulations" (interview 1997). The rhythm, flexibility, and mass nature of this suppression campaign ran in almost the exact opposite direction to the "stability, formality and professionalism" characterized by Stalinist legal formulations, which in turn were thought to be the necessary shell for any planned form of economic development. In the Soviet Union, at this time, one suffered the certainty of what one scholar has described as a Stalinist "jurisprudence of terror," and not the vagaries of a populist mass-based campaign (Sharlet 1977, 158, 163).

A logical, rational, and centralized economic model was always thought to require if not a legal shell then, at the very least, a technical, rational, and regulatory one.[25] Yet what the Chinese communists showed through the suppression of counter-revolutionaries and the Three and Five Antis Campaigns was that it was possible to develop a planned economic structure while politics was stabilized by Party-led popular indignation. Far from acknowledging the need for technical or legal stability or clarity, the Chinese campaign strategy seemed to mock it, giving voice instead to mass involvement and a blurring of the lines between official organs of state repression (the police) and popular, mass-line organizations harnessing indignation. It was as though the Chinese felt that the danger of depoliticization that centralized planning seemed to threaten could be rectified by mass vigilance and action.

Paradoxically, the promotion of mass action based on the production of political intensity was facilitated by the development of an organizational form that in appearance, at least, seemed to further confirm the scientific and objective quality of the centralized plan. That organization was known as the work unit system (*danwei*). The name itself seemed to imply a function. It appeared to be a unit of calculation for work undertaken (He Xinhan 1998, 43). Yet work units differed from ordinary economic enterprises insofar as their desire to overcome the alienation of labor led them to offer a wide array of services to members that effectively made the calculation of costs and outputs almost impossible. In providing a wide body of services, the work unit system replaced the transparency needed for calculation with an opacity that dominates everyday life. The result was a blurring of lines between work and life, but the appearance of a work site totally suited to Soviet-style planned economic development. For Chinese communists, this blurring of lines enabled the generation of political intensity and this then produced the activists who could be mobilized for campaigns. In a sense, work units were a dual production system, supplying the central plan with material resources and products while providing the Communist Party with an activist mass base.

Work units developed as an organizational response to the Marxist political and moral objection to a system of labor power and material resource allocation based on the vagaries of the market. This objection was twofold. First, markets were regarded as unscientific and inefficient and, second, they were thought to be exploitative and alienating. To avoid inefficiency, socialist distribution since Lenin turned on the planned allocation of goods and resources. To avoid an exploitative and alienating system they were organized to employ human resources in a manner that would not separate life from work. By merging life and labor into a single work-based structure, the Chinese communists believed they had discovered the means by which to fulfill both of these two requirements.

Hence this work unit system catered for all of life's needs if not its pleasures, and, in this regard, fulfilled both the moral and economic component of the socialist planning agenda. Built behind large compound walls that designated their areas of jurisdiction, work units established a labyrinth of small institutions such as shops, hospitals, schools, workers apartments, and entertainment venues, and, of course, mass-line protection organizations. In other words, and in a radically different context, for each work unit member they supplied what Marcel Mauss once referred to as a system of "total services" (1990, 5).

This system of total services was a precondition for an internal distribution system that decentered monetary incentives and markets but, increasingly, attempted to supply goods and services on the basis of "need." Indeed, the money economy was further decentered first by the fact that the introduction of ration coupons for most goods limited the use of money and second by an egalitarian push in the early fifties for a massive reduction of wage differentials.

With life and work merged, money decentered, and a more opaque system of distribution in place, work units increasingly developed an internal economic structure that then became the basis for what Mauss called a "gift economy." It is this facet of their operation that has led Chinese scholars, such as Lu Feng, to conclude that work units have a close kinship with traditional lineage group arrangements (Lu Feng 1998, 54–58). While this argument is not without merit, what it fails to mention is that the kinship promoted within the work unit is politically based, not family based. Increasingly, work units not only rewarded those who were politically active but also established a lived regime within which activism could be "naturally" produced and expended. With this type of economic structure underpinning its work, mass-line organizations were always going to have a ready supply of activists. So, for the Chinese Communist Party, this blurring of lines between what is conventionally known as state and civil society led to a clarification of political ones.

Work units blurred the lines between life and economy to promote economic production but in so doing produced the conditions for mass-line policing. In blurring the lines between the official organs of state security (the police) and popular, mass-line organizations that harnessed and chan-neled political indignation into police campaigns, work units helped resolve the resource problems police faced.

If a lack of resources became the mother of invention within the work unit, it was also the wet nurse that gave birth to the newly institutionalized Maoist idea of mass-line policing. That too was born of a scarcity of human resources. The time and date of this birth more or less correlates with the "high tide" of the Campaign to Suppress Counter-Revolutionaries.

It was because of this campaign that all the disparate mass-line defense organizations of China would come to be collectively named and given defi-nition. Of course, most of these mass organizations had existed in dispa-rate forms in earlier days. Prior to 1951, however, their status had always remained ambiguous, and they had always suffered from the confusion of a "multi-headed leadership" (Brugger 1981a, 99). While these forms had always shared a family resemblance, it was only during the high tide of this campaign that they became more than momentary structures to deal with immediate problems. At this time, and arguably for the first time, they be-came structured into Party considerations of government. It was Mao Ze-dong who first saw the need to formalize these organs collectively as "pub-lic order defense committees." Outlining their basic operating principles, he said, "In the current great struggle to suppress counter-revolutionaries, public security committees must be organized among the masses every-where. Such committees should be elected by the people in every township in the countryside and in every department and organization, school, fac-tory, and neighborhood in the cities" (Mao Zedong 1977, 5:52).

Established under the auspices of the work unit, resident, or village com-mittees these organs were charged with securing the "four protections" (sifang), that is, prevention of spying, theft, fires, and social order incidents. When work unit security organs combined with resident committees, they would form the "joint public order defense committees" (zhi'an lianfang wei-yuanhui), or "joint protection" (lianfang), as they were sometimes known. Not only were these disparate types of mass protection work more standard-ized in their form during this campaign, they were also sewn into the fabric of government. They became the base-level organs of the state's social con-trol system. With this inclusion, the mass-line expanded exponentially.

By the end of the suppression campaign in 1953, China had 170,000 resident or work unit security committees (zhi'an baowei weiyuanhui), with a mass activist base numbering 2 million people (Tao Siju 1996, 104; Outline of Public Security 1997, 268). These formed the front-line shock troops for a diminutive public security force. It was these organs that helped solve most crimes and assisted the police in maintaining community social order. They would keep tabs on the household registers and keep an eye on suspects. Operating under the leadership of the local public security organs, these committees formed a weblike structure that stretched across all facets of social life in China and offered comprehensive social control right down to the street and the work unit (Yu Lei 1992, 164). Because of this, they could also provide the security forces with help in solving another of their problems, namely, the monitoring of suspect or minor counter-revolutionaries whose crimes had been insufficient to warrant penal incarceration. This had become a significant problem as the campaign entered its second year and its first high tide.

From February 1951 onward, a high tide came into effect after the "Directive on the Punishment of Counter-Revolutionaries" ordered all work units to go in hard on counter-revolutionaries. This, in turn, produced huge numbers of counter-revolutionaries in need of punishment and then put pressure upon the fledgling prison sector, which was suddenly swamped. While this led to a massive expansion of the prison system, even this was not enough to halt the crisis. The reasons for this can be gleaned from the arrest figures of that time. Up until the "double ten" directive of October 1950, some 392,292 people had been taken into custody. From October 1950 through to 1952, the number of arrests jumped over eight times, to an amazing 3,239,481 people (confidential material 1986).[26] While an expanded prison sector would end up holding some 1 million people (Outline of Public Security 1997, 267), that still left nearly 3 million in need of management. Local community supervision through mass-line security organs offered the answer.

Sometime in 1951, "mass surveillance and control," or guanzhi, was devised as the best means by which to deal with the situation.[27] Guanzhi effectively meant that one's place of work and life, the work unit, would become the site where one was also under mass supervision and control.[28] Yu Lei has suggested that guanzhi was used for "historic" criminals whose level of criminality did not warrant the charge of counter-revolutionary being leveled against them but who nonetheless still required "certain restrictions" being placed upon their actions. Such restrictions were to last no more than three years, and any extension of this time period would require further approval. In rural areas, approval would come from the area- (*qu*) or township- (*xiang*) level people's governments that were to notify the county-level Public Security Bureau of the request, have the case checked, and then validate the approval. In the city, requests for guanzhi came from the local police station and were checked and approved by the city Public Security Bureau (Yu Lei 1992, 402–3). In practice, however, such strictures were a dead letter and rarely, if ever, impeded the use of guanzhi. Through this system, work units become open prisons for anyone placed under guanzhi. Moreover, as work units were pressed into the role of prison, prisons themselves were being transformed into sites of reform through labor or *laogai*.

With huge numbers of inmates pushed into the penal sector as a result of the suppression campaign, the jails and prison camps of China were finding it hard to cope. The state's response to this was to centralize control and regularize form. In 1950, with the approval of the Administrative Council, all prisons and prison camps in China came under the direct control of the Ministry of Public Security (Wang Zhongfang 1992, 53).[29] With complete control over the penal sector, the Ministry of Public Security, in May 1951, began to innovate. It introduced a split system of control for minor and major offenders. Those judged as criminals would henceforth be sent for laogai, or reform through labor, while minor offenders would be dealt with by other administrative means (such as guanzhi).[30] Despite this, revanchism and abuse still constituted a common and ongoing problem, forcing police to reform the system further. In June 1952, the ministry convened the First National Reform Criminals through Labor Work Conference, and it was here that they announced the establishment of a new penal system for China (A *Summary History* 1989, 85). The guiding ethos of this new system was to be "reform first, production second."[31] As one Chinese source notes, it was through the Campaign to Suppress Counter-Revolutionaries that reform through labor finally became a reality (*Outline of Public Security* 1997, 267). These were but a few of the (Maoist) innovations that are claimed to have emanated from this (so-called Soviet-style) campaign.

The Campaign Develops, the Battle Begins

The Campaign to Suppress Counter-Revolutionaries was of great help in establishing the people's democratic dictatorship and pushing it forward. After the establishment of the state, questions still remained. While the basic structures of the state had changed, it still wasn't clear which organs were to replace the old machinery or how this work was to be carried out. All these sorts of things were new issues. . . . It can be said with regard to the establishment of the machinery of the state that the influence of this [campaign] was very great. It helped raise the prestige of the police, the procuraturate, and the courts [*gongjianfa*] among the masses and made them realize that they had weapons of their own with which to protect their own interests. Government and legal organs also learned how to use these weapons to eliminate the enemy. Indeed, it enabled these organs to see the value of employing the mass line, which was now opening onto a new stage of development. Step by step, the [lessons of this campaign] became something of a tradition.

—WANG ZHONGFANG

The question of suppressing counter-revolution was the revolutionary question of 1949. Even as the state was being established in October of that year, upper-level cadres of the nascent Ministry of Public Security gathered to draw up a response to the question of counter-revolution. Their discussions form the earliest indications of an agenda that would take a full year to come into view. Public security teams, they decided, were to be organized and strengthened. In the cities, they argued, work should focus on uncovering spy networks, while in the countryside, they contended, bandits were to be eliminated (Luo Ruiqing 1994, 11). The question to be asked of this campaign, then, is not why it took place, but rather, why it was not until October 1950 that this early policing agenda was finally announced. By then, of course, this was no longer a police agenda, but a national *political* agenda. Indeed, even as early as March 1950, these issues were no longer confined to the police. At that time, the Central Committee, the Administrative Council, and the Supreme People's Court were already discussing the issues raised by the nascent Ministry of Public Security, and by June, the third plenum of the seventh Central Committee meeting more or less made the police agenda its own when it called for the elimination of bandits, spies, tyrants, and counter-revolutionaries (*Campaign to Suppress* 1992, 16). These "elements," along with "secret societies" (*huidaomen*), would become the five targets of the suppression campaign (*Questions and Answers* 1994, 71). As I have already stated, outside factors, such as American belligerence, also proved critical in heightening the tension and paranoia, but the campaign was already in motion some time before these external factors buffeted the Party's agenda further to the left.

In effect, the Campaign to Suppress Counter-Revolutionaries, conventionally dated from the so-called double ten decision of 1950 (that is, the decision of the Central Committee on October 10, 1950), was in preparation for a full year prior to this date. As was the case with the 1942 rectification campaign in Yan'an, it was the public prosecution of the campaign that came to be identified as its beginning, rather than its preparatory stages. Yet preparation for this campaign began almost the moment Mao stepped down from the podium on the gate of Tian'anmen in October 1949. What is important about this preparatory work is that it left the ethical status of the moderate leniency policy of the first year in some doubt. There appear at least some grounds to suspect duplicity. After all, as police were registering Guomindang members and promising leniency, the upper echelons of the Party organization were simultaneously preparing for a campaign that, as Brugger notes, would use these very same records as the basis for the attacks upon such "elements" (1981a, 73).

The first the public would know of this campaign came on October 10, 1950, in the form of the "Directive to Suppress Counter-Revolutionary Activity." This directive was authored by a small leadership group of five, including Liu Shaoqi, Peng Zhen, and Luo Ruiqing.[32] The key point they made was that greater stress needed to be laid upon the struggle against any rightist tendency of being too lenient (*Campaign to Suppress* 1992, 20).[33] To ensure that limits were in fact placed on leniency, in February 1950, the Administrative Council released the "Directive Strengthening People's Justice Work" that helped clarify the relationship between suppression and leniency: "In relation to counter-revolutionaries, the first thing to be done is to suppress them. Only once they have been suppressed will they admit guilt, and only once they have admitted guilt can we begin to talk about leniency" (qtd. in *Campaign to Suppress* 1992, 22). Five days later, the key agenda item of the Second Public Security Work Meeting was how to implement this. The answer, they suggested, was to get all Ministry of Public Security and Party branch resources to be channeled into the campaign. In this way the Party launched its war against counter-revolution.

Within months of the meeting, police in Fujian province claimed to have smashed seventy underground spying organizations and to have arrested over seven hundred people, while police in the northwest claimed to have cracked forty serious spying cases involving five hundred people. Meanwhile, in rural areas between November 1950 and February 1951, police in Shanxi, Hebei, Chaha'er, and Beijing began the attack on the so-called reactionary secret societies (*Campaign to Suppress* 1992, 21–22). As if the meaning of these raids was not clear enough, the government then enacted the "Regulations Regarding the Punishment of Counter-revolutionaries in the PRC" in February 1951. It then followed this up by publishing an editorial in the *People's Daily* that brought home to ordinary cadres the importance and urgency of such new measures (*Outline of Public Security*, 1997, 260). Action at a local level quickly followed.

On March 13, police carried out attacks on counter-revolutionaries in Chongqing, leading to 4,000 arrests. On March 27, Chengdu followed with some 1,200 people in all five targeted categories arrested. Shandong would follow these cities with its own campaign. On the evening of April 1, 1951, Shandong police launched an attack on counter-revolutionaries in which 4,053 people were arrested (*Campaign to Suppress* 1992, 25). City campaigning allowed for concentrated action and visible results. It offered, therefore, an ideal site from which the Party could further advance the campaign through a propaganda war that was, in terms of scale and depth of social penetration, claimed to be "without historical precedent. Every family and every home knew about the campaign and participated in it" (*Campaign to Suppress* 1992, 27).

The way the campaign proceeded in cities can be understood from the example of Beijing. Once again, the campaign progressed along familiar lines. The city leadership was mobilized in February 1951, and it then used its power to broaden the campaign. This broadening began in spring, when the city authorities organized 29,000 meetings throughout the city with 3.3 million participants in attendance (*Campaign to Suppress* 1992, 27–28). But it was not just in the cities that the campaign gained momentum; every village in the country seemed to be engaged in a scaled-down version of these events.[34]

The high tide of campaigning, however, was leading the Party into dangerous waters. There were simply too many arrests and deaths, and the fear of a significant backlash began to stalk Party leaders. Mao articulated just these sorts of concerns on April 30, when he said:

> In executing we should not kill too many for, if too many are killed, we will loose social support and we will also loose too much productive labor. . . . Serious criminals who should be sentenced to death, but who do not owe a debt of blood or whose actions have not resulted in mass indignation can be given a death sentence with a one- or two-year reprieve. This group would then be forced to undertake labor, then we can make a decision based on the results. (qtd. in *Campaign to Suppress* 1992, 36)[35]

But even as Mao spoke, the problem was already well out of hand. Within one year of the October 1950 decision to launch this campaign, around 700,000 people had been executed and more than 2 million arrested. The vast majority of these people, it seems, had been arrested between October 1950 and May 1951 (interview 1995).[36] Erroneous cases, overzealous cadres, and a fear of chaos brought on by an overreliance on populist political intensity led to growing Party leadership concerns about the progress of this campaign. Stronger Party leadership over mass exuberance was now the order of the day. This demand would come from Ministry of Public Security leaders who, following Mao, regarded it as a matter of "military urgency" to immediately correct the high tide of leftist deviation before more executions took place. In order to promptly rectify the situation, the Third Public Security Work Meeting was brought forward to May. This meeting would later be hailed by the Minister of Public Security, Luo Ruiqing. He would claim that the "correction of this potentially leftist deviation" and the "creation of conditions that enabled the smooth transition to the second and third stages of the campaign" held "historic significance" for both the Party and the police. Ultimately, he concluded, they "paved the way to overall victory" (Luo Ruiqing 1994, 409).

The resolution that came out of this May meeting, written entirely by Mao Zedong, would sum up the new "correct path" (*Campaign to Suppress* 1992, 74; Mao Zedong 1974, 9–10). The resolution stated that "in the Suppression of Counter-Revolutionaries Campaign, we must pull back and, for the next month, apart from implementing those detention measures necessary to prevent counter-revolutionaries from carrying out their wrecking activities, detention of people should stop, and the execution of counter-revolutionaries must be controlled and kept within bounds" (qtd. in *Outline of Public Security* 1997, 262).

Within a matter of months of this resolution, all cases other than those already under investigation were temporarily put on hold and police attention turned to the "long-pending cases" (*ji'an*). To efficiently carry out this work, a number of areas established specialist "counter-revolutionary case-checking committees" (*fangeming anjian shencha weiyuanhui*) that operated like the later work teams to check cases for error or pick up on cases that had slipped through the net (*Campaign to Suppress* 1992, 39–40; Luo Ruiqing 1994, 106, 108–9). These teams were a long way from the populist-based left actions of the earlier months. A new phase of the campaign now opened up as "expert" began to prevail over "red." This next phase would operate under a more disciplined expert leadership that stressed, as Mao had demanded, a greater emphasis upon the leadership role of the local Party committees (Mao 1977, 5:56). Indeed, from the time of the Third Public Security Work Meeting onward, all arrests at a county level would need the approval of the prefectural Party committee or the prefectural commissioner's offices, while all executions were to be passed on for a final decision made by the autonomous region or provincial-level authorities (*Outline of Public Security* 1997, 262). Once again, local Party committees were seen as the most appropriate mechanism to control the excesses of dyadic political forms at a local level. At a central level, all government organs and legislation now revolved around ratcheting down the political intensity of the earlier months.

Indeed, even when it came to advocating further action, the May "resolution" was cautious. While it called for further political work in a number of medium and larger cities, it argued that this work was not to be of a populist nature. Instead, the new key task was to expose the undercover professional spies who could only be brought to the surface by specialist investigative units (*Campaign to Suppress* 1992, 38, Mao Zedong 1974, 9). By the end of May 1951, the Central Committee announced a decisive shift away from populism toward a more professionalized model in its "Directive Concerning Cleaning Up the Question of the Middle Ranks and Inner Levels."

This redirected police energies away from populist campaigns and toward counter-espionage work within the army, government (the so-called middle ranks or *zhongceng*), and the Party (what was called the inner levels or *neiceng*). The immediate effect of this action was that around 1,080,000 people in various work units and education institutions from around the country came under investigation (*Campaign to Suppress* 1992, 53). These investigations, however, differed significantly from the mass actions of previous months. Professional skill, not mass indignation, now formed the core ingredient of the campaign.

Thus when the campaign moved back into the cities between June and September, it had both a different focus and a different dynamic propelling it. In the initial phase of the counter-revolutionaries campaign, hidden counter-revolutionaries in society at large (the so-called *waiceng*) had been the target. Attention now moved to the hidden enemy agents within the army, the government, and the Party (Luo Ruiqing 1994, 79–80, 85; *Questions and Answers* 1994, 75–76).[37] What might have seemed at the time like a minor shift would end up bringing forth a set of concerns that would ultimately lead to the Campaign to Suppress Internal (Party- and government-based) Counter-Revolutionaries. That, however, was very much on the distant horizon and, at this time, these shifts appeared to be anything but portents of things to come. Rather, they were attempts to wind back the suppression campaign and move it off the streets. This new phase of the campaign no longer constituted a mass-based populist purge. Instead, it was said to be based upon the spirit of rectification. Moreover, it was thought to be nearing its end (Mao Zedong 1977, 5:51; *Campaign to Suppress* 1992, 52). This line of thinking dominated the Fourth Public Security Work Meeting in September 1951. Counter-revolutionaries, the meeting concluded, were "badly beaten but not completely eliminated." The remaining tasks of this campaign were, in the main, to clean up work already in progress or pick up on areas left neglected (*Campaign to Suppress* 1992, 42–43). If the meeting thought these "tails" could be dealt with quickly, it was wrong. What would end up speedily emerging was not the end of this suppression campaign, but the need for two more: the Three and Five Antis.

Beginning in December 1951 and January 1952, respectively, the Three and Five Antis Campaigns would have separate but related agendas. The

Three Antis campaign would focus on corruption, waste, and bureaucratization while the Five Antis Campaign targeted bribery, tax avoidance, theft of government property, theft of materials, and theft of economic intelligence. The concerns of these two campaigns dovetailed neatly with the agenda of the suppression campaign as it continued to check for counter-revolutionaries within government, army, and Party ranks. Yet in effectively transforming the campaign into a series of counter-espionage tasks, the combative, hard style of open political campaigning was no longer thought effective. Indeed, other than in those areas where suppression formed an adjunct to land reform, the suppression campaign was more or less suspended until the end of the Three and Five Antis Campaigns in July–August 1952. Thus when delegates gathered for yet another Public Security Work Meeting in October 1952, all talk focused on reviving and finishing off the suspended suppression campaign (Luo Ruiqing 1994, 149). This Fifth Public Security Work Meeting would pick up where the fourth had left off and begin, once again, the work of rechecking cases for error.

This revival of professional specialist police work was further strengthened by a Party decision in January 1953 to launch a "new Three Antis" case-checking rectification campaign (*xin sanfan*).[38] In the circular that accompanied this campaign, many of the procedural problems that had plagued the first and populist phase of the suppression campaign were remembered and attacked. The report was scathing and called for "the strict handling and elimination of criminal breaches by illegal and ill-disciplined elements who have caused much hatred among the masses" (qtd. in *Campaign to Suppress* 1992, 88). The breaches it cited included wrongly sentencing people to periods of "mass surveillance and control" (guanzhi), employing the bi-gong-xin method of coercing people into making confessions or extracting confessions through torture, and forging or altering records to cover up police mistakes or misdeeds. By May 1953, reports of abuse from southwestern China in particular were regarded as so serious as to force the Ministry of Public Security to issue written instructions to its provincial-level bureau to take more vigorous preventative action (*Campaign to Suppress* 1992, 88). While the new Three Antis Campaign would end in July 1953, the issue of forced confessions and other abuses would remain. In November 1953, the ministry was forced to publish a small pamphlet called *Opposing the Forced Extraction of Confessions, Opposing Illegal Breaches of Discipline*, which was distributed to all branches and supposed to guide all future action (*Campaign to Suppress* 1992, 88). The problem was, however, that the issue was not that simple.

Campaigns relied upon an uneasy combination of popular enthusiasm and Party leadership. Constructed around leadership expectations of quick and decisive results, campaigns would employ mass organizations to administer severe strikes against chosen targets. Working off centrally designated arrest quotas and reliant upon harnessing ill-disciplined mass enthusiasm, campaigns always ran the risk of pulling to the left. The suppression campaign illustrated this, but it also demonstrated rectification practices that pointed to a less well-publicized tendency of campaigning. Away from the glare of the campaign spotlight, mechanisms were constantly being experimented with by those who believed in the binary logic of campaigns at a philosophical level. For these elements, experimentation proved necessary to work out the appropriate mix of mass action and specialist skills for different political events. Experimentation would lead to perfection, and the perfect mass-line technology would ignite passions but not lead passion into excess. Others within the Party likewise believed in the rectification process, but they did so for wholly different reasons.

For this latter group, campaigns constituted a technology of transition. They employed popular enthusiasm only on a temporary basis and only in order to establish the firm political ground on which a more formal and stable governmental structure could develop. As a technology of transition, the campaign would not only clear the ground of opposition, but it would also set the stage for the formal incorporation of the mass-line into the structures of government. With these mechanisms in place, policing, like politics generally, could be "regularized." This was more or less the view of the Central Committee in late 1954, when it noted that "the large-scale national, mass-based Campaign to Suppress Counter-Revolutionaries is already a thing of the past, and public security work has already entered a period of more regular forms of struggle" (qtd. in *Outline of Public Security* 1997, 272). It was likewise the view of Luo Ruiqing who suggested that from this time onward, a more professionally orientated reconnaissance work designed to aid the undercover struggle would be the focus of the socialist police force (1994, 208). Police did not turn their backs on mass organs, but simply slotted them into a structure that would limit their role to community policing. Here, then, was a way to both moderate the populism of the masses and yet maintain a commitment to the mass-line. A good example of how this would work was offered by the household registration system.

In July 1953, temporary national household registration laws accompanied the announcement of the first five-year plan. The registration laws effectively halted all unauthorized population movement, enabling economic planners to know what human resources were available in different locales (Dutton 1992, 217). The local police station was generally made the repository of these records, offering an effective means to police local communities at an intimate level. Moreover, police jurisdictions or beats were usually organized around these recording zones. In cities, a cluster of five hundred households usually made up a city beat, while in market towns, it was seven hundred households. Each would have an officer assigned to oversee work in the area, but the actual, daily work of checking on details was left to the village or neighborhood security committee (Xu Hanmin 1992, 22).[39] In effect, police tended to become the leadership organs of local community security work carried out, in the main, by community groups. These mass committees bore the biggest burden of basic community control as the public security forces began to concentrate on the more specialized and professional work of policing. It was this more professional, specialized, and limited agenda that emerged in May 1954 at the Sixth National Public Security Work Meeting.

At this meeting, the focal point of future police work was to be in defense of the economy, yet it was also at this point that the tectonic plates of two different worldviews would begin to clash and cause friction. While communist central planners trained in the logic of Soviet-style planning regarded law as the appropriate means to stabilize the state and, therefore, establish the ground upon which planning could commence, those committed to Maoist-style mass campaigns operated from a very different set of assumptions. Mass action, not law, they thought, would limit the process of depoliticization and therefore do a better job of protecting the political shell that guaranteed the implementation of the plan. At the heart of this new economically centered police agenda lay the task of uncovering wreckers who had managed to enter the Party or key industries (A Summary History 1989, 124). Police reconnaissance work and hidden struggle against wreckers in key areas and industries was now the order of the day. Ports, transportation points, military bases, and mines all became the focal point of police activity as the agenda of the police moved from arresting all of the five remnant counter-revolutionary elements to a concentration on just spies and enemy agents. In this realignment of duties, 156 key basic construction projects and 694 large and medium-sized enterprises were marked out by the public security forces for special attention. Police efforts would now be heavily directed toward strengthening mass security work in these places and over these projects.

Police leadership over security committees in these key areas was strengthened as was the internal enterprise security system. Internal protection units within key enterprises began to go through their personnel dossiers to ascertain the political purity of their staff (*Outline of Public Security* 1997, 272–73),[40] and, as they did, they began to uncover a range of suspected hidden enemies. To discern the signs of a hidden enemy, however, was much harder than finding an overt one. To ferret out a professional spy required a degree of professional skill and specialist expertise of one's own. This stress on skill—when combined with the 1954 "Regulations on Police Station Organization," the drafting of the criminal code, and the promulgation of the constitution (Xu Hanmin 1992, 111–12; Brugger 1981a, 104)—suggests that at this time, there occurred something of a move away from the mass-line toward a more formal professional justice system. Expertise, not mass involvement, now appeared as the order of the day, and the structuring of the 1955 internal sufan campaign around specialist work teams with a high degree of expertise in detective and investigative work reflected this trend. This campaign, however, not so much marked the death of the mass-line organs as their formal subordination into an increasingly professional policing system. Mass-line organs would still play a key role, for only they knew the "real" situation on the ground. Nevertheless, when it came to the key task of investigating evidence relating to hidden enemies, what was required was expertise, not enthusiasm. This appears to be the logic underpinning police actions during the Campaign to Suppress Internal Counter-Revolutionaries in 1955. Yet while this new more specialized and professional form of campaigning appeared tailored to a Soviet-style centralized planning model, the actual targets chosen for suppression suggest that appearances may be deceptive. While an array of lesser targets were chosen for suppression, easily the most important and significant were those cadres most closely associated with the Soviet Union and most committed to an idea of socialism built upon a dispassionate, "objective," and "rational" centralized economic plan. The campaign may have targeted such liberal figures as Hu Feng, but its real beginning was with the Gao Gang and Rao Shushi affair.[41]

From Regularization to Radicalization:
The Internal Suppression Campaign

QUESTION: What was the Campaign to Suppress Internal Counter-
  Revolutionaries [*nebu sufan yundong*]?
ANSWER: On May 12, 1955, the Supreme State Council meeting said:
  "Raise vigilance, clean out the enemy agents, prevent deviations, avoid
  injustices against good people." At the CCP Central Committee meeting
  on July 1, 1955, they issued "Instructions on the Opening Up of a Struggle
  to Clean Out Hidden Counterrevolutionaries." With this, the internal
  campaign to clean out these elements began. — *Questions and Answers*

Unlike the previous Campaign to Suppress Counter-Revolutionaries, the 1955 internal campaign would run along lines that would later be criticized as being "too Soviet" (interview 1995). Indeed, being "too Soviet" was to become one of the key reasons given for the failure of work styles at this time.[42] The main problem seems to have been that it worked less on the Maoist ideal of "taking the ideas of the masses and systematizing them" and more upon a model of sending in work teams to push the masses into action (interview 1997). Ironically, this Soviet-style campaign to purge internal enemies seems to have had its origins, at least in part, in an earlier purge of two of the Party's leading pro-Soviet luminaries, Gao Gang and Rao Shushi. The purge of these two figures not only sent shock waves through the Party and the country but, more significantly, it precipitated a search for those with links to this clique, which would, in turn, lead to the purge becoming a fully blown political campaign as evidence of other forms of counter-revolutionary activity began to emerge. The key events would play out in Shanghai.

At this time, China was divided into six administrative regions, each run by six separate bureaus. Gao Gang and Rao Shushi headed two of the six regional administrative bureaus. One of these was the economically powerful northeastern region, while the other was the politically influential eastern China region which included Shanghai. A central charge leveled at Gao and

Rao was that they had tried to develop their own regions into "independent kingdoms." As a result, the purge of the two men brought forth investigations into their support base among subordinates in these regions. It was none other than Mao Zedong, who, in early 1955 at the Party congress, called upon anyone associated with Gao and Rao to come forward and confess (Luo Qingchang 1995, 363), and this, in turn, precipitated a number of confessions. Easily the most sensational of these confessions would come from Rao's subordinates in Shanghai, and the first important associate to be so named was the head of the Shanghai's Public Security Bureau, Yang Fan.

The link between Rao and Yang that seems to have come under most scrutiny, involved the appointment of Hu Junhe as head of the intelligence committee of the city. While no one doubted Hu's qualifications for work in this area, few thought of him as being above reproach politically. He had, in fact, been a double agent in the past, having worked for both the communists and the Nationalists at various times. In addition, he had even been an assistant to Li Shiqun in Wang Jingwei's puppet government in Nanjing. Furthermore, he had played some part in arranging a secret meeting between the communists' spy chief Pan Hannian and Wang Jingwei. Clearly, Hu had a history that needed to be accounted for, and questions hung over Yang as to why he would appoint such a dubious character to such an important and sensitive position.

Questions about the loyalty of former Nationalist agents working for the communists were nothing new. In the winter of 1950, a group of former Nationalist intelligence agents who had gone over to the communists fled to Taiwan, betraying the Party. This led the central government to issue warnings about the dangers of using such agents. Hence, by the time Luo Ruiqing arrived in the city of Shanghai in 1951 to investigate the appointment of Hu Junhe, suspicions had become almost palpable. In light of the central government's warning and Luo's arrival, the Shanghai police decided to reinvestigate a number of unsolved terrorist attacks, including the 1950 bombing of the Shanghai power station. When Luo inquired into these incidents, he was told of the potential problems caused by employing remnant Nationalist intelligence workers. From this, it was clear that those who spoke to Luo were already pointing the finger at figures like Hu Junhe (Yin Qi 1995, 374). From very early on, Hu Junhe's appointment generated rumors that led directly back to Yang Fan. Moreover, any appointment by Yang would have to be approved by the head of the eastern China administrative region, Rao Shushi. When the Gao Gang incident surfaced and the charge of independent kingdom arose, Rao Shushi was identified as Gao's main ally. When this bombshell hit, connections between Rao and Hu began to be made. The earlier suspicions of treachery that had circulated around Rao because of the Hu Junhe appointment now seemed confirmed. This, of course, was bad news for Yang Fan.

On the last day of 1954, Yang was detained and sent to Beijing for interrogation (Yin Qi 1995, 379). To make matters worse, Mao himself would link the treachery of Rao Shushi directly to the police chief. He did this almost in passing as he explained that political alliances were rarely based on signed contractual documents. His "illustration" of this point put Yang Fan "in the frame." Mao said, "Then again, we haven't seen any pact between Rao Shushi and people like Xiang Ming and Yang Fan. Therefore, the idea that you cannot consider something an alliance if you have not found a written agreement for it is wrong" (Mao Zedong 1986, 1:535). History and a shared belief system, not a piece of paper, he seemed to suggest, bound these figures. Arrested and accused of shielding 3,300 Nationalist agents, Yang's fate was sealed (Yin Qi 1995, 379). As this maelstrom gathered pace, others within the Shanghai leadership began to nervously look over their shoulders as past events came back to haunt them. Of all the leaders, the one haunted most by ghosts from the past was the deputy mayor of Shanghai, Pan Hannian.

Fearing that the investigation might well raise skeletons from his closet, Pan decided to confess his past contact with Hu Junhe to his boss, the mayor of Shanghai, Chen Yi. His first memory of Hu Junhe dated back to the war years. At that time Hu served as an official in the Japanese wartime puppet regime of Wang Jingwei. Wang, the former left Nationalist Party leader, had, like so many others in the late thirties, thought the Japanese unbeatable and sued for peace. Setting up a puppet regime in Nanjing, he was interested in speaking to the communists about the possibility of an alliance against the Nationalists. As I noted in the preceding chapter, this was a time of increasing tension and suspicion between the two United Front partners, and Wang was keen to exploit this growing hostility to his own advantage. The communists, for their part, were suspicious of Nationalist Party intrigues. They wanted to know whether the Nationalists were planning an alliance with Wang's regime aimed at destroying them. Both Wang Jingwei and the communists were interested in speaking to one another, albeit for completely different reasons. Thus when a senior official from Wang's government, Li Shiqun, suggested they could share information about the Nationalists, Pan Hannian keenly opened up a dialogue (Yin Qi 1996, 216). To this end, intelligence agents, led by Pan, were dispatched by the Central Committee to investigate the possibilities of initiating discussions and closer ties with sections of Wang's government. For this course of action, the Central Committee had given permission. Nevertheless, fearing that the Nationalists might interpret the mission as the first signs of a "betrayal of the United Front," the communists wanted to keep it both secret and low level. To this end, the Central Committee expressly forbade any direct contact between Pan and Wang.

Once in Nanjing and in conversation with Li Shiqun and his assistant Hu Junhe, Pan found this final Central Committee order impossible to obey. Somewhere in the course of their discussions, Li invited Wang into the room to meet Pan. This meeting with Wang lasted no more than fifteen minutes. Despite its brevity, Pan realized its meaning—he had directly disobeyed a Central Committee directive. Fearing the consequences of such disobedience, he never divulged the meeting with Wang. This would all have been forgotten had it not been for the Campaign to Suppress Internal Counter-Revolutionaries.

It was these ghosts that came back to haunt Pan in 1955, and it was Chen Yi who would first listen and then transform Pan's fears into reality. Chen Yi listened to Pan, then went straight to Mao. Mao listened, then labeled Pan a counter-revolutionary. On April 3, 1955, the Central Committee concurred. Issuing a secret decision on the Pan Hannian internal spy problem, it ordered Pan's arrest. Tried in 1963, Pan received a fifteen-year jail sentence from the Supreme People's Court (Yin Qi 1996, 345–47, 368). In effect, for every minute Pan had spent with Wang, he was given one year of imprisonment. Later, in 1970, even that sentence was regarded as insufficient and was extended to life (Yin Qi 1996, 381; Tan Yuanheng 1996, 384).[43] Up until that time, however, Pan had been regarded as one of the most trusted of the inner-circle communists and privy to its most closely guarded secrets. Then again, so were Gao Gang and Rao Shushi.

What the investigation into the betrayal of these latter two senior Party figures revealed, however, were the weaknesses in the populist prosecution method of the earlier Campaign to Suppress Counter-Revolutionaries. This earlier campaign successfully rooted out historic counter-revolutionaries, but had failed to uncover and address even more serious breaches. The revival of concerns around the Campaign to Suppress Counter-Revolutionaries, therefore, was not about errors made and abuses in need of correction. Rather, the main concern in 1955 was that the Campaign to Suppress Counter-Revolutionaries had proven ineffective in attacking some of the regime's key enemies. Pursuing these types of enemies became the main agenda item for public security work in 1955.

The tasks ahead were outlined by Xu Zirong,[44] the newly appointed Deputy Minister of Public Security, on April 21, 1955, when he gave his "Summary Outline of Public Security Work in 1954 and the Key Points of Work in 1955" to the State Council. This outline, as well as the later Ministry of Public Security "Report for the Central Committee on Important Aspects of Public Security Work in 1954," set out the new plan of attack (Yu Lei 1992, 11). In May, the Central Committee concurred and hence, after a very brief respite of rectification, hard struggle was once again back on the agenda. Correcting erroneously heavy judgments and harsh work styles was said to continue, but it was quite clear that the wind had vanished from these sails. In place of this, the Central Committee document put stress on the dangers of leniency: "To sentence lightly severe criminals, or to not execute when execution is called for, is to commit a rightist error," it noted. By June, a new campaign was looming. Spies, espionage agents, criminal elements who disrupted the process of socialist transformation, and other hidden counter-revolutionaries were to be the new target criminals. In effect, the enemy within once again emerged as the communists' most-feared enemy.

Throughout the early part of the 1950s, this had not been the case. At this time, most counter-revolutionaries were regarded as remnants of the old order that could be dealt with by employing mass-line action. Party and government structures required intermittent rectification not because there was an enemy within but because, without occasional checking, it was feared erroneous work styles would proliferate. In other words, in the early 1950s, the enemy remained "without." By 1955, this assessment began to change. Mao, in particular, proceeded to blame wreckers within the party and government organs for any setbacks. As the rural collectivization program stalled, Mao adopted a line of thinking parallel to that of the early

Soviets who campaigned against Shakhtyite wreckers in industry and Kulak wreckers in agriculture.[45] Mao believed his political plans were being sabotaged by reactionaries and enemy agents who had "wormed" their way into the Party (interview 1996). Evidence to back up his claim came from a variety of sources. Apart from major cases such as the Gao-Rao betrayal, there were also more mundane examples that a paranoid frame of mind could interpret as "signs" of enemy activity. Police statistics on deaths and injuries in industry and agriculture in 1954 told of over six thousand suspicious homicides and eight thousand cadres and workers killed or injured in industrial accidents. Surely such a huge increase could not occur naturally? Surely sabotage was the key to understanding this? (A Summary History 1989, 129).

Yet to assess such figures as evidence of sabotage was also to suggest that the public security forces had not been alive to the problem of economic wrecking. This, at a time when China found itself in the throws of developing controversial agricultural cooperatives and nationalizing all remaining capitalist industries and businesses, was seen as a serious flaw that the Ministry of Public Security would quite obviously need to remedy. By the end of the following year, it had. The ministry began its process of rectification by adding three additional bureaus to its structure, so that it could cover, in a specialized manner, the type of protection work needed in industry, finance, and transportation. It also strengthened the mass-line component of the economic protection work, which effectively spread the power of the economic protection bureau into every work unit, enterprise, and farm (Outline of Public Security 1997, 283–84). In addition, it designated these economic domains the focal area for all suppression work in 1955 (Outline of Public Security 1997, 272–73). This had an immediate and dramatic effect.

In 1954, 419 espionage cases were uncovered nationwide. In the first four months of 1955, in the city of Shanghai alone, there were more.[46] As enemy infiltration became a major issue, the political line grew harsher. Luo Ruiqing captured the shifting mood in his final summary report to the Sixth Public Security Work Meeting. Prefacing his comments with a litany of complaints about unprofessional public security practices and leadership failures, Luo concluded that errors and oversights would only be corrected when a strong collective leadership was put in place and a culture of checking prevailed (Luo Ruiqing 1994, 229–30). This idea of strong collective leadership emerged as a response to the Gao-Rao affair and was, in part, brought in to stop the possibility of "independent kingdoms." Hence, by the time of the internal suppression campaign in July 1955, Luo's call for strong collective leadership and a culture of checking already formed part of the Party's "reform" agenda. Such strong collective leadership, it was thought, should come from the very top.

The Central Committee led other Party committees by way of example. It established an elimination of counter-revolutionary ten-person small team that became the model for all Party committees in each area and every work unit (Questions and Answers 1994, 85).[47] An office of this Central Committee small team was also set up within the Ministry of Public Security to ensure that its instructions were carried out "to the letter" (Outline of Public Security 1997, 279). These small teams would promote a culture of checking. Each team would carry out political checks on cadres in all government and Party departments, as well as in key industries and work units. They would check by carefully reexamining personnel dossiers. These cadre checks led to name lists which in turn led to arrests. In fact, this campaign promoted its own form of Stakhanovism whereby the arrest quotas for the year were not only quickly reached but, in most cases, easily surpassed.[48]

By September 1955, just three months after the official launch of the campaign, police had received more than 120,000 tip-offs from so-called mass informants and had cracked 2,000 cases of organized spying, espionage, and counter-revolution. By this time, the arrest rate had already come close to that planned for the entire year, and local Party officials, police, and mass organizations demonstrated their revolutionary credentials by petitioning to have these quota levels lifted so that more arrests could be made. The way this campaign escalated into a major purge is best illustrated from the ground up, and I will therefore turn to the prosecution of the campaign in Hunan to tell the remainder of the story of the "internal" campaign.[49]

Internal Suppression a Mistake? Hunan as a Case Study

In Hunan, the internal campaign began with a check of enterprises and cadres' files undertaken between January and October 1955. These checks revealed that during the period of investigation, there had been 413 cases of serious economic wrecking. One case alone—an arson attack on a factory in January—was said to have caused 90,000 yuan worth of damage. As in the rest of the nation, the Hunanese authorities believed that through a professional and specialized campaign to check records, suspicions about the counter-revolutionary nature of such industrial "accidents" would be confirmed. Investigations into wrecking in Hunan led to the uncovering of a range of reactionary organizations—the China Peasant Party, the Peace Party, the Democracy Party, and the Libertarian Freedom Party. The discovery that many of these organizations had successfully infiltrated Party, army, and government units proved even more worrying. Tight leadership was called for in pursuing this campaign, and the Hunan Provincial Party Committee modeled its organizational response on the ten-person small team.

In Hunan, the Party committee established an elimination of counter-revolutionary five-person leadership small team to lead the struggle. This team then ordered each of its local Party branches to set up work teams in every region, autonomous prefecture, city, and county. These teams were to be run by the Deputy Party Secretaries and the heads of the organizational section of the area concerned and were answerable directly to the local Party Committee. Their task was to go down to local work units and carry out detailed investigations into the political background of all local cadres and staff. Before embarking on such trips, however, the teams familiarized themselves with materials from the area and personnel files from the work units. From these materials they prepared a general report on each work unit for their local Party committee, and from the personnel files they designated a target population that should be monitored. While the teams carried out the initial investigations, they were not the organs that physically pursued suspect elements. That task was allocated to local activists, who were given the name lists of all those under investigation and ordered to check them out.

This type of limited mass involvement differed greatly from previous campaigns. In the past, the Party had responded to mass initiatives, and the mass-line organs were central to the prosecution of the campaign. This time around, with the discovery of high levels of treachery from an enemy within, the demands for action came from above. Local propaganda drives alerted workers and peasants to the dangers the target group posed. Goaded by such propaganda campaigns, it was the task of "the masses" to engage in "face-to-face struggle" with members of the target group. This type of struggle session formed the basis for further investigations, and these investigations resulted in a further broadening of the campaign. Once one person in the target group "cracked," he or she became a "special case," and the struggle was then transferred back to the work team for further investigation. The work teams were to recheck the case to ensure that the evidence in the case file was accurate and that other culprits had not avoided punishment. Finally, after checking the claims made in mass struggle sessions, verdicts would be given. "In this way," Hunanese police sources claimed, "the campaign ran smoothly" (PSHM 1992:1, V23, 126).

Smooth it may have been; accurate it was not. At a national level, one senior Chinese police source estimated that around one in every four people arrested and investigated during this campaign was later found to be innocent (interview 1996). In effect, the dynamics unleashed by this type of "professional" campaigning tended to ensure that the goal of capturing more culprits easily overrode any concern for accuracy. This is because, irrespective of the methods used, the leadership would always judge the success of any campaign in terms of quotas met or exceeded. In addition, campaigns tended to operate through a combination of olive branches and canes. Just about every campaign offered "leniency for those who are honest and harshness for those who resist." As honesty invariably meant implicating others, campaigning always had a propensity to move agendas to the left as suspects had an incentive to "reveal" their supposed fellow conspirators.

In addition to these general considerations, this campaign in particular employed an investigative technique that ensured high arrest rates. The rates were, in part, secured by the circular nature of the investigative process. In any given area, it was the work team that would first identify suspected internal enemies. The work teams drew up a list, passed it on to the local mass-line organs, and then waited for them to organize struggle sessions against suspects. After a violent session with mass-line activists, most suspects confessed. Allegedly to ensure no miscarriage of justice, these struggle sessions were then followed by a review of the evidence. Who undertook this review? The same work team that had fingered the suspect in the first place. In other words, under this regime, the work team became prosecutor and appeal court judge. As a result, few were found innocent. What this investigative technique did do was privilege the status of the professional interrogator who had come to lead all mass action. In the balance between red and expert, this campaign witnessed the emergence of expertise at the expense of the mass-line. It also demonstrated that the move away from populism did not, in itself, lead to moderation. The arrest rates attest to this.

While the exact number of arrests remains unclear, at least one Chinese source estimates that nationwide, by the end of this campaign, 100,000 internal counter-revolutionaries were discovered and 65,000 additional common criminals and minor counter-revolutionaries were unmasked. In addition, something like 1.7 million people had negative notations added to their personnel files (*Outline of Public Security* 1997, 280). Brugger goes further, suggesting that by September 1955, some 2.2 million people found themselves under investigation, with 110,000 of these finally designated as counter-revolutionary elements (1981a, 111). An examination of detailed internal statistics reveals that Brugger's higher figures may be closer to the truth. Internal public security statistics for this period reported almost half a million people arrested for counter-revolutionary crime (confidential material 1986).[50] This statistical anomaly (between two different Chinese government sources) may, in part, be explained by the fact that the word *arrest* in China did not necessarily mean that suspects would either be released or have criminal charges laid against them. In China, there is a third possibility: administrative sanction.

As noted earlier, by the mid-fifties, Chinese police had devised an array of coercive administrative sanctions. These were employed against those deemed insufficiently criminal to be given penal incarceration, but insufficiently innocent to be let off altogether. Coercive administrative sanctions helped the police deal with this problem. The huge number of arrests, coupled with the minor nature of many of the charges and the repentance of others, led police to call for a new way of dealing with any minor offenders. The police sought a means of enabling the removal of such elements from society, but wanted a system that did not lead to penal incarceration or social stigmatization. This was the ground on which the future "reform through education" administrative detention system was laid. In other words, it came about as a result of concerns that emerged in the course of the internal suppression campaign. Chinese sources make this quite clear:

> In the second half of 1955, we engaged in the campaign to eliminate hidden counter-revolutionaries. From a work unit and institutional perspec-

tive, it became important to clarify what was to be done with those whose offences were not serious enough to warrant criminal incarceration, but who were also not fit to be left to continue holding their work position. At the same time, if this group were to be simply flung back into society, they would add significantly to the number of counter-revolutionary and bad elements who remained unemployed. (Yu Lei 1992, 403)

It was in the somewhat liberal climate of 1956 that the Central Committee worked on this problem and eventually came up with an answer. On January 10 they issued a directive stressing the need for a noncriminal system of administrative incarceration. They suggested that minor counter-revolutionaries be removed from their workplaces and put under "concentrated surveillance" while new arrangements were made for their future employment. Initially, police and civil authorities ran this system jointly, but in August 1957, the State Council and the National People's Congress passed the "Decision Concerning the Question of Reform through Education," which brought into existence the reform-through-education system (Yu Lei 1992, 403; *Collection of Rules* 1992, 3).[51] All these deliberations took place in an increasingly moderate climate. The reasons for this have little to do with the campaign itself.

First, in the spring of 1956, the three big transformations (*sanda gaizao*) were proclaimed a decisive victory, and China was said to be quite close to its historic transition from new democracy to socialism.[52] Second, in March 1956, the Central Committee had lowered the national arrest quotas and demanded that more emphasis be placed on determining whether cases were being correctly designated (*Outline of Public Security* 1997, 279). Local policies began to reflect this national change in mood. In Hunan, the Party leadership began to argue that frank admissions could be gained more easily through "peaceful negotiations" rather than through struggle sessions. By April, the provincial Party leadership had even sent orders telling local officials not to adopt a quota system with regard to arrests. With a new moderate policy in place, great claims were now being made with regard to the lenient approach to campaigning, with area units reporting around 43.5 percent of those targeted for investigation choosing to frankly admit their crimes rather than resist.

The April Politburo meeting endorsed this moderate line, as did Mao Zedong. He held a somewhat more complex position, however, for while arguing for moderation, he also suggested the need for greater reliance on the masses. He was clearly unhappy with the Soviet-style of discipline that dominated the internal suppression campaign, for he believed it "tied the hands of the masses." At the same time, however, he recognized that neither he nor anybody else in the Party leadership had a ready-made answer to solve these problems (Mao Zedong 1974, 30). With no answer in sight, Mao returned to past experiences for inspiration, and, once again, he recalled the Yan'an model of rectification. Rectification in Yan'an had not resulted in any deaths and had led to only a few arrests, he noted. Executions, Mao said, should therefore remain limited. Mistakes can be made, but "once a head is chopped off, history shows it can't be restored, nor can it grow again as chives do after being cut" (Mao Zedong 1977, 5:299–300). In February, 1957, he reiterated his moderate stance announcing the end of "large-scale, turbulent class struggles" (Mao Zedong 1977, 5:395). At the same time, he called for a more nuanced approach to social contradictions. Haunted by the specter of the Hungarian uprising, Mao feared that the contradictions among the working people that were nonantagonistic, if handled incorrectly, might become so.[53] To ensure that Chinese intellectuals did not go over to the side of reaction, he called for "one hundred flowers to bloom and one hundred schools to contend" (Brugger 1981a, 125, 131; Mao Zedong 1977, 5:408).

At the April 1957 meeting of the Politburo, the "Directive on the Rectification Campaign" called for a nationwide critique of bureaucratism, factionalism, and subjectivism. As part of this drive, the one hundred flowers campaign encouraged intellectuals to criticize Party practices and work styles. While intellectuals offered criticism (with what would, a little later on, be regarded as far too much enthusiasm), the Party leadership turned once more to a detailed examination of its own practices and its own cadre force. While the mood at this time was moderate, the April Politburo meeting undertook a course of action that would change this dramatically. Examining the results of the one hunded flowers criticisms, it decided to investigate the motives of critics. To this end, it called for a deepening and speeding up of the internal suppression campaign. In addition, the Central Committee also refocused the internal suppression campaign by demanding that the individual historical records of Party cadres be opened up and investigated. The new task of the suppression campaign was to ascertain whether or not any of the Party's cadre force had suspect pasts. With lower-ranking Party members now targeted and, in many cases, found wanting, the mood on the ground once again began to change. The story of this transformation from moderation to radicalism in Hunan once again tells a bigger story.

After the Central Committee called upon its branches to open up the records of Party cadres, the authorities in Hunan called for the examination of 40,039 cadres' records. As seems to have happened elsewhere, they were surprised by what they found: of all records, 11.3 percent were deemed to indicate some historic problem or another. Of these, 2,055 local Party cadres were thought to have had serious problems that needed attention. To deepen the campaign, the Hunanese Party Committee targeted lower-level intellectuals for investigation alongside its own cadre force. As a result, 8,463 primary schools in ninety-one different counties and cities came under review between February and June 1957, and checks were conducted on over 60,000 people (PSHM 1992:1, V23, 130). In effect, the investigation of these two groups not only increased the arrest rates, but also made the Party nervous.

As a consequence, by late 1957, what the Party did in Hunan set the stage for what it would do nationally. Rectification and the one hundred flowers, it said, revealed "a very small number of bourgeois rightists who had used this opportunity to attack the Party" (A Summary History 1989, 144). In July, Mao began to revise his assessment of the dangers posed by the right. Where once he saw the right as dying remnants, he now had cause to draw a much bleaker conclusion. Mao was not alone. At the 1957 meeting of public security department (gong'an ting) and bureau (gong'anju) chiefs, they drew the conclusion that the enemy was, in fact, "gaining momentum" (Outline of Public Security 1997, 295). To stem this rising tide, it advocated "harsh treatment" (A Summary History 1989, 144).

Arrest figures once again reflected the change. Nationwide, only 229,012 people had been arrested in 1956, but by 1957, the number had more than doubled to 469,611 (confidential material 1986). Moreover, an additional 1,200,000 people were either subjected to public criticism or put under "supervision and control" (guanzhi) (Outline of Public Security 1997, 296).

Throughout 1957, this leftist mood grew, not only resulting in more arrests but also involving organizational changes to counter perceived slack work styles. Yan'an was again remembered, but this time it was the role of the army, not rectification, that reorganized agendas. By late 1957, this Yan'an-based army model informed all rectification work going on within the Party, and this line of attack was endorsed by the eighth Party congress in September. By December, the Ministry of Public Security's work style also came under scrutiny. With a Soviet style still dominant, it, too, required rectification, and it wasn't just the internal suppression campaign that demonstrated this.

Nineteen fifty-six had seen a huge increase in the number of worker and student disturbances. Police responses to such disturbances were anything but proletarian.[54] One case, in particular, brought forth a sharp rebuke. On March 26, 1957, in Hua county, Guangdong province, a disturbance broke out over the construction of a leper hospital. The deputy chief of the Guangdong Public Security Bureau, Chen Lida, ordered the People's Armed Police to open fire on the rioters, leading to some fourteen people either killed or maimed. When this was reported to higher-level authorities, their response was scathing. China was undergoing some large-scale changes, the report on the incident noted, and even leading police showed a lack of proletarian consciousness. Such people handled the new situations they faced in obsolete or erroneous ways. The report continued,

> A very small number of public security personnel, when implementing policy, do so in ways that are convenient to them rather than being convenient for the masses. They handle people oppressively and do not do things righteously. One can even go so far as to say that a small number of cadres do not differentiate between antagonistic and nonantagonistic contradictions, but use the same oppressive methods in relation to both. Such work styles are like those of the nationalists. It is necessary that public security personnel across the whole country draw the appropriate lessons from what happened in Hua county, Guangdong. (Qtd. in *Outline of Public Security* 1997, 291)

Lessons were certainly drawn, but what they taught the police was an altogether different matter.

In response to this and the many other problems plaguing work styles, the Ministry of Public Security advanced a highly contradictory two-pronged solution. On the one hand, the ministry demanded that police operate on the basis of the law to resolve problems such as these, but then it said that this should take place in the context of an overall police policy of being both red and expert. Only in this way, it said, would the police force operate in a truly proletarian manner. To structurally ensure that this latter point went beyond mere rhetoric, the ministry in 1956 resurrected the 1942 Yan'an policy of "better troops and simpler administration" and used this as an exemplary model by which to "rectify" work styles. The result was a drastic reduction in police numbers, with the majority of officers sent down to work with, and learn from, the masses (*Outline of Public Security* 1997, 288). It is unlikely that, from there, they would be working with, or learning of, the rule of law. In fact, with so many police sent into base-level production, there was hardly any security forces left to police the law, should that have been their intention.

The Party Central Committee enthusiastically endorsed this simplification of the Ministry of Public Security structure, as well as the rustification of most of its officer corps. The result was dramatic. The ministry's original twenty-three professional bureaus, along with their 3,300 staff, were reduced to just fourteen bureaus with 1,070 staff by the spring of 1959. The rustification of police cadres meant that most were to spend time in base-level production units. Some participated in industry, most in agriculture, but all were to go to base-level work units to learn from the masses. August 1958 statistics covering twenty provinces (autonomous regions and centrally administered cities) tell of 38,084 police officers sent down, including 27,645 sent to undertake labor and 10,439 cadres sent to do basic-level police work in lower-level units (*Outline of Public Security* 1997, 289–90). The purpose of this rustification program was to improve police work styles, increase production, and uncover yet more wreckers (*Gansu Provincial* 1995, 14).[55] What began to emerge out of this policy was not only a new and more radical version of mass-line policing but a set of practices that would foreshadow a new theory of the socialist dictatorship itself. What was being foreshadowed was a great leap into the darkness of populism.

Conclusion

On July 16, 1951, Zhou Enlai passed on to Luo Ruiqing the basic method that would eventually give the socialist police of China control of the streets: "First look downward," he said, "and then get on to the checking of household registers" (Tao Siju 1996, 107). Before that, of course, the police had "looked downward" and registered only the troublesome. Corralled into the categories of focal populations and businesses, the most obvious troublesome remnants of the old society had been neutralized and could no longer impede the forward march of socialism. The register would now spread to the overall population and become an inventory of human resources and their locations. But these registers would also become a key pillar upon which to build socialist policing. It was the Campaign to Suppress Counter-Revolutionaries that would show just how useful these registers could be.

"In revolution," Liu Shaoqi once said, "there is no before and after, but with counter-revolution, there is a fundamental difference" (qtd. in *Campaign to Suppress* 1992, 20). This difference between revolution and counter-revolution proved pivotal to policy and provoked a variety of public security responses between the years 1949 and 1957. From the leniency policy of 1949–50 to the high tide of repression in 1951, from the populist mass-line of the first suppression campaign to the specialist Soviet-style purging of the second, and from the constant resurrection of draft legal codes suggesting the need for a rule of law to the legal elasticity necessary for the operation of the mass line, Chinese responses to counter-revolution seemed to cover every conceivable option. Indeed, sometimes they seemed to occupy mutually exclusive positions simultaneously. It would be easy to read this simply as a chaotic jumble or a sign of an internal if unspoken inner Party two-line struggle. More accurately, I think, it constituted an example of the security forces grappling with the complexities of postrevolutionary life and groping toward a politically appropriate way of dealing with them. That differences in approach existed within the Party and the security forces is obvious, but it is equally true that for the most part, during this time, these were thought of as nonantagonistic and were certainly not reflective of fundamental internal political differences.

Thus, in 1953, when populist arguments in favor of making militia power the basis of state power were put forward as an alternative to the already articulated claims that the time of the mass-line had passed and a more formal legal structure was needed, it did not cause a schism. Neither of these two contending arguments were entirely condemned, although the security minister Luo Ruiqing would deem both inappropriate (Tao Siju 1996, 105). What the existence of these two contrasting positions tells us is not that a two-line struggle had emerged within the Party, but that there was, at this stage, a degree of indeterminacy concerning the correct path the revolution should take. Clearly, the fifties were a time of trial and error. At this moment, far less unanimity about the role or even longevity of many of the structural inventions of mass-line policing existed, even though many of these would later come to be viewed as lying at the very heart of Maoist politics. What the history of the police in this period suggests is that much of the mass-line was born of necessity and groped toward a particular, concrete form. From being a highly pragmatic and economic means of resolving the problem of police numbers and impurity within police ranks, the mass-line organizations would go on to become model forms of Maoism. Recognizing the lowly, pragmatic, and contingent origins of the mass-line, however, does not entail a dismissal of the subsequent theoretical claims made about it. Such *post factum* theorization by Chinese communists was not a mere afterthought or smoke screen covering up the "real" pragmatic intentions of the police and the Party. Rather, it is a post factum realization that whether by chance or design, the localized nongovernmental revolutionary structures put in place at this time perfectly reflected the unconscious dyadic political framework the Party had employed from its inception. The mass-line organs, the political campaign, and even the recourse to professional political experts all constituted responses from within this framework of politics, which was, ultimately, a politics of two lines.

One must remember that there were a variety of ways in which these problems could have been resolved and that the choice of the mass-line was but one of them. The reason why the mass-line would always emerge as an option was not simply because it was the best but because it best expressed these types of politics, the types Maoism had always relied upon. In this respect, the mass-line organs that came to life during this period were much more than a concrete expression of the mass-line in thought. They were the organizational expression of the dyadic politics of Maoism when compressed into institutional and governmental forms. How these organs developed and came to envelop all other contending renditions of dyadic political thought becomes obvious as the story of the police moves away from "expertise" and heads off in the direction of "redness." This is the story that will unfold next as the economic policies of the Great Leap start to produce a demand among the police to develop their own politically intense leap into radicalism.

4 The Years That Burned

TIMELINE 1957–1976

Date	Politics	Police
1957	Antirightist campaign begins	
1958	Great Leap Forward begins	Great Leap Forward in Ministry of Public Security
1959		**September:** Xie Fuzhi appointed as Minister of Public Security
1962	Sino-Soviet split **September:** Tenth plenum of the Eighth Central Committee meeting convened	**October–November:** Twelfth National Public Security Work Meeting
1963	**January:** Campaign to learn from Lei Feng starts	Fengqiao experiments with local mass dictatorship
1964	**February:** Campaign to "Learn from the People's Liberation Army" starts	**March:** Thirteenth National Public Security Work Meeting calls on public security organs to follow Fengqiao model
1965		**June:** Fourteenth National Public Security Work Meeting focuses on mass dictatorship

Date	Politics	Police
1966	Beginning of Cultural Revolution **August:** Eleventh plenum of the Eighth Chinese Communist Party "Sixteen Points Program" issued	**July:** Restructuring of the public security force along military lines
1967	**January:** Shanghai "January storm" starts campaign to seize power (*duoquan yundong*)	Ministry of Public Security releases "Public Security Six Points" Xie Fuzhi calls on radicals to seize power in public security organs **February:** Application of marital law to Beijing Public Security Bureau **December:** Application of martial law in public security organs
1968		**August:** Xie Fuzhi calls on radicals to "smash the *gongjianfa* to a pulp"
1969	**April:** Ninth Party Congress convenes	
1971	Lin Biao dies	Ministry of Public Security focuses on restoration of good order on transport routes in Beijing

Date	Politics	Police
1972	Nixon visits China	Li Zhen commits suicide
1973	**September:** Tenth Party Congress convenes; Deng Xiaoping rehabilitated Campaign to criticize Lin Biao and Confucius begins	
1975	Fourth Party Congress Campaign to Study an All-Round Dictatorship of the Proletariat begins	Hua Guofeng appointed as Minister of Public Security
1976	**January:** Zhou Enlai dies **March–April:** Tian'anmen Incident **September:** Mao dies **October:** Arrest of the Gang of Four	

I N FEBRUARY 1957, Mao Zedong announced to the world that "large-scale, turbulent class struggle of the masses characteristic of times of revolution have in the main come to an end" (Mao Zedong 1977, 5:395). With socialism announced in 1956, a new notion of political unity grew to rival class struggle as the internal organizing trope of the new revolutionary state. As this idea of the political unity of the people grew, so, too, did the demand by some for a more formal system of socialist law. This demand would emerge because political unity required the avoidance or supersession of tensions, antagonisms, and conflicting interests among the people, and legal forms offered the type of "binding normative order and form" that could both determine and limit the possibilities of action within any concept of political unity (Böckenförde 1998, 41). In circumstances where revolutionary emotions still ruled, however, this was not what would eventuate. Law did not become the basis of a new normative order among the people; flexible administrative regulations based on the political situation did. Indeed, as has been noted by others, even that most obvious monument to law, the constitution, was, in its 1954 incarnation, more a symbol of political unity than of the legality of the state (Schurmann and Schell 1967, 110).

In some respects, the position of the Chinese communists in relation to law bore something of a family resemblance to the formulations of the early Soviet legal theorists, the commodity-exchange school. This school would advocate the withering away of law and the employment of flexible, "technical rules" to administer political unity during the socialist transition phase.[1] This was because they believed law to be merely a contemporary means by which to adjudicate competing (class) interests. If this constituted the intrinsic nature of law, then it stood in sharp contrast to the needs of socialism, which required the fashioning, administering, and strengthening of political unity among the people. Where the adversarial nature of the law court was said to share a "close morphological link" with the duel, not to mention market competition (Pashukanis 1978, 63), the administrative-technical regulation would speak to a unity of purpose and, therefore, to the political unity of the people (Pashukanis 1978, 81). Law was an inappropriate means by which to administer things under socialism, the school argued, because "revolutionary legality is a problem which is 99 percent political" (qtd. in Leggett 1981, 280).

Even this brief description makes clear that much would separate the thoughts of these early Soviet legal theorists from their Chinese cousins. What they shared, however, was a view about the inappropriateness of law in handling contradictions among the people. Indeed, as John Hazard noted long ago, it was in 1957 that the Chinese communists realized this and began to advocate legal elasticity in the treatment of contradictions among the people (1969, 99). Unlike the commodity-exchange school, however, Chinese legal elasticity had little to do with the withering away of law or the state. Indeed, one key reason for the prominence of elasticity in China was that it facilitated state-sponsored programs of political education.

For the Chinese, political unity would be achieved through the ongoing policing and production of norms established in the course of political campaigns. These flexible norms were then embedded in an array of governmental and mass-line institutional and structural anchorage points that first became established in the course of the suppression of counter-revolutionaries campaign that ran from 1951 until 1953.[2] While law would continue to function, it would do so only to establish the outer limits of state tolerance. Read in a traditional Legalist fashion, the key task of law was to punish the enemy. Read thus, law was simultaneously rigid, harsh, and inappropriate for application in relation to contradictions among the people. For the people, a more flexible administrative and ameliorist means was needed. By 1957, China could boast just such a bifurcated socio-legal structure, and this seemed to mirror a political stance operating on the basis of the friend/enemy distinction. Strangely, however, it was the bifurcated nature of this socio-legal structure that would end up producing a distortion in the dyadic logic of the political.

In 1957, Mao offered theoretical justification for the bifurcation of the legal system. In doing this, he ended up complicating the dyadic political structure theoretically by introducing a ternary element. Mao would give voice to this complication not in the language of law, but through a reformulation of the notion of contradictions. In speaking of two types of contradiction—one of which was antagonistic and related to the enemy, the other being non-antagonistic and related to the friend—he appeared to reinforce the binary of politics. In fact, he introduced the possibility of a third element. If friend be governed by homogeneous political unity and enemy rendered as antagonistic contradiction, then the concept of the non-antagonistic contradiction raised the specter of a shadowy third element: the wayward friend, or, in the language of politics, the adversary. The introduction of a conceptual space that allowed for the presence in socialist polity of an adversary offered a new and more nuanced approach to the political. It also offered a path along which unity could be restored and socialism developed without violence. Socialist legality would therefore work between these two different worlds, and as socialism developed, violent class struggles would diminish and the harsh and punitive Legalist approach would give way to one in which wayward, adversarial elements were "cured" by administrative intervention. In this way, a unity of purpose among the people would be restored. That was the political theology of 1957.

Within ten years, it was turned on its head. The enemy would no longer be regarded as numerically weak, nor purely a "relic." Instead, it was now partly viewed as a negative side effect of the process of socialist state building itself. Even worse, this new analysis raised difficult questions in relation to the Party cadres. The question of cadre loyalty, of course, was nothing new. The internal campaign to suppress counter-revolutionaries that intermittently stalked police agendas from the time of its launch in 1955 until it was swamped by the Great Leap Forward in 1957 was organized specifically to combat bureaucratization, corruption, and treachery within cadre ranks. What was new, however, was the way in which the question was raised. Up until this time, any campaign that brought up the question of cadre weakness and error did so at an individual level. As an individual cadre problem, most errors would be treated as contradictions among the people. Once a cadre problem was rendered in a socio-structural rather than a psychological way, however, the world changed. What were once considered individual contradictions among the people were increasingly regarded as structural effects of power relations. Cadres were interpolated into a class position which was not of the people. As this analysis developed, any wall that may have existed between formal law on the one side and flexible administrative regulations on the other vanished. More than anything, it was the passion generated by a new understanding and application of the term *revisionism* that brought forth this change.

Revisionism forced the Party to attend to the effects of its own political structures. Had it not produced cadre privilege? Had it not allowed that privilege to become a habitual part of the collective life of cadres such that they began to develop their own collective viewpoint? Was it not a collective viewpoint that would, if left unchecked, eventually congeal into a class view-point? These were just some of the questions that would eventually lead Mao and the radicals to claim that elements within the Communist Party were beginning to form into a new bourgeoisie. The problem was that if this were true, then revolutionary political unity could no longer be guaranteed by the existence of a Party dictatorship. Only class struggle could guarantee the forward march of socialism. Only the mass-line campaign could channel class struggle toward revolution. New ways of operating based on this new way of thinking emerged. Thus while the language and concepts used by the Communist Party did not appear to change at this time, their meaning did. Nowhere was this more in evidence than in relation to law and the policing of it.

Right up until the high point of the Cultural Revolution, both law and the police would be described as crucial tools of the dictatorship. This would change as a different understanding of dictatorship developed. Where early renditions of dictatorship inherited from Lenin and imported from the Soviet Union closely tethered the notion to state power (Lenin 1964, 25:416–17), Mao began to read dictatorship as a concept allied to his notion of mass-line democracy. At first, this had little to do with his analysis of revisionism. If anything, it began as a pragmatic consequence of a decision to drive the economy by political means. Once the Great Leap required mass politicization, the mass-line legacy took on added significance. The structural significance of this heightened attention to politicization would lead to greater mass involvement and greater powers being ceded to a dictatorship of the communes. It is, therefore, with the communization of life that was the Great Leap Forward that a new notion of dictatorship would emerge. It would arrive on the scene not as a new theoretical formulation, but as a set of empirical practices put in place to pragmatically address the question of the economy. It is, therefore, with this development that we must begin if we are to understand the full import of later events and the way they were handled. It is, then, time to move on to the Great Leap proper and to examine more closely the contribution of the police.

The Beginning: The Great Leap in Policing

February 1957 was a time when Mao could foresee the end of class struggle. Policies adopted in December, however, would undercut this. It was at this time that the idea of a Great Leap Forward was proffered. Here was a policy that began life as a way of addressing the economy. In effect, it did this by employing political technology to address economic problems. The command economy model imported from the Soviet Union was, by the late fifties, showing signs of strain. Central planning had promoted industry over agriculture and had led to peasants being bled white in an attempt to rapidly develop the heavy industry sector. Industry developed, but not quickly enough. As a consequence, sectorial imbalances began to emerge, leading to bottlenecks, shortages, and peasant unrest. Nor did these constitute the only problems of the command economy model; bureaucratism and commandism also emerged as negative side effects. Even if these deviations did not emerge, the planning model still placed too much emphasis upon technical expertise over politics. Up until 1957, the Party had attempted to keep politics out of economic issues. The role of political campaigns had, in the past, done little other than create a protective shell around the command economy and ensure that wreckers and other enemies did not disrupt production. With problems of the planned economy now becoming central concerns of the state, a radical new plan of action was devised. Political intensity would be harnessed to drive economic production. After all, if intensity could drive a revolution, why not use it to drive a people to higher levels of production? Why not make the economy subject to the political?

It was in this way that political intensity would be unleashed upon the economy. Harnessing political intensity, however, required putting the mass-line, rather than the planner, in charge. Combining the idea of *xiafang*, which meant being sent down to the countryside, with a process of administrative decentralization created the conditions, it was hoped, to enable mass-line political intensity to be directed into a political campaign designed to develop the economy and increase production.

Security forces, too, would learn to utilize political intensity more effectively. They too would use it to increase their productivity. Mass-line policing and decentralization of policing powers became their contribution to the Great Leap. As Luo Ruiqing pointed out, the "Leap" meant more than sending police down to learn from the masses. In order to remain relevant to the new situation of socialism, he asserted, policing needed to keep abreast of the demands of this campaign and develop its own "Great Leap" (*Outline of Public Security* 1997, 296). Nevertheless, while police would eagerly participate, some within the leadership feared the consequences of politicization. If intensity was unleashed, there would always be the question of how to stop the "Leap" falling into excess. In the early days of the Great Leap, deputy minister of public security, Yang Qiqing, would directly address this problem. On January 22, 1958, Yang spoke to a meeting of seven provincial bureau and department heads, calling on them to "leap," but only after having sought "truth from facts." In some respects, Yang was simply listening to, and repeating, Mao who, ten days earlier, had railed against overzealousness and the danger in Party committees of being "red but not expert" (Mao 1974, 77). These cautionary remarks, however, do not seem to have been reflected in "The 1958 National Public Security Work Key Points." Indeed, in this document, it seemed that police, like the economy, would produce better, faster, and more economical results.

It was in the "key points" document of 1958 that their increased productivity was proclaimed. Quotas on cleanup rates for political cases would be increased to over 60 percent of all cases, while cleanup rates for ordinary crime were pushed above, or at least made equivalent to, the historically low level of 1956.[3] In terms of cracking ordinary criminal cases, quota rates were set at over 75 percent of all cases, and, for serious crimes, the target goal was to crack 90 percent of them. Fire-related incidents were also set to come down by between 15–20 percent of the then current levels, while the police fire division was to ensure that major fires did not cause over 50,000 yuan worth of damage (*Outline of Public Security* 1997, 297). In addition, police were to work more closely with enterprises and, following a call from Mao back in April, to recheck and clarify internal bad elements and any former landlords, rich peasants, or counter-revolutionaries whose labels had been removed (Mao Zedong 1974, 69). In a period of intense political passion, it seems unsurprising that in the vast majority of cases, these people were sent down to the countryside for work and reeducation.

If some of these key points seemed unrealistic, individual provincial responses to them bordered on the insane. In a series of outrageous competitive claims, provincial public security organs set the stage for a massive inflation in police claims. As in agriculture production, Hunan province would lead the Leap.[4] In all agricultural cooperatives, work units, enterprises, and educational institutions across the province, there were to be "four eliminations" (*siwu*). In agricultural cooperatives, the police promised to eliminate all major superstitious activities, all gambling, all thefts with a value of over fifteen yuan, and all fires that caused more than ten yuan worth of damage. In the work units, enterprises, and educational institutions, wrecking activities were to be eliminated, theft of goods with a value over one hundred yuan to cease, and no disaster to cause more than ten yuan worth of damage (*A Summary History* 1989, 145–46). This report from Hunanese delegates received enthusiastic endorsement from the Party leadership, which, in turn, put pressure upon other provinces to perform. The result was a revolutionary bidding war.

By February 1958, the Guizhou provincial police department reported that it, too, would launch an elimination campaign. Its campaign, however, involved not four but seven eliminations. The police promised to eliminate all fire-related incidents, all long-pending cases, all forms of banditry, theft, and social disturbance, as well as all drug trafficking and gambling in the province (*A Summary History* 1989, 146). "People who have read this Guizhou report have become really excited," the ministry enthused (Huang Yao and Zhang Mingzhe 1996, 341). They were not the only ones.

In Liaoning, police issued a so-called competition letter that challenged every other provincial police force to match their revolutionary targets. As the competition heated up, so too did the number of claims being made. In the end, some police stations promised productivity increases that involved 142 eliminations (Huang Yao and Zhang Mingzhe 1996, 34). In some places, they even claimed that they would eliminate family bickering (*Gong'an Jianshi*). By March, while most units were still dizzy with success and rattling off endless lists of things they would eliminate, the ministry grew concerned.

"In a number of places," the ministry stated, "the slogans of the Great Leap do not accord with the reality of the situation." As concern grew about these "elimination campaigns," the ministry began to rebuke what it called the "simplification of class struggle." Eliminations, they suggested, had to be local-level goals; it was simply "absolutist" and "impossible" to rid entire counties, much less provinces, of many of the social ills targeted. Like life itself, crime had its ups and downs, and one could not guarantee absolute elimination in such a short time span (*Outline of Public Security* 1997, 298; see also Li Jinping 1993, 274; Tao Siju 1996, 253–54). In an attempt to maintain revolutionary enthusiasm but contain excess, Luo Ruiqing and his deputies went in search of a more sober model. Touring a series of provinces, they convened local meetings to check on the success of the elimination program. In actual fact, they were on the hunt for a means by which to formulate a new rendition of the Great Leap Forward in policing that would not lead to excessive claims. In April, in Guangdong, they found what they were looking for.

Heeding ministerial calls to tie eliminations to local-level policing, the Guangdong police had implemented a series of work unit–based "security campaigns" (*anquan yundong*) (*A Summary History* 1989, 146; Tao 1996, 254). Through the localization of the elimination campaign, it was thought that the claims being made would be more realistic and moderate. While this logic may, in the end, have proven incorrect, the adoption of this model had immediate structural effects. Localization and intensification of mass-based elimination campaigns compelled the security forces to decentralize their policing powers. Political intensity worked by offering local people a sense of empowerment. As intensity took hold, police had to keep up with the mass-based campaigns, and one revolutionary way of contributing was to cede an ever-increasing number of coercive administrative powers to local mass-line authorities. This strategy sat well with the general political line of the time. Divesting powers to localities was being encouraged in all areas. This was because the Party believed that the local authorities had a better idea of what was going on at ground level (Teiwes 1979, 334).

It was on the basis of this logic that base-level police stations and neighborhood security committees obtained the right to gather intelligence and crack cases, while county-level police were given the power to detain, and the people's communes, who had more or less tethered local policing to the commune structure, took overall charge (interviews 1995).[5] With local communes in command, a massive increase in the number of arrests and detentions followed. Far from being a source of concern, this "success" was trumpeted as an example of red triumphing over expert.[6] In order to cater for this massive increase in arrests, local communes also received administrative detention powers. The first such power of detention given was (forcible) collective training, or jixun (interview 1997).[7]

Jixun was first employed in the 1955 sufan campaign as a means of forcibly incarcerating suspected counter-revolutionaries and transient criminals for education and checking. After the Great Leap, jixun would be revived and would form the basis upon which the now infamous system of shelter and investigation would develop.[8] During the Leap, however, it had other uses. It proved to be an appropriately flexible mechanism for the detention of bad elements who jeopardized the Great Leap Forward in production and adversely influenced social order. Being an ad hoc mechanism of campaign-style policing, jixun operated without any legal constraints. Being a discretionary power vested in local village authorities who were themselves driven by political intensity, it became a source of countless cases of abuse (interview 1996).

In April 1958, 233 people from Guangchang county, Jiangxi, were brought in for collective training after claims were made that they were involved in religious sects. Fifty-nine of them were labeled sorcerers, while the other 174 were described as sect members. Their crime? Vegetarianism. In the same month, police checked the records of "one thousand odd" jixun inmates in the cities of Huhot and Baotou. The result: over 70 percent were found to have been wrongfully incarcerated (Gong'an Jianshi). Jixun became the end point of a populist revanchism that swept the country. Virtually anyone holding opinions contrary to those of the local commune leaders or criticizing local cadres' work styles faced collective training. So, too, did members of dysfunctional families or husbands and wives who fought with one another (Gong'an Jianshi). As the Great Leap developed, so did this form of productivity. Moreover, it grew mostly on the back of the once ameliorist, flexible administrative regulation. By the end of the Great Leap, communes were even organizing their own reform-through-education penal camps. These camps were also to be the source of countless cases of abuse. They were, in fact, little more than slave labor camps in which inmates would be tied, beaten, and abused in the course of a day's work for the commune (*Gong'an Jianshi*).

Both the degree of abuse and the numbers arrested and incarcerated increased. For the first three seasons of 1958, arrest and detention rates showed an astronomical rise, reaching over 600,000 people. By the end of that year, internal police sources revealed that 1,014,238 arrests had been made (*Gong'an Jianshi*; confidential material 1986). With growing evidence of excess, the ministry, still wedded to the idea of expertise, grew alarmed. In August 1958, Luo Ruiqing tried to rail things in. He announced a move away from the tight control of the communes to a more lenient approach. To reinforce this, he also announced a policy of "three fewers": fewer executions, fewer arrests, and fewer people under control and surveillance or guanzhi (Luo Ruiqing 1994, 439).

At the same time, Luo realized that all these new measures would mean nothing if commune policing power remained intact. A slow rollback of commune power was quietly initiated. Reform through education was taken from them, and far greater strictures were placed upon their use of jixun. Even these modest changes made a massive difference. Detention rates in these two sectors plummeted. In 1959, only 180,000 people received jixun, while reform-through-education detentions dropped to a little over 116,000 people (*Gong'an Jianshi*). Under the new policy of the three fewers, the arrest rate dropped from over 1 million in 1958 to just 213,356 people in 1959 (confidential material 1986). If the productivity promoted by the Great Leap in policing caused concern, it was nothing compared to the concern generated around the effects of the Leap's politicization of the economy.

Estimates as to the extent of the problem vary wildly. Anywhere between 15 to 46 million people were said to have died in this period (Teiwes with Sun 1999, 5). Something had to be done to rectify the situation. As attention turned to economic recovery, the police set about to readdress the huge number of industrial accidents that flowed from bad work practices adopted during the Leap.[9] In this changed climate, the old political security campaigns began to emphasize safety and security and did so under the new guise of a so-called safety checking campaign (*anquan jiancha yundong*). Touting slogans such as "struggle against the enemy, struggle to promote safety and security" and "production must be safe for safety serves production," the Party effectively used security campaigns to downplay politics.

Police actions at this time must be understood in the light of this general retreat from the "Leap" that was taking place. Security forces had to cope with massive social problems and starvation following the failure of the Leap, the failure of the harvests, and the growing Sino-Soviet rift that saw Soviet advisors departing China. Security forces played only a minor role in many of these events, but the wild fluctuations in policing policy following the Leap were a direct result of varying assessments being offered about how to recover from it. For Luo Ruiqing, recovery meant only economic recovery. Industry and agriculture must be protected and the social order stabilized. Only when economic development was assured could socialism advance. Under conditions of economic difficulty, however, police needed to recognize that most contradictions would be of a non-antagonistic nature. When peasants attacked granaries or involved themselves in "heretical religious sects," these actions did not constitute those of an enemy. Luo, however, was no longer in a position to institute this moderate assessment of crime.

After the failure of the Great Leap, a major shake-up of both Party and army occurred. In particular, the head of the army, Peng Dehuai, who had severely criticized Mao, fell from grace and was replaced by Lin Biao. Lin Biao was an old army friend and comrade of Luo Ruiqing's and, in September 1959, Lin requested Luo's transfer to the People's Liberation Army (Huang Yao 1991, 165). The request was granted and Luo returned to the army, being replaced as Minister of Public Security by the more radical Xie Fuzhi (Yu Lei 1992, 18).

Xie would offer a very different appreciation of the failure of the Leap and what to do about it. Where Luo had argued for moderation, Xie framed everything politically. The social disorder created by the famine, far from being a non-antagonistic contradiction, had imperiled the revolution by offering counter-revolutionaries a range of new opportunities. Anti-social actions aided this cause and, after the discovery that large numbers of Taiwanese agents had been dispatched to the mainland to take advantage of the temporary adverse conditions, this view seemed to be confirmed by the facts. In these conditions, it was impossible to regard anti-social acts benignly (Outline of Public Security 1997, 304; Guilin City 1995, 17; Yu Lei 1992, 19–20). The politics of friend and enemy reasserted itself as a fear of invasion spread. As this fear spread, the space that once existed for non-antagonistic contradictions began to disappear.

It was this line of thinking that would come to dominate the Tenth Public Security Work Meeting in February 1960, and it was Xie who would articulate it. He suggested that public security forces should maintain the public appearance of moderation but secretly institute a tighter internal regime (*A Summary History* 1989, 149).[10] Under the influence of this policy the security forces began to redesignate many acts formally described as anti-social and non-antagonistic as crimes of the enemy.[11] These redesignations increased the fear of the enemy and by August 1960, Xie had grown so concerned about the possibility of a counter-revolution that he called for a new, large-scale "social suppression" campaign targeting "internal counter-revolutionaries" (*shehui zhenfan, neibu sufan*) (Guilin City 1995, 16). With the famine upon them, however, other more moderate voices prevailed. Thus, despite the radicalism of their minister, the ministry itself took a more moderate position.

At the Eleventh National Public Security Work Meeting in February–March 1961, Xie's line seemed to hold no weight. Instead of supporting Xie's radicalism, the ministry called on the police to focus on the protection of economic production. At the same time, they continued to strip the communes of their powers of arrest, detention, and "collective training." Indeed, they even sent out cadres from the political section to "help" security officers overcome populist errors in local public security work styles (*A Summary History* 1989, 150–51, 174; *Outline of Public Security* 1997, 313). By the time of the May harvest in 1961, the ministry's moderation seemed all too apparent. Calling on security forces to protect the harvest, they warned of hoarding, petty thefts, and fraud by commune members but made no reference to counter-revolutionaries. Instead, they advised security forces to tread carefully and not to incorrectly handle these contradictions by labeling people. Overstating contradictions, they noted, could easily lead to mass violence (*Outline of Public Security* 1997, 310–11; Yu Lei 1992, 18–19).

Despite this moderation, counterveiling tendencies continued to emerge. Indeed, it is at this time that we begin to see the first, rather shadowy, outline of a two-line struggle developing within the Party. While differences of opinion had always existed within the Party, it was really only after the "Leap" that these would be read as political signs. How the different approaches to recovery became political rather than merely tactical differences cannot be understood without some attention given to the looming figure of revisionism.

The Specter of Revisionism

Increasingly at odds over Marxist theory, international relations, and economic development strategies, the Soviets had withdrawn all aid to China in August 1960. By September 1962, the inter-Party dispute between the Chinese and the Soviets had reached the point whereby the tenth plenum of the Eighth Central Committee was ready to endorse Mao's labeling of the Soviet Union as revisionist (Brugger 1981b, 21). This would have a direct and immediate effect on public security. At the Twelfth National Public Security Work Meeting of October–November 1962, police preoccupation centered around sealing the borders and overcoming a series of (unspecified) problems caused by Soviet activities in Xinjiang and northeastern China (*Outline of Public Security* 1997, 319). This, however, was the least of the Chinese worries. Of far greater concern was the lesson Soviet degeneration would teach the Chinese Party about itself.

If, following Theodor Däubler, it can be said that "the enemy is our own question as a figure," then the Soviet Union, as the new enemy, became the central question for the Chinese Communist Party (qtd. in Meier 1998, 44). The Chinese Party, structured along Soviet lines, was, potentially at least, open to the same processes of degeneration that had transformed the Soviet Party into a revisionist one. After this category emerged to frame thinking, no cadre work style error could ever again be viewed innocently. For Mao, the question of how to combat revisionism led to a revival of the friend/enemy distinction, but this time, it would center upon an enemy within. With a new threat looming, the Party would once again come to rely upon intense class struggle and a populist mass-line. This time, however, these "technologies" would focus upon the new and rather abstract enemy within, the revisionist. The problem became one of how to make concrete this rather abstract concept of the enemy.

Because of revisionism, class enemies could no longer be rendered merely as remnant elements. Revisionism signaled the fact that new class enemies could emerge from the womb of socialism. Revisionism was the product of remnant but absolutely necessary capitalist production relations that still had a role to play in developing the socialist economy. As a result, in "socialist society, new bourgeois elements may still be produced. During the whole socialist stage, there still exist classes and class struggle, and this class struggle is a protracted, complex, and sometimes violent affair." (Mao Zedong, qtd. in Schram 1974, 168). Class struggle was no longer dying, but neither was it anchored in past property relations. Partly structural but principally ideational, it was about to become the greatest danger to the revolution.

To combat this new enemy required a new form of struggle. It required adopting a symptomatic reading which could identify the hidden presence of revisionism by its outward manifestations. Corrupt or shabby work styles could be telltale signs of a hostile class attitude; slips of the tongue or wayward hobbies might well be signs of a deeper malaise; even an apparently innocent joke might reveal a hidden meaning, code, or political tendency. Then again, as Freud once said, a cigar is sometimes simply a cigar. In psychoanalysis, it is the symptomatic reading that enables the unconscious thoughts that undergird the public statement to be brought to the surface. But this requires the skills of a trained analyst. Wouldn't the exposure of revisionism similarly require trained professional and specialist knowledge? Mao had, of course, long since rejected that opinion. He would instead advocate a combination of mass-line action and professional knowledge. "Professional work is necessary," he would say, "but the most important thing is to carry out the mass line under the leadership of the Party committee" (Mao Zedong, qtd. in Schram 1974, 169). Mao, therefore, looked back to Yan'an rather than to psychoanalysis for his answers. Security forces needed to rely upon the masses and not become "specialist kingdoms," he insisted (Mao Zedong 1974, 314–17). In Yan'an, the mass-line had addressed the issue of the enemy within, but it had not led to the bloodbath that was Jiangxi. Once again, Mao hoped to emulate that success. The socialist education campaign was launched with this in mind, and despite its innumerable problems, by 1963, it had, if nothing else, come up with at least one model that had something to offer.

Informed by the twin concepts of mass democracy and mass dictatorship, a new mass-line method of policing found compelling institutional expression in the model that emerged in the Fengqiao district of Zhuji county,

Zhejiang. Here, in 1963, an experiment in local mass-democratic dictator-ship was put into effect over retrograde elements. Still moderate in tone, this model would mold the ideas of mass-based action and dictatorship into a largely ameliorist program for dealing with adversaries. Boasting fewer arrests and fewer suspects, this model was said to offer a concrete render-ing of Mao's order to rely less on the government and more on local mass-dictatorial powers. In Fengqiao, they would do just that.

Instead of calling upon police to arrest local landlords, rich peasants, counter-revolutionaries, and "bad" people, the local authorities in Feng-qiao allowed representatives of the four elements to remain in production units, but ordered them to be supervised by the masses. Surrounded by good people, they were said to have reformed (Questions and Answers 1994, 96). Mao was pleased: "These are contradictions that should be resolved by the locality and not handed on to higher-level authorities," he said. Mao then ordered the Ministry of Public Security to summarize and generalize the Fengqiao experience.

As a model of how to rely upon "mass dictatorship" rather than govern-ment, it would be adopted as a working police model at the Thirteenth Na-tional Public Security Work Meeting that ran from February through March 1964 (Outline of Public Security 1997, 325–26). The meeting stressed that po-lice, in handling the four elements, needed to follow the Fengqiao model and "listen to the masses, discuss things with them, and hear what they have to say." "The last thing we want," it went on to say, "is a small group of cadres and the organs of the dictatorship simplifying things and acting on the basis of such simplifications." For this reason the meeting concluded by advising police units to allow the masses themselves to reform the four ele-ments, rather than simply handing them over to higher-level security organs for treatment. The effects of this recommendation had immediate signifi-cance and would herald a new approach to policing. More important for my argument, however, is the fact that if one reads this experiment in the context of an ongoing debate over the nature of dictatorship within social-ism, then Fengqiao forms the beginnings of a new and very different way of understanding the state.

With most potential enemies now being dealt with at a local level prior to them causing major problems, China witnessed a massive drop in the formal criminal arrest rate. While 1963 had seen 156,659 arrests, by 1964 the number had dropped to only 94,699. By 1965, it had fallen again, dropping to an amazing 64,186 arrests (confidential material 1986). At the Fourteenth National Public Security Work Meeting in June 1965, the Fengqiao experience became a key methodological component of the Chinese massline in policing. By this stage, mass dictatorship had become something of a mantra, but as the question of revisionism loomed ever larger, it was now joined by another "mantra," class struggle: "In instances where the political nature of the case is outstanding, use class struggle as the key and institute an all-round and complete mass dictatorship, but arrest as few as possible. Follow the policy that if there is no contradiction, then actions require no prior approval from above" (confidential material 1988). As class struggle grew in importance, the wall between "hard" Legalist actions that turned on struggle and punishment and "soft" localized corrective programs aimed at "educating" miscreants began to tumble. The soft administrative option hardened dramatically, and Fengqiao fell prey to this trend.

A "protective umbrella that covered the enemy classes" was how the Fengqiao model would come to be described (PSHM 1994:2, v32, 103). Accused of being bourgeois because of its lack of attention to class struggle, the model disappeared from the press (Zhou Changkang 1994, 5). Despite this disappearance, we should not underestimate its historical role. Fengqiao had played a pioneering role in developing a methodological breakthrough for mass-line policing and, despite later criticisms, it did lead to the idea of mass democracy and dictatorship migrating from policing into politics proper. The mass-based administrative "decisionism" that the Fengqiao model began to institute enabled mass-line decisionism to be directly sutured into government determinations. This would blur the line of authority that stretched between the state and the mass-line. It was just this type of blurring of state authority that enabled class struggle to be pressed beyond the realm of collective campaigning in a way that it could begin to touch individuals "to their very souls."

Thus while the humanism of Fengqiao would not survive, a more radical and harsher model of mass dictatorship would. It would fuel a political program that showed a marked divergence from orthodox Marxism-Leninism. Where orthodoxy located the dictatorship in the Party-State, Maoism had successfully relocated it in the actions of the masses. Seen in this light, Fengqiao gave a foretaste of things to come. When mass dictatorship moved beyond the confines of localized public security questions and began to intertwine with the class struggle to unmask those within the Party taking the capitalist road, it moved rapidly toward an event that history recalls as the Cultural Revolution.

From Mass Dictatorship to an All-Round Dictatorship

At the eleventh plenum of the Eighth Central Committee in August 1966, the Cultural Revolution became a large-scale mass movement.[12] For both culture and the police, however, this revolution had begun well before August. Radicalism had been looming for some time. Mao's new ideas on class and class struggle took shape in the course of an increasingly shrill polemic with the Soviet Union over revisionism. Arguably, from around 1962 onward, Mao's views were being radicalized by his increasingly grim view of Soviet socialism. As the Chinese Party and state structures were based upon the Soviet model, it seemed obvious that the same structural consequences that led Mao to accuse the Soviets of revisionism would find an echo in the Chinese Party. The question was—how much of an echo?

In order to limit the development of full-blown Soviet-style revisionism, Mao came to the conclusion that the Chinese Party must "never forget the class struggle," and it was this single line, coined in 1962, that would become the new methodological panacea. Class struggle as the solution to everything led to the political intensification of everything. Class struggle would educate the young, combat revisionism, lead to the correct level of enthusiasm in production, and advance Chinese socialism. It was within the army, rather than the police or the Party, however, that the effects of this stress on class struggle found its clearest and most detailed expression. This became evident in a number of ways.

First, the campaign to study Lei Feng, which was initiated by Luo Rui-qing, took a more radical turn when Mao Zedong wrote of it and transformed it into a mass-based army political campaign (Huang Yao and Zhang Mingzhe 1996, 449, 450). More than anything else, this campaign laid stress on Lei Feng's loyalty to Mao. It promoted the selfless lifestyle of the Red Army tradition immortalized in the Yan'an period, but it now did so under the aegis of loyalty to the Chairman. From the campaign to study the selfless, loyal army hero Lei Feng in January 1963 through to the "learn from the People's Liberation Army" movement of February 1964, the army began pushing the Party to the left and itself to the fore.

Second, in 1965, Lin Biao published under his name the famous essay "Long Live People's War," in which it was suggested that the countryside of the world (led by China) would surround and defeat the cities of the world (led by the United States).[13] This, according to Brugger, could be viewed as one of the opening shots in the Cultural Revolution (1981b, 53). It clearly functioned as such within the army. Henceforth those within the ranks of the army who laid any stress upon conventional military approaches at the expense of politics would be stigmatized. This would lead to the demise of the former Minister of Public Security, Luo Ruiqing, and this, too, would have repercussions for policing.

While the head of the army, Lin Biao, almost single-mindedly put politics and Mao Zedong Thought in command, Lin's former close friend and adjutant, Luo Ruiqing, was endeavoring to promote military competitions alongside political training. For Lin, Luo's employment of this red-and-expert approach was not only a sign of a lack of faith in politics in command but also a sign that Luo was insufficiently loyal to his minister (Huang Yao 1996, 456–70).[14] In the heady political atmosphere of the time, this combination of political and personal factors proved fatal. By the end of November 1965, Luo had disappeared from sight, and by December, he had been formally stripped of all his offices and responsibilities (Zeng Fanzheng 1998, 2:437). November 1965 proved a busy month in the revolutionary calendar. It was at that time that the idea of Cultural Revolution began to broaden out into a general and very public critique of politics in the cultural arena. Ironically, one of Luo Ruiqing's final acts would play a key role in this spread of politics into culture.

It was in November 1965 that a play by the deputy mayor of Beijing, Wu Han, was subjected to a bitter and public denunciation by the literary critic Yao Wenyuan. Yao's bitter critique of the play would first appear in the pages of the PLA Daily, but it did so only after the direct intervention of Luo Ruiqing (Teiwes and Sun 1996, 209). Ironically, Luo's final curtain call in the leadership group catapulted the radical Yao to national prominence. The effect of Yao's critique was electric. Arguably one of the opening shots of the Cultural Revolution, his critique concluded that this play, entitled "Hai Rui Dismissed from Office," was in actuality, nothing more than a "big, poisonous weed." The key reason for the huge impact of this critique, however, was that the Chairman had sponsored it. Despite this, the quixotic Chairman would later come to the view that even this criticism was too moderate. For Mao, "the Crux of 'Hai Jui [Hai Rui] Dismissed from Office' was the question of dismissal from office. In 1959 we dismissed P'eng Te-huai [Peng Dehuai] from office. And P'eng Te-huai is Hai Jui too" (qtd. in Schram 1974, 237). With the play read as analogous to the Mao-Peng dispute over the Great Leap Forward, Wu Han's fate was sealed. More worrying for the orthodox Party leadership, however, was that, politically, Wu was closely connected to the powerful mayor of Beijing, Peng Zhen.

By early 1966, things would come to a head. In March, Peng Zhen disappeared (*Great Cultural Revolution* 1968, 169). In April, criticism of him turned to struggle, and in May, struggle led to dismissal. By June, Peng was effectively replaced as mayor (Brugger 1981b, 59; Teiwes and Sun 1996, 56; *Great Cultural Revolution* 1968, 169). The implications of these two purges for the public security leadership group could not have been greater.

Because Peng Zhen and Luo Ruiqing both had a long and intimate association with the security forces, virtually every leading figure in the force became suspect. On June 7, 1966, every suspect leader was accused, and it was their own minister who was throwing around the accusations. Gathering together all leading cadres within the ministry, Xie Fuzhi would tell them that there was only one real revolutionary commander (*hongsiling*) within their ranks. The rest of the leadership group, he insisted, was all "black" (interview 1996). As if to demonstrate the extent of the problem empirically, he ordered police to study and further investigate the criminal conspiracies of Peng Zhen, Luo Ruiqing, and Di Fei (confidential material 1986). To push the point home and drive the existing leadership out, Xie ordered the left-wing work teams he had sent in to public security units to report their findings.[15] The findings were a revelation, and nowhere more so than in the capital.

Closely tied to the former city mayor, Peng Zhen, the Beijing bureau was under investigation by a work team led by senior leftist Li Zhao. On June 12, 1966, Li concluded his investigation and sent his findings to Xie Fuzhi. Xie then used these to authorize the arrest of five bureau chiefs. With the upper echelons of the Beijing Public Security Bureau leadership purged, Li Zhao took charge and instituted a root–and-branch reorganization of the force and a major change in personnel (confidential material 1988).[16] Across the road in the ministry, similar purges were underway. These struggles within the ministry reached a conclusion of sorts in August, 1966, when a new seventeen-member Ministry of Public Security Cultural Revolution Group took charge and effectively brought to an end the rule of the old police culture and old cadre leadership group (confidential material 1988).[17] While this old public security leadership group was being purged, street cops were in the process of being rectified.

On June 10, 1966, Xie offered ordinary street police an opportunity to avoid the fate of their leaders. In a notice to police, he advised them all to "remember well the proletarian dictatorship and stay close to the revolutionary movement" (confidential material 1988). Translated into action, this meant that police were to support the revolutionary actions of students and radicals. Whether it was in relation to the hanging of "big character posters" or violently attacking rightist factional enemies, the duty of the police was to protect their right to rebel (*Outline of Public Security* 1997, 330). In effect, police were being ordered to lean to one side and support student and left factions on the streets rather than their local Party leaders. With leadership structures tying them into their local Party committees and a notion of political policing linked to the Party-State dictatorship, police were never going to find this order easy to obey. Just how difficult it would be became obvious in August 1966.

At that time, radical students from Shaanxi province's Tongchuan Number One Middle School, spurred on by the idea of mass democracy, surrounded the city Party committee offices and demanded that the Party leadership stand aside. The Party committee refused, and a series of attacks on the building followed. The Party committee, fearing Red Guard violence, turned to the police. Security forces arrived and ordered the students to disperse. When they repeatedly refused, the police chief ordered his officers to open fire. The violence of the police shocked the left.

Xie Fuzhi would read of this incident and label it a "suppression of revolutionary student action." The security forces, it seems, needed to be rectified further. They also needed to be reminded that they were no longer the authority on the street, the radical activists were. The role of the police was to support, not attack, such actions. On August 22, 1966, Xie issued another notice, ordering security forces to stay off student campuses, to avoid interference in student rebellions, to refrain from detaining rebels, and to turn the other cheek if attacked by the left (*A Summary History*, 1989, 179–80; confidential material 1988). For the police, the idea of turning the other cheek when attacked was the source of some bitterness, particularly after the so-called Wang Lianyou Incident.

This incident arose shortly after Mao threw his weight behind the idea of revolutionary exchanges. As a result of this support, millions of Red Guards around the country crowded onto free trains to spread the revolutionary message (Ying Hongbiao 1996, 180). One of the most popular routes went from Shanghai to Beijing, and it was on this train that the Wang Lianyou Incident took place. Named after the police officer involved, it began when Wang Lianyou tried to stop a group of Red Guards from attacking and beating passengers. In trying to calm the situation down, Wang angered the Red Guard activists, who turned on him. Beaten and injured, he was dragged from the train and taken to a local police station where the Red Guards involved demanded his immediate arrest for trying to "dampen down rebellion" (*Outline of Public Security* 1977, 331).

Reports of this incident caused fear and concern within police circles. If Wang could be attacked, any officer could. Fearful yet angry, police still believed that the Party would somehow rescue them and correct such excesses. Police groups from around the country began making their own revolutionary pilgrimages to Beijing to petition the leadership about this and other such incidents and ask for more support (*A Summary History* 1989, 181; *Outline of Public Security* 1997, 331). After the Tongchuan Incident, however, such petitions fell on deaf ears. All that the petitions about the cases such as the Wang Lianyou Incident did was confirm the existing left viewpoint that the police force was utterly reactionary. Under siege from Red Guard groups and unaided by their own leadership, police simply abstained from work, joined rival Red Guard factions, or went on their own revolutionary pilgrimages. In effect, the entire public security system now began to collapse.

By late 1966, even the pretence of a unified national public security force was in tatters. Ordinary police within the ministry and its various branches were splintering into competing Red Guard factions forcing the ministry, in September, to institute a blanket ban forbidding any police participation in such groupings. Throughout this tumultuous period, the purges of the old leadership group continued. Starting with the disappearance of deputy minister Xu Zirong and his replacement by the leftist Li Zhen,[18] the ministry witnessed a string of dismissals, arrests, and purges. By December, the radicals had made a clean sweep of all ministry-level leadership positions. Deputy Ministers Xu Zirong, Liu Fuzhi, and Ling Yun were dismissed, as was the head of the political section, Yin Zhaozhi (confidential material 1988). In total, seven of the original eight Deputy Ministers, forty-three of the original forty-nine bureau chiefs and deputy chiefs, and sixty-six section (chu) heads and deputies were arrested and labeled traitors, spies, counterrevolutionaries, or "unrecoverable running dogs of capitalism."

The struggles against this old leadership, however, took many turns. Groups that began as radical "turned" when their parents ended up being victims. One such group was liandong, which, in December 1966, undertook a series of attacks on public security offices. Largely made up of children of denounced high-ranking Party officials, liandong opposed the radical leadership of Jiang Qing and Xie Fuzhi. Their most spectacular "coup" was a raid by about 139 of their members on the Beijing Public Security Bureau compound (Red Guard 1980, 3303–4). In total, liandong would mount six attacks upon the Beijing bureau but, rather than producing a "reversal of verdicts," these actions simply led to their arrest. To counter liandong's influence, Xie Fuzhi and Jiang Qing threw their support behind a more radical Red Guard group, the political science and law commune group. Comprised of older, less well connected students from Beijing's Political Science and Law Institute, the commune group also undertook a series of raids upon the ministry and the Beijing bureau, but they had a very different agenda to that of liandong. Far from desiring a reversal of verdicts, this group called for a "total transformation" of the "conservative" police structure and in doing so offered their own revolutionary alternative to policing. On January 15, 1967, the leaders of the commune group met with Xie Fuzhi to announce their plans. "We have to align ourselves with rebel comrades within the Public Security Bureau, and together we can take over and run the Beijing bureau," they would tell the minister. He enthusiastically endorsed their plan (Capital Red Guards 1967). He would do so at a time when the public security "revolutionary preparatory small groups" (gechou xiaozu) were being reorganized into "combat battalions" (zhandoudui) and sent out to criticize, and struggle against, local reactionary police chiefs across the country.

In Guilin, these combat battalions struggled against Su Yushan, the bureau chief and deputy mayor. In the end, Su and the entire leadership of the city's public security force would be dismissed, then arrested (Guilin City 1995, 19). In Shanghai, where the purges proved particularly severe, battalions focused upon the 1,700 police cadres said to have "a contradiction with the people." Of these, 113 were executed (*Outline of Public Security* 1997, 334). In Beijing, the battalions aligned themselves with the commune group and attacked the bureau and denounced its former leadership as an "anti-revolutionary clique." On January 17, the Political Science and Law Commune, with the backing of the combat battalions and the acquiescence of the minister, dispatched hundreds of students to the Beijing Public Security Bureau in one final push that would lead to the occupation of the administration building and the seizure of power. While the students bombarded the headquarters, the battalions arrested the former leadership group that was now denounced as "the nucleus of an anti-revolutionary gang employing traitors and spies." As a result of these actions, almost half the 10 bureau chiefs and deputy chiefs, along with 72 of the 155 section and deputy heads, were accused of being traitors, spies, or counter-revolutionaries. The former bureau chief Xing Xiangsheng and his deputies Min Buying, Li Yiping, and Zhang Lie, as well as 16 section-level cadres, were all labeled "major criminal counter-revolutionaries" and thrown into prison.

While the alliance produced a victory in the center of the city, out in the suburbs, violent struggles were breaking out over who would control the suburban stations. Guided by Lin Biao's idea that in revolution, the countryside must surround the city, commune members went out to suburbs such as Fangshan and Shijingshan and struggled to gain control of the local police stations (interview 1997). Both their plan of attack and their tactics gained the enthusiastic endorsement of the minister: "Your actions have been great, you have done a great job. Well done! You have all been very brave. All the revolutionary comrades in the Ministry of Public Security welcome you warmly and support your revolutionary actions firmly" (Capital Red Guards 1967). While both the takeovers and the support of the radical leaders would prove to be Pyrrhic in the long run, for a very short period, it appeared as though a new libertarian-populist order was about to be announced in China.

Across the nation, the wedding of mass democracy and class struggle was leading to calls for a total transformation, until they reached a peak in early 1967.[19] By January, the idea of a Shanghai commune was being floated, and there was to be a "campaign to seize power" (*duoquan yundong*). The January storm had begun. From January 1967 onward, it also became clear that revolutionary policing now had nothing to do with the defense of the Party. This became evident on January 13, 1967, when the ministry released the now infamous "Public Security Six Points." Apart from offering a traditional Legalist understanding of law by which counter-revolutionaries would be punished and an abstract notion of the revolutionary masses protected, this document employed a third notion—loyalty. Loyalty, however, was no longer given to the Party. Instead feelings became personified and loyalty was transformed into a threat: Anyone who "scurrilously attacks the great teacher Chairman Mao or his closest comrade in arms, Comrade Lin Biao, is a counter-revolutionary and is to be punished on the basis of the law," the document stated (*Supplementary Edition* 1979, 26–27). Drafted by Xie Fuzhi and Zhang Chunqiao, and approved by the Central Committee in February, this document not only reduced all police operations to just six points but simultaneously operated like a formal legal code governing all police actions in this period (*A Summary History* 1989, 182; *Outline of Public Security* 1997, 336).

It was under these very general pressures that Mao had launched the campaign to oppose the reactionary capitalist line (Ying Hongbiao 1996, 182–83). The effect of this campaign was to further increase pressure on the Party and reinforce the idea of direct mass rule. With the radical leadership and Mao all seemingly expressing loyalty to this idea, radical students began to act. They would "bombard the headquarters," to use Mao's expression, carrying out a string of attacks that led to Xie's infamous call on August 7 to destroy the entire legal system. Xie began by pointing out the nature of the task: "From the time the Cultural Revolution began right through until this year's [1967] January storm, the vast majority of public security, procuraturate, and court units stubbornly held onto power and went on the capitalist road suppressing the revolutionary masses" (*A Summary History* 1989, 185; *Supplementary Edition* 1979, 357–58). Faced with such intractability, the only revolutionary choice was to smash the *gongjianfa* (public security, the procuraturate, and the courts) and, on this point, Xie had the full backing of the

Chairman. "At least eight times, if not ten," Xie recalled, Mao called upon him to "smash the gongjianfa" (CCPRET 1973, 329). As this radical line of the Cultural Revolution advanced, so, too, did the ferocity and frequency of these kinds of calls, which in turn resulted in further attacks upon public security forces.[20]

As students and radicals gained control of the ministry, the Beijing bureau, and many local suburban police stations, it was now the turn of the "reactionary" police to suffer. Xie Fuzhi proved quite adroit at utilizing the new Red Guard factions to clean out this "enemy within." Despite such advances, the question still remained as to whether these groups would be strong or united enough to institute the mass dictatorship buried within the rhetoric of total transformation. Total transformation, therefore, may have been the ideal for all the left but all ideals needed to be demonstrably correct in practice. Tests were needed to determine whether or not the students were strong and united enough to carry out total transformation.

From Xie's office came the suggestion that mass policing required a period of experimentation rather than instant transformation. He himself put forth this idea in a meeting with leaders of the commune group: "Can't we set up a place to experiment with this idea? We can set up the Beijing public security western city section and [the students] can take care of that area" (*Outline of Public Security* 1997, 331). This suggestion, however, was never acted upon.[21] No doubt after the high point of revolutionary enthusiasm in January, realism had to temper the utopian claims of total transformation. Nowhere did this tempering become more apparent than in the heartland of radicalism, Shanghai.

It was in Shanghai in January 1967 that the need to have new structures to replace the rapidly crumbling power of the Party organization became irresistible. As this struggle intensified, over a million people would take to the streets to applaud the ideas of the radical Marxist theorist Zhang Chunqiao, the literary critic Yao Wenyuan, and the young revolutionary worker Wang Hongwen.

On February 3, 1967, Zhang would proclaim the advent of a new form of revolutionary political power for Shanghai. He and his companions would call this new form the Shanghai Commune. Deliberately modeling itself on the Paris Commune of 1871, they hoped this idea of a commune would spread like wildfire around China, promising a new form of state organization. If this was the radicals' plan, it quickly turned into an illusion, and it was the Chairman himself who would kill it off.

While in early January 1967 Mao had talked about the revolutionary powers in Shanghai bringing "hope to the whole country," by February he clearly thought they had gone too far. He labeled the commune an example of extreme anarchism and raised the fundamental question of how state power could be maintained if this structure was adopted nationwide. In discussions with Zhang in early February, he made the crucial remark that "communes are too weak when it comes to suppressing counter-revolution" (qtd. in Schram 1974, 278). He then went on to recommend that the city adopt a different model based on the structures put in place in Harbin and Shanxi province after radicals had seized power there. In these two places, it was the army that had played the most active role in the power seizures, and the structures instituted reflected this. In these two places revolutionary committees had been formed based on the triple alliance of mass revolutionary organizations, old Party cadres, and the army. From this time onward, and despite surges to the left in 1968, the basic issue for Mao was not about mass democracy but about how best to suppress counter-revolutionaries. The enemy would once again define the structures of the friend. Perhaps even more significantly, however, Mao came to reject the Paris Commune model on grounds raised by Marx and stressed by Lenin. Like Mao, Lenin in particular had rejected this structure because he found it too weak when it came to defending the revolution.[22]

Lenin had made this point in 1917. In *State and Revolution* he argued for a strong proletarian dictatorship during the socialist transition period. It was this structure that enabled the proletariat to exercise power over the bourgeoisie in a way that the libertarian-inspired commune could not.[23] While the importance of this idea as a concrete political practice was not lost on Mao, it would take some seven years before it was made into a general point and theorized in Marxist terms. This theorization would take place in the course of the 1975 campaign to study the all-round dictatorship of the proletariat. Back in 1967, however, it was not the dictatorship of the proletariat that was being stressed, but the revolutionary nature and role of the People's Liberation Army. In conditions that bordered on anarchy, the unity of purpose, discipline, and power they displayed would prove crucial.

The Army Moves In

The story of military-style socialism begins more or less at the moment that Mao called into question the Shanghai Commune model of mass dictatorship and mass democracy. The army became the only viable alternative as doubts were raised about the ability of commune structures to suppress counterrevolution. As the army began its takeover, it focused its attention upon any remaining aspects of the state repressive apparatus. By November 1967, the army had completed its purge of the Beijing Public Security Bureau. In all, a total of 1,693 police officers and their families from the bureau were killed, arrested, or put under supervision. Among their number were 124 heads and deputy heads at a departmental and sectional level, 117 sub-bureau heads, and 10 deputy or bureau chiefs (confidential material 1988). This was but one of many actions undertaken nationwide as the army took over all public security work (Yu Lei 1992, 22; confidential material 1988).

On December 9, the army took over the ministry. On January 25, 1968, thirty-two military officers were sent in to cull staff and run key areas of ministry work. By February 7, there were only eighty-five of the original public security cadres left. This massive reduction of police staff was made possible by the narrowing scope of army interest. Its primary concern was securing the political case files of the old leadership group. Xie Fuzhi, Wu Faxian, and Wang Dongxing took charge initially, but in February, a new military officer, Zhao Dengcheng joined the ministry, and, by April, he took charge of this work. Under Zhao's leadership, seven hundred transferred army cadres began to sift through all political case files in search of evidence of counter-revolutionary activity (confidential material 1988). They would not leave empty-handed.

In May 1968, a whole series of exposés appeared that scandalized the country. On May 13, under express orders from Kang Sheng and Xie Fuzhi, the Beijing City Public Security Bureau military commissioner, Liu Chuanxin, released the so-called 513 Report.[24] It was said to expose the "espionage activities undertaken by the intelligence agencies of the United States and Chiang Kai-shek along with the counter-revolutionary revisionist activities of the old Beijing Public Security Bureau" (confidential material 1988). Luo Ruiqing, Xu Zirong, Wang Jinxiang, Yang Qiqing, Wang Zhao, and Ling Yun were all denounced. Luo Ruiqing was variously described as a U.S. spy and a

Guomindang agent, and that was, of course, when he was not being called a deep-cover mole for the Russians. In any event, his fate was sealed. On May 28, in the so-called 528 Report, similar charges were laid against most senior cadres in the ministry. As a result, seven deputy ministers, forty-three bureau chiefs and deputies, sixty-three chiefs and deputies of public security provincial sections, and ninety-two chiefs and deputies at a divisional level were all labeled enemies. "When power was in their black hands," the report concluded, "they were able to transform this ministry from a proletarian dictatorship to a bourgeois dictatorship" (A Summary History 1989, 187; confidential material 1988).

With investigation into the cadre files of the old leadership revealing such dark and dramatic secrets, the radicals decided they needed to broaden their investigations. On July 3, 1968, they did just that. The seals on all ministry files were broken and thrown open to a campaign-style investigation. This work would continue until February 1970. While the workload was enormous, it was nothing compared to the political pressure. On three separate occasions, Mao Zedong, Lin Biao, Xie Fuzhi, and the Central Committee Cultural Revolution Group came to the ministry and demanded that more charges be laid. Under such pressure, the investigating cadres obliged.

In little over a year, they checked through 30,000 individual personnel files, 290,000 case files, 104,000 separate documents, and 640,000 reference works. In the course of their investigations, over 90,000 case files were closely examined, leading to 5,700 people being found guilty of counterrevolutionary crimes. In 223 cases, they found enough material to support charges of treason and, in a further 84 documents, they discovered evidence of espionage (confidential material 1988). From these investigations, the wild accusations that had been leveled at the old police leadership now became generalized accusations leveled at all police cadres. The catch cry of August 1967 to "smash the gongjianfa" had become a reality. On the basis of incomplete statistics for all areas barring Tibet, over 34,000 police were put under investigation. Of those, over 3,600 were "forced to wear counterrevolutionary hats," 1,300 put in prison, 3,600 beaten and left with serious injuries, and over 1,200 beaten to death (A Summary History 1989, 186).

Given the predominantly intelligence-based backgrounds of many of the members of the public security force,[25] the dubious investigative and evidentiary methods employed by the army, and the increasing demands of the left leadership group for more evidence of counter-revolutionary duplicity, it hardly seems surprising that a mountain of evidence would translate into an avalanche of claims. This, in turn, reinforced the conclusion that the whole of the public security system was tainted. It was Xie Fuzhi who summarized this conclusion: "The seventeen-year history of public security work demonstrates that while we could not say every action was in conflict with Mao Zedong Thought, we could nevertheless say . . . [that] . . . the basis of such actions was the revisionist line" (CCPRET 1973, 330).

Given the collective guilt of the ministry and all its sections, it was decided to solve the problem by banishment.[26] According to one of the banished, when the day of departure came, Xie Fuzhi was there to send them off with the parting words, "Your period of life as high officials is over, your lifestyle based on the principle of 'serving the people' has only just begun" (interview 1996). Thus, after the spring festival in 1969, more than one thousand cadres were sent to the northeast to a prison farm just outside the town of Jiamusi. In March, a further one thousand ministry cadres and their families were sent to Bijia mountain reform-through-labor camp in Jixian county, Heilongjiang, or to Shayang reform-through-labor farm in Hubei province. They would be joined on March 6 by disgraced cadres from four other units—the Supreme Procuraturate, the Supreme Court, the Internal Affairs Ministry, and the Internal Affairs Office—and the total number of banished cadres stood at 2,400 which, when families were added, came to over 3,000 people (A Summary History 1989, 187). Conditions in these places were reported to be harsher than even in the worst reform-through-labor camps.[27] It was under these extremely harsh conditions that the public security cadres were told to remodel themselves into new people. They would remain in these camps until the revolutionary tide ebbed. When it did, one year later, a small trickle of cadres returned.

The process of return was instituted at the Fifteenth Public Security Work Meeting convened between December 1970 and February 1971 at Zhou Enlai's behest (Yu Lei 1992, 23). At this meeting a very limited reversal of some verdicts was announced.[28] Yet even this limited return did not take place without a struggle. Reiterating the left line that had underpinned the decision to banish, the Deputy Minister of Public Security, Li Zhen, argued that the seventeen-year history of the ministry had been one of betrayal. The mercurial Chairman Mao, however, now found grounds to disagree:

"With regard to public security work," Mao would say, "one needs to adopt an attitude of one divides into two. There are still good things about public security work, and one shouldn't view everything as having been bad" (qtd. in Gong'an Jianshi). Adopting this more conciliatory line, Mao actively intervened in conference proceedings. He would end up commenting on ten of the fourteen reports of the meetings' subcommittees and would conclude that the majority of public security cadres were good or relatively good. He then critiqued the left line as ahistorical and argued that it needed to be reformulated (Gong'an Jianshi). A debate then ensued around the question of the applicability of "one divides into two" in relation to police work.[29] This debate emboldened Zhou Enlai, who used Mao's comments and this debate to run an agenda of his own.

Zhou was careful never to directly attack the politics of the left. Rather, his critique rested on the question of efficiency. He pointed to areas of weakness that had resulted from the left military line, demanding administrative simplification.[30] In place of this, he called for a return to a more specialized and professional approach to policing. His volleys at the left proved incendiary.

On December 31, 1970, he complained about the lack of professionally trained and experienced police cadres within the military-run ministry. Investigative and detective work had all but ceased, he noted, and as a result, police organs were left without their specialized "eyes and ears" (confidential material 1988; Outline of Public Security 1997, 448). In May 1971, he read a report on the treatment of Japanese war criminals still held in Chinese prisons.[31] Between 1966 and February 1971, 33 imprisoned war criminals died of contagious diseases, and 3 died under mysterious circumstances. Moreover, of the 143 war criminals still in custody, 13 were seriously ill. Again, a lack of specialized medical attention was said to be the cause. As Zhou Enlai would conclude: "To refuse to treat sick criminals is not in accord with Chairman Mao's views and policies" (confidential material 1988). His criticism forced a volte-face from the left and constituted something of a minor victory for Zhou.

The immediate result was that the "simple administration" program instituted under the auspices of the military left leadership of the ministry was abandoned and specialized units were reformed, including ones covering intelligence work, as well as the reform-through-labor penal sector.[32] To reinstitute a more professional approach, 450 banished police cadres from Heilongjiang were recalled to the ministry (*Gong'an Jianshi*). The left military tide had clearly ebbed, hastened, no doubt, by the redefinition of the Cultural Revolution as a movement to consolidate the Communist Party and, even more significant, by the scandalous demise of Chairman Mao's chosen successor, Marshal Lin Biao.

The redefinition of the Cultural Revolution took place in April 1969, at the Ninth Party Congress (Meisner 1986, 365). It led to the revival of the more traditional Party committee structure and to the winding up of the three-in-one revolutionary committee structure. The abandonment of the three-in-one committee structure may have been aimed at undermining Lin Biao's power base and may have contributed to his attempted coup, if indeed such a coup was ever contemplated.[33] Needless to say, the details of this coup and subsequent demonization of Lin lie outside the parameters of this current study. The fallout from these events, however, does not.

The Lin Biao affair effectively brought to an end the military model of socialism and, with that, a crisis in the ranks of the remaining civilian radicals. After the rejection of the Shanghai model, the notion of mass dictatorship replaced that of mass democracy. With the army returning to barracks, the return of the old police force was but a matter of time. Yet given their history, how could these officers be relied upon to police a radical left political agenda? While the Party right was concerned to emphasize the need for an efficient policing of social order, for the left, there was a lot more at stake. Tethered to an authoritarian model of "policing Chinese politics," the crisis of the left was a crisis of the political, and while the left could rely upon the militia to police the streets, the theoretical issue of how to advance the revolution and halt revisionism still was, for them, the key task of the moment.

In order to generate mass involvement, the left needed to create ever-increasing degrees of political intensity. In the past, this had been attempted through the politico-police campaigns. Police were no longer of interest to the radicals, but in the fight against revisionism, the radicals still needed to generate political intensity. The generation of political intensity around revisionism, however, proved much more difficult because of the complex nature of this struggle. Revisionism was not only hard to uncover it also proved difficult to explain. A key role of the left campaigns, therefore, had to be educational. They had to teach the masses how to protect the gains of the Cultural Revolution.[34] For the radicals, one of the greatest gains of the Cultural Revolution was the development of a disciplinary model of socialism strong enough to combat revisionism. This model was first practiced under the aegis of the military, but it would subsequently need revision in the light of Lin Biao's demise and the gradual withdrawal of the military from civil affairs. In the remaining years of radical Maoist influence, campaign themes continued to promote a civilian version of this disciplinary model as a necessary support for the ongoing process of class struggle.

The departure of the military from the political scene, therefore, signaled a subtle but important change in the overall left vision of policing Chinese politics. While military forces were no longer designated the shock troops of the revolutionary state, the idea of a disciplinary form of socialism that they heralded still held importance. Without this disciplinary model, the left had no way of addressing the question of revisionism. Hence the various political campaigns the radicals ran in the remaining years of Mao's life displayed a kind of disciplinary push designed to protect and advance their conception of socialism through an extension of class struggle. It was this idea of disciplinary push that gained clearer definition in the twilight years of the left. Paradoxically, for a group long associated with the "Lin Biao clique," the first signs of this new conception of the state would emerge in the course of a general attack being mounted on Lin by the Party.

The Campaign to Criticize Lin Biao and Confucius (*pi Lin pi Kong yundong*) was announced at the Tenth Party Congress in September 1973. Through it the radicals attempted to lay down the groundwork for a disciplinary model that no longer relied upon the army, but that could, nonetheless, offer an alternative, disciplinary frame with strong "Chinese characteristics." In attempting this "Sinification" of the debate, this campaign was drawn to the ancient Chinese debate over the nature of humanity and the role of the state. Two very different schools of thought would contend on this point. One was the ancient Chinese Legalist school of harsh punishments, the other, their Confucian opponents who believed in the rule of the virtuous. In returning to this component of the pi Lin pi Kong campaign, one comes to appreciate the novelty of the radical endeavor.

The Dystopia of the Party "Left":
Heading toward an All-Round Dictatorship

For the left, the Cultural Revolution offered a twofold lesson. First, the Cultural Revolution was credited with drawing attention to the potential for a new form of capitalist class to grow out of the Party bureaucracy in the socialist transition period. In other words, communist cadres could, and sometimes did, change color. Second, and this was far more worrying, while the Cultural Revolution focused attention upon this issue, it had failed to come up with an adequate structural or theoretical response. Both the mass-democracy model and the idea of a military dictatorship had failed. In effect, the radicals had identified the problem but had not developed an adequate solution.

The initial ideas of mass democracy wedded to a theory of continuous class struggle had resulted in a flirtation with the Paris Commune model. After the rejection of this model in Shanghai in 1967, left efforts went into developing a more punitive model. This followed Mao's rejection of the commune-as-government model, itself based on arguments previously advanced by Lenin in 1917. At that time, Lenin, too, rejected the Paris Commune model as the framework for a future socialist state. For Lenin, the criticisms of the commune were twofold. First, following Engels, and somewhat like Mao Zedong, Lenin believed that the commune did not adequately utilize the repressive power of governmental authority (Lenin 1964, 25:443–44). Second, the commune had failed to take over the banks and thus failed to expropriate the expropriators. In other words, it had failed to halt the redevelopment of conditions that would enable a capitalist restoration (Lenin 1962, 13:476). At a time when "restorationism" was central to the attacks being mounted against Lin Biao, Lenin's comments proved insightful. Nevertheless, while Lenin's work proved useful in offering a basis upon which to reject the commune model and forewarned of the dangers of restoration, his analysis failed to offer anything more than fragments toward the construction of an alternative.[35]

Piecing together these fragments, the radicals made Lenin's position on restoration central to their own concerns and a key reference point for their own campaigns. In particular, they would find inspiration in his idea that bureaucratic degeneration could be halted only by the development of a strong state and an institutional structure that could administer constant checks and counterchecks upon communist bureaucrats (Lenin 1966, 36:573–74). This idea struck a chord largely because it was, for the Chinese, already intuitively known. Indeed, it proved central to the founding debate of traditional Chinese statecraft, having been expounded upon by the ancient Legalists in their lengthy dispute with Confucianists. The Confucian tradition rejected regulation as inadequate. Good government, its proponents argued, emanated from virtuous souls (Confucius 1971, 146). For Legalists, government by virtuous souls was simply another means by which officials usurped the power of the sovereign. Virtue, they believed, flowed from punishment (Fu Zhengyuan 1996, 74).[36] Here, then, were two quite distinct cosmologies of government and a dispute within ancient Chinese political philosophy that spoke to the heart of contemporary radical concerns. Indeed, according to the radicals, Confucianism could be read as a "screen allegory" for reactionary politics and restorationist agendas in general (Hong Guangsi 1974, 42–45; Kang Li 1974, 54–57).

Nevertheless, while Confucianism could stand in for all forms of reactionary politics, Legalism, rendered by the radicals as the dominant ideology of the ancient landlord class, hardly constituted a suitable allegoric partner for Marxism. Certainly in comparison to Confucianism, Legalism was historically progressive and might even hint at the direction critique could take. As the radicals never tired of pointing out, however, it was "only the working class that could completely criticize and overcome Confucianism, for only they were the true revolutionary class that had no limitations on their criticism" (Hong Guangsi 1974, 42–45). Despite limitations, Legalism proved useful in "Sinicizing" Lenin's dictum that a strong state organized around a comprehensive dictatorship was needed to suppress opposition (Liang Xiao 1974, 127–31). It was, however, only with the addition of the Marxian notion of class struggle that such a strong state could halt restorationist agendas. With this additional line of argument, the radicals came full circle back to Marx and Lenin.

With the 1967 rejection of the good morals or good governance argument that was the commune model, the obvious conclusion to be drawn was the need for a strong, centralized state. Yet the history of failure that was Legalism's legacy also pointed to an anomaly.[37] Strong centralized states also required highly developed bureaucracies to administer them. How could one stop the degeneracy of that bureaucratic class that Legalism had failed to halt and Lenin failed to adequately address? The radicals' answer was more class struggle, and it was with this move that we discover them returning, once again, to the question of friends and enemies.

In the years that followed, their ideas developed further. In the process, the campaign that had centered upon the ancient dispute between Legalism and Confucianism was "translated" into the language of Marxism. This translation took place in 1975, and the new campaign was named the Campaign to Study an All-Round Dictatorship of the Proletariat. This new campaign reiterated similar sorts of arguments to those proffered in the earlier Campaign to Criticize Lin Biao and Confucius, but did so in the more familiar language of Marxism-Leninism. In other words, even though the terminology and categories had changed, the general concerns had not. Traditional Legalist concerns about a strong, centralized state were replaced by an equally strong and authoritarian notion of an all-round dictatorship, while the ancient concern about the parasitic scholar-gentry class became the basis of the radicals' concern about Party revisionists and restorationists. All would be remedied, it seemed, by an ongoing emphasis upon class struggle. Only this would solve the problem of class degeneration.

Beginning in early 1975 with two major articles written by the most influential and theoretically inclined of the radicals—Yao Wenyuan and Zhang Chunqiao—the Campaign to Study an All-Round Dictatorship heralded the most detailed mass investigation of the theoretical works of Marx and Lenin on the state ever undertaken. The study materials for this campaign turned on Lenin's claim that a strong proletarian dictatorship was necessary to halt a reversal of the socialist transition. Attention would turn to the issue of bourgeois right and the necessity of limiting it to achieve a halt to restoration. Much would be made of Lenin's critique of tendencies that could lead to the reversal of the proletarian victory. Lenin had, of course, said that "small-scale production engenders capitalism and the bourgeoisie continuously, daily, hourly, spontaneously, and on a mass scale" (Lenin 1966, 31:24). This, the radicals noted, demonstrated two things: First, that Mao had been correct to talk of socialism as a period of intense and continuous class struggle that could end in reactionary rule, and, second, that necessary but essentially capitalist forms of production operating within socialism could, if left unmonitored, engender bourgeois attitudes and values.

Marxism-Leninism had always assumed that socialism would be built on a high level of development of the productive forces. Socialist states would achieve this by building upon the productive forces inherited from capitalism. As Marx famously said—and the Chinese endlessly repeated—socialism "in every respect" is "still stamped with the birthmarks of the old society from whose womb it emerges." Because of this, what Marx referred to as bourgeois right would continue to exist under socialism. The private ownership of commodities, the circulation of money, as well as commodity production itself, all constituted essential preconditions of economic development. Unfortunately, they also constituted the means by which bourgeois right would be reasserted. What was needed was a means of ensuring that these things would continue to promote production but would not engender capitalism. What was needed was an all-round dictatorship and class struggle.

Thus, in 1975, the radicals began to emphasize the need to protect certain limited forms of bourgeois privilege and inequality so as to encourage production. At the same time, they needed to heavily restrict the overuse of such incentives, so that they would not develop into a capitalist restoration. To ensure that this balance between production and backsliding was maintained, rights would be restricted rather than eliminated. As with Legalism, the idea of a strong state offered the basic guarantee. The problem was that one is left guessing as to how the radicals would differentiate between which of the various bourgeois rights were necessary and which were unacceptable. More pragmatically, one is left guessing how they ever intended to police such divisions given their own rapidly declining influence in the security sector.

Under the period of military rule, radical influence in security matters spread from the ministry through to the grassroots with the dispatch of military officers to virtually every functioning police station. For the most part, this proved ineffective, for these military officers lacked both the numbers and the professional experience to make any impact. In the main, most army officers tended to divest themselves of as much policing responsibilities as they possibly could.[38] Into this void, the radicals tried to insert the local people's security organs of the revolutionary committees (interview 1995). These security organs, staffed by activists who were often ex-Red Guards, were strongly committed to the left political agenda. They carried out the local-level investigations into special cases, ensuring that the Cultural Revolution attack on revisionists and traitors would spread well beyond the confines of government agencies into every town and village (interviews 1995–1996). While they combined the authority of the public security units, the procuraturate, and the courts, they were less interested in maintaining social order than in keeping alive a high degree of political intensity. In this respect, they were not law enforcement officers but campaign instigators. These organs were powerful, however, only while they had army support.

With the fall of Lin Biao, the withdrawal of the military from policing, and the rehabilitation of the old police and Ministry of Public Security cadres, this was no longer the situation. Increasingly, the arguments proffered about the need for a professional and specialized police force began to gain ground and, as they did, the weakness of the radicals' position became increasingly clear. Nowhere did their weakness become more visible than at the national discussion meeting of Public Security Bureau chiefs that the radicals convened between June 14 and July 2, 1976. Shi Yizhi made the running for the radicals (confidential material 1977).

The key question for the radicals was the first one posed by Shi: "Who are our enemies and who are our friends?" he asked,[39] and by the time he returned to the public security leadership meeting to give his closing address, this distinction and the way to address it had become the body of his speech. Entitled "Toward a Dictatorship of Capitalist Roaders," Shi's speech laid out the radical agenda: "The capitalist class has entered the ranks of the Communist Party, and the organs of the dictatorship have a new special function. . . . It is necessary that this judgment becomes our guiding principle and that the special function [of the police] will be to research the current enemies' activity, determine what rules it makes, combine our experiences, and use these to gradually strengthen our struggle against them" (Gong'an Jiianshi).

Here was a program of action reliant upon a police force that for the most part, had only recently returned from exile after the last radical call to action against revisionism. Now the radicals were again attempting to make this the national agenda. This time, however, senior police knew what was coming. Delegates refused to endorse this radical agenda, and the newly installed Minister of Public Security, Hua Guofeng, made sure that it never came into effect. Power was slipping from the radicals, and this meeting would do little other than highlight this fact. Right pragmatism, it seems, was about to have its day in the sun.

The Pragmatists of the Party Right: From the Tian'anmen Incident to the Fall of the "Gang"

As the 1970s progressed, the Party right began to reassert itself. In the area of public security, they would effectively build on the lacuna left by the abject failure of the military model and the lack of an effective radical left alternative to that model. The military model of policing was increasingly shown to be a failure, and it was only the political power of Lin Biao that had ensured its survival. The problem for the radicals was that any withdrawal of military personnel from the ministry now meant the gradual return of those police officials whom the radicals had earlier purged and banished. On July 9, 1972, the Central Committee made this recall from banishment official. The banished police cadres would return to their old posts, replacing a military rule that had "provided a historic role and should now be wound up" (confidential material 1988). The return of the old cadres was slow, but, by 1975, it was complete (confidential material 1988).

The call for a return of these old cadres was, in part, a pragmatic recognition of the fact that policing did require specialist skills the army demonstrably lacked. A whole string of internal reports and events that began to emerge at this time effectively underlined the failure of the military-run security service. These reports told of shocking abuses of power and lamentable failures of leadership. In effect, these reports highlighted the fact that under military control, the policing of the social order had all but collapsed. Low crime figures merely reflected the collapse of police research units in charge of compiling them. The figures available were ridiculously low. Such a low number of cases at a time subsequently described as the third high tide of crime suggested serious problems in the policing domain (Yu Lei 1993, 42).[40] This was underlined by the fact that as crime rates grew, cleanup rates dropped precipitously. By the early 1970s, cleanup rates for common crimes dropped to a little over 50 percent, and this was despite the most draconian measures being employed to extract confessions and detain suspects.[41]

With politics in command, however, the only cleanup rate of interest to the left related to political crimes. In relation to these, the military had been quite successful in producing a massive penal Gulag based on arbitrary arrests and punishment. Incomplete ministerial statistics from twenty-five provinces in early 1972 indicated the nature of the problem. Of the 846,000 people estimated to be in detention at this time, many places detained up to half of these without ever laying charges (confidential material 1988). Once detained, the prisoners faced a constant diet of beatings, torture, and general neglect. Things even reached the point whereby Mao Zedong would be shocked by the treatment being meted out.

On December 18, 1972, Mao commented on letters he had received from the wives of Liu Jianzhang and Liu Shuqing that complained about conditions in Beijing's notorious Qincheng prison. In his comments on these conditions, Mao said: "This is a type of fascist investigative mode, who was the person or persons responsible for this? No matter who it is, this must be stopped." It was Zhou Enlai who would take up this issue as a stick with which to beat the left. On the very day Mao spoke, Zhou acted. He demanded that such practices be immediately stopped and then said: "All these fascist methods, torture techniques, and bashings mentioned by the Chairman must be brought to the surface, and they must be publicly repudiated. From now on, all arrested criminals must have their arrests publicly announced. If criminals are brought in, they are to be punished in accordance with the law, but we must permit them the right of defense" (confidential material 1988). Further research revealed that such bashings, abuse, and torture of detained criminals were commonplace. In addition, it was discovered that prisoners were being starved, refused water, given little or no exercise, and forced to endure grossly unhygienic conditions in inadequate clothing (confidential material 1988). Drawing on such findings and on the disgust of the Chairman, Zhou called for an increase in the pace of pardons handed out to exiled professional police.

In addition to this, Zhou further strengthened his argument by pointing to the adverse effects of bad policing upon economic development. He pointed to the regrettable state of public order on the railways, the high numbers of accidents on trains, and the chaos that reigned in an industry described as "an artery of our national economy" (confidential material 1988). Through such arguments, he succeeded in having many former rightists rehabilitated, including the former number two capitalist roader, Deng Xiaoping, who was put in charge of dealing with crime on the railways. Thus, while Party radicals pursued highly publicized but essentially confusing politico-educational campaigns or abstractly railed against the specter of a new bourgeoisie within the Party, the moderates offered a series of pragmatically based, concrete strategies that related to specific problems in need of address. The left's plans began failing because they were unable to generate the necessary degree of political intensity through abstract populist campaigns around theories of the state. The death of Zhou Enlai changed all that. Political intensity would return, but not quite in the way the left had anticipated.

On January 8, 1976, the cancer that had incapacitated Zhou for over a year finally took his life. China went into mourning. His funeral on January 15 also functioned as the last public appearance of Deng Xiaoping, who, with the death of his mentor, immediately fell victim to the political machinations of his radical enemies. Rumors abounded of a last will and testament of Zhou Enlai, and despite radical attempts to silence such rumors, they persisted. By the end of March, huge crowds amassed to lay wreaths at the foot of the Monument to the People's Heroes in Tian'anmen Square to commemorate Zhou's death. This was around the time of the traditional Qing Ming festival when Chinese mourn their dead. It was also the time when the all-round dictatorship could be used by the left to silence such tributes, which they read as political attacks on them. Plainclothes police were therefore sent into the square to track people back to their work units, take pictures, record what was being said, and take down car registration numbers in preparation for a campaign about to be launched against participants.

By April 4, the day before the Qing Ming festival, the left was ready to act. On the evening of that day, 50,000 militia, 3,000 police, and 5 battalions of garrison troops were sent to Tian'anmen Square to suppress the mourners, who were now labeled counter-revolutionaries. So began what was later to take the name the "April Fifth Movement." Apart from suppressing those in the square, the left also acted against so-called rumor mongers who continued to speak of the last will and testament of Zhou Enlai. On April 1, the Ministry of Public Security produced "A Notice Concerning the Investigation into the Unfounded Counter-Revolutionary Rumors about the So-Called Premier's Bequeathment Letter." In this notice, the ministry called upon the Party to criticize "the right-wing reversal of verdicts" and demanded that a campaign against counter-revolutionary rumor mongering begin. As this campaign advanced, the number of victims grew. By May 13, some 236,600 counter-revolutionary rumor-mongering handbills had been confiscated and 1,662 people detained. In addition, a further 390 people were arrested on criminal charges (confidential material 1988).

While police went through the false rumors, the radicals attacked the mourners. One of the key radicals, Wang Hongwen, suggested that the "five bad elements" of landlords, rich peasants, counter-revolutionaries, bad people, and rightists were all strongly represented among Zhou's mourners. The leaders of these mourners, however, were said to be the "capitalist roader factions" within the Party. A new campaign to implement a dictatorship over these capitalist roaders was, therefore, launched, with Deng Xiaoping as its main target. Within the Ministry of Public Security, it was the radical Deputy Minister Shi Yizhi who would lead this charge at the previously mentioned national discussion meeting of Public Security Bureau chiefs. It would begin as a radical charge and lead, ultimately, to a routing of the left. But it was not the power of the right that would halt the radicals in their tracks. Fate, too, played its part.

While the beginning of July 1975 focused national attention upon the counter-revolutionary enemy within, by month's end, it was nature and not politics that preoccupied police, Party, and nation. The city of Tangshan had been flattened by an earthquake that left 200,000 people dead and millions injured and homeless. At a time when the Tangshan relief work was said to be grossly inadequate, the radical leaders' obsession with the political continued. Utilizing their control over the media, they exhorted earthquake survivors to continue the political campaign against Deng Xiaoping and other capitalist roaders (Meisner 1986, 426). As the rubble of Tangshan was cleared away, the creaking edifice of the all-round dictatorship remained only as long as Mao drew breath. When he breathed no more, the final flickers from the radical flame died with him.

Mao died on September 9, 1976. His wife barely made it to the funeral. On October 6, the Gang of Four, as Jiang Qing, Wang Hongwen, Zhang Chunqiao, and Yao Wenyuan were now being called, were quietly arrested as counter-revolutionaries. Their few remaining supporters tried a forlorn, last-ditch stand in Shanghai, having been tipped off about the secret arrest of the "Gang" by Zhu Jiayao on October 8. By November 20, the Ministry of Public Security convened a meeting of all its staff to pass on instructions from the new Central Committee. The next police campaign was to be one to expose and criticize the crimes of the "Gang." The ministry set up a special office to check and counter the things the Gang of Four had done to usurp Party power and to begin an investigation into the people they had promoted (confidential material 1988). After their long period of banishment in Heilongjiang and the constant fear that they would be sent back there, this was a task police would undertake with relish.

Conclusion

It is an oft-employed tactic of scholarship on the Cultural Revolution to treat the transition from the apparent anarchism of the Shanghai Commune to the Stalinism of the all-round dictatorship as little other than a ruse to hide (rather than guide) the personal leadership ambitions of those in power. At best, this shift in thinking is read as leading to a cynical act of betrayal of a noble revolutionary goal. At its most severe, this change is presented as evidence of a cynical leadership ploy, a smoke screen hiding naked ambition from the very start. While neither of these readings is without supporting evidence, neither is totally convincing either. Through reading this historical trajectory from what appears to be the anarchism of the Shanghai Commune through to the all-too-obvious Stalinism of the all-round dictatorship in terms of the policing of Chinese politics, one gains a slightly different appreciation of events. For me, this transition to Stalinism was simply another example of the very best of revolutionary intentions leading to the very worst of results. Once again, the combination of groping for a solution coupled with a heightened intensity brought on by the political distinction of friend and enemy proved to be a potent combination that fueled the tanks of those traveling down the road to Cultural Revolution. That this pathway led to a heightened sense of the mass-line, and to the most extensive and detailed critique of Party revisionism yet seen, seems hard to reconcile with its later incarnation as a movement of Party consolidation that led to a (Stalinist) "all-round dictatorship." Certainly, the Cultural Revolution appeared to be going somewhere else when it first drew breath.

Back in 1955, when a different kind of cadre error was being revealed through the "internal" suppression of counter-revolutionaries campaign, the ongoing and recurrent problem of vertical leadership, and therefore

"Stalinism," that plagued that campaign seemed to suggest the need for a more mass-based form of surveillance and policing. The later Fengqiao model appears to have initially offered something of a solution to this problem and to that of recalcitrants. While Fengqiao provided a more libertarian approach to mass-line policing, problems would remain. After all, within a few short years, the problem of revisionism would grow, and as it did, calls for an extension and deepening of class struggle would also develop. Under these circumstances, when a new form of revisionism led some to "doubt everything," how would a local, mass-line form of libertarianism offer an adequate means to deal with this new and more insidious threat?

Fengqiao was a mass dictatorship that operated without the usual populist and politically intense edge. It pioneered retraining techniques such as social help and education and simultaneously gave the children of the four black categories a chance to work toward a new life (PSHM 1994:2, V32, 108–10). This was the solution Fengqiao held out. Yet it was a soft solution always threatened by the intensity that would follow any revivification of class struggle. After all, how could one not respond more harshly when the friend/enemy distinction had become more pronounced and when enmity was being felt more intensely? Surely this was the key weakness of the Fengqiao community model? With one eye on the general political picture at the time and another on the weaknesses of Fengqiao, one begins to note some striking parallels.

When Mao Zedong told Zhang Chunqiao in February 1967 that communes were too weak when it came to the suppression of counter-revolutionaries, he was speaking of the Shanghai experiment. He could just as easily have been talking about Fengqiao. It was only after these remarks (in early 1967) that the Fengqiao model was abandoned (PSHM 1994:2, V32, 103).[42] When the dominant attitude turns away from rehabilitation and reform toward "killing the unrepentant capitalist roaders," is it any wonder that the Fengqiao model ends up being denounced as "an umbrella protecting snakes and monsters"? (PSHM 1994:2, V34, 109). Little wonder, too, that with the emphasis placed upon armed struggle, it would be a more visceral and dictatorial version of the mass-line that would emerge alongside class struggle and not the reintegrative shaming model of Fengqiao.

This was the time of the Red Guards. Their youthful vigor, their loyalty to Mao, and their combative version of the mass-line offered a means to combat the tired, complacent, and ultimately revisionist Party. Very quickly, however, their strengths came to be regarded as weaknesses. That they were not tied to the structure of the state may have freed them from claims of revisionism, but it also meant they lacked an understanding of the subtleties of power. That they operated solely on the basis of loyalty to a distant Chairman meant that their loyalty took on an almost religious zeal, yet lacked any basis upon which to build unity and discipline. As a result, it quickly descended into infighting. This was hardly the force that could ensure the unitary national character of security when the Ministry of Public Security was "smashed to a pulp." As in the past, when faced with crisis, the only force that could simultaneously hold a gun in its hand and still have the power of Mao Zedong Thought in its head was the army. It was to this force that the radical leadership of the Cultural Revolution group would turn in order to maintain a semblance of unity and order. Far from being a cynical betrayal, however, this transition to an army takeover of the security organs appears as little other than the logical outcome of a series of linked arguments concerned less with means than with ends. Moreover, employing the army in this way was far from heretical, new, or novel. Indeed, it was classical Mao.

Back in the early days of Yan'an, and with the excesses of the Jiangxi Soviet still very much on people's minds, the army had offered tutelage to the discredited security forces. In those early days in Yan'an, it was the army that supplied the security forces with a new organizational structure and a suitable model to emulate. Learning a mass-line approach from the military and adopting a shadow Party committee structure to give it leadership, the security forces would again take up the leading role of protecting the internal security of the base camp areas and the Party. Clearly, the Cultural Revolution was not Yan'an, but the memories of the models employed there still played a role in orienting political concerns. With the political decline of the left military model, but an ongoing need to suppress revisionism, an alternative to this Yan'an military model was needed. As I have suggested, that would take many years to develop and would move the policing of Chinese politics well away from the security forces. From early attempts to explore traditional Chinese state theory, the radicals eventually arrived at an "all-round dictatorship of the proletariat." This offered a new model of state that centered upon Maoist ideas of continuous revolution, the mass-line, and class struggle all being deployed to combat revisionism. It may not have been a pretty sight, but there can be little doubt that it addressed the types of practical and theoretical issues that spawned the Cultural Revolution. Yet while the radicals burrowed away with their Stalinist alternative, the harshness of their model was beginning to lead even Mao to rebuke them. More than any other, it was Zhou Enlai who was responsible for transforming Mao's critique of the radicals' "fascism" into a call for greater levels of pragmatism and professionalism. As the excesses of the penal system were revealed, the inadequacies of military policing became apparent. The result was that in the shadows of radicalism, an alternative vision of public security was beginning to take shape.

This would emerge most definitively in the rather modestly configured campaign model adopted by Deng Xiaoping in 1975 when he was put in charge of solving the problem of crime on trains. To deal with this problem, Deng would redraw the revolutionary map and put pragmatism center stage. In Deng's campaign, one would not hear of abstract ideas like all-round dictatorship or continuous revolution. Instead, his campaign would result in bodies arrested and threats overcome. This pragmatic and concrete redrawing of the Maoist political campaign would become a model for policing in the early days of economic reform. It would provide a transitional model that pointed back to a memory of Mao and revolution, but which simultaneously stripped this model of any political intensity. It is in this decoupling of policing and the political that Deng's maneuvers hint at a new understanding of the political. They mark, at the very least, the end of the policing of Chinese politics through the security forces. It is how this decoupling of police and the political is achieved that will, in fact, be the focus of the next chapter.

5 The End of the (Mass) Line?

CHINESE POLICING IN THE ERA OF THE CONTRACT

The Roman slave was held by fetters: the wage-labourer is bound
by his own invisible threads. The appearance of independence is kept
up by means of a constant change of employers, and the *ficto juris*
of a contract. — KARL MARX

In our country, we are establishing legal views on the commodity
economy, and these help us reflect upon traditional legal theories and
legal systems. . . . The system of the contract (*qiyue zhidu*) is the most appropriate legal shell for the commodity economy. It clears away blockages
in personal relationships caused by status-based evaluations that are
formed because of low or high evaluations of bloodlines and pushes forward a process that releases the great capabilities of the society's productive forces. It also leads to a renewal of legal concepts and turns law into a
"holy writ of human freedom." — KONG LIN AND ZHANG WEIGUO

TIMELINE 1978–2002

Date	Politics	Police
1978	**December:** Third plenary session of the Eleventh Central Committee of the Communist Party; Deng Xiaoping replaces Hua Guofeng as China's paramount leader Economic reform begins	
1979		Eight organs called on to solve the problem of juvenile crime
1980		PRC Criminal Code comes into effect
1981		**May:** The five cities of Beijing, Tianjin, Shanghai, Guangzhou, and Wuhan convene a security conference and put in place comprehensive management **August:** First Severe Strike Campaign starts
1983	**December:** Anti-spiritual pollution campaign starts	

Date	Politics	Police
1984	State Council issues "Temporary Regulations on Residency Identity Card in PRC"	**January:** Second Severe Strike Campaign starts Implementation of the residency identity card system China becomes a member of Interpol
1985		Police city patrols begin First private security company set up in Shenzhen
1986		**January:** 110 emergency number system begins **March–October:** Third Severe Strike Campaign **October:** Reform of traffic policing commences
1989	**June 4:** Tian'anmen Incident	Campaign to Eliminate the Six Evils
1992	Deng Xiaoping undertakes southern tour and launches the consumer revolution in China	

Date	Politics	Police
1994		PRC Prison Code comes into effect
1995		Police Law comes into effect
1996		Abolition of shelter and investigation centers
		New Severe Strike Campaign launched
1997		Revised Criminal Code comes into effect
1999		Falungong religious sect banned and repressed
2000	**February:** Jiang Zemin's "three represents" first raised	
2001		New Severe Strike Campaign launched
2002	**November:** Sixteenth Party Congress	

From the Political to the Economic

IN DECEMBER 1978, China's new party chairman, Hua Guofeng, announced to the world that "large-scale, turbulent class struggles of a mass character have, in the main, come to an end" (*Peking Review*, December 29, 1978, 11). While this did not quite flag a leap back in time, the repetition of Mao's famous dictum from 1957 did, at least, capture something of the desire within Hua and the party to clothe their radical policy changes in the garb of the fifties and the uniform of Mao. Indeed, even Hua's radically heterodox economic program—which involved wholesale borrowing from the West—would be dubbed the "Foreign Leap" as a way of genuflecting and linking his project back to that other "Great Leap" undertaken by that other Chairman back in the fifties.

This is not the place to rehearse these events nor tell of Chairman Hua's personal attempts to look, sound, and act more like Chairman Mao than the old Chairman himself. What is important to highlight, however, is the way that these shifts in politics and policy began to depoliticize society. With economics in command, the intensely felt and lived dyadic politics of Mao began to give way to a very different way of life, with quite discrete practices operating in different domains. Under these conditions, the policing of the political dyad by security forces slowly gave way to law enforcement, just as the friend/enemy binary gave way to the legal/illegal distinction.

Paradoxically, it was the radical left that made much of this depoliticization possible. Not only did they create a climate of political exhaustion that more or less necessitated a new mode of mobilizing the masses but, with the notion of an all-round dictatorship, they also provided the means to achieve this change. The all-round dictatorship strengthened notions of state sovereignty but ceded it to the Chairman. Had Hua not inherited this highly authoritarian rendition of state sovereignty, the policy changes that followed would have been unimaginable. The irony is, of course, that the political purge of the radical Gang of Four was facilitated because of the sovereign powers vested in both Party and Chairman by this notion of an all-round dictatorship. Once Party and Chairman turned against the Gang, however, the all-round dictatorship did its job.

At the same time, the Party "moderates" and Hua could employ the power of this all-round dictatorship without being identified with its creation. Hua benefited by using its power against the Gang, but was simultaneously viewed as having liberated China from it by the purge of the Gang. Moreover, once the Gang had been arrested, the Party then used its dictatorial powers to pursue a nationwide political campaign against them. This would constitute the last major state-initiated eruption of mass-based "class struggle" in China. It would be conducted with such cathartic intensity that it would produce a popular feeling of liberation and willingness to experiment with very different renditions of socialism far removed from a valorized notion of class struggle promoted by the Gang of Four. The arrest of the Gang, therefore, produced another shift in the tectonic plates of state. This was the movement away from state legitimation based upon the operation of the political dyad to one in which economy and development held center stage. This return of the economic was facilitated by the language and logic of orthodox Marxism. This change could, therefore, be rendered as a return to Marxism after years of error and exaggeration.

Through the careful deployment of the language of Marxism, the initial moves away from the political, therefore, appeared as little more than a restatement of an orthodoxy swept away by the radical but false prophets of Marxism, the Gang of Four. Their anthropomorphically driven notion of class struggle was politically charged because it produced and reproduced living enemies. Under Hua, and later and more elaborately under Deng Xiaoping, class struggle would be transformed into a struggle against nature. Indeed, it was this that would end up forming the basis upon which Jiang Zemin developed the first of his "three represents" of the Party.[1] With class struggle reconfigured in this way, the modernization drive unleashed by Hua and developed by Deng became central to the Party's new rendition of struggle and its conception of Marxism.

At the same time, ways had to be found to halt the redevelopment of political intensity. The Communist Party did this by mimetically reconfiguring all potential political eruptions into agonal forms before they could become intense. If economic reform could reconfigure Marxism to once again highlight economic concerns, political reform would mimetically transform potentially intense political events into more limited and agonal forms. Hence, in 1983, when the struggle against spiritual pollution emerged as a potentially decisive political issue, it was quickly transformed from a potential passion play into a morality lesson. Its potential passion derived not from the fact that it campaigned against a version of Marxism that was humanist and existentialist, or even because it attempted to combat various expressions of bourgeois values on the streets. It was potentially passionate because the anti-spiritual pollution campaign worked against particular renditions of personhood that were concrete, empirical, and lived. From women's makeup through to fashion and on to lifestyles and belief systems, spiritual pollution was said to be gnawing away at the fabric of Chinese socialism. In acting against such telltale signs of pollution, the Party once again saw itself threatened with an intensification of class politics. In response, the Party changed its rhetoric and mimetically transformed the nature of the anti-spiritual pollution campaign.

Shifting from a stress on the eradication of pollutants to one that emphasized civilization produced a new type of campaign. No longer would bourgeois dress be attacked on the streets anymore than attacks on humanism would give rise to mass action. Instead, moral education would be stressed. This change of rhetoric dissipated the power of street-level attacks and promoted a new moral pedagogy. If state-sponsored violence continued in any way in the reform period, it took the form of the "severe strike" against criminals and turned not on the division between friend and enemy but on the social divide between the legal and the illegal. Such, then, was the power of this mimetic revolution that all signs of intensity could be dissipated or corralled into legal forms. It is this power of the mimetic that one finds employed time and again in China as the economic reform agenda ratcheted down any signs of political intensity.

"[T]he illusion of mimetic power adorns objects with a value that is not their own," writes Bruno Latour (1993, 45), and if this is employed to inform an examination of the tactics of reform, one discovers that in these small mimetic transformations a different type of politics was being articulated. Indeed, the first signs of this emerged in embryonic form even before Mao's death. It was Deng Xiaoping who would be the architect of this transformation. As far back as 1975, Deng had devised a means of surreptitiously moderating key elements of the radical left political agenda by reconfiguring their concerns into a limited and pragmatic form of struggle. In effect, he would transform an overtly political campaign against counterrevolutionaries on trains into a law-and-order campaign. He did this by mimicking and reworking the Maoist campaign—a key "revolutionary" technique of the continuous revolution—so that it could be employed in this concrete, pragmatic, and limited way.

It was the dramatic increase in crime on trains in 1975 that occasioned the employment of this tactic of mimesis. Faced with this crime problem, the Party demanded action and it was Deng who came up with a workable solution. He transformed the language and largesse of the Maoist mass movement into the discrete and pragmatic anticrime campaign.[2] In this seemingly innocuous move, Deng mimetically transformed the campaign—a key pedagogical, mobilizational, and disciplinary device of Mao's theory of continuous revolution—into a simple, punitive, and pragmatic tool of policing. It proved a stroke of tactical brilliance, for it enabled Deng to both pay homage to Mao and the revolution and simultaneously transformed the intrinsic meaning of the Maoist mass-line in a way that made it more pragmatic than "revolutionary."

In a series of moves that reversed the uncanny revolutionary techniques first pioneered by Mao in Yan'an, Deng set about to tactically transform the revolutionary into the utilitarian by a process of mimesis. In the Yan'an era, the revolutionary was carved out of local traditions by a series of sly subversions. Hence familiar traditional folk songs were transformed into revolutionary anthems by the substitution of lyric lines, or traditional Chinese operatic forms were pressed into the service of a revolutionary plot line. Here was an example of the Freudian uncanny at work in the interests of revolution. In the case of folk music, the tunes remained intact and, therefore, eerily familiar. It was the change in lyrics that led to them becoming "estranged." The result of this uncanny process was a revolution one could sing to! Yet if Mao's revolutionary techniques turned on producing this uncanny effect, Deng's revisionism played on an absolute reversal of this process.

Through mimesis, Deng replaced the revolutionary content of the political campaign with one that proved more pragmatic and manageable. He would, nevertheless, leave the political shell intact and thereby disguise his political deviation by making his new content fit into an utterly familiar form. To affect this type of pragmatic change, Deng needed to miniaturize the Maoist campaign model so that it became concerned only with achievable goals. By doing this, the grandiose was made simple. He would thereby jettison the heavily didactic and politico-ideological component of the campaign and thus turn the utopian into the functional. He would also lay the groundwork for a ratcheting down of the political by hinting at the possibility that the friend/enemy division was nothing other than the divide between the legal and the illegal. By the time of economic reform, Deng could add even more radical innovations to his repertoire of revisionism. With the spiritual pollution campaign we see this process at work once again. As significant as that campaign may have been, by far the greatest conjuring trick of Deng Xiaoping was to, quite literally, put the key political structure of the Maoist state, the mass-line, on a contractual basis. In so doing, he changed the nature of campaigning and mass-line politics forever. Without wishing to reduce the state to its economic program, it was in developing this contractual form of mass-line policing that China witnessed the dawn of a new and very different era. Contractualization spoke not just of the reform of the police but to the heart of the reform process. It enables us to understand how the economic reform era continues to limit the political while still finding a means by which to enthuse the masses. It is the monetarization of society in general, and policing in particular, that proves central to this process, and it is for this reason that I have "bent the stick" and focused almost entirely upon the contractualization of policing and its significance.

Money Talks

Police, or, at the very least, the now familiar Western concept of them as law enforcement agencies, only began to arrive at the scene of the crime in China after economic reform.[3] From this time onward, police increasingly claimed to be operating on the basis of the law, not Party dictates. The problem was that as the Party dictatorship faded, the police sirens no longer seemed to stir the masses to action. Increasingly, it appeared as though the only thing that would open the eyes of the people was money (*jianqian yankai*). Nor was this attitude confined solely to the urban populace. As the old Maoist slogan about the forward march of socialism (*yiqie xiangqiankan*) was parodied and replaced by a new colloquial expression that spoke of the forward march of money,[4] millions of peasants packed their bags and marched to the city in search of work and wealth. Some found it, but others lost their way. Those who were the losers, aptly named the "floating blind" (*mangliu*), became the rabble from which emerged the urban fear of a new, mobile, and dangerous criminal class.[5] While this transient or mobile criminal group would remain one of the most intractable problems facing contemporary China, it was far from being the only one. Indeed, it was as though market reform had, quite literally, produced its nemesis—criminal reform.

New crimes began to emerge just as old ones, long considered vanquished, reappeared. Moreover, all crimes, new and old, appeared in unprecedented numbers. The market not only produced a new moneymaking ethos and new social mobility but brought in its wake a dangerous and paradoxical situation: crime figures would rise just as the old social control structures fell. These latter structures would begin to crumble because they had been built upon the political activism of local, Maoist-inspired massline organs and been kept in place by a tight system of demographic policing organized around the household register. This system had worked well in the era of the plan, but it would prove far less successful in the depoliticized and fluid conditions produced by China's new marketized economy. From the pull of the cities, with their need for labor, through to the tug of a newly monetarized economy, with its fetishization of material things, reform produced a new demographic and social mobility that eroded the old Maoist social structures and the ideological certainties upon which they were built.

No longer could China claim to be the land where "no one picked up others' things from the road and no one needed to lock their door" (*lubushiyi, yebubihu*). Instead, it turned into the land of crime waves where the new high tide of crime (*gaofeng*) seemed never to recede (see table 4).[6] Little wonder, then, that this new and quite unprecedented wave of crime occasioned something of a social panic, which, in turn, led to calls by Party and government officials for a reform of policing.[7] Hence, just as the Great Leap had called forth its own "Great Leap in Policing," economic reform now demanded its own version of police reform. And just like the Great Leap initiatives of the police, this new period of police reform would closely follow the

Table 4. The Number of Criminal Cases Opened and Solved

Year	Total Pop.	Cases Opened	Cases Solved	Crime Rate (per 100,000 people)
1950	551,960,000	513,461	361,477 (70.4%)	93
1951	563,000,000	332,741	258,207 (77.6%)	59
1952	574,820,000	243,003	162,326 (66.8%)	42
1953	587,960,000	292,308	130,077 (44.5%)	50
1954	602,660,000	392,229	260,048 (66.3%)	65
1955	614,650,000	325,829	192,565 (59.1%)	53
1956	628,280,000	180,075	119,210 (66.2%)	29
1957	646,530,000	298,031	211,304 (70.9%)	46
1958	659,940,000	211,068	197,771 (93.7%)	32
1959	672,070,000	210,025	204,774 (97.5%)	31
1960	662,070,000	222,734	201,574 (90.5%)	34
1961	658,590,000	421,934	330,796 (78.3%)	64
1962	672,950,000	324,639	n/a	62
1963	691,720,000	251,226	199,473 (79.4%)	36
1964	704,990,000	215,352	167,514 (77.8%)	31
1965	725,380,000	216,215	142,378 (65.9%)	30
1966	742,060,000	174,678	107,021 (61.3%)	24
1967	760,320,000	161,377	64,520 (40%)	21
1968	781,980,000	165,820	69,882 (42%)	21
1969	803,350,000	195,691	74,736 (38.2%)	24
1970	825,420,000	230,040	107,181 (46.6%)	28
1971	847,790,000	323,623	149,201 (46%)	38
1972	867,270,000	402,573	218,228 (54.2%)	46
1973	887,610,000	535,829	340,641 (63.6%)	60
1974	904,090,000	516,419	337,372 (65.3%)	57
1975	919,700,000	475,432	327,345 (68.9%)	52
1976	932,670,000	488,813	317,258 (65%)	52
1977	945,240,000	548,415	400,132 (73%)	58
1978	958,090,000	535,698	385,782 (72%)	56
1979	970,920,000	636,222	439,696 (69%)	66
1980	982,560,000	757,104	538,425 (71%)	77
1981	1,000,720,000	890,281	650,874 (73%)	89
1982	1,016,540,000	748,476	579,039 (77.4%)	74
1983	1,030,080,000	610,478	431,292 (70.7%)	60
1984	1,043,570,000	514,369	395,550 (76.9%)	50
1985	1,041,084,298	542,005	427,100 (78.8%)	52

Table 4. (continued)

Year	Total Pop.	Cases Opened	Cases Solved	Crime Rate (per 100,000 people)
1986	1,053,972,907	547,115	433,315 (79.2%)	52
1987	1,069,164,090	570,439	463,767 (81.3%)	53
1988	1,086,540,493	827,594	624,833 (75.5%)	76
1989	1,103,560,506	1,971,901	1,111,166 (56.4%)	179
1990	1,129,543,033	2,216,997	1,265,240 (57.07%)	196
1991	1,141,907,793	2,365,709	1,460,622 (61.7%)	207
1992	1,152,428,217	1,582,659	1,079,517 (68.2%)	137
1993	1,162,765,740	1,616,879	1,211,888 (75%)	139
1994	1,173,537,000	1,660,734	1,298,005 (78.2%)	142
1995	1,184,676,966	1,690,407	1,350,159 (79.9%)	143
1996	1,195,462,742	1,600,716	1,279,097 (79.9%)	134
1997	1,205,826,819	1,613,629	1,172,214 (72.6%)	134
1998	1,214,980,875	1,986,068	1,264,635 (63.7%)	163
1999	1,224,915,376	2,249,319	1,375,109 (61.1%)	184
2000	1,236,722,424	3,637,307	1,644,094 (45.2%)	294

Sources: The 1950–80 figures of total population, cases opened, and partial indication of crime rates are drawn from Wang Zhimin and Huang Jingping 1992, 49–67. Figures on cases solved for 1950 until 1981 are drawn from confidential material 1986. The 1981–2000 figures are based on volumes of the *Law Yearbook* (1987–2001), except for the 1981–84 figures of total population, which are drawn from *China Population Statistics Yearbook* 1993, 352.

contours of the main social agenda, which was now economic reform. This meant that the politico-moral methods once used under Mao to improve police performance would give way to a series of money-based bonus systems, responsibility systems, and other contractual arrangements favored by Deng Xiaoping. In terms of content, reform would bring forth the rhetoric of professionalization, specialization, and adherence to the law. The trouble was, as we shall see, the methods used to improve performance, namely, the monetarized reward system, would end up driving the professionalization, specialization, and respect-for-the-law agenda off course.

Publicly, of course, the Chinese police admitted no such conflict between form and content. Instead, the professionalism, specialization, and adherence to the law of the new police reform agenda would be highlighted. Much would be made of the new police academies and the new professional specialist courses. Much was also made of the fact that formally taboo disciplinary areas, such as Western criminology, criminal psychology, and the rule of law were now being taught in these institutions.[8] On the streets, reform was said to have led to the adoption of a range of new policing techniques. From the institution of mobile police patrols to the adoption of the Japanese *koban* (pillbox) system, from the emphasis on forensics to the promotion and spread of the 110 emergency number system, the Chinese public security forces appeared to be following a reform program that drew heavily upon Western policing practices. Taken together, such reforms implied that the "open-door policy" was leading toward the adoption of a scientific discipline of law enforcement.[9] The Western concept of the police, it seems, had arrived in China.

Yet there was another side to this police story, one no less inspired by economic reform, but one which sent policing practices spiraling off in an entirely different direction. Rattled by rising crime rates and the gradual erosion of their once strict but static form of community control, the Chinese police opted for a partial revival of their political traditions. This included a more visceral and populist response to crime and, as this began to take shape, it came to shadow and problematize the process of professionalization, specialization, and rule of law promised in the rhetoric of scientific law enforcement.[10] Foremost among these more visceral and populist responses were the Maoist-inspired police campaigns and the so-called comprehensive management of social order.

While campaign-style policing emerged as a significant strategy in May 1981 after the Five-City Security Conference,[11] it was not until 1983, with the announcement of the first of the Severe Strike Campaigns against crime, that its full consequences became apparent (H. M. Tanner 1999, 72).[12] Leading to the arrest of over 1.5 million people overall, it would follow the traditional Maoist three-stage approach to campaigning perfected in the 1950 campaign against counter-revolutionaries (see tables 5 and 6; see also H. M. Tanner 1999, 83–104). This campaign, as well as subsequent ones, would adopt methods similar to those of the pre-reform period to deal with new problem crimes. This was not the only thing the police would borrow from the past. While campaign-style policing focused upon the short, sharp shock, the other significant innovation revisiting the socialist past was re-

Table 5. Results of an Investigation into the Handling of
Those Arrested during the First Severe Strike Campaign

Unit: People	Arrested	Reform through education	Youth reform	Public order penalties	Educated and released	Released from shelter and investigation	Total
First stage	696,144	126,851	4,392	77,903	14,933	143,507	1,063,730
Second stage	200,710	20,522	590	9,850	11,263	18,444	261,279
Third stage	127,911	19,466	916	7,682	3,315	19,012	178,302
Total	1,024,765	166,839	5,898	95,435	29,511	180,963	1,503,411

Source: Confidential interview material 1986.
Note: The figures listed above cover the period only to August 31, 1984. At that time, a further 27,000 arrests were made, but there has been no time to analyze these newer figures.

ferred to as the comprehensive management of social order (H. M. Tanner 1999, 66–72). Where this differed from the campaign was that it was said to offer a more lasting and reintegrative crime-fighting model. Thus while both campaigns and comprehensive management relied upon a wide range of local social forces coming together under the leadership of the Party and the police, the former focused on attacking crime, while the latter emphasized the longer-term goal of crime prevention and social reintegration.

This idea of comprehensive management emerged in June 1979 with a call from various organs for the Party to pay more attention to juvenile crime (Wang Zhongfang 1989, 8).[13] By the time of the 1981 Five-City Security Conference, comprehensive management was offered alongside campaign-style policing as a solution to the rising crime rates nationwide. Given that both comprehensive management and the police campaign relied upon the participation of community activists, they required not only the reemphasis of Party committee leadership (Dai Wendian 1991b, 253) but also the revival of the increasingly moribund mass-line security organs. It was with regard to the revival of the latter that the use of monetary incentives began to make its appearance within community policing. As this style of policing was revived, it almost inevitably bumped into the rhetoric of scientific law enforcement. With the strategic need to coordinate all social forces to effect campaigns and comprehensive management strategies, local Party

Table 6. Situation with Regard to Arrests Directly Emanating
from the First Severe Strike Campaign

	Arrested	Sent to re-education through labor	Sent to youth retraining centers	Criminal detention	Shelter and investigation	Total
First stage of campaign (Aug.–Dec. 1983)						
	269,279	29,839	954	50,124	732,655	1,082,851
Second stage of campaign (Jan.–March 1984)						
	186,589	15,893	393	12,043	57,446	272,364
Third stage of campaign (April–July 1984)						
	97,926	14,993	693	17,039	71,613	202,264
Total	553,794	60,725	2,040	79,206	861,714	1,557,479

Source: Confidential material.

committee leadership was once again thrust to the fore. This ran counter to the rhetoric of specialist and professional leadership and could, potentially, even challenge the rule of law. The rule of law, however, was to be challenged by these innovations in a more fundamental, subtle, and paradoxical way.

Mass-line organs, as products of the Mao era, had always and would always require a degree of legal elasticity in order to operate effectively, and this, quite obviously, was in conflict with the new and highly publicized commitment to the rule of law. Nevertheless, the revival of these organs did not signal a return to Mao, but rather the return of something anathema to his thinking, namely, the use of monetary, rather than political, incentives. Ironically, the revival of populist Maoist-inspired forms of organization in the reform years signaled the demise, rather than the rebirth, of left politics. It was this slow process of political and ideological drainage that would change the nature of mass mobilization in China forever. The new dynamic fueling the development of mass-line policing not only led to the diminution of politics but also, for the police, to a politics of dependence. Police reliance upon monetary incentives was to have its own hidden costs. The more the police employed financial incentives to bring back the mass-line, the less they could rely upon their old political ways of mobilization. In the end, the police were left with no options other than to allow the spread of monetary incentives throughout the entire policing system.

Police stations, police beats, even "snouts" were all put on contract. Mass-line organs would sell their household registration licenses to finance their own incentive schemes, just as police increasingly invoked fines to finance theirs. Even private policing was introduced, in part, to offer police a profitable sideline. Effectively, economic reform reshaped the nature of policing in China and fundamentally altered the basis upon which it would recruit, mobilize, and operate. It is at this point that one notices another side to the economic reform process. China has, in effect, become the land of the economic contract, and good social order has become the product that police are contracted to supply.

It was Max Weber who once insisted that the spread of money and market mentalities required law and the law of the contract (1978, 671–72). In terms of Chinese policing, what I want to argue is that the growth of the contract actually led to the revival of organs that, in quite important but modest ways, challenged substantive law. In other words, the rule of law would be seriously compromised by the expansion of the contract form when this form was used to resurrect paralegal organs and promote paralegal policing tactics. Economic reform produced not only the need for the rule of law but also the mechanisms that enabled its (partial) abnegation.

Economic Reform: From a Covenant of Grace to the Contract

The year 1978 was a turning point in China. In contrast to the single political covenant of Mao, the legitimacy of the economic reform era rested upon a multifaceted modernization program with a rhetoric of economic efficiency, and not politics, in command. Deng Xiaoping would, in this way, break up the unity of the friend/enemy distinction which had monopolized all discourse in post-1949 China. He would do so by introducing a series of economic changes that brought forth an endless array of localized contractual arrangements organized around the production of goods and services.

These would eventually become the hallmark of a new type of government in China. Indeed, it was these modest local-level contracts that would end up turning the logic of the economy into that of government.

Begun in 1978 with the announcement of the "responsibility system in agriculture," the economic reform agenda would soon spread to other domains. Indeed, as the economy filled with "responsibility systems," "bonus systems," and "contract systems" of various sorts, other, more socially orientated areas of life became infected with the language and logic of economic reform. Where once everything operated under the aegis of Mao, everything now, it seems, was put under contract. Where once Mao's covenant of grace with the people operated under the sign class struggle, in Deng's society of the contract, every new arrangement was signed with the word *economy*. Law was essential to this process, for without a strong legal code, there could be no contractualisation of the social and, without this, no new (materially based) incentive system (Kong Lin and Zhang Weiguo 1987, 6).

The foundation of the modern contract, as Sir Henry Sumner Maine had long ago argued, lay in the historic transition from family dependence to individual obligation (Maine, 1970, 168).[14] While the Chinese trajectory may be differently configured, it is similarly inspired. The desire to replace the Maoist-induced collective dependence upon the politicized state with a notion of rationally calculable individual obligation was central to Deng's reform program. It was the contractually based notion of individual obligation that fueled China's economic reform program and, as a result, the development of a substantive legal code would, by necessity, become an essential component of this process. It is, after all, through law that contracts are made legally enforceable (Weber 1978, 669).

In the China of Chairman Mao, there was neither individual obligation nor a commitment to substantive law. Indeed, as the Chinese press in the time of Mao made clear, any discussion of law presupposed the centrality of legal elasticity.[15] Without such legal flexibility, everything from the mass dictatorship of the fifties through to the all-round dictatorship of the seventies would have proven impossible. Legal elasticity was the hallmark of both the Maoist-style continuous revolution, as well as his campaign style of political life. Little wonder, then, that the much-vaunted criminal code circulating within Party ranks from 1954 until the early months of 1957 was never ratified and fell victim to what later Chinese scholarship would describe as Mao's legal nihilism (He Qinhua 1991, 3). China under Mao was ruled by generalized, publicly promulgated regulations, specific and detailed internal Party edicts, and *People's Daily* editorials and commentaries. The land that produced a political "covenant of grace" and thereby unified the people and their leader also promoted a form of governance that demarcated legitimate and illegitimate actions not on the basis of the law but on the basis of Mao's friend/enemy dichotomization of life. Such a covenant of grace would come to bury any notion of formal legal equality. Indeed, by 1959, legal circles talked freely of the need for the "rule of man" (*renzhi*) rather than the "rule of law" (*fazhi*) (He Qinhua 1991, 3).

It was just this type of legal flexibility that became the target of a series of debates in China after economic reform resurrected the need for law. The rule of man would become the target because, as Chinese legal scholars have continuously pointed out, "the market economy is a legal-system economy" (Albert Chen 1996, 4). If law was essential to guarantee stability, then elasticity was the dragon that must be slain to ensure the success of the economic reform program. As the ongoing series of critiques within Party and legal circles began to accumulate, they cleared away the few remaining defenders of legal flexibility and established the theoretical ground to justify the Party program of legal construction. Thirty years after the rule of man seemed to have been set in stone, the rule of law made a comeback.

In the debates that followed, legal reformers overturned the left view that law merely reflected the will of one dominant ruling class. Instead, reformers suggested that socialist law increasingly embodied all social needs and the common good (He Qinhua 1991, 17, 36). As this form of classless socialist law developed, it would increasingly serve a multiplicity of ends and reinforce a range of "objective economic conditions." It therefore became impossible to tie law back to class (see, for example, Zhou Fengju 1980, 39; Wu Buyun 1980, 11).[16] These types of arguments all helped bolster the stability and legitimacy of the newly developing legal culture which, in turn, was said to contribute to the process of economic reform. As the Chinese legal scholar Zhang Shuyi makes clear, the "basic point" in establishing the legal system from 1979 onward was to promote the socialist commodity economy. He notes that "the legal system was established in accordance with the needs of the commodity economy, and it is being developed in concert with the development of the socialist commodity economy" (qtd. in He Qinhua 1991, 51).

As emphasis began to be placed upon the development of a legal-based culture, the legislative basis upon which policing was undertaken was also questioned. As law won the day, a vast array of legislation was devised and then enacted to ensure that policing, too, was placed on a legal footing. In the twelve-year period between 1979 and 1991 alone, over 50 percent of all the nation's laws and regulations governing public security were enacted. In the same period, local governments and the regional People's Congress passed a further six hundred regulations governing police actions (*Outline of Public Security* 1997, 404). With laws beginning to dictate and delimit police actions and procedures, the security forces' traditional Party-based function as defenders of the dictatorship began to erode. This shift from a covenant of grace to a legally based society of the contract not only seemed to herald the arrival of policing as a form of law enforcement but it also looked like the Western history of policing was about to be retold with Chinese characteristics.

Europe as Precursor?

Under very different political conditions, in a different time, and with different specificities, similar sorts of rearrangements of life and economy as those currently being witnessed in China began to unfold in late seventeenth-century Europe. These European shifts not only led to the reification of the contract form but, more significantly, they marked the birth of the modern bourgeois state. In Europe, this modern bourgeois constitutional state developed secularized contractual relations that drew upon the religiously based covenant of grace that had proven central to the constitution of Christian faith.[17] Little wonder that Carl Schmitt would remind us that "all significant concepts of the modern theory of the state are secularized theological concepts" and lead us away from an omnipotent God toward an omnipotent lawgiver (Schmitt 1985, 36). Be that as it may, secularization proved central to these sorts of changes for, as Oestreich notes in his "sociological synopsis" of this European transition, it was the shift from the cleric to the lawyer that marked the opening moments of a phase we would come to call modernity. Oestreich plots the transition succinctly: "At first there is an approximate balance between clerics and officials of the court, the state and the towns, including medical men, but from the last decades of the seventeenth century onwards the business of writing gallant verses is taken over mainly by lawyers" (1982, 165). These new "gallant verses" of the early modern era would be written as statutes and their poetry styled in the language of the contract. Tied to the market, this emerging form of constitutionalism would avow a blindness to past forms of privilege and power. Economic transactions were legitimized under a code that claimed an autonomy and independence from all political arrangements. Yet this was, quite obviously, a fiction. The development of the market could not take place independently of politics, for it was through the law of contract that the market order was actually constituted (Collins 1986, 4, 6). For market-orientated economic relations, the law of the contract lay at the intersection of market and state power and, as such, was (and arguably still is) central to the constitution of the modern bourgeois state (Collins 1986, 11). Under these types of politico-legal arrangements professional policing came into existence. Only under this universalized code of law, operating as a secular and social contract, could the police begin to develop the character of a secular force for legal enforcement. This secularization of policing, witnessed in Europe in the early modern period, was accompanied by a process of professionalization brought on by other, more earthly, concerns.

Early European definitions of police related to the maintenance of good government with regard to the interconnected concerns of the moral, political, and economic order (see Foucault 1979, 11). Around the seventeenth century, this *oeconomy* of policing began to break down as the static, stable rural communities of Europe began to break up.[18] At this time, there was a huge movement of the population into towns and cities, which not only increased urban density but produced social dislocation and new lifestyles. It also created a social panic leading to increased demands being made upon the government to offer a more effective and professional answer to the growing list of social problems. Community self-policing began to give way to professional policing, and this, in turn, resulted in the reinvention of police as a force charged with the new, specialized task of crime prevention (Oestreich 1982, 156).

Similar concerns fueled a very different but no less professional model of policing in England after the War of Austrian Succession in 1748.[19] Philip

Rawlings (1995) chronicles the growing list of concerns that led in this direction. He argues that from around the latter part of the seventeenth century, a whole range of social problems emerged to fuel the fires of the later Fielding brothers' reforms. The unparalleled economic expansion of the time, coupled with the beginnings of industrialization, accentuated the already existing pull of the towns, but added to this potent mix some radical new social problems.

The development of industries increased the degree of wealth disparity, leading to increased degrees of social envy and crime. Struggles over the introduction of new labor-saving technology resulted in Ludditism and similar social movements. New industries and technologies increased the need for labor in the city, which, in turn, upset the demographic stability of city populations, further exacerbating existing social divisions. Marx, of course, had pointed to just these problems when he spoke of the disenfranchising effect of the enclosure laws upon the peasants. But while Marx would examine this period to understand the formative moments of the working class, Rawlings examines it to understand the social conditions that led to the need for professional policing.

"It was not just that there appeared to be more crime," Rawlings argues, but, "the crime was also perceived as being of a particular frightening type, unpredictable, violent and committed by gangs who preyed on all social classes" (1995, 136). With violent new crimes emerging and social dislocation the dominant motif, radical action was called for. The actions taken would lead, eventually, to the formation of a professional police force. It was in this regard, rather than as the fathers of the Bow Street Runners, that Rawlings believes the Fielding brothers made their greatest contribution:

> The effect of their work was to lay down key ideologies of the modern professional police bureaucracy, and, in particular, to emphasize a more proactive law enforcement method, at least with regard to serious crimes. . . . They stressed the difficulty of their job, thereby endeavouring to demonstrate that it required professional expertise allied both to adequate financial and legal support and to a criminal justice system which did not obstruct the work. Within this model, the role for popular involvement was essentially limited to supplying information. In effect, the Fieldings began to rearticulate policing around public officials rather

than victims and communities.... The implication of the Fieldings' work was that only experts could separate the criminals from the generality of the labouring poor. (1995, 139)

The new social mobility of the poor not only brought forth crime in the cities but simultaneously broke up the old agnatic bonds of community that had enabled the community policing regimes of the oeconomic past. This, in turn, eventually led to the establishment of a new, professional, and specialized force in 1829, when Robert Pell, the home secretary, pushed through the Metropolitan Police Act. Initially quite unpopular, the force authorized under this legislation won over the population because of its discipline and its ability to bring law and order back to the streets of London (Sklansky 1999, 1202–3). If we now return to the streets of China, we discover similar processes impelling change.

As the old command economy gives way to market socialism, the life-world of China is being transformed. The "agnatic," almost rural, nature of the Chinese cities was to be changed forever by this process. The once all encompassing 'rustic' work unit that took care of all aspects of a worker's life is being transformed into an economic enterprise, while peasants, once tethered to the land by a castelike system of household registration (Gong Xikui 1998), are being transformed into "free" workers and drawn into the city in ever-increasing numbers. Greater wealth disparities coupled with greater degrees of social and demographic mobility spell the beginnings of this now familiar story of social dislocation that we call the history of modernity. It is under these conditions that the Party cleric is slowly being replaced by the professional lawyer and the Chinese police are beginning to speak of the need to professionalize, specialize, and, because of the new-found respect for law, legitimize their work. It was with this latter goal in mind that the Chinese police somewhat hesitantly began to question their own traditional role as a tool of the Communist Party.

Rethinking Policing

It was in 1988 that the preeminent Chinese police studies journal *Public Security Studies*, borrowing from the spirit of earlier, reform-era legal debates about the status of law as a class tool, opened up the issue of policing and law under a people's democratic dictatorship. Momentarily, it appeared as though police debates would closely follow those that, in the early and mid-eighties, had solidified the resurrection of the rule of law. If that was the intention, it quickly went awry.

As the student protests of 1989 loomed, a new hard line began to emerge within the Party and the police. Despite this impending disaster, the advocates of policing as law enforcement still had time to advance their position. It was the liberal police scholar Liu Zaiping who offered the most cogent defense of this line of argument. Beginning with a critique of policing as a tool of the dictatorship, Liu suggested that this position obscured the inherently democratic function played by the force in the era of economic reform. This position, he argued, not only overstated the coercive role of the police but masked the changing function of the security forces in the period of reform (Liu Zaiping 1989, 8). This not only led to misunderstandings about the nature of the force but also ignored the special nature of the dictatorship that prevailed in China.

In contemporary China, Liu noted, the "special quality" of the dictatorship promised citizen sovereignty and an equality of rights. Policing, under these circumstances, worked to uphold socialist principles, promote socialist law, and guarantee social order (Liu Zaiping 1989, 9). By promoting the rule of law, police helped establish a stable social order, which formed the precondition for the development of both democracy and the economy (Liu Zaiping 1989, 11). Moreover, with economic reform, Liu seemed to suggest, democracy would develop both at the economic base as well as within the superstructure.

"The social base for a democratic politics," he provocatively argues, "rests upon a commodity economy." This, in turn, means that the role of the police in defending the socialist commodity economy against corruption, profiteering, and other acts of criminality not only benefits the people but also helps advance the democratic process (Liu Zaiping 1989, 11). But this was not the only way the Chinese police force advanced democracy, he contends. Of equal importance was their new primary role as law enforcement agents.

In Liu's view, economic reform resulted in significant changes in the nature of policing. Police were no longer a force designed simply to protect the Party, but had become "relatively autonomous" of both Party and government. Their overarching guide to action in the period of economic reform, he insists, comes "first and foremost" from the roles allocated to them under the constitution (Liu Zaiping 1989, 11). As police duties gain legal specificity and recognition, the security forces themselves begin to invest in law and democracy. These, in turn, rely on and are founded upon the principle of equality. While a defense of law will always require an acknowledgment of its coercive powers, Liu suggests that as democracy expands, the dictatorial function given over to the police will diminish (Liu Zaiping 1989, 12). With major student protests just around the corner, however, the diminution of police powers seemed far from the political agenda, and Liu's argument would find little public support. Particularly after 1989, this kind of argument gave way to a chorus of calls for a return to a more class-based form of "total" policing.

These conservative voices bemoaned the decline of the preventative Maoist policing model and the lack of class analysis that had accompanied the headlong rush to promote economic development and the rule of law (Liu Wenqi 1990, 21; Yang Zhaomin and Wang Gongfan 1990, 8). Even a cursory glance at the categories used by the police force in designating crime in the reform era bears out these complaints. Police have consciously avoided using such politicized categories as counter-revolutionary crime in the prosecution of cases. Indeed, in clear contrast to the pre-reform years, counter-revolutionary crime has become a marginal category in contemporary China. Only about 0.1 percent of all cases have been treated under this banner in the reform era. Moreover, even this small number declined over time.

In 1979, nearly one thousand criminal cases involved the charge of being counter-revolutionary, while in the prisons about 7 percent of all inmates were so labeled. In 1990, after the arrests that followed the political protests of June 4, there were even fewer counter-revolutionaries in prison and far fewer up on this charge. In that year, about four hundred counter-revolutionary cases came before the courts and only 4 percent of the prison population were regarded as counter-revolutionaries. The reason why this category has become dispensable, then, is because police are no longer interested in establishing links between politics and crime. Indeed, the reverse seems to be the case. Police seem intent on criminalizing political dissent rather than politicizing crime. The treatment of those arrested in 1989 after the Tian'anmen protests bears witness to this fact.

In the months that followed the June 4, 1989, protests, *Public Security Studies* offered a breakdown of the motivations of those arrested. They "discovered" that nearly 30 percent were unreformed recidivists who were said to harbor deep resentment against the authorities and 50 percent were social dregs that the police already knew about but had neither arrested nor prosecuted. Apart from these two groups, 3 percent were said to be profiteers and corrupt officials and another "small but highly active group" spies and secret agents of foreign powers (Yang Zhaoming and Wang Gongfan 1990, 10). In other words, well over 70 percent of the participants arrested in these protests were defined as common criminals. So little used was the politicized category of counter-revolutionary criminal that it disappeared altogether from the amended criminal code of 1997. In place of this category came the new charge of "endangering national security."

The decline and final abolition of this category of counter-revolutionary crime, however, was merely a symptom of a greater malaise. In effect, what these left conservatives were highlighting was not simply the shift away from overt political policing but the movement away from a Maoist model of "total" policing that enabled comprehensive preventive strategies to be employed in a new and more familiar Western model of policing that was principally reactive. It was in this regard that they also highlighted and critiqued the tawdry state of politico-ideological education in reform-era China, which, they argued, had left Chinese youth unprepared for the seductions of capitalist ideology and the money economy. Tying these complaints together and employing the language of critique Mao had once used against Yugoslavia and the Soviets, one senior police commentator even wrote of the events of 1989 as part of a worldwide movement to bring about the peaceful evolution of socialist China (Tan Songqiu 1990, 3). If the "sugar-coated bullets" of the West were seducing the youth of China, then action had to be taken. Only a renewal of mass-line policing, along with a return to a class analysis of crime and a reliance upon campaign-style coercion and propaganda, could start to set things straight.[20] Through these methods, the police could revive the structures that had given them such stability in times gone by.

The Mao era had given police a ready-made set of work methods and organizational forms that even in the reform era, still formed the bedrock of policing. These structures and "ways of doing" were still maintained, partly as an inherited structure the police could pragmatically not operate without, partly as an ideological imperative many within the force felt socialism could not live without. Thus, long after most other domains had abandoned the mass-line in everything but name, it appeared to live on in the realm of social control. Yet the conservative arguments of police scholars like Tan Songqiu unsettle these assumptions by pointing to the way policing has changed in the reform era. The continuation of mass-line policing in the reform era may have given the appearance that little had changed since the days of Mao, but in truth, everything had. In particular, it was no longer the site through which political intensity would be generated. Instead, the mass-line would be mimetically transformed by Deng Xiaoping's "all-round dictatorship" of the economic relation. The shell-like structure of this once intensely political mass-line organizational form would remain, but its political mode of operation would be transformed. In the reform era, the mass-line would still produce activity among organizational members, but it would not produce this by igniting and harnessing their political passions. Instead, another mode of operation would come to prevail. The "sugar-coated bullet" of this whole mimetic transformation process was nothing other than the contract.

The Spread of the Contract

The spread of the contract into noneconomic domains such as mass-line policing was an effect of its stunningly productive success in agriculture, where it had been introduced at the beginning of the eighties (Zweig et al. 1987, 320; Xu Hanmin, 1992, 149).[21] So successful was it in producing peasant enthusiasm for work and a calculable set of material outcomes that contract forms were thought worthy of emulation and adaptation in other, more distant, domains. In the end, the spread of the contract led to a virtual contractualization of Chinese life. This not only transformed the economic opacity produced by Mao's politics in command into something more calculable and productive but, in the process, revolutionized both urban and rural lifestyles and mentalities.

In terms of economic relations, the employment of a "purposive contract," as Weber would no doubt have called it,[22] broke down the established politico-moral bonds within traditional Maoist arrangements and reordered them into a discrete series of calculable domains and items. Under Deng, the Maoist homologization of all facets of life under the rubric of politics gave way to a dispersed set of economic calculations modeled upon the disaggregation of things. Thus while Deng had his Four Cardinal Principles to protect and promote the Party,[23] most emphasis in the reform period would be placed upon economic development and upon establishing a means of achieving calculability and profitability. It was as an extension of this logic that a new contractual model of social life emerged. While contracts had begun as a relatively simple means of developing the economy, their spread into social domains ate away at the political certainty and unity of the Party. And the more the moral core of the Party was eaten away, the more the Party required the economic contract to produce enthusiasm for the work of modernization upon which Party legitimacy rested. In the end, even the public security forces succumbed to the contractual temptation. The irony is that it was principally Maoist-style mass-line policing organs that were being brought back to life by this core mechanism of capitalism.

Beginning in the early 1980s, increases in the overall crime rates, in recidivism, and in the number of prison escapees had begun to cause great concern about social order and the ability of the police to deal with it. Worried that such instability would offset economic gains, Party authorities began demanding that the public security forces improve their performance. They called upon the police to return China to the halcyon days of stability represented by the social order situation of the mid-1950s. Given the changed nature of social relations brought on by economic reform, however, many within the force knew that such demands were utterly unachievable.[24] Nevertheless, it was clear that Party orders had to be followed. What better way for the police to demonstrate their determination to bring down crime rates to the levels experienced in the fifties than by reviving fifties-style policing techniques. Moreover, as transient criminals, drug addicts, and prostitutes constituted the new face of crime, the problem areas of eighties policing looked eerily similar to those encountered successfully by public security cadres back in the fifties.

From the early 1980s onward, police began to focus upon these problem crimes and review and revive earlier solutions. But to revive the past involved trying to recreate the conditions of the past, and this meant trying to restabilize society by reintroducing controls on population movement. Police could not do this, for they had neither the resources nor the backing of the Party to do so. After all, economic reform required population mobility. Allowing such mobility ensured that a relatively cheap rural labor force was always available to urban developers. Along with mobility, however, reform also required stability. What the police would therefore end up doing was to insert into the demographic debate the notion of legitimate and illegitimate travel. In this way they hoped to find a means by which to limit the flow of peasants into the cities and thereby recreate the semblance of order without jeopardizing the necessary flow of labor. With the tight internal migration laws having become something of a dead letter, by the 1980s this task would prove daunting. Huge numbers of peasants were entering the cities in search of higher-paid work.[25] How would the police limit that flow without throttling economic growth? To deal with this seemingly intractable problem, they would employ both a carrot and a stick.

The "carrot" came in 1984 when police modified household registration laws to enable the introduction of the resident identity card system. This effectively attempted to streamline procedures for those making legitimate travel arrangements. By this stage, the biggest of the "sticks" was already in place. In 1982, police cracked down on illegitimate travelers by reinvesting in shelter and investigation centers. These had proven useful in dealing with transients both in the famine of the early sixties and during Deng Xiaoping's campaign against crime on trains in 1975. In the face of rising illegal migration that reform brought in its wake, security forces thought that these centers might, once again, prove useful. Just how useful they would end up becoming was greatly influenced by the 1986 refocusing of the severe strike law and order campaign.

From 1986 onward, it was decided that the spotlight of this campaign should shine more directly upon transient criminal (liucuanfan) activity and criminals on the run (zaitaofa). To facilitate this new stage in the Severe Strike Campaign, shelter and investigation centers augmented their role and became the key detention centers for suspected transient criminals. The problem was that these establishments were run down and insufficiently funded. Indeed, even the ministry that ran them suggested that they had become the worst form of detention in China ("Ministry of Public Security" 1985,

188–89). Of even greater concern than living conditions, however, was the flexible nature of the regulations governing them.

According to Chinese regulations, suspects could be detained in these centers for no more than three months. Any extension to this would require approval from higher-level authorities. The problem was that the calculation of the three-month detention period only began after the verification of the detainee's name and address ("Ministry of Public Security" 1988, 229–31). With many of the detainees suspected of being transient criminals or prison escapees, gaining even this information proved difficult. In one study undertaken in Hunan in 1989, for example, it was found that more than 30 percent of the detainees had been held for longer than the stipulated three-month period. Indeed, some detainees had been held for two, three, and even five years, during which time nothing had apparently been done to solve their cases (Li Kangrui et al. 1989, 63). By the nineties, shelter and investigation had come under scrutiny from Western human rights groups who successfully lobbied for its abolition, which occurred in 1996. This, however, proved a Pyrrhic victory, for the revised 1997 criminal code extended police detention powers in such a way as to reintroduce the caveat that had enabled the police to hold suspected transient criminals indefinitely (see figure 5). Ironically, the desire to control crime would lead to a revival of a limited degree of legal elasticity, just as the promotion of Maoist forms of stable community policing would come to reinforce the new power of money. Nowhere was this latter point more in evidence than in the rural regions.

The revival of policing in the countryside turned on a partial resurrection of the old static model of community control. This revival was made possible by funds emanating from direct state financial investment, as well as by the use of techniques pioneered in the reform era. The state's investment in rural policing resulted in an enormous increase in the number of rural police stations,[26] but it also included the use of financial incentives to revive rural mass-line policing methods. From the early eighties onward, police began to employ monetary inducements to reinvigorate the rural village security pact system. Success in this arena led to further incentive-based reforms. Soon afterward, financial incentives were also employed in relation to factories and mines, where all internal security arrangements became subject to contracts.

By June 1981, all police stations in the five main cities of Beijing, Tian-

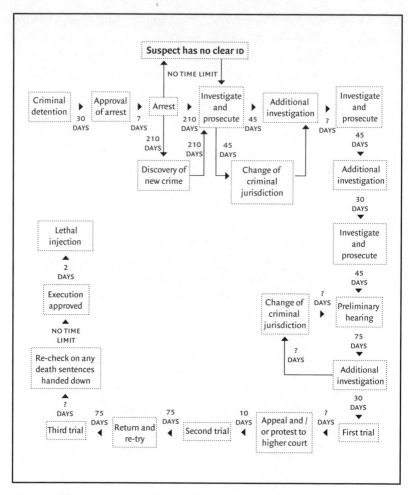

Figure 5. Chinese Document Indicating the Process of Prosecution

Source: This material is provided by the Public Security Bureau's Preliminary Hearing Bureau.

Notes

1. During the investigation period, if any of the suspects is discovered to have carried out serious crimes, then these can be counted only once.

2. There can be only one change of court or procuratorial jurisdiction.

3. The suspect can be detained for no more than 1,187 days during the criminal procedure unless the suspect refuses to provide a genuine name, address, or identity, or reexamination of the death penalty is under way.

jin, Shanghai, Guangzhou, and Wuhan were ordered to implement the responsibility system in policing which directly linked police officers' financial remuneration to their success in maintaining law and order.[27] By the mid-1980s, and after the success of this and the rural and factory security responsibility systems, contractual arrangements were employed on a trial basis throughout China's remaining cities. By August 1982, financial remuneration was also said to be "the key" to the successful implementation of the "comprehensive management of social order" (*Collection of Rules* 1992, 9; Wang Zhongfang 1989, 9).[28] Other than being fanned by monetary reward, however, such policing innovations ran absolutely counter to the logic of economic reform.

Whereas Deng's economic innovations had principally involved a disaggregation of things, police reform programs like comprehensive management constituted an attempt to totalize and unify social forces in the fight against crime. Indeed, one might go so far as to suggest that comprehensive management gave yet another example of the miniaturization and specialization of the basic attributes of the Maoist all-round dictatorship of the proletariat, for both comprehensive management and the all-round dictatorship turned on a desire for total control based upon mass-line organs. With comprehensive management, however, this desire for total control only ever extended to the maintenance of social order; yet in the logic underpinning the way it operated, it differed little from that of the old Maoist politico-ideological campaign for an all-round dictatorship.

Formal state police agencies were closely linked to the work of mass-line organs, educational institutions, and work unit security sections. Together, these organs would devise and build up a comprehensive system of crime prevention (Wang Zhongfang 1989, 8–15; H. M. Tanner 1995, 297–99). From social help and education through to establishing jobs and training schemes for ex-criminals (Liu Chenggen 1995), the comprehensive management of social order craved the type of total control central to the Maoist strategy of an all-round dictatorship.[29] Yet financial inducements, not socialist inspiration, drove this crime prevention model. Without financial inducements, such innovations remained impossible because, as Xu Hanmin makes clear, a "reliance upon mass consciousness . . . has left many areas with organizational names but little else" (1992, 149). To maintain social order, the police clearly required more than names; they needed monetary inducements.[30]

From the mid-eighties onward, even the Maoist-style police campaign would be brought to life not by revolutionary enthusiasm but by monetary incentive. In 1983, during the Severe Strike Campaign, police began a trial run of the responsibility system in policing. The success of these experiments led to it being fully adopted nationwide at the beginning of the second stage of this Severe Strike Campaign in 1984. In authorizing contract-based policing, the Central Committee pointed to experiments that had taken place in Guangzhou. Through the use of the contract, one area boasted that its overall crime rates had dropped by 18 percent and that breaches of the public security regulations had diminished by 20 percent (Xu Hanmin 1992, 149). In alluding to this example, the Central Committee summarized the changes undertaken in policing in the following manner:

> In Nanhai and Shunde, two counties in Guangzhou province that have a well-developed commodity economy, they have actively pushed forward the idea of security committee small groups and peasants signing up to security and protection contracts [zhi'an baowei chengbao]. These contracts enabled financial remuneration to go to participants and offered a method of financially rewarding and penalizing people. This strengthened the base-level work, strengthened the patrol and watch-house work, and, by strictly implementing the "village pacts," led to a situation where we could rely upon the masses to turn around the security situation and bring about clear results. The masses reflected upon this innovation in the following manner: "These 'packages' are a really smart way of doing things in terms of productivity, but they are also a really clever way of dealing with security work. This experience is worth drawing lessons from and extending to other places." (Collection of Rules 1992, 113)

And draw lessons and extend this idea they did. By the beginning of 1985, the idea of financial remuneration was already clearly established. In January, Chen Pixian insisted that all neighborhood committees, village committees, and mediation workers receive remuneration packages that combined "spiritual support" with "material rewards." Only with this combination, he concluded, would these organs once again become active (qtd. in Bai Yihua and Ma Xueli 1990, 194). In the following year, Qiao Shi announced the contractualization of base-level police work, and, from that time onward, the purposive contract became one of the key devices used to ensure an active base-level policing operation (*Collection of Rules* 1992, 52–55).[31] Through contracts, local police and mass-line organ results were made predictable and, for local activists, profitable. Moreover, because they could renew the ranks of their mass-line security organizations using monetary incentives, the police continued to rely upon and even strengthen the traditional area-based system of policing they had inherited from the Maoist era.

Not all of the effects of such financial-incentive schemes, however, could be labeled "best-practice" policing. Financial changes put pressure upon the so-called *tiaotiao kuaikuai*, or dual leadership system. This system came into existence with the accession of Mao to the Party leadership in the Yan'an period. It was one of the organisational reforms designed to ensure that Chinese security organs operated very differently from those in the Soviet Union. Whereas Soviet security organs had become a law unto themselves, the Chinese Party insisted upon local and Party political control over all security. From that time onward, the security system operated under a dual leadership system. This meant that they would be led by local governments and local Party committees at the same administrative level as the police units concerned (this was called horizontal leadership, or *kuai*). For professional leadership, however, they would look to higher-level public security organs (vertical leadership, or *tiao*). While this system had worked well throughout the Mao era, it was significantly challenged by the forces unleashed by the reform program.

Theoretically, this type of dual leadership was challenged by the demand for police to professionalize, specialize, and obey the rule of law. These demands pointed to the need to strengthen professional, technical, and legal leadership over local police branches. Yet this was being argued at the very time that financial pressures militated against any strengthening of this type of leadership. Basically, whoever paid the bills played the tune, and on the ground, an ever-increasing portion of the financial burden for local policing was being pushed onto the shoulders of local governments rather than onto professional, technical, or legal leadership bodies. As a result, the cash-strapped and overworked local governments began demanding that "their" local police collect their taxes and grain allocations, police the one-child policy in their jurisdictions, and carry out a range of other nonpolicing tasks that were essentially the responsibility of local government (Li Wennan and Jin Lu 1998, 25). In effect, local governments were employing the police as their administrative assistants, just as the party had formerly used them as its tool.

Even more worrying was the fact that many of the local governments found themselves in such financial difficulty that they had no capacity to fully maintain local police station work. So they, in turn, passed on the financial burden to the local police stations, more or less telling the police to partially self-fund their activities. The result was disastrous. In Gansu, for example, reports began to filter in of local governments refusing to fully fund police stations and demanding that the local police plug the budgetary gap. Local police stations reacted by extensively exercising their powers to levy fines and fees. They did this not as a means of deterrence, but simply to pay the wages of their officers (Wan Shengzi et al. 2000, 23). Increasingly, fines began to replace punishment,[32] and nowhere was this more in evidence than in those ambiguous administrative areas that lay on the edge of criminality. Prostitution was one area subject to "administrative sanction" that lent itself to the extended use of the fine.

As noted earlier, prostitution had become one of the problem crimes of the reform period. Nevertheless, police and Party officials continued to hold the view that prostitutes were victims not criminals. Hence criminalization was thought inappropriate in most cases, and in place of that, a dual strategy of education and deterrence was put in place. The educative side of this strategy relied upon the revival of the once successful fifties strategy of detention and education. From 1982 onward, women's education and support-through-labor units began to appear that would operate in a very similar fashion to the earlier Womens' Production, Education, and Fostering Institutes. These latter institutions had been established shortly after the revolution in 1950 to reform prostitutes by putting them to work in factories and farms. While the role and responsibilities of these units in many respects resembled the prison sector's reform-through-labor program, they differed in that they were not based on the criminal code. Indeed, initially, they were developed without any legislative basis whatsoever.[33] Women could therefore be sent for rehabilitation at the behest of city-level public security bureau chiefs alone (interview, 1990).[34] Given the enormity of the problem, however, only a very small percentage of the prostitutes caught were actually sent. Instead, the police devised another method to deal with lesser offences. That, of course, was the employment of the fine.

Cash-strapped police forces began to employ the new financial logic of economic reform to try to remedy the ancient problem of prostitution. Increasingly, however, police began to look at prostitution as a milch cow that would pay, through fines, for the vast array of financial-incentive schemes and other costs that held the local public security system together. A mechanism that began life as a deterrent had very quickly degenerated into a moneymaking business, as the police critic Song Haobo explains:

> Lots of people, including law enforcement agency staff, were enticed by money, and this was to have a negative influence upon them and resulted in the commodification of administrative management. Hence there was an exponential growth in the use of fines, and this malady became quite serious. It created situations in some places where the law enforcement agencies took prostitutes and their clients in not to detain, control, or educate them, but simply to extract fines. (1994, 3)

With such an ethos coming to dominate, the situation deteriorated well beyond the use of fines to finance bonus packages. In one area, the local government even allowed the police to invest a percentage of the money they had "earned." The amount proved so great that police began investing in a range of office buildings which the general public then began to call gambling and prostitution buildings, for it was common knowledge that these purchases had been financed through fines levied on these two particular industries. According to Song Haobo, this led inevitably to the "commodification of legal implementation" and ensured that "criminals with money could avoid the detention, education, and other control measures" (1994, 3). By the time of the Six Evils Campaign in late 1989,[35] which specifically targeted prostitution, the fine had become so ubiquitous that the authorities had to introduce very strict and detailed guidelines limiting its use. Justice, they feared, was being seriously eroded because of its overuse.[36]

Fines may have distorted justice, but the money it brought into the system kept the justice system afloat. While some of these expenses would be covered by government expenditure, rising costs and the added outlays associated with the spread of the police responsibility system meant that the system would always face financial pressure. The problem was that it was only through contracts and responsibility systems that local police were able to keep a lid on crime, or at least that seemed to be the case. Indeed, endless statistics could be cited to that effect. Yet closer scrutiny of these figures suggests something else. In effect, they revealed that the decreases in local crime rates after the introduction of the responsibility system occurred more on paper than on the street. The responsibility system in policing, it seems, was producing a decrease in police reporting without an actual decrease in the number of crimes committed.

This disjunction between the statistic and the street first came to light in 1987 when the Fujian provincial police department undertook a nationwide study of police records from fifty-seven different stations. The study revealed a huge gap between the number of known or "real" crime cases and the number of cases reported. Indeed, reported cases constituted only 12.75 percent of the total number of all known cases. Even in relation to serious crime, where stricter procedures operated, the investigators discovered a glaring discrepancy between known cases and those actually being pursued. In this instance, only 58.33 percent of all "serious cases" were recorded (Fujian Public Security Department 1989, 332–40). The reasons for such a low rate of reporting, it was later discovered, related principally to the performance criteria of the security responsibility system.[37]

Expectations upon local police were simply too great. Quotas set on cleanup rates in some places were as high as 85 percent, while cleanup rates for serious cases were set at 95 percent. This proved impossibly high, and certainly much higher than existing cleanup rates, which ran at a little over 70 percent of cases (Fujian Public Security Department 1989, 337; Yu Lei 1993, 491). As a result of this discrepancy between existing cleanup rates and expectations, police were seriously in danger of missing out on their bonuses, and, worse still, of incurring a penalty for failing to reach their allotted targets. In effect, underreporting was their way of coping. Not only did this tactic help police avoid the penalties associated with missing their targets, but it also had the added advantage of allowing them to avoid the mundane paperwork associated with opening cases. Best of all, it meant that they would still gain their financial bonus as well as receive praise: nonreporting translated into nonexistence in police statistical work (Fujian Public Security Department 1989, 337).

While the Fujian police study acknowledged a lack of sufficient statistical evidence to make any definitive claims on this front, further studies have tended to support these findings (Yu Lei 1993, 47, 562). Indeed, a more recent nationwide study of the problem undertaken in 1997 discovered that even at this time, only 80 percent of known cases were being reported and only 30 percent of these were actually recorded. Of the 30 percent, only 37 percent would actually be solved (Wu Zhongfei and Chen Yuanxiao 2000, 27). Other studies point to the way this problem of underreporting is not restricted to the formal police force. Responsibility systems, it seems, are distorting the crime profile right across the mass-line (Yichang Administrative Area 1989, 344).

In 1989, the Yichang police undertook a study of the effects of the responsibility system on neighborhood security committee policing and the internal protection sections of work units (Yichang Administrative Area 1989, 345–46). Again, the study found a similar trend to that which was taking place within the formal public security force. Indeed, responsibility systems were proving such a disincentive to crime reporting that even ordinary staff at enterprises failed to report crime. In one incident in a department store in Zhijiang county, Yichang, the fear of being financially penalized for not meeting the contractual obligations of the security responsibility system led staff to cover up the theft of four watches and pay for the cost of their loss out of their own pockets (Yichang Administrative Area 1989, 346). Despite such anomalies, neither the police force nor their mass-line could survive without these sorts of financial incentive systems. They formed the basis upon which police had been able to reinvigorate their work and revive the mass-line parapolicing support base still essential to police work. This could not have happened without the use of such "incentive schemes" (Yu Haibing 1989, 28). Unfortunately, this slavish adaptation of the methodology of economic reform to parapolicing organs had other hidden costs that only become visible when one closely scrutinizes the adoption of these systems within the mass-line organizations themselves.

The Monetarization of Mass-Line Organs

With a whiff of financial ammonia, it was thought, the basic level Maoist mass-line security committees could be brought back to life and help solve the deteriorating crime situation, much as these organs had done in the political past. The first phase of this revival strategy involved raising the basic wage levels of participants. By the 1980s, reforms were instituted to massively increase wages paid to mass-line activists. For too long, it was argued, local governments had used the October 1954 City Residency Committee Organizational Regulations, which stipulated a monthly stipend not in excess of 15 yuan (US $2) per committee member. Inflation and a new money-based economy made this wage rate completely untenable. By the early eighties, the mass-line committee structures were falling into disarray at an alarming rate. One study found that 20 percent of these organizations at a village level and 25 percent of them at a city level were either inactive or totally paralyzed. In 1989, the Ministry of Civil Affairs conducted a nationwide survey and found that in addition to the decline of these mass organs, 20 percent of all grassroots Party and government organizations at a village level were inactive, while a further 25 percent of them were completely paralyzed. Meanwhile, in the cities, street committees and local security groups, lacking a capacity to generate income, shriveled up, while internal protection sections within work units often existed in name only (Yu Lei 1993, 234). To deal with the decline of mass organs, a new regime was instituted that raised participant wage rates to over 100 yuan (US $12) per month and, in some cases, over 300 yuan (US $36) per month (Bai Yihua and Ma Xueli 1990, 184). In addition, a number of city-based security committees began offering monthly bonuses of over 100 yuan per month for heads and deputies who put in a good performance (Bai Yihua and Ma Xueli 1990, 162).[38] Through such methods, the police were able to stabilize and begin to redevelop, albeit unevenly, the local-level security committees and small group structures that constituted the backbone of all local-level community-based policing arrangements (see tables 7 and 8). Despite this, the vagaries of financial opportunities were to leave their mark.

In cities where other, more lucrative financial opportunities existed, security committees and groups still tended to rely heavily upon an ever-aging group of retirees (see tables 9 and 10). In contrast, rural areas could still rely upon philanthropic local traditions and a lack of other work opportunities to ensure a large number of youthful recruits to the mass-line organizations. This difference resulted in a major age disparity between rural and city committees and groups and, as a consequence of that, a huge discrepancy in the value of these committees to police operations. While less than

Table 7. Public Security Committees and Personnel

	Internal	City and town	Village	Total number
COMMITTEES				
1986	291,548	154,804	728,824	1,174,456
1989	309,366	170,525	695,619	1,175,510
1990	319,382	163,560	711,668	1,194,610
1991	317,867	216,087	717,074	1,251,028
PERSONNEL				
1986	1,580,426	858,943	2,866,078	5,305,447
1989	1,574,887	951,519	2,656,167	5,182,573
1990	1,664,592	884,810	2,728,069	5,277,471
1991	1,564,331	857,719	3,464,249	5,886,299

Sources: All figures drawn from information given in Wang Zhongfang 1989, 1991 *Law Yearbook*, 1992 *Law Yearbook*, and 1993 *Law Yearbook*. After 1993, no information was available.
Note: *Internal* means internal to the enterprise and work unit.

Table 8. Public Security Small Groups and Personnel

	Internal	City and town	Village	Total number
COMMITTEES				
1986	407,763	394,300	2,247,696	3,049,759
1989	394,199	474,849	1,617,866	2,486,914
1990	433,162	472,953	1,719,692	2,625,807
1991	422,091	472,671	1,624,389	2,519,151
PERSONNEL				
1986	1,312,576	1,083,385	4,347,475	6,743,436
1989	1,344,700	1,291,364	3,950,499	6,586,563
1990	1,455,800	1,293,810	4,321,080	7,070,690
1991	1,448,384	1,303,877	4,697,617	7,449,878

Sources: All figures drawn from information given in Wang Zhongfang 1989, 1991 *Law Yearbook*, 1992 *Law Yearbook*, and 1993 *Law Yearbook*. After 1993, no information was available.
Note: *Internal* means internal to the enterprise and work unit.

Table 9. Number of Retired Workers and Cadres Involved in Public Security Committee Work

	Internal	City and town	Village	Total number
1986	44,298	248,967	34,737	328,002
As % of all participants	2.8	29	1.2	6
1989	69,112	301,109	46,136	416,357
As % of all participants	4.4	31.7	1.7	8
1990	89,143	304,231	52,802	446,176
As % of all participants	5.4	34.4	1.9	8.4
1991	84,835	304,674	57,644	447,153
As % of all participants	5.4	35.5	1.7	7.6

Sources: All figures drawn from information given in Wang Zhongfang 1989, 1991 *Law Yearbook*, 1992 *Law Yearbook*, and 1993 *Law Yearbook*. After 1993, no information was available.
Note: *Internal* means internal to the enterprise and work unit.

Table 10. Number of Retired Workers and Cadres Involved in Public Security in Small Groups

	Internal	City and town	Village	Total number
1986	45,195	359,985	39,799	444,979
As % of all participants	3.4	33.2	0.9	6.6
1989	82,152	450,922	59,235	592,309
As % of all participants	6.1	34.9	1.5	9
1990	106,932	479,997	69,244	656,173
As % of all participants	7.3	37.1	1.6	9.3
1991	95,807	483,880	69,954	649,641
As % of all participants	6.6	37.1	1.5	8.7

Sources: All figures drawn from information given in Wang Zhongfang 1989, 1991 *Law Yearbook*, 1992 *Law Yearbook*, and 1993 *Law Yearbook*. After 1993, no information was available.
Note: *Internal* means internal to the enterprise and work unit.

2 percent of all rural committee and group members were retirees, in the cities, retirees make up around 35 percent of all members. In quite a number of cases, however, retirees made up 60 to 70 percent of committee and group members (Basic Outline 1987, 247). The large number of retirees in city committees and groups prompted two Chinese scholars to speculate that "there may be no more cadres after this generation of neighborhood committee members" (Bai Yihua and Ma Xueli 1990, 184). Their only chance of survival, in fact, lay with a more extensive use of the incentive schemes. The only problem with such an extension, however, was who was going to pay.

Costs involved in running such incentive schemes devolved to the local communities themselves as the economic reform program ensured reliance upon a "user pays" ethos. Hence, in neighborhoods, "resident users" emerged as the greatest source of financial support for these committees and groups (Course in the Uses 1990, 247). Unsurprisingly, the introduction of monetary incentives became quite unpopular with local residents, and increasing public resentment forced police and the committees to experiment with other methods of recouping the costs of local neighborhood security work. One method involved charging visitors' fees for residency rights.[39] Another scheme involved trying to redevelop neighborhood solidarity and reinvent the voluntary basis of the neighborhood security system that had predominated in the past.[40] In this regard, one discovers the rather unlikely revival of the spirit of Fengqiao.

Once a Maoist model of mass democracy, Fengqiao was now adjusted for use in the new era in which "spiritual civilization" rather than class struggle was being promoted. In the era of reform, Fengqiao no longer served as an example of mass democracy, but became known, instead, as the Fengqiao community crime control model. This time around, the work principle that "small matters are dealt with locally without being passed on to the village, big matters are dealt with at village level without being sent on to the town, and contradictions are not sent to higher authorities" no longer indicated the masses taking charge of their own political struggles, but rather the "spiritually civilized" organizing themselves and bringing peace and harmony to their community (Zhou Changkang 1994, 1–5). Thus even when money was not involved in the revival of activism around law-and-order issues, neither was politics. The rekindled spirit being promoted was not revolutionary but philanthropic. It was based on the idea of community service that lay buried at the heart of all rhetoric about socialist spiritual civilization. Generally, policing methods derived from this revival of a community spirit tended to prove more effective in the countryside where notions of solidarity still reigned. They were much harder (although not impossible) to implement in the cities where money talked. Partly in recognition of this, police knew that the professionalization of policing was the key to lowering the crime rates in the cities. While volunteers might have proven a useful supplement, police increasingly turned to hired help. This trend even spread to the informant system and even here, one finds, "professionalization" involved the "dumbing down" of politics.

From Eyes and Ears to Snouts

Informants have been an important source of police intelligence since the formation of the Yan'an city police squad back in May 1938.[41] As in contemporary policing, the Yan'an city police relied upon mass-line organizations to carry out their grassroots work, but, given the wartime setting, they were particularly reliant upon those within the mass-line whom they described as "backbone mass-line elements." These people became known as lianluoyuan, or liaison personnel. It was their job to give the police detailed information about the political reliability of neighborhoods and families in which they themselves lived (Basic Outline 1987, 262). After 1949, this system of activist-informants was expanded and formalized. In 1950, the Ministry of Public Security issued an internal document called "The Methodology for Temporarily Managing the Focal Population (Draft)," which placed special emphasis upon the role of the activist-informant in assisting police to control those deemed politically suspect. The task of the liaison personnel was to carry out covert surveillance of these people and report anything untoward to the police. To effect this, the public security forces secretly selected and recruited local, politically pure activists from within the ranks of the mass-line organizations.

From 1956 onward, information on those deemed politically suspect was held in a subcategory of the household register known as the focal or special population register. Local activist-informants undertook covert surveillance of the suspicious, and anything important they discovered would be added to the household registration details. Because most of this additional information came from the liaison personnel, they became known as the eyes and ears of the household register (*hukou ermu*). Like much else, this system dissolved during the Cultural Revolution but was revived in a depoliticized way in the era of economic reform. No longer politically inspired or directed, the new role for the liaison personnel took them away from the covert surveillance of the special population and directed their gaze instead toward common criminals. As this shift took place, they moved from being the eyes and ears of the household register to being "the eyes and ears of public order" (*zhi'an ermu*).[42] Far more significantly, however, they moved from being politically inspired eyes and ears to being dubiously motivated hired help.

Particularly in the cities, mass-line organizations no longer offered the type of symbolic capital necessary to compensate activists for their voluntary work. Dominated by the profit motive, even work units had been transformed into economic enterprises. China no longer worked in that overtly political fashion and, as a result, the mass-line organs could no longer guarantee a young activist base from which to recruit "eyes and ears." Instead, police were forced to rely upon minor criminals to do this work. It was estimated that in some cities, 60 to 70 percent of all eyes and ears were ex-criminals. No doubt because of this they had a network of criminal contacts that proved to be an enormously useful resource to the police. On the basis of police statistics covering nineteen cities and provinces from October 1984 until February 1985, 60 percent of all the crucial evidence enabling police to crack cases came from eyes and ears, while a further 58 percent of all clues that helped solve cases also came from them. In the same period in Zhejiang province, eyes and ears not only provided clues in over 5,129 cases, but their information was directly responsible for the cleanup of 2,059 criminal cases.

The shift away from recruiting politically dedicated activists to employing petty criminal informants may have helped police maintain social order, but it came at the cost of a further monetarization and depoliticization of the policing system. While police documents insist that the informant system is nonprofessional in character, eyes and ears are now "owned" by particular police stations that recruit, register, and pay them for all information given. Indeed, the leadership of a police station must approve their nomination, and their status as informant must be entered into their personnel file along with other details relating to their work. In effect, eyes and ears are now almost identical to registered police informants in the West.

If money can be said to have fundamentally altered the nature of mass-line policing within the community at large, on the other side of the work unit wall, it was having an even more deleterious effect. Ironically, the financial-incentive schemes used to keep the appearance of the mass-line alive in the wider society have proven to be the very devices that have more or less begun to kill it off within enterprises and work units. Internal work unit security organs have all been put on contract and, as a result, they have increasingly concerned themselves only with their own workplace. This is a far cry from their original mass-line role.

Internal Protection Units

Internal protection work began in Ruijin in September 1931, but it was only later, in Yan'an, that protection units started to develop into a regular feature of work unit life. Not until the takeover of the cities and the development of a stronger communist industrial base, however, did these protection units become a prominent and ubiquitous feature of Chinese city life, and only after 1948 did work units recruit their own security staff. Prior to that they relied upon specialized protection cadres from the Party's Social Section. While work unit staff would come to completely replace the professional security agents the Party sent in, the political influence of this latter group never disappeared. Thus even when the system of internal protection became formalized and standardized across the country in 1949 and security units were made entirely enterprise based, they still clearly remained "Party" in nature (*Internal Protection* 1991, 19–21). Indeed, as Mao himself pointed out, "Protection work must especially stress the role of Party leadership and, *in real terms*, it must get direct leadership from the Party committees, otherwise things could become very dangerous" (qtd. in *Internal Protection* 1991, 25; emphasis original). Economic reform tended to sever this link with the Party, and, as a result, the situation within work units has indeed become very dangerous, especially for the Party's much cherished concept of comprehensively managing social order. The beginning of this diminution of Party influence within work units began as a direct result of economic reform.

To raise production, enterprise administrative autonomy was encouraged

and the role of the Party committee restricted to overtly ideological matters. As a result of this administration-Party split, internal protection work
was said to have "drifted" into the enterprise administrative sphere (*Internal Protection* 1991, 25). With managers administering their own workplaces
and a reward system geared to production, security matters tended to drop
from workplace agendas (Hu Yongming 1993, 58). Hence, despite the massive growth in the number of enterprises in China over the reform period,
the number of protection workers has remained more or less at the level it
was in the fifties, that is, at around 100,000 cadres (Hu Yongming 1993, 60;
Gao Feng 1988, 19). These new administrative arrangements, however, not
only made security organs short of staff but also changed the nature of their
work.

Prior to reform, protection units focused upon public and covert action designed to stop counter-revolutionary wreckers disrupting production. This reading of protection work as part of the policing of the political established it ideologically as identical to the policing of the social.
Moreover, on a practical basis, it became an integral part of the comprehensive security system that flowed from work units back into society. In
post-reform China, while the focus of enterprise protection work would remain on practices that adversely affected production, neither the protection
work nor the disruptions were coded politically. Instead of engaging in a
search for politically inspired wreckers, the protection units began to focus
on safety matters and work practices within the enterprise that proved deleterious to production. This new more limited and internally driven focus was
further reinforced when a contract responsibility system tying security unit
salaries to improvements in safety and production was brought into effect
in the eighties (*Internal Protection* 1991, 29). Where once the internal protection sections within work units had served as backbone elements in social
and community policing and had proven central to the formation of parapolicing lianfang groups (the joint protection defense groups), their agendas now focused almost exclusively upon enterprise production, industrial
espionage, and internal work unit affairs (Zheng Yuhua and Cen Shengting
1992, 7; Gao Feng 1988, 19).[43] With this new agenda, these organs had little
to do with the formal police force, and they were no longer interested in, or
tied to, police professional leadership.

With enterprise managers in charge and an agenda geared to increasing enterprise production, the right of public security units to determine internal protection unit appointments, stipulate security staff numbers, and set security agendas within work units was withdrawn.[44] This decline in police influence within the internal protection units would create significant problems for the police generally and for the concept of comprehensive management in particular. In the past, work unit security organs had fed directly into police work. They had established dossiers on those within the work unit deemed dangerous,[45] they had carried out surveillance on such people, had investigated and interrogated suspects, and opened criminal and administrative cases for the police. While none of these powers had ever been legislated, they were, nevertheless, seen as an acceptable and legitimate devolution of police powers. After all, work unit protection duties could never have been fulfilled without these extensive powers. Given the deliberate policy of the past to maintain a very small police force so as to ensure that security forces were always reliant upon the mass-line, such mass-line parapolicing organs were not only essential politically but also practically. Indeed, without the local knowledge of these units, the impressive cleanup rates of the police would have been seriously threatened.

It is estimated that about 70 to 80 percent of all work unit–based administrative and criminal cases had, in fact, been cracked by internal protection units. Thus, despite constant complaints from within the police force that these internal units were "professionally weak," the police nevertheless depended upon them (Gao Feng 1988, 18–19; Hu Yongming 1993, 60). Today, however, their usefulness is severely limited by both an enterprise management system that increasingly looks only at the bottom line (profit) and by a criminal code that limits the powers of nongovernment parapolicing units. Given these problems, the police have attempted to deal with the problem in a novel way.

In 1985, with enterprises increasingly taking control of their own internal security, larger enterprises began to request and require a more formal police presence within their workplaces. Indeed, what they wanted was a hybrid force answerable to them but also endowed with many of the powers and training of the formal police force. Their requests were met with support from the police. Thus, despite the lack of any legal basis, by the early nineties in the province of Hunan alone, some 979 enterprises had established their own public security units, employing some 7,596 cadres (Zhou

Rongzhao and Yang Ming 1991, 49). All that was needed for the establishment of police units was the approval of the local government and a higher-
level police unit. Despite the need for governmental and higher-level police
approval, it was, once again, enterprises that would pay the wages and, as
a result, these new structures very quickly began to run into familiar problems. Paid by enterprises rather than by the government or the police, these
units ended up following enterprise orders rather than those issued by public security units. The result could sometimes lead to unforeseen and quite
deleterious consequences.[46]

While such enterprise police would often wear police uniforms and carry
public security identification,[47] they were, in fact, not part of the formal
police force. Neither the quality of recruits nor the training they were given
met with formal police standards. Indeed, one survey undertaken into the
quality of enterprise policing revealed that in ten enterprise police stations
with fifty-one officers, around 80 percent of the staff had received no training whatsoever, while a further 30 percent could not even perform basic
police duties (Zhou Rongzhao and Yang Ming 1991, 50). This particular attempted reform of internal enterprise policing, therefore, merely replicated
the problems that plagued the internal protection units. While all attempts
to reform and revive mass-line–based enterprise policing have proven prob-
lematic, one new reform that relies upon the experience of Western policing
has proven to be a great success and has surreptitiously increased the power
of the formal public security forces within enterprises and work units. There
is a double irony in this. First, this "other reform" came about because of
foreign investor pressure, rather than because of any concerns about Party-
mindedness. Second, it emerged not through any attempt to revamp mass-
line structures, but actually in an attempt to avoid them. The development
I am alluding to is the establishment of a private security industry.

Private Security Firms

The first private security firms (bao'an fuwu gongsi) in China came into existence at the behest of foreign investors and private enterprises. These investors wanted a type of security organization within their enterprises that
concerned itself with economic not social profit and would abide by the
law of the land rather than Party "Red Banner documents." In these types

Table 11. Private Security Companies

Year	Number of companies	Number of personnel
1985	1 (Shenzhen)[a]	over 50
1988	99	many 10,000s[b]
1991	1,000	over 100,000
1995	2,200	over 200,000[c]
1998	n/a	over 300,000[a]

Sources: (a) Interview with head of the Beijing Private Security Company (August 1998); (b) *Public Security Studies*, no. 3 (1988): 39 and *An Outline of Public Security 1997*, 384; (c) *1996 Law Yearbook*, 168 and Ye Huaming 1989, 24–27.

of foreign-owned or partially foreign-owned enterprises, the Party organization was not allowed to participate in management or in administrative, security, or specialized police work (Chen Du and Gu Xinhua 1988, 31). While theses types of enterprises all recognized the need for workers to have unions, they were far less sanguine at the prospect of having communist mass-line security forces within their ranks and requested another form of security more in keeping with international business practices. The result was the development of a private security company system.

Given this background, it hardly seems surprising to discover that the first private security company appeared in 1985 in the Shenzhen special economic zone (Ye Huaming 1989, 25). In 1986, a similar security company was set up in Beijing, and within a few years, most other major cities had them. The growth of these companies has been spectacular (see table 11). By 1998, they collectively employed over 300,000 employees. In Shanghai alone, private security guards were said to number 27,000 officers, which makes their operations about half the size of the Shanghai city police force. In Beijing, the growth has been even more spectacular. There are over 34,000 security guards in the Beijing company, which, in terms of officers, means that it is about the same size as the city Public Security Bureau (Ni Minle and Fang Lei 1998, 64; interviews 1998).[48]

Chinese private security companies differ from those in the West, however, in that they are all wholly owned subsidiaries of the local branches of the Ministry of Public Security whose bureaus directly operate these businesses. Not only do the public security forces have a monopoly over this industry but they also have complete control over staffing. Police control over these security forces, however, should not be read as a sign of renewed political control but as a sign of profit and "professionalism." Separating these forces from the police yet maintaining control over them allows for profitable efficiencies to be made. At the same time, by bureaucratically allocating all senior staff positions within these companies to trusted high-ranking police officials, authorities are able to claim that professional standards are being met. This is something they could not have done had they merely reintroduced mass-line security units.[49] Profit and the appearance of professionalism are therefore what is being secured.

It is estimated that these companies now cover about one-third of all police work in the cities, and it is from guarding banks, restaurants, and other such establishments that they derive most of their profits. Ironically, then, police control over enterprise security is strongest where it appears least communist. More important, perhaps, the emergence of private security takes the ongoing commodification of security matters which the police reform agenda has promoted to an even higher level (Spitzer 1987, 50). With the emergence of these firms, the point being made here, at a general level, breaks to the surface. Security has become commodified and, like any other commodity, it is increasingly up for sale.

This commodification of security was, I would argue, the inevitable end point of the ongoing process of contractualization. This is because the contract not only makes things calculable or economically viable or visible but also produces new mentalities and value systems that lead to a reification of money and the commodity economy. The contractualization of most parts of the Chinese lifeworld therefore offers the crucial means by which to "train" Chinese out of their politically imposed egalitarianism and into the new egalitarianism of contractual and market relations. The police have played their part in promoting this new mentality. The real irony is that the organization most closely associated with the Maoist revolution, and most feared by Western entrepreneurs as they entered China, has now become the principal vehicle for the promotion and training of capitalist values among the reddest of the country's revolutionaries. The mass-line in security has become one vast network of tiny little workshops that repeatedly trains cadres to think in terms of the market, the contractual relation, and the monetary reward. It is, in effect, marketization with a Maoist face. This marketization is a gift delivered via the contract from economic reform, and, as holds true for any gift, the only thing really given has been time (Derrida 1992, 41). Time for the police to reform their own structure in line with the new demands of a modernizing China; time for them to shift tact and move from a preventative to a more responsive form of policing; time, too, for them to plug the structural holes in the system and change things so that a code of professionalization can replace a system that required revolutionary zeal. One might, therefore, suggest that this gift of time was essential and, while the police scholar Zhang Min does not quite suggest this, he does offer evidence in support of such a conclusion (2000, 31–33).

Zhang Min argues that policing in the reform period can be divided into three overlapping stages. In the first, which lasted from the beginning of the reform period until the early nineties, a revival of the traditional socialist system of policing occurred. This revival turned on the development and expansion of the police station system that would operate as the leadership backbone of a vast network of parapolicing security committees and groups operating under the stations' purview. This was the predominant trend until the early nineties. From that time until the mid-nineties, a second stage of development took place. This turned on the development of new policing strategies to augment the revived mass-line system. Effectively, these two stages constituted little more than two different jurisdictions of reform. The first stage involved the revival of policing in rural areas, while the second stage turned on developing appropriate methods for policing the cities. In particular, Zhang Min notes that stage two involved the development of the police patrol system in the cities, for the mass-line here required augmentation rather than revival.

Economic reform has, in many respects, begun to return the cities to their old prerevolutionary form. Back in 1949, the communists had originally begun to transform them into revolutionary cities. Now, with economic reform, the tide has turned again. In 1949, the communists had begun to rustify the cities. They had started to transform all existing enterprises into small industrial villages that came to be called work units. These units helped produce a structure and a mentality that would enable mass-line policing. Economic reform led to a reversal of that process of rustification. It heralded the revival of ideas of commercial and business centers, as well as shopping streets and arcades, which had all but disappeared with the Maoist dream of pastoral, political cities. As economic reform increasingly disaggregated work and life, the old mass-line–based residency and work unit policing strategies proved structurally inadequate to the new tasks of city policing. Mass-line organs constituted area-based protection units, and the question now posed was how to deal with the new types of city areas that were neither residential nor controlled by work units. By the end of 1995, this question brought forth an answer in the clarion call to professionalize policing. By that stage, 2,217 large and medium-sized cities had established police patrols and, nationwide, the police patrol force boasted some 110,000 officers. From the mid-nineties onward, while still relying on the revived area-based mass-line to maintain order in certain places, city police started to become more mobile. They developed command centers in their stations from which they would monitor and react to calls placed on the emergency police number 110. By 1996, over two hundred stations had set up this particular type of system (Ye Ming 1998, 65), and this, for Zhang Min, demonstrates the story of growing police comprehensiveness in an era of social mobility in this, their third stage of reform (2000, 31).

While one may doubt the triumphalist tone, the evenness of this transition, or even the smoothness of the trajectory Zhang Min plots, one thing is clear: the first brick in the edifice of this new security system was the revival and mimetic transformation of the mass-line policing structure. Its revival, however, did not flag a return to the political past, but its opposite. Contracts prevailed where politics had once dominated. In effect, the contract bought the police time, and in the time they had, they set about establishing more radically mobile and reactive policing techniques that are now coming to dominate city policing. Nevertheless, whether one turns to the more traditional system still operating in rural China or looks to the bright new professionalism encouraged in the cities, one thing is clear: all reforms are utterly dependent upon monetary incentives. This is the road down which the public security forces are now traveling, and it is one that flags the end of a long Maoist tradition of socialist policing. Irrespective of where it leads from here —whether it is to the law-based system desired by the West or to the more authoritarian but apolitical form that seems to suit the Party—is unclear but no matter were it goes, it can truly be said to be the end of the mass-line.

Conclusion

In 1988, when the police began to formally question their status as a tool of the people's democratic dictatorship, the script line for their new life as a law enforcement agency seemed clear enough. For economic reform to succeed, stability must prevail, and that, in turn, depended upon overcoming any remnants of the so-called rule of man in favor of the rule of law. Under these circumstances, police would become law enforcement agencies. Economic reform produced a sea change in attitudes, and new policing practices reflected that. The growth of police academies and the teaching of legal studies within them, coupled with a new professional attitude and desire for specialization, all suggested that police were in step with these changing times. As the role of the dictatorship in legitimating police actions diminished, law came to replace it, and, as it did, it more and more framed police actions. Law proved central to economic reform because it was through law that stability could be achieved and calculable outcomes forecast.

At the same time, however, while economic reform required stability, it did not produce it. On the contrary, it created the conditions for social dislocation. In some respects, economic reform was to be a trip down memory lane. The redevelopment and rustification of cities that took place from 1948 onward and resulted in a system of urban and industrial villages known as work units is in the process of unraveling and returning the Chinese city to a form it knew before the arrival of the communists. The stilling of the population upon which planning and socialist policing were predicated has given way to a new social mobility. Mobility is, of course, a requirement of market economies hungry for labor to fuel the development of city construction and the service industries. Yet in relying upon the market, in promoting a money economy, and in "freeing" the population to move in a manner dictated by the economy, the old social ills of capitalism have returned. Drug addiction, prostitution, economic crimes, and an endless sea of troublesome transients have been but a few of the negative side effects of the reform program.

At first these social ills proved embarrassing. After all, curing them was one of the great boasts of the Chinese revolution. If nothing else, the relapse into crime, vice, and other social ills that accompanied the development of the economic reform program suggested that there were lessons to be learned from the history books of an earlier socialist policing era. Perhaps also, the Party's demands to return China to the crime-free days of yesteryear also suggested that the solutions of the past might still have some purchase. Whatever the reasons, and there were many, the mass-line was still very much in vogue in the early reform years. This was despite the very real and growing emphasis within the police force upon professionalization, specialization, and a respect for the rule of law. It is also in spite of the fact that in order to operate successfully, mass-line organs would always require a degree of legal elasticity rather than formal law. Pragmatically, there was little else the Chinese police could do other than to rely upon a structure they had built up over the proceeding decades and which they had exalted to such a degree that to think beyond it was, initially at least, impossible.

This situation resulted in a potential contradiction between the rhetoric of legal reform and the need to maintain stability. That is because the maintenance of stability required a reliance upon mass-line organs, and that, in turn, meant opening the door to legal elasticity. Because of this potential contradiction, there would always be attempts to square the circle by putting the mass-line in policing on a new and legal footing. And while such rules and regulations proved to be important, it was another type of law, the law of the contract, that became the crucial catalyst of change. This is not to disparage claims by Chinese commentators that the Chinese police are increasingly a law enforcement agency. Rather, it is to broaden this issue and ask a more profound question about the type of societal policing they are being called upon to carry out and the type of law they are to enforce.

Past mass-line communist solutions to crime had succeeded precisely because they were "holistic" (comprehensive) and involved turning their backs on the money economy. Instead of capital, communist cadres offered activist participants in their system a form of symbolic capital. The mass-line was a vision of a communist future and enthusiastic participation in it the cost of the entry ticket. With economic reform, however, this historical materialist vision came crashing to earth. But from the rubble a new type of materialism emerged. It offered a new means by which the Chinese police could mobilize and enthuse the masses in a world where comprehensiveness was no longer possible. That new means was, of course, money. Moreover, because money was always tied to performance, local communist cadres would be retrained and disciplined into the work habits of the market economy. By slowly commodifying mass-line policing through contracts, responsibility systems, and bonus programs, the authorities, in effect, would unwittingly transform the mass-line into one long conveyor belt of capitalist values. Ironically, then, it was these most communist of organizational forms—the mass-line organs—that became the schoolhouses of this new value system. In this light, the rhetoric about the need for the "rule of law" takes on a very different hue.

"Only in commodity production does the abstract legal form see the light," wrote the onetime doyen of Soviet jurisprudence, Evgeny Pashukanis (1978, 118). His argument was simple enough. All legal relations were "relations between formally equal subjects" (Pashukanis 1978, 41), and this legal equality mimicked the myth of equivalence that was central to market economics, in general, and the contract in particular. The dominance of a money-based contract system, therefore, signaled the dominance of an ideology of equivalence, and it was through this myth that markets and commodities came to appear both normal and even natural despite the fact that they were utterly alien to the planned socialist economy of the past.

Economic reform, in this light, constitutes one vast program of reform through labor in which one learns to think outside the inequality of the friend/enemy dyad and is instead inculcated with the equality of the money economy. The contract responsibility systems that economic reform has relied upon reinforce this myth of equivalence that is central to the new money economy. Moreover, the police, in devising their own money-based version of this strategy in order to reinvigorate the mass-line, have bought into this ethos, becoming, in the process, one more agent of change—despite the fact that they are all too often regarded as a conservative (read leftist) force in the West. Police have indeed become law enforcement agencies and are themselves increasingly subject to the law. But the main law they are subject to and their main task of enforcement is with regard to the law of the contract. It is this law that has transformed the mass-line into a mass production line for the maintenance and extension of values that the revolution once fought against. This perhaps, marks the final irony and lasting legacy of the mass-line in policing, and quite possibly the end of socialist mass-line policing in China. If nothing else, it signals, if not the end, then, at the very least, the demise of the political.

Concluding Reflections

To know oneself and to know the enemy
will lead to victory in a hundred wars. —SUN ZI

A CONCLUSION IS A LAND of opportunity. An opportunity to reflect upon what has been written, to tease out from the empirical detail some barely concealed theoretical concerns. Let me seize this opportunity then and reflect upon this empirical work as a localized instance of the life cycle of the political. To redescribe this book in these terms is to reveal the submerged structure that both framed and propelled the narrative, and, if the narrative is to be believed, the history as well. I have named that history "political" and claimed its exit point was marked by the development of the contract. The reasons for naming this work a political history, therefore, was twofold. Empirically, it was obvious from the very beginning that in terms of content the book described political history. Theoretically, however, things were different. It was not at first apparent to me that what I was writing was, in some respects, a history of political form.

The ability to name this work a political history in this latter sense emerged almost by accident. The theoretical and historical coincidence that occasioned it was the discovery that the lived revolutionary line of Mao Zedong also constituted the abstract theoretical line drawn by one Carl Schmitt. Indeed, Mao's very first revolutionary question was, as I have repeatedly pointed out throughout this text, nothing other than Schmitt's concept of the political. Because of this coincidence of the experiential and the theoretical and the influence of this on the revolutionary history of Maoist China that followed, we can in fact describe this history as political history in the Schmittian sense. In many respects, all I have done is to bring this deeper semiotic tale of the code of the political and its effects upon the Chinese lifeworld to the surface.

I have done this not by focusing on Schmitt but by depicting the birth, life, and death cycle of the friend/enemy concept in its various concrete and empirical guises in China. I have no interest in Hitler's so-called crown jurist beyond this. Nevertheless, the consequences of even this modest investment in Schmitt prove significant. I started with the rather obvious point that if his concept of the political is in any way valid, then the Maoist period constituted politics in its purest form. Maoist China lived life politically and, in the process, transformed everything into a binary political question framed in the language of class. No longer would class operate as a purely economic category. Instead, it became the crucial point of decision dividing the world of Mao into friend and enemy. It was around this category of class that struggle developed a concrete form. And it was through this that the abstract concept of the political acquired existential intensity. This intensity proved strong enough to power a revolution. In some key moments, it actually overpowered it.

With politics in command, class struggle proved almost impossible to control. The various attempts to institute what Denis Hollier might refer to as an "ethics of constraint" (1988, xxvi) by political means were far less successful than the attempts made to harness and extend the struggle. Rectification, united frontism, Party committee leadership, and even the mass-line could all be thought of as attempts to limit or channel the violent intensity of the political, just as the ideas of nonantagonistic contradictions could be viewed as an attempt to inlay into the dyadic political structure a moderating trinitarian element. To deal with the enemy, Chinese communists employed quite traditional dynastic appreciations of the law that always depicted it as both harsh and swift. In Mao's China, this traditional Chinese Legalist understanding of law was supplemented by a Soviet-inspired desire for legal flexibility. What was powerful and harsh within traditional Legalism thereby became unrestrained under Mao. The lived threat of a dangerous political enemy would always lead to this wedding of the harsh and the flexible for nothing should restrain a Party caught in a life-and-death struggle with its enemy. Yet legal flexibility had another side. It would also undergird the ameliorist and humanist tendencies of this regime.

As Mao intermittently attempted to open a third way for the political which did not turn on the either/or nature of political decisionism, a different set of measures unfolded that demonstrated an ameliorative face to "flexibility." Rectification was nothing if not the flexible employment of campaign technology. It would attempt to harness political intensity but avoid the bloodletting. United frontism pushed the boundaries of friendship into new terrain by transforming the enemy into a stranger-foreigner and extending the possibility of friendship to all Chinese. Party committee leadership and mass-line organs both offered flexible technical leadership over the struggle at a local level. If political problems could be dealt with at this more intimate level, the chances of excess were, it was thought, diminished. Finally, with the arrival of the nonantagonistic contradiction, we begin to see the solidification of this flexible dualistic framework. In the dual legal structure that grew from this, the enemy would be dealt with harshly by severe laws, but contradictions among the people would be handled with care by ameliorative technical-administrative means. This division of the legal and the technical-administrative constituted nothing less than the division of the world. For the onetime doyen of Soviet Marxist jurisprudence, Evgeny Pashukanis, it described the difference between capitalism and socialism.

"Historically," says Pashukanis, "law begins with dispute" (1978, 93). Where law begins with the assumption of conflicting interests, the ameliorative technical-administrative regulation that socialism would develop, he notes, assumes a commonality of purpose and a unity of interests. Famously described by Pashukanis via the train timetable, this distinction between the bourgeois legal form and the technical-administrative form that will come to dominate under socialism is axiomatic both for his argument about the withering away of formal law under socialism and for the Chinese Communist claims that they employ reintegrative justice alongside class justice. It is, however, in Pashukanis that the theoretical stakes of this division become clear.

The punitive quality of railway liability law stood, says Pashukanis, in stark contrast to the commonality of purpose encouraged by the regulation of train timetables (1978, 81). While the former law is punitive (designed to determine where liability lies), the latter is regulative (how do we all work together to ensure that the trains run on time?). For Pashukanis, socialism marked the transition from the former, punitive mode to the latter, regulative one. This view would eventually cost him his life. Nevertheless, in the time between his demise and his death, he would attempt to save his physical life by sacrificing his intellectual one: "[My] grossly mistaken position, foreign to Marxism-Leninism, distorts the meaning of the proletarian state, distorts the meaning of proletarian communist morality, and distorts the meaning of Soviet law as the instrument of the proletarian state which serves as an instrument in the construction of socialism" (1936).[1]

Such statements were but the final forlorn moments in a reluctant transition that led Pashukanis and the Soviet Union from a flexible legal transfer culture, which promised a withering away of law because of its inherently bourgeois quality, toward a culture in which the legal superstructure of the state was strengthened and emphasis placed upon the "stability, formality and professionalism" of the law (Sharlet 1977, 158, 159). This latter model would end up forming the basis of a jurisprudence of terror under the erstwhile student of Pashukanis, Andrei Ianuaryevich Vyshinsky.[2] In an oedipal move masked by Marxist pretense, Vyshinsky the student-son denounced his father-teacher.

So it was that in January 1937, Pashukanis, and not law, "withered away." Indeed, so completely was his work torn from the pages of socialist legal theory that if one were to leaf through the innumerable Chinese texts outlining socialist theorizations of law, few would mention his name, and even fewer would give him anything more than a passing pejorative appellation.[3] Nevertheless, the concerns he raised were ones that would continue to shadow socialism. Where Pashukanis saw law withering away and being replaced by technical regulation, the Chinese believed that these two spheres, one coded ameliorative, the other punitive, should work in tandem. It was as they attempted to get them to work in tandem that they established a distinction between law and administrative regulation.

The power of the political, however, constantly undercut the introduction of ameliorative administrative measures. Where the communists desired an ameliorative administrative system of regulation to run alongside the punitive legal system, politics constantly compressed the space of moderation, forcing all decisions into an either-or framework. As this took place, the technical and administrative formulations of the Party faded in the face of the political passions aroused by the various political campaigns. More often than not, the administrative regulation ended up being valued for its flexibility of application rather than for its ameliorative spirit. Indeed, the ameliorative could really only ever acquire full voice when there was little at stake, and it is Schmitt who shows us why this is the case. Disparaging the humanism of ameliorist regulatory models (such as those suggested by Pashukanis in his example of the train timetable), Schmitt suggested that any unity of purpose built only on the basis of economics or the "technical regulation of traffic" was no more of a social entity than "tenants in a tenement house, customers purchasing gas from the same utility company, or passengers traveling on the same bus" (1996, 57). His conclusion is that an "interest group concerned exclusively with economics or traffic cannot become more than that, in the absence of an adversary" (1996, 57). Yet the minute such an adversary appears, of course, one is thrown back into the either/or question of politics.

It is the threat of the enemy that strangles any broader unity of purpose. It tightens around the group that shares the same worldview and does so strongly enough to make it feel a sense of righteous indignation that it then directs against its enemy. Commitment politics, by definition, always speaks in defense of its commitments, and in this respect, it is always, in part, defined in relation to what threatens these. The revolutionary virtues of martyrdom and the ethic of the heroic forces one to defend what one holds dear by committing acts that take one beyond oneself. As one is moved beyond oneself, there is no room for ameliorist compromise. This is a battle to the death, and, as such, it is fought bitterly. It is a battle which not only takes one beyond oneself and makes one chance the sacrifice of life but it also moves one beyond the moral norms that govern and guide the everyday. Paradoxically, and from a subjective perspective, the more noble the sacrifice to be made, the more it appears as the wet nurse of excess. Commitment politics, then, is defined and defining of both the collective and the individual. Collectively we are drawn to a cause, individually and existentially we transform that cause into a way of life. Both collectively and existentially our cause becomes the touchstone of who we are and who we want to be.

"The enemy is our own question as a figure," Schmitt once remarked (qtd. in Meier 1998, 44). Mao clearly agreed. From *ziwo piping* (self-criticism) through to *dousi pixie* (struggle against self, criticize revisionism), the problem of the enemy was brought home to the subject. This, therefore, was not just a question for the collective revolutionary body but also an issue for the individual body of the revolutionary. Indeed, this collective question becomes the individual revolutionary's own existential one. In the realm of the political, and in the era of Mao, China was enveloped by this double question. We come to define ourselves not in an agonal and endless contest of "self-testing," but through an intimate and intensely charged acknowledgment of the threat posed by the enemy. And while I am not fully sure I agree, others have suggested that we only have friends because we have enemies (Strauss 1996, 86). Be it in the singular or in the collective, then, the enemy defines us. This logic should come as no surprise, for we live it quite readily in other domains. Remember the legal trial which gains meaning only as a result of a legal breach or the criminal code where the phrase "thou shalt not" reigns supreme (Meier 1998, 41, 52, n. 73, 39)? If negative definitions are far from strange, why does it appear odd to insist that we are driven to, and defined by, our own perceptions of the opposite?

This ability to define self emerges alongside a (self-) awareness of what it is to be right and proper. Both emerge out of a brush with what we see as the immorality of our enemy. Just as Jeremy Bentham once mused that law creates right not by and in itself but by creating crime, so, too, the moral thought gains concrete form only in the reflection of what it is not (Pashukanis 1978, 167). But where the law of Bentham would aspire to impose an ethic of limit by carving out a reason of correspondence between misdeed and punishment, politics always remains potentially limitless. It is always, potentially, a fight to the death. It is this that propels it beyond any ethic of limit or technical-administrative clause we may care to impose upon it. To offer oneself in a potential fight to the death is to go beyond reason. It is here that the power of commitment politics becomes all too apparent. It instills within the committed a concrete existential sense of righteousness that offers "a material power which mere 'ideas,' 'rational ends' or 'normativities' lack" (Meier 1998, 31). It produces an ethic of heroism which is, of course, merely one of the many faces of the ethic of excess. We are caught in the bind of fearing that which, in other circumstances, we might most admire. We desire that sense of moral purpose, yet refuse to face its likely consequences. Ultimately, we must come to accept that as a paradoxical art of the emotions, the political forms part of what makes us human.

How, then, was it possible to collectively turn a nation's face away from this type of political enchantment? Certainly, adopting ameliorative measures from within politics itself seemed to offer no solution. If it shows nothing else, the concrete history of Chinese socialist policing demonstrates that any solution that works within the folds of the political constitutes no solution at all. But this is precisely what makes the story of economic reform in China all the more remarkable. It offers a clear example of a moment when the enchantment of the political is no more. Enchantment itself remains, but, like the migrant workers of China, it has left the village of politics for the cities of the consumer. Thus unlike the political solutions of Mao, economic reform offered seductive solutions that did not confront the political directly. Economic reform was a war of maneuver against the political. Its proscriptions never directly challenged the institutional political order in any significant way. It never broke into the realm of the overtly political and therefore avoided challenging commitments and forcing the either-or question to the fore. Rather, the reform of the economy appeared as a mere extension of some natural (economic) law, and it is in this regard, not in its grand contest with the rule of man, that the rule of law plays a crucial role in reconfiguring post-Mao China. To understand how requires returning to Pashukanis.

"The development of law as a system," writes Pashukanis, "was not predicated on the needs of prevailing power relations but on the requirements of trading transactions with peoples who were precisely not yet encompassed within a unified sphere of authority" (1978, 95). The historic shift from patriarchal to contractual relations, Pashukanis insists, constituted nothing other than the arrival of the modern bourgeois subject, and law was to be its vehicle. It is in the famous dictum of Sir Henry Sumner Maine that we become alert to this. In the historic shift that takes us from family dependency to individual obligation, the basis for an abstract theory of the contract is laid (Maine 1970, 168). The contract, therefore, is but the abstract legal expression of the play of equal, "autonomous" wills (Pashukanis 1978, 121). This process of abstraction, so central to the constitution of law, also proves central to the constitution of capitalist relations. Just as law requires an abstract legal subject, so, too, commodity forms require the notion of abstract labor. In the abstract, everything can be rendered equal, and the contract, borne in abstraction, becomes an almost "natural" means by which to reify the idea of "relations between formally equal subjects" (Pashukanis 1978, 41). The contract does this by rejecting everything not connected with the nature and purpose of the economic transaction. This made it appear as a mere technical expression of some natural law of the economy (Pashukanis 1978, 95). Such a process of naturalizing the concept of free, abstract, equal individuals who bear rights and responsibilities carried within it the seeds of a new world. It is for this reason that Pashukanis reads contract law as the "concept central to law" (1978, 121) and why he reads legal form as inherently bourgeois. Thus even though it appeared to be of little consequence, the reification and naturalizing effect it had upon bourgeois notions of a transcendental subject made the contract central to the early development of capitalism.

The contractual form presents the world as a series of atomized relations between formally equal subjects (Pashukanis 1978, 41). The disparities of wealth, position, and power that exist in concrete circumstances are never recognized within abstract contractual relations. In fact, inequality is occluded by the formal equivalence given to both parties. It is this that underpins the faux equality of the legal myth and, at the same time, makes law a further means to reinforce the myth of commodity and market equivalence. Pashukanis therefore concludes that the essential form law takes ties it to the same specific set of social circumstances that produced the commodity relation. The legal relation between subjects is simply the reverse side of the relation between products of labor which have become commodities, he says. Both work on an exchange of formal "equivalences" that mask significant differences. One leads to the occluded, "always the same" quality of the commodity (Adorno and Horkheimer 1979, 9), while the other points us to legal equivalence and the occluded privilege Marx referred to as bourgeois right. So while the commodity always appears different but is essentially always the same commodity form, law always appears equal, but only by disguising the built-in privileges it offers the wealthy.

The spread of the contractual form in China plotted in my final chapter takes on added significance when read alongside this theoretical formulation. Yet what I wanted to stress here was not the issue of equivalence so much as that of repetition. Part of the power of the contract to naturalize equivalence came from its repeated use. Once the contract form was habituated, it produced new desires that led the Chinese subject to think not of a political revolution but of a consumer one. In light of this, the story of Mao, Deng, the Party, and the police becomes more than a historical narrative of a particular security agency. Essentially, and very much in the margins, it is a tale of the seduction of the political, rather than of its forced demise. Life lived through the logic of the political binary was seduced by the forms thrown up by the market. Market seductions would never directly confront the political. They remained beneath the threshold surface that we might label *resistance*. Yet they moved the political more than any overt practice of resistance could possibly have.

It is at this point that one needs once again to recognize the novelty of this tale. More than a history of a particular political organization, this history reveals a specific, concrete, ongoing tale of the policing of politics. This way of attending to the political, however, is never on the agenda of standard accounts of Chinese political history. They miss this because they feign an apolitical, "objective" stance. Yet far from being apolitical, such works are, like the legal contract or the commodity form, utterly bourgeois. Fighting words . . . so let me explain.

The Two-Line Struggle

At the very beginning of this book, I suggested that in order to understand the concept of the political, one need only turn to the first line of the first page of the first volume of Mao Zedong's *Selected Works*. Now, at the very end of this work, I want to turn to the first line of the first page of another work and say the opposite: If you want to misunderstand the nature of the political, turn to (the first line on the first page of) Thomas Kampen's recent political history of Chinese communism. There, as an opening gambit in his revisionist account of elite communist politics, Kampen states, "For about half a century, international research on the rise of Mao Zedong and the CCP leadership . . . has been dominated by the idea of a 'two-line struggle'" (2000, 1).[4] This, says Kampen, is both a simplistic and historically inaccurate method through which to analyze political history (2000, 3–5).

Kampen is not alone in his criticism of this method. Indeed, he is merely the latest in a long line of revisionist political historians of the Chinese Communist Party to revisit and debunk this model of historical causality (Teiwes 2000, 243). Indeed, I can think of no recent contemporary political history of China, other than those written by members of the Communist Party themselves, that would not agree with him. Moreover, they all seem to agree upon the best method of demonstrating the falsity of this two-line struggle method. Just look at the historical facts; they speak for themselves. Turn to the detail and the detail will reveal the lie of this method.

Like so many historians of Chinese politics before him, Kampen does just that. He corrects the historical record with the eye of an erudite scholar. He marshals the archival material to produce a dense and detailed portrait of elite politics that belies a simple binary interpretation. History reveals from its archive a myriad of political positions emerging under the imprimatur of various leading Party lights. The case is made. History is irreducible to just two lines, and the evidence from the historical record proves just that. Kampen is, of course, historically speaking, absolutely correct. History is always more complex than two lines. The problem for Kampen and all the other critics of the two-line struggle who argue their case in exactly this way is that they all fail to recognize that while history is more complex than this, politics is not. Indeed, it is precisely in its ability to transmogrify the many into the few that the power of the political lies. It is in its ability to reduce everything into a concrete existential distinction between friend and enemy (Schmitt 1996, 26) that commitment politics produces the intensity that propels political history forward. The dynamic of history, that force that enables political history to be written in a manner that is indeed historical rather than static, requires locating, in a concrete empirical setting, that spirit of intensity that gives rise to (historical) movement. To render the political anthropomorphically as a series of (nonbinary) power plays robs history of that dynamic. It forces history into a barely disguised version and variation on the "Great Man" view of history. Ultimately, with China, the "Great Man" was Mao. Here, then, we have a Western version of the cult of Mao returned to us in an inverted and methodological form.

If, however, the political is precisely the question of two lines (those of friend and enemy), then the error of these political histories seems obvious. In their very attempts to rectify the simplicity of the two-line method by adding empirical complexity, they occlude the political. By complicating history through the addition of supplementary dissenting morphologies, they lose sight of the power of the political that lies precisely in its ability to reduce *everything* to a dyadic question. They forget the importance of Mao's words when he called upon the revolution to hunt down the principle contradiction. In failing to do this, these complex Western accounts become the inversion of the simplistic approach they criticize. Western historicization of the political leads to the occlusion of the political in much the same way as Chinese politicization of the historical leads to the elision of the historical. Paradoxically, it is the Chinese error that proves the error of the Western approach. What the Chinese anthropomorphization of the two-line struggle method of history writing shows is that everything, including historical narratives themselves, are pulled by the gravity of the binding political question, "Who are our enemies, who are our friends?"

Thus rather than complicating the idea of a two-line struggle by adding additional dissenting voices, I have tried to complicate the tale in another way. I have tried to show how this single question came to dominate the Chinese lifeworld in a myriad of complex ways. I examined how it was transformed into a problem in Yan'an; how it was structured into the organs of state and the considerations of government immediately after the revolution; and how, over time, it developed into a nascent theory of the state. I have tried to offer a historical account of its development which belies its Schmittian transhistoricism. I have, however, borrowed from Schmitt the observation that we are dealing here with more than a question of method. The power of the political lies in the fact that it becomes a way of life. An entire national ethos built around various expressions of this dyadic political form, everyday objects infused with political symbolism, personal and emotional commitments that shone brightest and most clearly under the intensity of this dyadic form—these, I have argued, were but some of the effects of living in a state of the political. Historically, and in a classically Schmittian sense, Mao's China was, as I have stated earlier, a state of commitment politics lived on the knife edge of a binary division. It produced a life both extremely dangerous but also utterly life-affirming. It gave purpose to one's existence and offered a sense of belonging that would fill one's soul.

This, not Reason, was the "spirit" that would guide this particular history. It is a spirit, I would suggest, guiding any expression of commitment politics, and it is for this reason that its implications go well beyond the empirical tale in which it is set. Without tracing what one might call the spirit of intensity—that unreason of the political—one is left with only half-baked and half-correct pragmatic accounts of History's revolutionary unfoldings. This spirit of intensity, then, has little to do with Reason. From Hegel to Habermas, we have been led to believe and to instill within our histories a sense of Reason, a Reason of History. Historical progress, it seems, is ultimately propelled by this telos of Reason. Yet where is the Reason in states that lived the political as China did under Mao? What counts as Reason in such a (mental and political) state is nothing other than a commonwealth of commitment. Commitment produces the ethic of the heroic in the name of something, and in that name it pushes us beyond Reason. Only the two-line struggle, in highlighting the politically charged nature of relations with the enemy, offers us an opportunity to register this other side of Reason. It is this, in a myriad of different ways depending upon concrete circumstances, that offers us the possibility of history. It is a historical method that loses its raison d'être only when political commitment fades. Only then does the two-line struggle method appear simplistic. Only then does it become redundant.

Contemporary Western political histories of China that dismiss the two-line struggle because of "new facts" made available as a result of the open-door policy are, therefore, tied to the new era in a much more profound way than by the mere availability of new facts. Just as the new era of reform has complicated Chinese lives by disaggregating things and thus disengaging them from the single, simple dyadic political question of Mao, so, too, the historiographic method of the new era dissaggregates past politics by adding new, more detailed historical evidence. The resulting histories are more complex than the two-line analysis allowed, but they lack any historical dynamic save for the personalized machinations of the leadership group. As a result, commitment politics is rendered as little more than a smoke screen to mask the "real" venal pragmatic play of power politics.

If, however, one puts weight upon commitment, the veil of complexity that masks the dynamic of history is cut away by the razor-sharp knife edge of the either-or decisionism forced upon us by the two-line struggle. This method, however, only works when politics is in command. This is the moment when commitment reigns and when political intensity forces us into this either-or form of decisionism. To explain theoretically how the magic spell of this form of commitment politics was broken by the revisionist brilliance of Deng Xiaoping requires an explanation that went beyond both Schmitt and Mao. Essentially, what I have suggested is that just as the old political binary logic began to wane, another mode of simplification came to reign. If commitment politics produced simplicity by constantly reiterating the either-or choice of class struggle, economic reform simplified social questions not through binary political intensities, but through the condensation of all relations into monetary forms ordered around the contract. In this way, the Chinese lifeworld was turned on its head. Put simply, the strictures on wealth generation once held in place by political commitment and enforced by an elastic legal code gave way to a changed ethic and a very different relationship to law. Law in the reform era began to solidify into a stable code at the very time that economic restrictions upon wealth generation were lifted. Just as the coincidence of Mao and Schmitt highlighted the nature of commitment politics, so, too, this new coincidence pointed to something of great significance. And it was in the theoretical work of the commodity-exchange school that the significance of this became clear.

While politics subsumed all domains so that they became localized sites of the friend/enemy distinction, the economic domain worked through contracts to cover the social body such that everything was rendered potentially equivalent. The dominance of economic rationality led to the dissolution of the singular Maoist political covenant and the emergence of an array of contractual forms. Nevertheless, this new era also had a unifying social core. Repeated employment of contractual forms across the social landscape helped to naturalize its assumptions and to give it an abstract transcendental quality. It thereby bleached away the "unnatural" power of the political. As the power of the political distinction dissipated, an endless series of contractual distinctions emerged to mimic the binary form of the political dyad, but drain away the passion that had infused intensity into all relations. In each and every domain, and irrespective of their own particular localized distinctions, the practices once undertaken out of passionate commitment to a political program were now to be underwritten and disciplined by the dominant economic distinction of profit and loss. In this sense, and only in this sense, did the economic distinction come to replace the political one. Yet even at this moment of economic success, when profit was the signature that underwrote every social contract, the economic domain failed to evoke the same degree of authoritativeness and intensity that the political distinction had once achieved. The result was a disillusioned world that no longer spoke of anything with passion or intensity. It spoke of a materially prosperous future that lacked a soul. Caught between the Scylla of passion and excess and the Charybdis of alienation and order, the Chinese Communist Party would finally choose the latter. The cost of limiting excess, it seems, would be to place mental constraints on life. In this new, passionless world of the commodity society, the excitement of revolution gave way to the faux excitement of manufactured commodity desire. This would relive the past in mimicked forms rendered safe and salable for every consumer. The excesses of the past had finally vanished, but so, too, had the life-affirming victories of the revolutionary line. Perhaps this is the cost of an ethic of limit. Life-threatening intensity can only be limited by limiting life itself. Perhaps this is the real lesson of economic reform. Perhaps this is the final lesson of the political.

GLOSSARY OF CHINESE NAMES, PLACES AND TERMS

Names

Bai Ziming	白子明	Fu Zhong	傅钟
Bo Yibo	薄一波	Gao Gang	高岗
Chen Changhao	陈昌浩	Gao Kelin	高克林
Chen Duxiu	陈独秀	Gu Bo	古博
Chen Gongbo	陈公博	Gu Shunzhang	顾顺章
Chen Guofu	陈果夫	Gu Zuolin	顾作霖
Chen Lida	陈立达	Guan Xiangying	关向应
Chen Lifu	陈立夫	Guo Hongtao	郭洪涛
Chen Long	陈龙	Hai Jingzhou	海景州
Chen Mingren	陈明仁	He Long	贺龙
Chen Pengnian	陈彭年	Hu Di	胡底
Chen Pixian	陈丕显	Hu Feng	胡风
Chen Tianfang	陈天放	Hu Gongmian	胡公冕
Chen Yi	陈毅	Hu Jian	胡健
Cheng Cheng	程诚	Hu Junhe	胡均鹤
Cheng Qian	程潜	Hu Zongnan	胡宗南
Cheng Shicai	程世才	Hua Guofeng	华国锋
Dai Jiying	戴季英	Huang Gonglüe	黄公略
Deng Fa	邓发	Jiang Jieshi	
Deng Xiaoping	邓小平	(Chiang	
Di Fei	狄飞	Kei-Shek)	蒋介石
Ding Ling	丁玲	Jiang Qing	江青
Dong Biwu	董必武	Jiang Zemin	江泽民
Du Liqing	杜里卿	Jin Wanbang	金万邦
Duan Dechang	段德昌	Kang Sheng	康生
Dun Liangbi	段良弼	Lei Feng	雷锋
Fan Dawei	樊大畏	Li Baifang	李白芳
Fang Zhimin	方志敏	Li Chuli	李楚离
Fu Bocui	傅柏翠	Li Dazhao	李大钊

Li Fuchun	李富春	Liu Xiangsan	刘向三
Li Jishen	李济深	Liu Xuewen	刘学文
Li Kenong	李克农	Liu Zhidan	刘志丹
Li Lisan	李立三	Lu Dingyi	陆定一
Li Qiang	李强	Lu Dongsheng	卢冬生
Li Qingchang	李清昌	Luo Ronghuan	罗荣桓
Li Ronggui	李荣桂	Luo Ruiqing	罗瑞卿
Li Shaojiu	李韶九	Ma Mingshan	马明山
Li Shiqun	李士群	Ma Wenrui	马文瑞
Li Tianhuan	李天焕	Ma Wu	马武
Li Wenlin	李文林	Ma Xingwu	马星五
Li Yimang	李一氓	Mao Zedong	毛泽东
Li Yimin	李逸民	Meng Xianjia	孟宪嘉
Li Yiping	李一平	Min Buying	闵步瀛
Li Yiqing	李一清	Nie Hongjun	聂鸿钧
Li Yutang	李玉堂	Nie Rongzhen	聂荣臻
Li Zhao	李钊	Niu Yuhe	牛玉和
Li Zhen	李震	Ouyang Qin	欧阳钦
Liang Botai	梁柏台	Ouyang Yi	欧阳毅
Liang Guobin	梁国斌	Pan Hannian	潘汉年
Lin Biao	林彪	Peng Dehuai	彭德怀
Lin Meitin	林梅汀	Peng Guocai	彭国才
Lin Yizhu	林一株	Peng Zhen	彭真
Ling Yun	凌云	Qian Yi	钱毅
Liu Bingwen	刘秉温	Qing Ying	钱英
Liu Chuanxin	刘传新	Qian Zhuangfei	钱壮飞
Liu Di	刘敌	Qin Bangxian	秦邦宪
Liu Fuzhi	刘复之	Qu Qiubai	瞿秋白
Liu Haibin	刘海滨	Rao Rushi	饶漱石
Liu Jianfu	刘坚夫	Ren Bishi	任弼时
Liu Jianzhang	刘建章	Rong Wusheng	戎伍胜
Liu Jingfan	刘景范	Shen Zemin	沈泽民
Liu Junzhi	刘俊之	Shi Guangping	石广平
Liu Juying	刘居英	Shi Yizhi	施义之
Liu Lantao	刘澜涛	Shi Zhe	师哲
Liu Minghui	刘明辉	Su Yushan	苏玉山
Liu Shaoqi	刘少奇	Sun Yatsen	
Liu Shuqing	刘淑清	(Sun Zhongshan)	孙中山

Sun Zi	孙子	Yang Guomao	杨国茂
Tan Zhengwen	谭政文	Yang Jie	杨杰
Tao Zhu	陶铸	Yang Qingshan	杨青山
Wang Chu	王初	Yang Qiqing	杨奇清
Wang Dongxing	汪东兴	Yang Sen	杨森
Wang Hongming	王宏鸣	Yang Xianzhen	杨献珍
Wang Hongwen	王洪文	Yao Wenyuan	姚文元
Wang Jiaxiang	王稼祥	Ye Jianying	叶剑英
Wang Jingwei	汪精卫	Yin Zhaozhi	尹肇之
Wang Jinxiang	汪金祥	Yu Jisheng	余继生
Wang Lianyou	王连友	Yu Sang	于桑
Wang Ming	王明	Zeng Kuoqing	曾扩情
Wang Shiwei	王实味	Zeng Wei	曾威
Wang Shoudao	王首道	Zhang	
Wang Xuren	王须仁	Chunqiao	张春桥
Wang Zhao	王昭	Zhang	
Wei Dingyuan	魏定远	Dingcheng	张鼎丞
Wu De	吴德	Zhang Guojian	张国俭
Wu Faxian	吴法宪	Zhang Guotao	张国焘
Wu Han	吴晗	Zhang Keqing	张克勤
Wu Lie	吴烈	Zhang Lie	张烈
Wu Zhuozai	吴拙哉	Zhang Pinghua	张平化
Xia Xi	夏曦	Zhang Qirui	张其瑞
Xiang Ying	项英	Zhang Ranhe	张然和
Xiao Bin	肖彬	Zhang Xihou	张锡侯
Xiao Hua	肖华	Zhang Xiushan	张秀山
Xie Zichang	谢子长	Zhang Zuolin	张作霖
Xu Jianguo	许建国	Zhao Cangbi	赵苍璧
Xu Zirong	徐子荣	Zhao	
Xi Zhongxun	习仲勋	Dengcheng	赵登程
Xie Fuzhi	谢富治	Zhou Enlai	周恩来
Xie Hanchang	谢汉昌	Zhou Heng	周恒
Xing Xiangsheng	邢相生	Zhou Xing	周兴
Xiong Botao	熊伯涛	Zhou Yang	周扬
Xu Jishen	许继慎	Zhu De	朱德
Yan Xishan	阎锡山	Zhu Jiayao	祝家耀
Yang Fan	扬帆	Zhuo Xiong	卓雄

Places

Central Base Camp	Jiangxi-Fujian	中央革命根据地
Chuan-Shaan	Sichuan-Shaanxi	川陕
E-Yu-Wan	Hubei-Henan-Anhui	鄂豫皖
Gannan	southern Jiangxi	赣南
Ganxi	western Jiangxi	赣西
Ganxinan	southwestern Jiangxi	赣西南
Hai-Lufeng	Haifeng-Lufeng	海陆丰
Huainan	southern Huai	淮南
Huazhong	Center China	华中
Ji-Lu-Yu	Hebei-Shandong-Henan	冀鲁豫
Jin-Cha-Ji	Shanxi-Chahar-Hebei	晋察冀
Jin-Ji-Lu-Yu	Shanxi-Hebei-Shandong-Henan	晋冀鲁豫
Jin-Sui	Shanxi-Suiyuan	晋绥
Jinxibei	northwestern Jin (Shanxi)	晋西北
Ludongnan	southeastern Shandong	鲁东南
Luxinan	southwestern Shangdong	鲁西南
Minxi	western Fujian	闽西
Min-Zhe-Gan	Fujian-Zhejiang-Jiangxi	闽浙赣
Shaan-Gan	Shaanxi-Gansu	陕甘
Shaan-Gan-Jin	Shaanxi-Gansu-Shanxi	陕甘晋
Shaan-Gan-Ning	Shaanxi-Gansu-Ningxia	陕甘宁
Su-Lu-Yu	Jiangsu-Shangdong-Henan	苏鲁豫
Xiang-E	Hunan-Hubei	湘鄂
Xiang-E-Chuan-Qian	Hunan-Hubei-Sichuan-Guizhou	湘鄂川黔
Xiang-E-Gan	Hunan-Hubei-Jiangxi	湘鄂赣
Xiang-E'xi	Hunan-western Hubei	湘鄂西

Baiqueyuan (White Sparrow Garden)	白雀园
Bijia Mountain	笔架山
Boshan	博山
Fengqiao	枫桥
Fuping county	阜平县
Futian	富田
Harbin	哈尔滨
Huachi county	华池县
Hubian	湖边
Huxi	湖西

Jiaodong	胶东	
Jiamusi	佳木斯	
Jixian	集贤	
Liao county	辽县	
Lin county	临县	
Nanliang	南梁	
Panlong	蟠龙	
Pei County	沛县	
Qincheng Prison	秦城监狱	
Qinghe	清河	
Ruijin	瑞金	
Shanxi	山西	
Shayang	沙洋	
Shenyang	沈阳	
Suide	绥德	
Taihang	太行	
Tailaibian	泰莱边	
Taishan	泰山	
Taiyue	太岳	
Tongchuan	铜川	
Xi'an	西安	
Xueshan	学山	
Yan'an	延安	
Zhuji	诸暨	
Zunyi	遵义	

Terms

A-B *tuan*	A-B 团	A-B League Reformist Faction
anbaozu	安保组	security protection group
anquan baowei zerenzhi	安全保卫责任制	safety security responsibility system
anquan jiancha yundong	安全检查运动	safety checking campaign
anquan yundong	安全运动	security campaign
baiqu gongzuobu	白区工作部	white area work section
banshizu	办事组	office group
bao'anchu	保安处	security division

bao'an fuwu gongsi	保安服务公司	private security companies
baoweihui	保卫会	protection section
baoweiyuan	保卫员	protection worker
banhu renjia	半户人家	half household
bi-gong-xin	逼供信	forced confessional technique
canmouzhang	参谋长	chief of staff
cc pai	cc 派	cc faction
chengqian bihou, zhibing jiuren	惩前毖后，治病救人	learn from past mistakes to avoid future ones, and cure the sickness to save the patient
chiweidui	赤卫队	red protection terms
chujianbu	锄奸部	elimination of Traitors Bureau
danwei	单位	work unit
daoxia liuren, tingzhi buren	刀下留人，停止捕人	stop the killing, stop arresting
daxingzhengqu	大行政区	large administrative area
dayuejin	大跃进	Great Leap Forward
dipi liumang	地痞流氓	local riffraff or hooligans
diqu gongzuo weiyuanhui	敌区工作委员会	Enemy Areas Work Committee
diqu/qu	地区/区	Region, prefecture, area
diwei	地委	Prefectural Committee
dousipixiu	斗私批修	struggle against self, criticize revisionism
dui	队	team
duoquan yundong	夺权运动	Campaign to Seize Power
ertongtuan	儿童团	children's corps
fangeming anjian shencha weiyuanhui	反革命案件审查委员	counter-revolutionary case checking committee
fazhi	法治	rule of law
funü shengchan jiaoyangyuan	妇女生产教养院	Women's Production Education and Fostering Institutes
Futian shibian	富田事变	Futian Incident
gaizupai	改组派	Reformist Faction

gaofeng	高峰	high tide
gechou xiaozu	革筹小组	revolutionary preparatory small group
gong'anchu	公安处	public security section
gong'anyuan	公安员	public security personnel
gong'an yushen bumen	公安预审部门	public security preliminary hearing department
gong'an zhuliyuan	公安助理员	public security helpers
gong'anbu	公安部	Ministry of Public Security
gong'an hexin xiaozu	公安核心小组	core leading group of the Minister of Public Security
gong'anju	公安局	public security bureau
gong'anke	公安科	public security division
gong'anting	公安厅	public security department at provincial level
gong'an yuan	公安员	public security personnel
gongjianfa	公检法	public security, procuraturate and courts
gongnong baodongdui	工农暴动队	worker-peasant insurrectionary terms
gongzuo wangyuan	工作网员	work networker
guanxundui	管训队	supervised training teams
guanzhi	管制	mass surveillance and control
guojia zhengzhi baoweiju	国家政治保卫局	State Political Protection Bureau
hongjun gongzuobu	红军工作部	red army work section
hongqidang	红旗党	Red Flag Party
hongsiling	红司令	revolutionary commander
hukou ermu	户口耳目	eyes and ears of the household register
huidaomen	会道门	secret societies
Huxi shijian	湖西事件	Huxi Incident
ji'an	积案	Long-pending cases
jianchake	检查科	Inspection sub-section
jianqian yankan	见钱眼开	eyes open when money is in sight

jiapu	家谱	lineage record
Jiefang Ribao	解放日报	*Liberation Daily*
Jieji yiji fenzi	阶级异己分子	alien class element
jieyansuo	戒烟所	anti-drug smoking clinics
jingji chengbao zerenzhi	经济承包责任制	economic contract respon-sibility system
jingwei dadui	警卫大队	security teams
jixun	集训	collective training
jizhong guanzhi	集中管制	concentrated surveillance
juan	卷	volume
juesihui	决死会	Life and Death Teams
juzhang	局长	bureau chief
kanshousuo	看守所	detention centers (watch house)
kongsuhui	控诉会	accusation meeting
laogai	劳改	reform through labor
laojiao	劳教	re-education through labor
liandong	联动	name of a Red Guard group
liandui	连队	company
lianfang	联防	joint protection
lianfang zhi'anchu	联防治安处	joint defense protection of public security depart-ment
liang	两	a unit of weight, equal to 50 grams
lianluoyuan	联络员	liaison personnel
Liening zhuyi zuoyi fanduipai	列宁主义左翼反对派	Leninist Left Opposition Faction
liucuanfan	流窜犯	transient criminals
lubushiyi, yebubihu	路不拾遗，夜不闭户	no one picked up other's things from the road and no one needed to lock their door
mangliu	盲流	floating blind
mishuzhang	秘书长	secretary

neibu sufan yundong	内部肃反运动	Campaign to Suppress Internal Counter-Revolutionaries
neiceng	内层	inner levels
neiwubu	内务部	internal affairs bureau
pi Lin pi Kong yundong	批林批孔运动	Campaign to Criticize Lin Biao and Confucius
putonghua	普通话	Mandarin Chinese
qiangjiu shizuzhe yundong	抢救失足者运动	Campaign to Help Those Who Had Lost Their Footing or Rescue Campaign
qingbaobu	情报部	Intelligence Bureau
qingqidui	轻骑队	*Light Cavalry*
qiyue zhidu	契约制度	Contract system
qu	区	area
quwei	区委	Regional committee
renmin baowei zu	人民保卫组	People's security organs
renshiju	人事局	Personnel Bureau
renzhi	人治	rule of man
sandagaizao	三大改造	three big transformations
sanfan	三反	three antis campaign
sanguang zhengce	三光政策	three mop-ups policy
sansanzhi	三三制	third-thirds system
sanwei yiti	三位一体	three in one
sanwu	三无	three have-nots
Shaan-Gan-Ning bianqu	陕甘宁边区	Shaan-Gan-Ning Border Region
Shaan-Gan-Ning bianqu bao'anchu	陕甘宁边区保安处	Shaan-Gan-Ning Border Region Security Division
shanxi kangri jiuguo xisheng tongmenghui/ Shanxi ximenghui	山西抗日救国牺牲同盟会/山西牺盟会	Shanxi resist the Japanese, save the nation through sacrifice society
shaonian guanjiaosuo	少年管教所	youth retraining centers
shaoxiandui	少先队	Young Pioneers
shehuibu	社会部	Social Section
shehui minzhudang	社会民主党	Social Democratic Party

Shehui zhenfan, neibu sufan	社会镇反内部肃反	social suppression campaign targeting internal counter-revolutionaries
shengan yundong	审干运动	Campaign to Check on Cadres
shi junshi guanzhi weiyuanhui	市军事管制委员会	City Military Committees
shourong shencha	收容审查	shelter and investigation
sifang	四防	four protections
siwu	四无	four eliminations
Sufan	肃反	Campaign to Eliminate Counter-Revolutionaries
sufan weiyuanhui	肃反委员会	Committee to Eliminate Counter-Revolutionaries
teke	特科	special branch
tepaiyuan	特派员	special agents
tewei	特委	special committees
tewudui	特务队	special branch teams
tezhong hangye	特种行业	special business
tezhong hukou dengji	特种户口登记	special household register
tiaotiao kuaikuai	条条块块	vertical and horizontal leadership/organization structure
tiaozheng	调整	adjustment
tinghuadui	听话队	listening brigades
tuanzhang	团长	regimental commander
tuhao lieshen	土豪劣绅	local tyrants and evil gentry
waiceng	外层	outside the party, in society at large
wangyuan	网员	networker
wufan	五反	five antis campaign
xiafang	下放	send down to the countryside
xiang	乡	town/township
xingshi juliu	刑事拘留	criminal detention
xingdongtan	行动探	activity detective

xin sanfan	新三反	New three antis
Yuan	元	Chinese dollar
yanda	严打	Severe strike
yifadaixing	以罚代刑	Use of fines to replace punishment
yige busha, dadou buzhua	一个不杀，大都不抓	don't execute a single one, and arrest only a few
yiqie xiangqiankan	一切向前看	to look ahead (to socialism)
yiqie xiangqiankan	一切向钱看	to only have eyes for money
yikuhui	忆苦会	meeting to recall past suffering
yujinyuxian	寓禁于限	tight control within limits
yushenke	预审科	interrogation and detention sub-section
yushenzu	预审组	pretrial interrogation and detention group
zaitaofan	在逃犯	criminals on the run
zhandoudui	战斗队	combat battalions
zhengwuyuan	政务院	Government Administrative Council
zhenchabu	侦察部	investigative section
zhenchake	侦察科	investigative sub-section
zhenfan	镇反	Campaign to Suppress Counter-Revolutionaries
zhengfeng=shengan=sufan	整风=审干=肃反	rectification = cadre checking = the elimination of counter-revolutionaries
zhengwei	政委	political commissar
zhenwuyuan	政务院	government administrative council
zhengzhi baowei dadui	政治保卫大队	political protection big teams
zhengzhi baoweidui	政治保卫队	political protection teams
zhengzhi baowei jiguan	政治保卫机关	political protection organs
zhengzhi baoweiju	政治保卫局	Political Protection Bureau

zhengzhi baoweizu/ zhengbaozu	政治保卫组/政保组	political protection group
zhengzhibu	政治部	political department
zhengzhichu	政治处	political section
zhi'an baowei chengbao	治安保卫承包	security and protection contracts
zhi'an baowei weiyuanhui/ zhibaohui	治安保卫委员会/ 治保会	resident or work unit public security committees
zhi'an baowei (xiao) zu	治安保卫(小)组	public security (small) group
zhi'an baoweizu/zhibaozu	治安保卫组/治保组	public security protection group
zhi'an chengbao zerenzhi	治安承包责任制	security contract responsibility system
zhi'an ermu	治安耳目	eyes and ears of public order
zhi'an lianfang weiyuanhui	治安联防委员会	joint public order defense committees
zhidaotan	指导探	detective instructor
zhixingbu	执行部	implementation section
zhixingke	执行科	implementation sub-section
zhongceng	中层	middle ranks
zhongyang baowei weiyuanhui	中央保卫委员会	Central Protection Committee
zhongyang junwei	中央军委	Central Committee Military Commission
Zhongyang junwei gong'anbu	中央军委公安部	Public Security Ministry of the Central Committee's Military Commission
zhongnan junzheng weiyuanhui	中南军政委员会	South-Central Military Control Committee
zhongyang shehuibu/ zhongshebu	中央社会部/中社部	Central Committee Social Section
zhongyang teke	中央特科	Central Committee special branch
zhongyang zongxuewei	中央总学委	Central Committee General Study Committee

Zhuanshu	专署	prefectural Commissioner's Office
ziwo piping	自我批评	self-criticism
(zizhi)zhou	（自治）州	(autonomous) prefecture
zu	组	group
zuotan	坐探	sleeper/stationary detective

NOTES

Introduction

1 *The Selected Works of Mao Tsetung*, vol. 1, dates this text as March 1926. Schram and Hodes, however, have traced it back to December 1, 1925 (1994, 249). I have followed the official dating.

2 This is a standard trope in Western accounts and seems to cover the full gamut of books written about this period. From serious scholarly accounts, such as Patricia Stranathan's book (1998) on the Shanghai underground Communist Party, through to more popular historical narratives such as Faligot and Kauffer's (1989) work on the secret police, CCP history becomes a series of factional disputes and betrayals. This approach tends to focus on individuals and factions rather than institutions.

3 The first communist special branch was actually formed in Wuhan after the communist leadership was forced to flee Shanghai during the massacre of communists. This organ, however, lasted for only three months.

4 This is the case, even when the narrative "invents" a later beginning to socialist policing. Wang Qiuxia, for example, sees the first signs of the characteristically Chinese "mass-line in policing" coming into being in the Soviet base camps after the failure of the Autumn Harvest Risings in 1927. By looking back over the mass protection work first developed there, Wang observes, one gets a sense of the tradition of contemporary public security in China. Yet all these manifestations of mass protection work—including the "red protection teams" (*chiweidui*), the "worker-peasant insurrectionary teams" (*gongnong baodongdui*), the young pioneers (*shaoxiandui*), and the children's corps (*ertongtuan*)—were all invented in the process of class struggle. See Wang Qiuxia 1994, 58–61.

5 One may rightly object that, in the age of "seeking truth from facts," the reduction of more recent police stories to variants of the "two-line struggle" plot line is unfair. Certainly, if one were to compare what was once told with what is now told, the lines are different. Nevertheless, while one focused on the clarity of the two-line struggle, the more recent accounts focused on how the lines were blurred. They therefore share a strange, if somewhat distant, kinship.

6 This phrase is famously associated with Carl Schmitt and he would, in fact, eventually lay claim to it. As Heinrich Meier points out, however, the person who coined the expression was not Schmitt but his friend Theodor Daubler (Meier 1998, 44).

7   The idea of a narrative chain is borrowed from Bakken. For Bakken, this chain links back to an original act that violates social norms and sets deviants off on a course that leads to crime (see Bakken 2000, 318–25). My usage differs only slightly insofar as it turns this coin face up, pointing to the way the chain can also link exemplary sites to contemporary institutions, thus promoting a sense of tradition and belonging.

8   Virtually all serious mainland Chinese material on socialist policing is classified and only available to workers within the Public Security Ministry or related security units. It is for this reason that I claim that these texts are self-referential. For a detailed explanation of the Chinese classification and censureship system for written documents, see Zhen Yuegang and Guan Shu 1993, 338–53.

9   As a method, the mass-line can be summed up in the words of Mao as taking the ideas of the masses and systematizing them until the masses accept them as their own. More concretely, the mass-line is also a set of local level volunteer organizations that take up the Party agenda in relation to certain issues.

1. Friends and Enemies

1   In March 1928, the Soviet government announced that it had unmasked a counter-revolutionary conspiracy to wreck production in the mines of the Shakhty district of the Donbass. This was alleged to have been carried out mainly by technical staff and engineers hostile to the communists and in league with foreign reactionaries. For more details, see Carr and Davies 1969, 621–22.

2   There were a whole range of other targets such as the Big Sword Society, the Young Boys' Army, and the Pacification and Protection Units, but the ones examined were the main three. (For a listing of some of the other organizations, and the Big Sword Society in particular, see Lötveit 1979, 102.)

3   The Nationalist Party Reformist Faction (*gaizupai*) was formally known as the Chinese Nationalist Party Reform Association. It began in 1927, when conflicts within the Nationalist Party between Jiang Jieshi and Wang Jingwei were at their most intense. Wang lost and was forced to leave the country. As a result, Chen Gongbo took up the reformist cause, calling for changes within the Nationalist Party organization and forming this "faction" in November 1928 in Shanghai. The idea behind the organization was to revive the 1924 spirit of reform within the Guomindang and to utilize the teaching of Sun Zhongshan (Sun Yatsen) against the military dictatorship of Jiang Jieshi. The group demanded reform of the Nationalist government in Nanjing and, for their trouble, were crushed and their organizers arrested. In January 1931, Wang announced the dissolution of this faction from Hong Kong. Despite this, in April 1934, the communist leader Zhang Guotao (said to be buoyed by the "leftist line" of the Party leader Wang Ming and by his own ambition) went to the E-Yu-Wan base camp and used claims of spying by this organization to launch a massive purge of base camp cadres. See Huang Jinlin 1988, 75; and *Gong'an Jianshi*.

4   Even the name of the organization was subject to contestation. Some have suggested
    that the name derived from the British Anti-Bolshevik League (Dai Xiangqing and Luo
    Huilan 1994, 39–52). Others, such as Chen Tianfang, who actually organized for the
    league, would later tell the historian Wang Jianmin (1965 2:528) that the name was
    purely organizational. On the basis of this understanding A stands for the provincial-
    level organization, while B stands for the county-level one. Together, A-B meant the
    overall development of a grassroots organization. In April 1927, after the communists
    briefly seized power in Nanchang, the Nationalist forces either escaped or were arrested
    and the A-B League was dissolved. The name nevertheless remained, but from this time
    on, it took on a new meaning which had nothing to do with the original organization
    (Sima Lu 1981, 45–46; Dai Xiangqing and Luo Huilan 1994, 39–52).
5   After the massacre, the Party was indeed decimated by acts of betrayal. By 1929, the
    Nationalist government had decided that this was such an important way to destroy the
    Party that they instituted the "Law on Communists Who Recant." This offered a "car-
    rot" to all those demoralized and alienated Party cadres willing to change color. With
    this law, any captured communist who swapped sides was given the chance of a new life
    if he or she was willing to work actively against the Party, which often meant working
    undercover. This law, coupled with near endemic factionalism within the Party, ensured
    that the CCP never found itself in a position to consolidate. Between 1928 and 1931,
    the Nationalists arrested fifteen high-ranking cadres, eighty middle-ranking ones, and
    fifteen thousand ordinary Party members, most of whom fell into Nationalist hands
    because of betrayal (*Gong'an Jianshi*). There could be no more dramatic example of the
    success of the Nationalist policy of encouraging betrayal than the arrest and subsequent
    "turning" of the key communist wet work specialist, Gu Shunzhang. For details, see
    Wakeman 1995, 151–55; and Xu Enzeng 1962, 56–63.
6   Fang Zhimin was a former provincial boss in Jiangxi, purged by the A-B League in Janu-
    ary 1927. Later, as secretary of the Min-Zhe-Gan area committee, he became a key
    figure in winding back the Elimination of Counter-Revolutionaries Campaign in that
    base area (*Gong'an Jianshi*; Benton 1992, 199). Fang Zhimin asserts that at this time, base
    camps were dominated by "an erroneous theory that took the elimination of counter-
    revolutionaries as the key link that took precedence even over (civil) war preparations"
    (qtd. in Zhang and Han 1987, 1:316).
7   With the proclamation of a Jiangxi provincial Soviet government in October 1930, a two-
    tier system of Committees to Eliminate Counter-Revolutionaries was, simultaneously,
    put into effect. One was for the province, the other, the county. Other places had three
    tiers: provincial, county, and village levels, and the names of the committees varied. See
    Li Jinping 1993, 62.
8   Not all committees were like this. In January 1932, the Chinese Soviet Republic Cen-
    tral Committee Implementation document suggested that the Committees to Eliminate
    Counter-Revolutionaries were much more ad hoc. The document states: "In areas where
    there has been an uprising, or ones where the Red Army is in control, those masses who

were active in the uprising elect the Committees to Eliminate Counter-Revolutionaries to carry out work under the worker peasant revolutionary committee" (Guo Hualun 1969, 2:279).

9   Wang explains the functions of these teams in the following manner: "The insurrectionary teams used spears and air rifles as their weapons. The town (xiang), was their work unit, and every town had one team, and the number of people in each team was calculated on the basis of the number of the people in the town. The professional duty of these teams was to eliminate the counter-revolutionaries, protect the township government authority, and, when the enemy comes, to help the Red Army and the 'red protection teams' fight the battle" (Wang Qiuxia 1994, 58).

10 On the question of the political credentials of team members, the central governmental committee of western Fujian put forth a draft on military matters on August 25, 1930, that stipulated that membership of such teams "must be completely made up of comrades, and it is absolutely not tolerable for noncomrades, and especially hooligans, to join their ranks" (PSHM 1990:2, VI6, 11).

11 According to Taiwanese sources, Deng Fa was in charge from November 1931 until the end of the Long March. After the arrival in the Shaanbei region in 1936, however, Deng was replaced by Wang Shoudao. See Guo Hualun 1969, 231; and Cao Boyi 1969, 414–15 for more details. Other sources say the bureau lasted from the end of 1927 until the spring of 1931, when it was replaced by the political protection organs (zhengzhi baowei jiguan).

12 The State Political Protection Bureau order number 7 stated that secret agents had to meet the following criteria before being accepted into the bureau (qtd. in Gong'an Jianshi):

> 1. They had to have had a variety of revolutionary experience in such things as uprisings or guerrilla warfare. Moreover, they were to be "unquestionably loyal."
> 2. They were to be from good, stable class backgrounds (in the main, of worker or peasant stock) and to have been a member of the Party or the youth league for more than one year. Intellectuals were also acceptable, but conditions for them would be stricter.
> 3. They had to have very clear political, economic, and organizational views that would not be shaken when confronted with the alternative viewpoint of the enemy.

13 For further details of these charges, see the Central Bureau of the Jiangxi Soviet "Draft Decision Concerning the Work of Eradicating Counter-Revolutionaries in the Soviet Areas" January 7, 1932 (CCA 1991, doc. 8, 18–2/).

14 Zhang Pinghua would go on to become the first Party secretary in Hunan province after liberation.

15 A further complicating factor is noted by Stephen Averill. At a local level, the A-B League and the communists both recruited from the same pool of people. This meant that old school and friendship ties often cut across both groups. In addition, communists also recruited former bandits who were similarly "tainted." Under these conditions, investi-

gations into suspicious connections among Party members would always have the propensity to get out of hand and lead to a purge (1995, 91).

16 To "encourage" a suspect to speak is known as *bi*, to extract a confession is called *gong*, and to believe the truth of what was being beaten out of the "suspect" was *xin*.

17 Was this, as Roger Faligot and Remi Kauffer suggest, Mao Zedong's first great act of betrayal (1989, 156)?

18 Mao Zedong associates the rebellion with the dying moments of the erroneous Li Lisan line within the Communist Party. See Snow 1977, 205–6.

19 Nationalist newspapers depicted it as a Red Army revolt against Mao Zedong. In this account, the soldiers were opposed to the partitioning of land and to the allegedly free-wheeling sexual practices adopted toward women in the Soviet (*Huabei Ribao*, August 2, 1931, qtd. in Hu Chi-hsi 1974, 475). Averill (1995) also points to the centrality of local rivalries and to the role of the Jiangxi leader, Li Wenlin, in the affair. Ronald Suleski calls this the Huangbo (Huangpi) incident and suggests that well over four thousand soldiers were arrested, but he makes no mention of executions (1969, 2–4).

20 One explanation for Li's decision not to arrest Liu is that Li and Liu came from the same village (PSHM 1990, V16, 100; Averill 1995, 105).

21 Kampen argues that there were no radio communications between Shanghai and the base camps at this time (2000, 53). Li Qiang ran the Shanghai communications section, which was fully operational and running an underground transmitter and training radio operators by October 1929. At first, communication between the various branches of the Party remained limited, but a second transmitter came "online" in Hong Kong in December to make communications between Hong Kong and Shanghai possible. By January 1930, these communications were regularized. While this connected Shanghai to the Comintern, keeping in touch with, and therefore staying in overall charge of developments in the newly developing rural base camps, required more time and energy. In January 1930, the communications section of the Party sent trained cadres to the Central Soviet base camp, as well as to the base camps in E-Yu-Wan and Xiang-E'xi. Not until September of the following year, however, could the transmitters communicate with Shanghai (*Outline of Public Security* 1997, 15).

22 See Duan Liangbi's "Report to the Central Committee" of December 30 in *Gong'an Jianshi*.

23 An example of his "ruthlessness" can be found in his response to the defection of Gu Shunzhang, which, as I have already noted, precipitated Zhou's flight to the Central Soviet. Tipped off about Gu's arrest and betrayal by a Party mole high up in the ranks of the Nationalist Party intelligence organization, Zhou promptly set forth plans to evacuate all key CCP figures to the rural base areas, but also ordered the undertaking of one last crucial task—namely, the massacre of Gu's entire family. The only concession the executioners would make was to leave his young boy alive (Wakeman 1995, 158; Stranahan 1998, 119).

24 This meeting was convened to commemorate the struggle against revisionism carried out by Lenin, Rosa Luxemburg, and Karl Liebknecht on the occasion of the seventh anni-

versary of Lenin's death and the twelfth anniversary of Luxemburg and Liebknecht's deaths.

25 Other accounts say he reported it to the Fujian Soviet government, which then took action. See Huang Jinlin 1988, 74.

26 This is because his rehabilitation would not take place until 1985 (Gao Hua 2000, 49).

27 In 1929, the Comintern sent the Chinese communists four letters emphasizing that right opportunism was international communism's greatest danger at the present time. They suggested that the CCP needed to conduct its own struggle against the right and against factionalism within Party ranks. For reproductions of these letters see CCA 1990, doc. 5, 605–23; 688–99; 744–48; and 791–99. There is considerable evidence that the Campaign to Eliminate Counter-Revolutionaries in part constituted a response to this admonition, for it was shortly after these letters, on November 13, 1929, that a central instruction letter to the Jiangxi provincial committee required them to "actively enlarge the anti–A-B League united front." See "An Open Letter from the Central Committee to All Party Branches and Comrades," reproduced in CCA 1990, doc. 5, 543–48.

28 Mao then went on to suggest that compensation of 5,000 yuan should be given to each victim of the campaign (PSHM 1990:2, VI6, 109). According to Gregor Benton, Zhang, who was close to Mao, had opposed the purges of social democrats and been accused of vacillating as a result (1992, 132).

29 Lin Yizhu worked with Deng Fa in the western Fujian Committee to Eliminate Counter-Revolutionaries until the latter was transferred to the Central Soviet in 1931. For details see Li Jinping 1993, 62.

30 The history of the Political Protection Bureau in Xiang-E'xi began in April 1930, when the E'xi base camp, formed of five counties, established the joint government Political Protection Bureau. In October, this changed its name to the Xiang-E'xi Joint Counties State Political Protection Bureau. In December 1931, it became Xiang-E'xi Provincial Political Protection Bureau, headed first by Peng Guocai, then by Ma Wu.

31 This is where the idea of ideological smoke screens comes into play. Yet smoke screen explanations simply produce the same problem, but make it once removed. That is to say, they proffer the idea that people are impelled by ideology to kill, but that such ideology is manipulated by cynical Party leaders who direct it against their rivals. In other words, the leaders are somehow free of the encumbrance of ideology, whereas the masses, of course, are duped by it.

32 This fourth encirclement campaign would be launched against all base camps in February–March 1933.

33 Apparently, Xu was an old Huangpu Military Academy friend of a Guomindang commander, Zeng Kuoqing. Xu was offered the leadership of the Fourteenth Army Division of the Guomindang should he defect. He refused the offer and had the spies who came to persuade him arrested (E-Yu-Wan 1989, 4: 502). Nevertheless, the fact that it was possible for him to defect with his troops does tell us something of the nature of loyalties within the CCP at this time. According to Mark Selden, the "prevailing military system" of this time was such that "troops owed allegiance and their livelihood to their immedi-

ate superiors, who were in turn bound to a warlord general or, in the case of a militia, to prosperous landlords. This meant that a defecting brigade or regimental commander often retained command of his men" (1995, 26).

34   As earlier noted, *The Selected Works of Mao Tse-tung*, vol. 1, dates this text as March 1926. Schram and Hodes, however, have traced it back to December 1, 1925 (1994, 249).

2. From Class to Nation

1   A small diversionary force was left behind at the original base camp under the leadership of Xiang Ying. Dai Xiangqing says he was a member of the Politburo, deputy chair of Central Soviet government, and then made secretary of a newly established central branch, as well as being a central military commander, and a political commissar. While Xiang Ying was secretary of the Jiangxi branch of the Central Committee, Chen Yi was made responsible for the Soviet government's central office work, and Liang Botai became his deputy (Dai Xiangqing et al. 1986, 681–82). Under these two organs, there was also a Political Protection Bureau, headed by Wang Jinxiang. It was to prepare the ground for the continuation of the struggle underground, but it was not until February 1935, after the Zunyi meeting and the effective replacement of Wang Ming by Mao, that the Party branch was given the order to go underground, dismantle the bureau, and take up guerrilla activities (PSHM 1992:3, V25, 17). There has also been some suggestion that those who remained held heterodox views. This was later the opinion of Otto Braun who suggested that both Qu Qiubai and Xiang Ying opposed Mao in the later years of the Jiangxi period. See Heinzig 1970, 132; and also Benton 1992.

2   The idea of differentiating between primary and secondary contradictions, while central to Mao's text and his understanding of dialectics, was not an original contribution. Based heavily upon M. Shirokov et al., *A Course on Dialectical Materialism*, it offered what was, at that time, an orthodox interpretation. Where Mao's originality would shine through was in the text's application to China; "On Contradiction" specified the implications of this understanding for China's class struggle. I wish to thank Nick Knight for this information. He offers further details of the relationship between this text and Soviet philosophy in his forthcoming book, *From Qu Qiubai to Mao Zedong: Marxist Philosophers and Philosophy in China, 1923–1945*.

3   The three-thirds system demanded that the composition of base camp governments be one third left-leaning progressives, one third Communist Party people, and one third so-called intermediate elements. The three-thirds system came into effect across all communist base camps in March 1940 (Wang Jianmin 1965, 228–30).

4   Thanks to Michael Schoenhals for this toilet-stop story.

5   In February 1934, Liu Zhidan and Xie Zichang led the worker-peasant Red Army to Nanliang in Huachi county and established the Shaan-Gan border revolutionary committee under which were established six specialized committees. One of these was the Committee to Eliminate Counter-Revolutionaries, which constituted the earliest protection organization in the area (*Gansu Provincial Gazetteer* 1995, 8). In the summer of 1935, the

Central Committee Northern Bureau sent cadres to the northwest base camp, and they established the Shaan-Gan-Jin Provincial Committee and the Political Bureau (PSHM 1992:3, v25, 18) .

6 This revolutionary base camp declared itself a Soviet government in the summer of 1935, after it had expanded into a range of new areas and counties (Gansu *Provincial Gazetteer* 1995, 8–9). It should be said that, while repercussions were felt among certain branches of the Shaanbei Party for these actions, the top leadership more or less avoided any lasting penalties. See Apter and Saich 1994, 52–53 for details.

7 Thomas Kampen insists that it was not Wang Ming but Zhou Enlai and Qin Bangxian who were criticized over the loss of the Central Soviet. See Kampen 2000, 98. Most Western sources agree that Mao's ascendancy within the Party was not complete until much later. Zunyi was, therefore, merely the beginning of his rise. Before Mao would reign supreme, however, there were further leadership battles to be fought with Wang Ming and Zhang Guotao, but, for the most part, the specifics of these battles lie outside the scope of this current study. For a highly detailed revisionist examination of Zunyi that suggests the Zunyi conference was even less significant than that in terms of the rise of Mao Zedong, see Kampen 2000, 66–77.

8 Along with Liu, many other local leaders of the Shaanxi base camp also suffered. Prominent figures who fell include Yang Sen, Gao Gang, Xi Zhongxun, Mao Wenrui, Liu Jingfen, Zhang Qingfu, Zhang Ce, and Zhang Xiushan (*Outline of Public Security* 1997, 64; Apter and Saich 1994, 52). In all, over one hundred of the top local Party echelon would fall (Selden 1995, 50).

9 This, of course, offers but a very schematic rundown of the events because it is still surrounded by controversy. There are rumors, for example, of ambivalence within the ranks of local communists toward Mao and his troops when they first arrived (Selden 1995, 50–51). Indeed, there is an even more scandalous rumor that Liu Zhidan was killed not by the Nationalists, as official accounts suggest, but with a bullet in the back ordered by the head of the protection bureau, Kang Sheng. Liu's localism, it is said, was always a cause of suspicion (interview, 1997). Mainland scholars strongly deny these rumors. The rumor that Mao and his troops were not welcomed is a confusion, they say, while they consider the claim about Liu's assassination a complete fabrication. The grounds on which these rumors are rebutted are intertwined and, in relation to the first accusation in particular, quite compelling. Mao's arrival in Yan'an signaled the beginning of the rehabilitation of the local popular cadres led by Liu Zhidan. This was clearly a very popular act and one which won Mao enormous local support. The arrival of the other main army force under Zhang Guotao was, however, said to have been quite unpopular and the local animosity toward his southern forces palpable. Liu's enormous stature after death, leading both to his national-hero status and to a county being named after him, are given as evidence of the value the Communist Party placed upon him. Given this high valuation, the argument goes, the Party was unlikely to have had him killed. The rumors nevertheless continue. Another scholar, talking of his trip to Shaanbei, confirmed that locals there still believed Liu was assassinated and pointed to the status given to him

in death as one indication of Party guilt. Another circumstantial piece of evidence they draw upon is that a cadre of Liu's rank would normally remain to the rear of the fighting, but Liu was killed in action on the front line. What would he be doing there, locals suggested, if it were not for the fact that he had been sent in to die (interviews, 1997).

10 Dai Jiying was the Rear-Guard Military Commission Chair and Shaan-Gan-Jin Political Protection Bureau Chief (Wang Shoudao 1983, 25). Despite this high rank, within a month of the arrival of the Long March veterans, Dai faced the precipice. Along with his deputy, Nie Hongjun, he was the subject of a major Central Committee Northwest Bureau resolution on November 30 that gave him "his very last warning" (*Outline of Public Security* 1997, 65).

11 The Central Committee document quoted here is entitled "An Outline of the Discussion on Targeting in the Campaign against Counterrevolution," cited in the *Gansu Provincial Gazetteer* 1995, 9.

12 Three interrelated reasons can be given to explain the swiftness of their investigations. First, the factional nature of the purges and the similarity of charges made against them meant that the investigation work was relatively easy. Second, local animosity had reached near boiling point, and there was a fear of a peasant rebellion against the Party unless they moved quickly. Third, while investigations were underway, further killings took place (interview, 1997).

13 The Xi'an incident revolved around the kidnapping of Jiang Jieshi by generals he had sent to blockade the communists, but who, instead, forged an informal nonaggression pact with them. These troops, drawn principally from Manchuria, felt that the Japanese constituted their main enemy. Manchuria had, after all, already been taken over by Japan so the soldiers had good cause to feel this resentment. Jiang, on hearing of their treachery, flew to Xi'an to sort things out. He was kidnapped, and demands were made that he forge an anti-Japanese United Front with the Communist Party. He refused but, on Christmas day 1936, he was unconditionally released. He did, however, sign the United Front shortly after that.

14 On July 7, Japanese and Chinese troops clashed at the Marco Polo bridge just outside Beiping. At first, both the Nanjing government and the Japanese tried to broker a deal, but on July 17, Jiang Jieshi ruled out any more compromises and moved reinforcements into Hubei. The Japanese military had successfully forced the hand of their government, resulting in war (Harrison 1972, 276).

15 The move to Yan'an took place in January. In March, they set up a special Shaan-Gan-Ning area government, which, in September, officially established itself as the government of the special region (*Questions and Answers* 1994, 22).

16 Structurally, it remained pretty much identical to the previous bureau and, in terms of personnel, it was still run by Wang Shoudao's replacement in the Northwest Political Protection Bureau, Zhou Xing, and still had Xu Jianguo (or Du Liqing, as he was sometimes known) as its deputy. Other deputies would later replace Xu. These included a veritable who's who of important Party security figures, including Tan Zhengwen, Liu Haibin, Liu Bingwen, Zhao Cangbi, Li Ziming, and Shi Zhe (Li Jinping 1993, 12; PSHM

1992:3, V25, 23; *Questions and Answers* 1994, 22; *Outline of Public Security* 1997, 74). This base camp security organization had the minor and rather dubious distinction of being the only one that could directly trace its organizational lineage back to more radical days. This, as I have already mentioned, of course, was only possible because it had been thoroughly purged of any leftist influences with the arrival of the Communist Party center back in late 1935.

17 This plenum also proved important to Mao Zedong whose leadership position was greatly strengthened vis-à-vis Wang Ming at this time. For details, see Gao Hua 2000, 171, 173; and Hu Qiaomu 1994, 271–72. It should be noted, however, that Mao would not become undisputed leader of the Party, and Mao Zedong Thought its guiding ideology, until after the Seventh Party Congress in 1945 (Knight 1996, 232).

18 The two base camps with this arrangement in place were Shaan-Gan-Ning and Jin-Cha-Ji. Shaan-Gan-Ning was the seat of communist power and had Yan'an city as its capital. Jin-Cha-Ji was an anti-Japanese border camp covering an area spanning northeastern Shanxi, central Hebei, western Hebei, and southern Cahar. It was established in July 1937, when the Eighth Route Army under the command of Nie Rongzhen entered the area and took control. It was a particularly important base in terms of policing history because Peng Zhen was a leader there. For further details on the nature of such arrangements, see "The Central Committee Resolution on the Elimination of Traitors Struggle" of October 10, 1939, in CCA 1991, 12:181–85.

19 Apart from Yang Qiqing and Luo Ruiqing, the other members of the committee were Zhu De, Peng Dehuai, and Zhou Heng. These three, along with Yang and Luo, were said to have played a crucial role in the formation of this unit (*Outline of Public Security* 1997, 75; PSHM 1993:4, V30, 2). Prior to this five-person committee, Yang Qiqing had lead a three-person protection committee made up of himself, Fu Zhong, and Lu Dingyi. See *Outline of Public Security* 1997, 75.

20 The Jin-Sui anti-Japanese border base area was made up of parts of northwestern Shaanxi and the southwestern part of Suiyuan (currently known as the western section of Inner Mongolia). This base area was formed in September 1939, when the 120th Division of the Eighth Route Army under He Long set up base in northwestern Jin and then expanded into Suiyuan. The Jin-Ji-Lu-Yu base area was a region north of the Huang river and south of the Jin-Cha-Ji area. It was a border region organized around four provinces: Shanxi, Hebei, Shandong, and Henan. The base camp was set up by the 115th and 129th Divisions of the Eighth Route Army and consisted of four strategic zones: Taihang, Taiyue, southern Ji, and Ji-Lu-Yu.

21 At that time, Bo Yibo was secretary of the CCP Shanxi provincial worker's committee and director of the Shanxi provincial third administrative area. More significant, he was a leader in the Shanxi Resist the Japanese, Save the Nation through Sacrifice Society, which Yan was also associated with. Rong Wusheng served as director of the Shanxi provincial fifth administrative area. Taiyue mountain area counties were generally divided between the third and the fifth administration areas, that is, between Bo Yibo's area of responsibility and Rong's (PSHM 1993:4, V30, 4).

22   Indeed, the United Front in some ways made it much more difficult for the Party to operate openly at this time. Especially in area takeovers, the CCP had to be particularly careful not to antagonize the Nationalists. Hence they adopted a variety of methods to infiltrate and gain control over areas. In the case mentioned above, they covered their tracks by using patriotic front organizations. In other places, they employed different means. In Sui-De, for example, the existence of Nationalist Party officials controlling key areas within the base camps hampered the consolidation of Party rule. The Nationalists could not be attacked directly, so the CCP used other means. In the case of one senior Nationalist commissioner, He Shounan, the communists made use of his corruption as a basis by which to demand his recall, stating that the masses demanded his resignation and that the CCP could do little to resist such calls (interview, 1997).

23   The associations used were the Shanxi Resist the Japanese, Save the Nation through Sacrifice Society (or, as it was sometimes known, the Shanxi *ximenghui*) and the Life and Death Teams (*juesihui*) (PSHM 1993:4, V30, 4).

24   The 129th Division had been particularly active earlier in the establishment of the protection section (*baoweihui*) of the political department run by Yang Qiqing (PSHM 1993:4, V30, 2).

25   It became the third special region, eastern office of the Public Security Bureau.

26   "The Decision of the Secretariat of the Central Committee of the Communist Party of China to Establish the Social Security Sections" of February 18, 1939, selected from the Central Committee Social Section, *Articles on Elimination and Protection in the Anti-Japanese War Period* (December 1948), reproduced in PSHM 1987, v6; see 3–4.

27   According to Zhong Kan, this organ was established in or around August 1938. See Zhong 1982, 77, 347.

28   Point 3 of the founding document of the Social Section states: "This resolution is top secret, it is not for dissemination outside Party ranks. Nor is the concrete role of the Social Section for transmission to lower ranks within the Party. Violations of this point are violations of Party discipline and will be punished." PSHM 1987, v6, 3.

29   Before putting Kang Sheng in charge, the Party had undertaken a number of moves to revive its intelligence work. The Central Committee had already established the Central Protection Committee (*zhongyang baowei weiyuanhui*) or, as it was sometimes known, the Enemy Areas Work Committee (*diqu gongzuo weiyuanhui*). This was designed to strengthen Party leadership over the elimination of traitors work in so-called white-held areas and was under the direction of Zhou Enlai. Zhou would be replaced in this position by Kang Sheng in late 1938 after the sixth plenum.

30   The Social Section may have begun life as a counter-espionage agency, but by December 1941, it was replaced in that role by an even more specialized and secret organ called the Intelligence Bureau (*qingbaobu*), which came into being after some harsh words at a Central Committee meeting about the "shallowness," "emptiness," and "subjectivism" of many intelligence reports. Demanding a new, more comprehensive approach, the Central Committee called for "an investigation and research organ within the Central Committee to collect information on domestic and international politics, as well

as on military, economic, cultural, and class relations (CCA 1991, doc. 13, 174). Even in its first document, the Intelligence Bureau called for closer links between the world of intelligence agents, the public elimination of traitors protection agencies, and the so-called secret enemy work sections. All of these, it suggested, should come under its leadership (*Outline of Public Security* 1997, 107–8). Effectively, that meant the leadership of the Social Section was also the leadership of the Intelligence Bureau. Indeed, the formation of the Intelligence Bureau owes much to the concrete policy directives given by the Central Committee Social Section and approved by the Central Committee. Two key documents from the Social Section in 1941 more or less framed the nature and organization of the Intelligence Bureau: "Instructions on Intelligence Work to all Levels" and "Instructions Concerning the Development of Intelligence Work behind Enemy Lines." Soon after this, the Social Section formulated the "Regulations on the Protection Network Organizations," the "Notice Concerning Measures to Be Taken against Japanese Special Agents," and the "Instructions Concerning Seeking and Collecting Japanese Special Agents Secret Documents," which more or less established the bureau's brief (*Outline of Public Security* 1997, 107).

31 On October 10, 1939, the Central Committee passed the "Resolution of the Central Committee of the Communist Party of China Concerning the Struggle against Enemy Agents," which stated that Party branches must: "Establish specialized work departments (social sections) or specialized personnel responsible for regular work in this area. Because the type of cadres needed in this work must be meticulously selected and are not easy to find, one should use the methods listed below to help in making the decision:

1. If the Central Committee bureau, area Party committee, or provincial level Party committee have cadres within their ranks who are politically resolute and loyal and have great ability, then these are the types that must be recruited into the Social Section.

2. If no such cadre is found over a lengthy period, then it is permissible to temporarily allow the Party Secretary, together with departmental heads, to do the task. It is also permissible for deputy department heads or very good workers who are loyal and reliable to get on with this job, but it will always be carried out directly under the Party Secretary's leadership.

3. In that temporary period when an organizational department head is in charge and the deputy or a hard worker is getting on with the job, preparatory training in independent work for cadres should be offered.

4. The special committees (*tewei*), county committees, or regional committees (*quwei*) that do not have suitable cadre candidates can temporarily refrain from building up such a specialized department. That is to say, they can let the Party committee and the Party secretary take responsibility, but they must allocate one person to the task of taking responsibility for the collection of intelligence on enemy spying activity."

From *Reference and Study Materials from the History of the Chinese Communist Party*, reprinted in PSHM, 1987, v6, 6–7.

32 The focus upon the political quality of the Party cadre had been a concern of the Soviet Union even in its early days. Lenin had, in fact, talked about the fight against bureaucracy as turning on the selection of the correct personnel and checking their performances (Claudin-Urando 1977, 82).

33 The CC faction was led by the two Cs, Chen Guofu and Chen Lifu. It had launched the abortive New Life Movement in 1934, which attempted to save China by returning to Confucian virtues. It emerged as a dominant group within the Guomindang throughout the war years. Because of its strong Confucian bent, it regarded the communists not only as outlaws but as moral heretics whose views were alien to core Chinese values (Harrison 1972, 267).

34 With the excesses of Jiangxi still within living memory, it would not remain thus. On April 4, 1941, the Central Committee Social Section or, as it is usually abbreviated, *zhongshebu*, issued the "Organizational Regulations on the Protection Network (Draft)," changing the name of networker (*wangyuan*) to protection worker (*baoweiyuan*). The protection workers were to be led by the elimination of traitors protection units. Three to five workers would make up a protection group, two to three would form a team (*dui*). The group and team leaders reported to the elimination of traitors units, although, in some cases, protection workers would directly liaise with the elimination of traitors units (*Outline of Public Security* 1997, 87).

35 To give but a few examples, it features in Mao Zedong's May 1937 paper entitled "The Tasks of the CCP in the Period of Resistance to Japan," in which Mao speaks of "our enemies, the Japanese imperialists, the Chinese traitors, the pro-Japanese elements, and the Trotskyites" (Mao Zedong 1975, 1:269), and also in his report to the sixth plenum of October 6, 1938, entitled "The Role of the Chinese Communist Party in the National War" (Mao 1975, 2:195–211). Party reports on the enemy also featured it extensively.

36 He was to return on the same plane as Wang Ming on November 14, 1937. According to Kampen (2000, 89), he picked up Chen Yun in Xinjiang on the way. There is, in fact, some controversy surrounding the exact date of Wang Ming and Kang Sheng's return, with some commentators saying they returned in October or December, not November as Kampen suggests. See Kampen 2000, 88–89 on the significance of these different dates.

37 The full title of this piece is, Central Committee Social Section, "A Directive from the Social Section of the Central Committee of the Communist Party Concerning the Policy with Regard to the Elimination of Traitors," is dated September 1, 1940, and was originally published in *Articles on Elimination and Protection in the Anti-Japanese War Period* in December 1948.

38 The details of this are as follows: In November, the Su-Lu-Yu branch head, Peng Mingzhi, heard complaints about the way this campaign had been conducted and carried out his own investigation. He then reported his findings to the 115th Division political commissar, Luo Ronghuan, and to the Communist Party Shandong branch secretary, Guo Hongtao, who immediately went to Huxi and ordered a halt to the campaign and the re-

lease of all those arrested. Wang Xuren was taken into custody and a full investigation undertaken. Military defeats forced a troop withdrawal and left this matter in abeyance. Not until March 1940 did the Central Committee Shandong branch and the 115th Division send the branch social section chief, Liu Juying, and an observation team to Huxi to further investigate the matter. After two months, they produced a document entitled "Summary Report Concerning the Elimination of Trotskyites Campaign in Su-Lu-Yu Border Region," which concluded that Wang Xuren and Wang Hongming had used torture to extract confessions. It reported that these two had irresponsibly killed many innocent people and that Bai Ziming had been complicit in the affair (PSHM 1988:3, v9, 161–64; PSHM 1992:3, v25, 37–38).

39 On June 1, 1940, the Shandong branch issued "Orders Following the Summary of the Elimination of Trotskyites Campaign in the Fifth Division Regional Party Committee (the Huxi Regional Party Committee)." Qtd. in PSHM 1988:3, v9, 162.

40 Other sources claim that Wang Xuren was executed as a traitor (*A Summary History* 1989, 63).

41 There was a perverse aftermath to this when the case was reopened during the Cultural Revolution, resulting in another round of purges among the original Huxi victims. This led to the issue once again gaining importance and forcing, yet again, another "reversal of verdicts" in the Deng era. Consequently, on May 26, 1983, a report entitled "The Report Concerning the Handling of Remaining Problems Relating to the Huxi Anti-Trotskyite Campaign" was given to the Central Committee. The report pointed out that the decision to regard Wei Dingyuan and the other six people as "Trotskyite faction members" was completely wrong. It suggested that Wei and the others should be rehabilitated. It added that anyone else victimized because of this event should be rehabilitated. On December 23, the Central Committee approved this report, and the Central Organizational Department issued it to all Party members (PSHM 1988:3, v9, 164; PSHM 1992:3, v25, 38–39).

42 So began the "liberal" period in the Yan'an era. During this time, Mao would write "On New Democracy" (January 1940), the three-thirds system of government was propounded (March 1940), and the base camps would begin to undertake massive elections (*Gong'an Jianshi*; Apter and Saich 1994, 210–17).

43 According to the CCP, the Japanese redirected their attention to communist base areas during 1941 and 1942. At this time, they employed 83,000 soldiers in 132 "mopping-up" operations against various communist base camps. In 27 of these attacks, more than 10,000 soldiers were involved. The Shandong base camps had more than 70 mopping-up campaigns directed against them, and 9 of these produced major battles and saw tens of thousands of troops deployed. The Japanese army's chief of staff for the northern China zone admitted that 7,700 new blockhouses had been built in the northern China theater and that the line of the blockade had reached 11,860 kilometers in length. This was six times the length of the Great Wall and a quarter of the length of the earth's circumference (*Outline of Public Security* 1997, 99).

44 Apart from the factors thus mentioned, others existed. The factional struggle against Wang Ming, for example, was one of these. What I highlight here, however, are those aspects that have an immediate bearing on security. For an account accentuating the power struggle as a key contributing factor, see Byron and Pack 1992.

45 On February 1 and 8, 1942, Mao gave two speeches to the Central Party School in Yan'an, entitled, respectively, "Rectification of Study, Party Style, and the Style of Writing" (reproduced in Compton 1952, 9–32) and "Oppose the Party's Eight-Legged Essay (Party Formalism)" (reproduced in Compton 1952, 33–53). These two speeches marked out three erroneous tendencies in Party work: formalism, subjectivism, and sectarianism. The two reasons given for such errors were that recently arrived intellectuals lacked experience and, also, the continuing influence of the Wang Ming group. For more details, see Apter and Saich 1994, 280ff.

46 I neither wish nor intend to enter into the once heated debate about Mao's Marxist credentials. The claim of romantic pastoralism posited here is not designed to imply that Mao was a deviant Marxist. One only need, in fact, recall Marx's own words from "The German Ideology" about life within communism being given over to hunting in the morning, fishing in the afternoon, herding cattle in the evening, and criticizing late at night, to realize that Marx, too, sometimes dreamed in pastoral colors.

47 Harbin was in chaos at the time of the communist takeover. The anti-city attitudes of many soldiers, coupled with the rapid growth of the army, contributed to the rather high level of insubordination and illegal activities said to be continuously increasing at the time. The Party quickly moved to nip such activity in the bud.

On July 1, 1947, the Harbin garrison headquarters and the Harbin Public Security Bureau jointly established The Army-Police Joint Checking Office to examine all cases of misconduct. Within two months and ten days of its establishment, it had arrested 39 soldiers and government officials involved in speculation or having broken Party and government policies. A further 36 people were found to be corrupt and had employed prostitutes, while 29 soldiers had deserted, and 150 stole oil and other things (PSHM 1987, v5, 47–48). Perhaps what is most remarkable about this is that it was so rare. By the time larger cities such as Beijing, Shanghai, and Tianjin were liberated, the military had restored its exemplary record.

48 The five stages of the Stalinist unilinear view of history are primitive society, slave society, feudalism, capitalism, and communism. Socialism marked the transition from capitalism to communism. See Mellossi 1977, 8.

49 On recification methods in Yan'an, see Li Jinping 1993, 130–31; on the methods of city takeovers, see Dutton and Li 2002.

50 Li Kenong makes this clear in his letters to Xu Jianguo and other comrades, dated October 23, 1948 and quoted in *Outline of Public Security* 1997, 149.

51 The term *volumes* (*juan*) needs qualification. In Chinese, it can mean anything from a formal volume right through to a slip of paper.

52 According to Teiwes and Sun (1995, 371), Kang Sheng also became head of a cadre

screening committee in the fall of 1941. Zhong Kan (1982, 348) dates this as being be-tween July and August and suggests that it was to serve as the precursor to the screening of cadres campaign that began in the following year.

53 As Selden correctly notes, however, the difference between the communists and the Nationalists, on this count, could not have been clearer. Indeed, the reduction of mas-sive inequalities allowed under warlord and Nationalist rule stood as one of the move-ment's most compelling claims (Selden 1995, 122).

54 Dai Qing (1994, 43) claims that it was Li Yuchao, one of Kang Sheng's cousins, who leveled the Trotskyite charge against Wang at a meeting on May 27. Wang admitted to having contacts with Trotskyists, but he denied membership of any Trotskyite organiza-tion. Kang, however, remained unconvinced: "Wang Shiwei is a Trotskyite element. . . . He is different from other people. His is not a problem of ideology." From here, Wang slipped into the enemy camp and was arrested on April 1, 1943. He was said to have re-mained in jail until 1947, when a Guomindang offensive forced the evacuation of the Yan'an base camp. It was at this time that Wang was executed, either on the orders of Kang Sheng, or, more likely, of Li Kenong (see Byron and Pack 1992, 176). The fact that Li replaced Kang as head of the Social Section in June 1946 and that Kang, by this time, was in Shandong, does suggest some circumstantial evidence to support the Byron and Pack proposition. Xu Linxiang and Zhu Yu, however, argue that Kang gave the order orally, and at least two other commentators, Lin Qingshan and Zhong Kan, agree (Xu Linxiang and Zhu Yu 1996, 152; Lin Qingshan 1988, 120; Zhong Kan 1982, 95, 354). Meanwhile, Dai Qing argues that it was neither Kang Sheng, who was, as mentioned earlier, in Shandong, nor Li Kenong, who was deeply apologetic to Mao about Wang's death, who gave the order. The order, she argues, came from He Long (1994, 167). In 1962, Mao Zedong would speak about Wang's death. He claimed at this time that no leader had authorized his shooting, but that the local security organs had made the de-cision (Schram 1974, 185). Irrespective of which theory one follows, the point is that all claims remain highly speculative and no real evidence exists to adequately point the finger at any one person. All we know is that Wang was taken to Lin county in north-western Jin and executed by local cadres. We also know of Mao's reaction. On hearing of Wang's execution, he apparently slammed his hand on his desk and repeated three times, "Bring me back Wang Shiwei" (interview, 1997). Mao, of course, would later make a more public but far less fulsome expression of regret over Wang's death. See Schram 1974, 184–85.

55 In my opinion, the heavy focus given to the Wang Shiwei affair leads to an overemphasis on the discursive side of the various struggles and gives undue attention to the intel-lectual purges. As a result, the complicated events framing these purges that were hap-pening in other spheres go underestimated. Without fully appreciating the widespread nature of such purges, it is easy to read other motives behind them. One of the more re-cent studies of campaigning in the Yan'an period by Seybolt (1986) perhaps best exem-plifies this. Seybolt argues that "the widespread fear that they [the counter-espionage campaigns] engendered was intentionally provoked, and must be considered an impor-

tant ingredient in the Communists' formula for success" (39). In response, and on the basis of the evidence I have seen, any intentionality is, I suspect, *post factum*.

56 His real name was Fan Dawei.

57 Teiwes (with Sun) offers a slightly different version of this story (1995, 372).

58 The chilling sequel to this "radish theory" of underground Party members came in the Cultural Revolution when, once again, being a former underground member of the Party led to suspicion. As in the days of old, any underground member who had been arrested was simply seen as a traitor who had escaped unmasking. Indeed, during the Cultural Revolution, Kang Sheng again raised the Zhang Keqing case with cadres and officials from Gansu when he said: "Your province has an important historical problem in the case of Zhang [Keqing]. You should detain him." As a result, Zhang was once again arrested and released only after Kang's death (Kang Sheng qtd. in Lin Qingshan 1988, 120).

59 Seybolt draws a different conclusion: "It is possible that the Guomindang threat at this time was greatly exaggerated, if not totally fabricated, so as to enhance Mao's power, and promote his policies" (1986, 58). Meanwhile, Teiwes puts a different slant on the event, suggesting that Hu Zongnan used the dissolution of the Comintern as an excuse to call on communist and fellow traveler writers sympathetic to the cause to lobby the CCP to dissolve itself. In these circumstances Kang Sheng began to "discover" large numbers of spies in the base areas (Teiwes with Sun 1995, 372).

60 Chen Yongfa (Chen Yung-fa) argues the campaign started on April 3, 1943, along with the release of the decision. Documents from the Central Committee that launched this part of the campaign have never been revealed. Chen pieced this information together from a range of other sources and commentaries. For his arguments supporting this date, see Chen Yongfa 1990, 69–71. Gao Xinmin and Zhang Shujun (2000, 370) claim that April 3 marked the beginning of the cadre checking campaign. The rescue campaign did not, in their view, start until around July 15.

61 Ironically, at least part of the reason accusations of treachery could so easily be believed lay with the liberal recruitment policies employed by the Party in the United Front period prior to rectification. Under Wang Ming, the Jiangxi period of recruitment had been limited mostly to those who came from very good class backgrounds, whereas under Mao in Yan'an, Party ranks were opened to all classes. (Even those deemed to have come from unsuitable class backgrounds were allowed in, although they were forced to spend a longer period as provisional members and underwent more careful screening.) The result was that by this stage, the majority of local communist leaders had come from "unsuitable" class backgrounds and were easily charged with class errors and erroneous attitudes (interview, 1997).

62 The six-point principles governing counter-espionage work were (1) leaders must take responsibility, (2) take responsibility for one's own actions, (3) carry out investigations and undertake research, (4) determine the various degrees of culpability separating light from heavy offences, (5) try to win back those who have lost their footing, and (6) educate cadres.

63 Mao's opposition to this campaign flies in the face of an assertion by Saich, itself based on the work of Seybolt, that this constituted a means by which to strengthen Mao's hold and his line within the Party. See Saich 1995; and also Seybolt, 1986, 39–73.

64 Mao insisted that the contents of this letter be published, and it was in this way that the famous "Nine-Point Policy" came into the public domain. It was published in *Experiences of Counter-Espionage* 6 in August 1943 (Mao Zedong 1996, 52; Dai Wendian 1991a, 19).

65 The "basic regulations" demanded the following from security workers: (1) in the absence of evidence to back up cases or without evidence emanating from the interrogation, the interrogator is prohibited from subjectively asserting that someone is definitely a counter-revolutionary; (2) physical torture or the use of any other torture techniques is strictly prohibited; (3) the method of continuous or round-the-clock interrogation by a team is strictly prohibited; (4) it is strictly prohibited to plant weapons on people or to verbal them; (5) to prevent false confessions under interrogation, it is prohibited to feed names, crimes, or other things to suspects; (6) verbal abuse or the use of foul language is prohibited; (7) it is impermissible to take advantage of any physical defects of a suspect; (8) make sure that any oral confession is written down, and do not exaggerate what is said or add things; (9) the confession is not to have any suggestions added to it by the interrogator; (10) in the process of interrogating, if the person being interrogated tries to get hold of weapons, tries to make a run for it, tries to commit suicide, abuses the interrogator, or yells counter-revolutionary slogans, then they are not to be bashed, but are to be treated severely under the law (*Outline of Public Security* 1997, 118).

66 According to Teiwes (with Sun), this occurred at the behest of Ren Bishi. Both Ren and Zhou were responsible for underground Party work at this time and were outraged by the slur that this campaign was casting on their operations and the possible effects it might have on the operations and recruitment of underground branches. See Teiwes with Sun 1995, 373; see also Zhong Kan 1982, 93.

67 According to Zhong Kan, the figures are much higher. In fact, he claims 90 percent of espionage cases uncovered were later found to be false (1982, 94).

68 Speaking of his own complicity in the turmoil of the Cultural Revolution, Mao would say, "Since it was I who caused the havoc, it is understandable if you have some bitter words for me." Qtd. in Schram 1974, 271.

3. The Government of Struggle

1 The Central Committee Social Section and the Northern Social Section had, in fact, been amalgamated in April 1949 (PSHM 1993:1, V27, 46).

2 Indeed, Liu Shaoqi said that 80 percent of all public security personnel must be Communist Party members (Tao Siju 1996, 162).

3 On this point, Mao was quite insistent. Policing was one area where Soviet advisors were "frozen out." Indeed, the Soviet advisors were quite hostile to the mass-line style of policing adopted by the Chinese and objected to it strongly. Later, it was said, they conceded that it had been correct (interviews, 1996).

4   Brugger points to the possibility of a political battle between the advocates of a more formal legal system and those who, under the influence of Yan'an, opted for a radical alternative (1981a, 101).

5   It should be noted that publicly available figures from Tao Siju, the former Minister of Public Security, do not correlate with the internal figures cited here. Importantly, it should be pointed out that neither does his method of calculation. Tao's figures not only include Ministry of Public Security personnel but also the predominantly army-based public security armed divisions and even sections of the army's field troops. Taking into account these inclusions by June 1950, Tao states that the total public security force numbered 240,000 people. This is about four times larger than figures used in the internal document cited above (Tao Siju 1996, 157). Interestingly, Tao's figures for later periods, when this crisis of numbers was largely over (i.e., 1952–53), increasingly correlate with those given in the internal document cited above (for these later figures see Tao Siju 1996, 160).

6   Schurmann quotes a Taiwanese source estimating that remnant officers made up around 60 percent of the new communist police force (1968, 372).

7   The most notable exception to this rule was in Tibet, where the Social Section was maintained throughout the fifties to offer leadership to all public security operations. Preparations for a Tibetan Social Section can be dated from April 1951, when the Central Committee approved the formation of the Chinese Communist Northwest Tibetan Workers' Committee in Lanzhou and, at the same time, had cadres and youth from the northwest bureau and the northwest military units sent in to set up the Northwest Tibetan Social Section under Du Shu'an. When the Central Committee decided to merge the Northwest and Northeast workers' committees on January 9, 1952, the reshuffle of the social sections resulted in the formation of the Tibetan Workers' Committee Social Section under Wang Huaren, with Du Shu'an and the former head of the Chengdu Public Security Department and Chengdu branch of the Workers' Committee Social Section, Zhang Xiangming, as his deputies. The original cadres for the Tibetan Workers' Committee Social Section and public security force came from five different groups:

1. The Eighteenth Army sent in section and department heads from their protection agencies.

2. About one hundred people from the army's Henan-Anhui-Jiangsu sector were transferred to Tibet as backbone forces.

3. The northwest bureau and northwest military area sent in personnel.

4. The southwest Ministry of Public Security sent in Yang Zhengfan and a group of backbone elements to establish a Lhasa Public Security Bureau. They also sent in two groups of cadres to form the Tibetan Public Security teams.

5. After entering Tibet in 1950, a number of Tibetan youth also began to participate in public security work.

By July 1952, every Tibetan city had a public security unit. At that time, the Tibetan Social Section had about forty members, while by year's end, the public security forces in Tibet numbered 365 police officers (PSHM 1992:4, V26, 100–101). I have been reliably informed that the Social Section remained active in Tibet until 1964 and only then began to merge into the regular police force.

8   This would put the strength of the force midway through 1950 at about 127,000 cadres. This comes somewhere between the 1950 figure of 72,684 police and the 1951 figure of 130,873 police offered in one highly confidential public security source consulted.

9   This armed branch of the force was quasi-military in character, having a separate line of command and quite unique duties that included a posting in Korea during the war. Armed police in China were nothing new. What was new was this attempt to shift such work away from the military. This formally occurred on September 22, 1950, when the military commission of the Central Committee communicated "Telegram Orders on the Structure of the Leadership of Public Security Detachments" and nominated Luo Ruiqing as its commander in chief and political committee member. Cheng Shicai was made his deputy commander, while Li Tianhuan was made deputy head of the political committee. Wu Lie was made chief of staff, while Xiong Botao became deputy chief of staff. Ouyang Qin was responsible for the political department (zhengzhibu), while Li Yimin was made deputy of the political department (Tao Siju 1996, 158).

10 The organizational form put in place in November 1949 was as follows: Each large administrative area (daxingzhengqu) established a People's Government Public Security Ministry, each province set up a Public Security Department (gong'anting), while each centrally administered city government had a Public Security Bureau (gong'anju). Prefectural Commissioner's Offices (zhuanshu) had departments (gong'an chu), while counties had bureaus (gong'anju). Areas (qu) had public security helpers (gong'an zhuliyuan), while villages had Public Security Personnel (gong'an yuan). In less than one year, this structure covered the entire country. While modifications followed—for example, the large administrative areas changed their Public Security Ministries into bureaus, and in June 1954, that rung of government was abolished altogether—this basic structure has remained in place ever since (Questions and Answers 1994, 66–67; Outline of Public Security 1997, 246).

11 The organization of the personnel sections within the ministry was worked out at the first national conference of personnel work within the Ministry of Public Security in June 1950. After this meeting, a three-tiered structure was established. Hence there was the central force that was the Ministry of Public Security, under which there were the large administrative-area public security ministries, and, finally, the provincial or city forces called either ting (department) or ju (bureau). This three-tiered structure was drawn directly from the army (Hu Zhiguang 1986, 56).

12 The actual structure approved by the Central Committee in March 1953 was as follows: Within the Ministry of Public Security personnel section, a political department (zhengzhibu) would be established. Each provincial, city, or autonomous regional public security department (gong'anting) and bureau (gong'anju) would set up a political section while every area and city bureau and section (gong'anchu) would set up a political

section, *zhengzhichu*. Moreover, all basic-level units would have specialists or part-time political work personnel assigned to them. See Hu Zhiguang 1986, 56–57.

13   Hu Zhiguang says that this meeting of public security workers decided to use the army's Gutian meeting decision and their "Report Regarding the Question of Political Work in the Army" as the ideological basis for all future political work in the public security arena. The Gutian decision is so named because it was taken in Gutian village in Shanghang county, Fujian province, at a CCP meeting in December 1929. The report from this meeting was written by Mao Zedong and was to ensure that while the army fired the shots, the Party always held the gun. For more details, see Hu Zhiguang 1986, 58.

14   Yang Jie was a former Guomindang general who went over to the communists during the civil war. Li Jishen was the chairman of the revolutionary Guomindang and vice chairman of the Central People's Government. Cheng Qian was a Chinese People's Consultative Committee member and member of the Central People's Government. Chen Mingren was a prominent member of the military in Hunan. Ye Jianying, Peng Dehuai, and He Long were leading communist military leaders. Tan Zhengwen was the communist security chief in Guangdong and Chen Yi and Pan Hannian were security chiefs for the communists in Shanghai.

15   Sources within the Ministry of Public Security told me that in 1949, Duan Yunpeng was sent to the mainland three times to carry out assassinations. He was given permission to kill anyone over the rank of general, and if he succeeded, he would be given 50 liang of gold for every murder (interview, 1995).

16   In relation to prostitution in Shanghai, Henriot points out that this figure of 800 drops to 518 brothels immediately after liberation. Henriot also suggests that the CCP seriously underestimated the actual number of prostitutes in the city. According to her, there were probably around 50,000, whereas police estimates placed the figure somewhere around 30,000 (Henriot 1995, 470).

17   This category would find legal form after August 1951, when the Administrative Council passed laws relating to industries using wireless equipment or that were engaged in engraving work. Also falling into the special business category were hotels, secondhand shops, pawn brokers, antique dealers, repair shops, and amusement centers. These categories would alter over time, narrowing particularly after 1957 when industry was nationalized (Xu Hanmin 1992, 33–35).

18   The figures given in this text (*Questions and Answers* 1994, 79) claimed that 1,303 prostitutes were held in Beijing centers and that 1,259 had STDs. The discrepancy between this figure (of 1,303) and the figures cited in the main text is due to the later date of the check and the likelihood that other prostitutes were brought into these centers after that first evening sweep.

19   In contrast, Gail Hershatter dates the official claim of eradication as 1958 (1997, 304).

20   The reality was, of course, quite different. Very small-scale prostitution would continue in China, but it existed underground and was usually dealt with by the public security forces under the rubric of "hoodlum activity." The one documented exception I have

found where prostitution was formally named as a problem came from a rather obscure and curious notice recorded in a regional gazetteer. As a diary entry highlighting police actions in 1964, in the city of Guilin, this note indicates that the situation with regard to prostitution was still quite serious and a campaign was needed to turn the situation around. The launch of this internal campaign was announced in the following manner: "1964, 19 November. Guilin Party Committee passes on to the City Politics and Law Party Group their 'Opinion Concerning the Development of the Work of Attacking Rapists and Hoodlum Prostitutes,' which calls for them to more vigorously pursue rapists and hoodlum criminal activities. The report was concerned with the fact that prostitution and rape were being treated in a similar fashion. It advised authorities to take care not to muddle these two types of contradictions and suggested rectification work was needed to ensure that this did not take place" (Guilin City Public Security Bureau 1995, 18).

21 Zhou Yongming disputes this link between the drug industry and counter-revolutionary activity. Instead, he suggests that it formed part of an image-making operation by the CCP. He argues that while this link was stressed, those cases that involved links with industry and the commercial sector were downplayed because the Five Antis Campaign had already led to a decline in production and the CCP did not want to scare the nation's capitalists any further. Zhou may well be right about the image-making quality of this link, but from police documents I have read, it also appears that the police themselves bought the line and policed accordingly (see Zhou Yongming 1999, 93–111).

22 The role of youth in denunciations would expand over time. The Three Antis Campaign saw an even more developed use of this technique. For a comparison of the role of youth in the fifties campaigns and the later Cultural Revolution, see Raddock 1979, 511–28.

23 Luo Ruiqing's text calls this county Shouning, not Jianning. See Luo Ruiqing 1994, 28.

24 Schurmann is not alone in this description of the first major post-liberation campaign. See, for example, Meisner (1986, 80) who also highlights the terror components of this campaign. Indeed, if it is dealt with at all in the literature (and it is often dealt with in the most perfunctory manner), it seems to be presented as quite different from the Maoist campaign style. Mainland police literature presents a very different picture of this campaign, suggesting, instead, that it constitutes the epitome of Maoist forms of campaigning. In terms of policing, this latter argument is quite persuasive, as I will attempt to show.

25 Even the most extreme anti-law thesis offered by the commodity-exchange school presupposed the growth of rational technical regulation in place of punitive legal forms. The example that Pashukanis famously used was the train timetable which set in place a radically different regulatory system to one based on liability. Where the former is predominantly technical (how does one get the train in on time), the latter is legal (who bears legal responsibility for any breaches) (Pashukanis 1978, 79). The failure of the regulatory model is manifold, but in terms of Maoism's friend/enemy distinction, it presupposes the absence of an adversary and reduces the social totality to an interest

group (see Schmitt 1996, 57). The main point to make here, however, is not this. It is simply that no matter whether one follows the commodity-exchange school or the proletarian law school of Vyshinsky, formal rules, not emotion, dictate action.

26 These figures vary wildly from those publicly available (see chapter 5 for a summary of these figures). All that can be said about this discrepancy is that the figures quoted here indicate the actual number of people detained, not of cases opened, whereas the publicly available figures refer only to the latter.

27 This idea of guanzhi or mass control and surveillance work was authorized by the "Temporary Methods Used to Put Counter-revolutionaries under Surveillance and Control." These "Temporary Methods" framed discussions at the first meeting of guanzhi workers organized by the ministry in October 1952. This meeting placed the onus on local areas to deal with their own counter-revolutionaries (*Outline of Public Security* 1997, 265). According to Yu Lei, however, guanzhi was already being widely used. He mentions it in relation to the Central Committee notice issued on October 10, 1950, entitled "Instructions Concerning the Elimination of Counter-revolutionary Activities." It stated that "concerning the comparatively minor criminals who show contrition, that is, those who could be described as lower-level spies or members of reactionary parties or cliques, we should immediately implement guanzhi and, through this, keep tabs on them." It was not until July 7, 1952, however, that these actions were made lawful by the State Council which, at that time, approved the Ministry of Public Security–drafted "Temporary Methods." See Yu Lei 1992, 402.

28 The structuring of the mass-line policing organs into the overall mechanisms of state control may well constitute a deprofessionalization of an earlier program put in place at the time of the city takeovers. In 1948, the communists were faced with the large number of remnant Guomindang officials who had run areas for the old regime. For the communists, securely holding such areas demanded that the former rulers be kept under tight surveillance, for they may have offered a potential threat to communist control. The way they dealt with these people was to establish supervised training teams, or *guanxundui*. These teams were made up of so called Nationalist Party backbone elements gathered together, held in disciplinary confinement, and checked. Ordinarily, such teams were put under the leadership of the public security preliminary hearing department (*gong'an yushen bumen*) and operated only for a short time (Yu Shubin 1992, 110).

29 So begins a struggle between two branches of government over who controls prisons that was thought resolved in 1983 when control was handed back to the Ministry of Justice, but which, behind closed doors, continues to this day.

30 This dual system still operates in a modified form today, as does the reform-through-labor system.

31 This is not to say the reform-through-labor system had no precursory forms. It did have, and these existed in both the Jiangxi and Yan'an periods. Indeed, as one gets closer to revolutionary victory, one finds many of the key tenets and structures of the system coming into existence. Hence the system can be traced back to the Jiangxi Soviet

when an extensive, if underdeveloped and underfunded system of penal incarceration took the name "Institute of Labor Persuasion." Alternatively, one could begin such a history in Yan'an, when these institutes reemerge. After all, as Griffin notes, it was out of the Yan'an experience that the ethos of the later reform-through-labor system first emerged in embryonic form. It was here, for the first time, that productive work was suggested to have an educative effect upon prisoners' ideology (Griffin 1976, 122–23). Indeed, this was one of the key goals of the Yan'an system, said to be to "organize prisoners into productive labor so that the material wealth of society can be increased and, at the same time, they can be reformed through labor and take on workers' ethics and learn their techniques of production" (Yu Shubin, PSHM 1992:4, v26, 109). It was not, however, until after 1941 that a systematized form of incarceration emerged with the justice department holding common criminals and the security forces controlling political criminals (Yu Shubin, PSHM 1992:4, v26, 107). Moreover, it was not until the communists entered the cities in 1948 that the system began to expand and develop one of its earliest innovations, the labor camps. It was at this time that the various liberated area prison authorities entered the cities and were faced with ever-increasing numbers of people to detain. Prisons were already overcrowded and, consequently, a number of area-level justice units decided to leave the cities and move prisoners to the countryside where they could develop farms and mines productive both of material goods and a new prisoner consciousness (Yu Shubin, PSHM, 1992:4, v26, 111).

32 This fact surely must cast some doubt on claims that Liu Shaoqi was more legally oriented than his comrades.

33 It is said that this draft document was completed at 1 a.m. on the morning of October 10. It was then sent to Mao, who checked through it, made a number of changes, and put his stamp of approval on it by 8 a.m. It was then sent straight off to press and published that very day (*Campaign to Suppress* 1992, 20).

34 Statistics from August 1951 on serious cases show that 44.6 percent of all cases involved bandit chiefs or professional bandits. A further 34.2 percent were described as "despotic tyrants," 13.5 percent as "special agents and local area military commanders for the Guomindang," and 7.7 percent as "leaders of secret societies and reactionary Party backbone elements." See *Campaign to Suppress* 1992, 26; Luo Ruiqing 1994, 98.

35 From this came the current sentence of death with a two-year reprieve offered in the criminal code. Having said this, however, one must also recognize that this suspended death sentence has a long history in China and can be traced back to dynastic times (Scobell 1990, 512). See Mao Zedong (1986, 189), edited by Michael Y. M. Kau and John K. Leung, for an English translation of this comment.

36 These figures differ dramatically from those offered by Zhou Yongming who states that by May 1951, 500,000 had been executed and that the total number of executions for the whole of this campaign lay between 500,000 and 800,000 (1999, 105, 176 n. 21).

37 The more lenient policy now in place was said to be more appropriate at a time when investigations were shifting away from society and moving toward elements within the Party, government, and military ranks, as well as into the fields of education, commerce,

religion, the democratic parties, and various peoples' organizations (*Campaign to Suppress* 1992, 37). Indeed, the Public Security Work Meeting resolution stated that even in cases of counter-revolutionaries found within Party ranks (i.e., the so-called neiceng counterrevolutionaries) and of those whose crimes were serious enough to warrant a sentence of execution, they should generally not be executed. To underline this, the authorities set a quota whereby only one- to two-tenths of those sentenced to death had their sentence carried out. The remainder would receive death with a two-year reprieve (Luo Ruiqing 1994, 77). This position largely reflected the views taken by Mao Zedong in May 1951. See Mao Zedong 1977, 5:54–56.

38   The new Three Antis Campaign was launched in January 1953 to mobilize against bureaucratism, commandism, and illegal breaches of regulations.

39   In villages, a similar schema prevailed. In country areas where there was no police station, however, the village governments established the registration areas and appointed responsible cadres to lead the work. All this work was, however, ultimately under the leadership of the police (Xu Hanmin 1992, 22).

40   Space does not permit a closer examination of the role of the personnel files in campaigning. Suffice it to say that the work unit filing systems only really began in 1952, when the Administrative Council passed a provisional measure for dossier collection for Administrative Council work units. The Party-held dossier system of organization was employed within work units from this time on. In 1954, a conference on the question of dossiers was organized and, in 1955, approval for a series of general temporary measures enabling their collection and use was put into effect. By the end of 1956, the first national governmental conference on personnel files was being convened in Beijing, and the detailed system of cadre, worker, and student files came into being around this time. Naturally, however, dossier work in these early days remained incomplete, with the most accurate and detailed dossiers being held on cadres and upper-level unit personnel. Worker and student dossiers have always been much simpler, but it is unlikely that they existed at this time in lower-level units (*Handbook* 1988, 448–49). For further details on the way files are currently employed in checking of work unit personnel, see *Handbook* 1988, 133–47.

41   For details of the Gao Gang and Rao Shushi conspiracy, see Teiwes 1990.

42   This was the critique offered by Xie Fuzhi, who was minister of public security from 1959 onward. See CCPRET 1973, 328–30.

43   Pan was rehabilitated on August 23, 1982.

44   A major structural reorganization took place in early 1954 with the abolition of the large administrative areas. This facilitated the transfer of a number of senior cadres into the Ministry of Public Security, and they took up leadership positions to help strengthen the collective leadership of the ministry. In January 1954, the newly established State Council appointed Xu Zirong, as well as Yang Qiqing, Xu Jianguo (known before the revolution as Du Liqing), Wang Jinxiang, Chen Long, and Wang Zhao as Deputy Ministers of Public Security (*Gong'an Jianshi*).

45   In the late twenties, the Soviets launched campaigns against what they called Shakhtyite

wreckers in industry. This campaign focused on the Shakhty region of the USSR, where so-called white agents were said to be engaged in sabotaging Soviet production. This industrial sabotage, so the story goes, ran alongside Kulak hoarding, and both events became linked together as signs of capitalist plots against socialism.

46 In the first four months of work in Shanghai in 1955, 430 cases of counter-revolutionary activity had come to light (*A Summary History* 1989, 130).

47 The members of this Central Committee team were Lu Dingyi, Luo Ruiqing, Zhou Yang, Liu Lantao, Liang Guobin, Qian Ying, Xiao Hua, Gao Kelin, Li Chuli, and Yang Qiqing (*Outline of Public Security* 1997, 279).

48 If Shakhtyite was the name that stood for wrecker in Soviet industry vocabulary, then Stakhanov emerged as the beautiful twin. In 1935, the model Soviet coal miner Alexei Stakhanov managed to achieve an output fourteen times greater than the norm and, in so doing, launched the term *Stakhanovism* into the socialist vocabulary. For details of the original tale, see Nove 1969, 233.

49 Unless otherwise stated, the material in the following section is drawn from "The Internal Campaign against Counter-revolutionaries in Hunan Province" (PSHM 1992:1, v23, 123–51).

50 Mao Zedong also commented on arrest rates in December 1956. He said that since the Pan Hannian and Hu Feng cases, over 4 million people had been investigated and, of the 160,000 suspects, only 38,000 were counter-revolutionaries (Mao Zedong 1974, 40).

51 Supplementary regulations were passed on December 29, 1957, and these stipulated the formation of management committees in cities and villages. These committees were in charge of sending people to reform through education. They were also responsible for the establishment of the processes by which people would be sent to do reform through education. The committees were initially made up of local government, police, and labor ministry representatives (interview, 1995). The supplementary regulations also set the term of incarceration from one to three years, with a possible fourth-year extension. The idea was that after their term was complete, the inmates would suffer no discrimination in work or study. Nor would the family or children of such people be discriminated against. Further supplementary legislation was enacted in 1982 (Yu Lei 1992, 403–4; *Collection of Rules* 1992, 6–7). By 1983, reform through education was no longer a shared police matter, but the responsibility of the Ministry of Justice. Incarceration, however, was largely determined by the police, for while reform through education may have been ameliorative in design, the operation of the system was anything but. In interviews, a number of police and justice officials said that in actuality, the management committees rarely operated. Instead, it was often left to the discretion of the local police chief, in consultation with work units and neighborhood security committees, as to who should be incarcerated and for how long.

52 These transformations were that socialism was being established, people's consciousness was being raised, and the people's democratic dictatorship was being consolidated.

53 Teiwes regards this document as a significant refinement of the rectification model, for it brings to the fore the idea of nonantagonistic contradictions (Teiwes 1979, 15).

While this holds true, it also constituted the culmination of a series of trends already in process. The idea of a more variegated treatment of lesser enemies was already developing before Mao put his stamp on the process and theorized it. Like most things, Mao's writings tended to grow out of experiences gained in practice, rather than from theoretical musings.

54   In the later half of 1956, a number of areas noted a deterioration of the social order situation. On the basis of incomplete statistics, the half-year period from September 1956 until March 1957 witnessed scores of worker strikes and mass petitions across the country. Numerous cities also witnessed student strikes and the petitioning of authorities at schools and colleges. In the rural sector, there was an ever-rising trend toward social disorder. In Zhejiang province, more than 1,100 social order incidents occurred in rural areas alone.

55   Quite apart from the ideological effect this was thought to have on police consciousness, there was also the added benefit that it saved money by turning police into workers. This was far from a minor consideration. After all, something like 51,349 officers were retrenched and reallocated work in economic production at this time (confidential material 1986).

4. The Years That Burned

1   There were two wings to this school. The radical wing of the commodity-exchange school was dominated by Evgeny Pashukanis, while the more moderate wing gained expression in the writings of P. I. Stuchka. These latter writings in particular have largely been forgotten. Easily the best collection available in English is Stuchka 1988.

2   For other related domains, somewhat different conditions charted their progress. For developments in the procuraturate at this time see, Ginsburgs and Stahnke 1968, 82–132. Briefly, however, it was in 1954 that the first constitution was promulgated and early drafts of a criminal code floated. More mature drafts of a criminal code were created in subsequent years. Indeed, the last draft (the thirty-third) appears to have been floated in the early days of the Socialist Education Movement. For further details, see H. M. Tanner 1999, 8.

3   In 1956, the cleanup rate peaked at a historic high with just 2.9 percent of all common crimes remaining unsolved (confidential material 1986).

4   In agriculture, it was the Hunanese who, at the beginning of the Great Leap, had promised to ensure that crucial aspects of the twelve-year agricultural program, such as increasing by 100 percent grain yields, ensuring comprehensive water conservation, and eliminating pests and illiteracy, would, in their province, be accomplished within one year. Mao, while striking a much more cautious pose publicly, tended to encourage such wild promises by promoting interprovincial competition among leaders. One can note the degree of similarity here between such economic competition and what was going on within the police force. For the Hunanese claims and the ensuing competition between it and other provinces, see MacFarquhar (1983, 42–43) for details.

5   On paper, at least, police were supposed to operate under a dual-leadership system so that professional leadership would come from the Public Security Bureau and local leadership from the people's commune. In most cases, the reality was different and it was the local commune that ran things (interview 1995).

6   From Liaoning's public security department came reports that in a fifty-day period, they had cracked 18,000 cases across the province. Gansu's public security department proudly stated that in sixteen counties, they had already reached a cleanup rate for counter-revolutionary and ordinary criminal cases that went into "the double one hundreds" (i.e., 100 percent cleanup rates on counter-revolutionaries, 100 percent on ordinary common criminals). Yunan's public security department boasted that all its cases, new and old, had been cleaned up in a high tide of case cracking.

7   Generally, collective training lasted for a few months (interview 1996).

8   In March 1958, the Ministry of Public Security issued "A Notice on the Situation in Shandong's Tancheng County Public Security Bureau Concerning the Clarification of Those Who's Situation Remained Unclear." It was with this notice that large-scale checking of those who formed part of the floating population and whose identities were not clear took place. With this, the conditions for the eventual use of shelter and investigation came into being (confidential material 1988).

9   On the basis of incomplete statistics, in the sixteen-month period between January 1958 until April 1959, damage caused by cutting corners or "experimenting" led to over 155,000 people being injured and more than 20,000 dying. In terms of economic costs, over 200 million yuan worth of economic damage was said to have been caused (*Outline of Public Security* 1997, 303).

10 Xie introduced his policy of outwardly appearing lenient while internally maintaining strict controls with the following words: "If one only sees an ever-diminishing degree of struggle against the enemy, and cannot see that it could flair up in the transition such that it is deepened and even becomes fiercer, then the rightist crime is very severe indeed. We are now entering a new period of socialist construction and the Party Central Committee has already said that in ten or fifteen years, we will realize the four modernizations. Socialist construction will continue with the Great Leap, and public security work must also have an appropriate Great Leap. Hence, in terms of the direction of public security policy, police should use the good situation to gradually tighten the noose in the struggle against the enemy, control them ever more tightly, and clean out these types thoroughly. We need to clean them out so that the enemy poses no more threats and thereby create an even better situation with regard to public order. This so-called tightening doesn't mean more detentions, more death sentences, or more supervision. Rather, it means tightly controlling attacks so they don't lead to chaos. It means more surveillance over reactionaries and controlling them more tightly. It involves transforming them more rigorously and working more diligently. We should have an outward appearance of leniency and an internal regime that is tight. In summary, then, we should strengthen the dictatorship, actively advance on the enemy, more actively control them,

and stop them from speaking and acting with impunity. By suppressing them, we can ensure that their destructive acts are reduced and the situation improved" (qtd. in *Outline of Public Security* 1997, 304–5).

11 The meeting discussed the nature of four types of criminal activity (*Outline of Public Security* 1997, 305–6):

> 1. Under the category of *contradictions among the people*, eight types of crimes could be considered counter-revolutionary. These were (a) going over to the enemy or going to a foreign embassy and asking it for political asylum; (b) participating in conspiracies to undertake violent actions; (c) committing murders, arson attacks, carrying drugs, or plotting to harm people; (d) organizing or participating in anti-revolutionary cliques; (e) encouraging the masses to take part in actions that wreck things or endanger life or state resources; (f) creating trouble in factories, mines, or enterprises, or, in rural areas, wrecking irrigation works, killing livestock, or adversely affecting rural production in a serious manner (g) writing or putting up counter-revolutionary things, writing counter-revolutionary letters, or producing political rumors; and (h) selling state secrets to foreigners.
>
> 2. If well-to-do peasants, cadres, or any members of the masses express dissatisfaction but do not engage in wrecking activities, or if they hold reactionary views or do very small illegal things, then these actions can be treated as contradictions among the people and dealt with as such. But if the people who do these things are historic counter-revolutionaries or former members of the Japanese puppet regime, then it is a different matter. They will be treated as counter-revolutionary actions.
>
> 3. Regarding corruption, theft of state or commune property, speculation for profit, or the beating up of cadres, the degree of culpability must be determined before assessing the nature of the offence. Only then can it be determined whether indeed they are contradictions between the people and the enemy.
>
> 4. For crimes such as hiding true production figures and then dividing up the dividends between individuals, taking advantage of someone, thieving, or buying a small amount for resale, criticism and education should be given. Such crimes must be clearly demarcated from ones in which people engage in corruption, serious theft, or speculative activities.

12 This was with the passing of the famous "Sixteen Points." For a translation, see Robinson 1969, 70–79.

13 There is now considerable evidence suggesting Lin was not the author of the document "Long Live People's War." Teiwes and Sun (1996) suggest that it was "primarily written by Wu Lengxi who was in the 'revisionist' Central Propaganda Department." See Teiwes and Sun for a fuller account of the actual drafting process (208).

14 Luo Ruiqing's advocacy of military performance–based competitions was particularly galling for Lin Biao, for this line of argument drew considerable support from Marshal Ye Jianying and Marshal He Long of the "military establishment." Such was the nature of Luo and Lin's relationship that the more Luo received support for this approach, the

more Lin felt betrayed. Their relationship had not always been so troubled. From 1930 until the anti-Japanese war, Luo had been Lin's close friend and deputy. Thus when Lin became minister of defense after the Lushan plenum, he turned to his old friend Luo for support and lobbied for him to be made his deputy. The relationship would remain close until around 1961, when Lin, suffering from an ever-debilitating illness, was forced to cede an increasing number of powers to Luo. Luo was even given the right to report directly to Mao on military matters, but the more he did this, the more Lin believed that Luo was trying to usurp his position. This growing personal dispute, coupled with Luo's lukewarm support for politics in command, ensured that their relationship grew increasingly frosty and took on a decidedly political hue. For more details on this and other personal aspects of the dispute, see Huang Yao and Zhang Mingzhe 1996, 436–97; Huang Yao 1991, 49–64; Zeng Fanzheng 1998, 2:433–37; and Teiwes and Sun 1996, 22–32, 203–16.

15   This report was left uncorrected until June 22, 1979, when the Ministry of Public Security Party cell wrote a report to the Central Committee entitled "A Report on a Number of Questions Concerning the 1966 Dispatching of Work Teams to the Beijing City Public Security Bureau to Seize Power." In this report, this seizure was acknowledged as quite wrong (confidential material 1988).

16   His deputies were Liu Jianfu, Ma Xingwu, and Cheng Cheng.

17   A standing committee was appointed that consisted of Li Qingchang, Niu Yuhe, Xiao Bin, Meng Xianjia, Wang Chu, Yang Qingshan, and Shi Guangping. Li Qingchang was put in charge, while Niu Yuhe and Wang Chu served as deputies.

18   The new lineup behind Minister Xue Fuzhi was Yang Qiqing as first deputy minister and first deputy secretary of the Party cell. Li Zhen served as third deputy minister behind Wang Jinxiang and second deputy secretary in the Party cell; he was also the cadre in charge of daily business. That left Yu Sang as fourth deputy minister (confidential material 1988).

19   From October 1966 onward, left actions became broadened, radicalized, and sharpened. The broadening occurred in early October as a result of a comment in the official Party organ Red Flag announcing that the Cultural Revolution should no longer be considered an inner Party struggle, but should, instead, be one that involved and relied upon the broad masses. The actions became radicalized when the Military Commission and the People's Liberation Army General Political Department issued an "urgent directive" putting "big democracy," and not the work team and Party committee leadership, in charge. They were sharpened after Chen Boda wrote "The Struggle between Two Lines," which acted to reinforce the idea that the masses, rather than organizations, should be in charge (Great Trial 1968, 280–84).

20   Precise dates regarding the Red Guard attacks proved quite difficult to ascertain. Some sources suggested from memory that much of the activity took place in early 1967. Other sources suggested that late 1966 was the time when the Red Guards' activity in the public security units was at its height. Much of this information has been drawn from interviews with students and teachers who participated in China's Political Science and Law

Commune or from police within either the Beijing Public Security Bureau or the ministry.

21 Some suggested it lasted only a matter of days, others told me that it was never implemented (interviews 1995, 1996, 1997).

22 In this respect, I disagree with those commentators who argue that the use of military power signaled a growing "Bonapartism" in Mao (Meisner 1986, 349; Domes 1976, 9–22). The term *Bonapartism* comes from Marx. It was first used in this way in Marx's discussion of the rule of Napoleon III in his text *The Eighteenth Brumière of Louis Bonaparte*. From this, Marx discerned a number of traits of authoritarian rule, and he labeled these Bonapartism. This term was repeatedly used pejoratively throughout the Russian revolution. It was first used in the analysis of Trotsky's rise to prominence and then, more important, by Trotsky himself when analyzing the emergence of Stalin. Generally, the key traits of Bonapartist leadership are: a reliance upon and the prominence of one-person rule, an emphasis upon the narrow political base of the leader, and a form of personal rule dependent upon the military. While it could be argued that Mao's rule at this time displays all these features, it is no less true that an alternative thesis (such as the one being mounted here) shows these features to be epiphenomenal.

23 It should be noted that there is some debate among Lenin scholars about this. Harding (1996) argues that Lenin opted for a one-party dictatorial model in the face of the overwhelming defeat of the world revolution in 1920. In response, Brinkley (1998) points out that Lenin's views about socialism were always "statist," and, to demonstrate this, he, too, points to relevant sections of Lenin's 1917 text *State and Revolution*.

24 This meant that it was reported to the central government on May 13, 1968.

25 Many of the leading members of the public security forces were former Social Section operatives. As mentioned earlier, the social section traversed the line between policing and espionage, and its operatives similarly crisscrossed that line. What hope was there for operatives whose work necessitated mixing with the enemy to extract information? In particular, as I have already mentioned, the Cultural Revolution saw a revival of the Gansu Red Flag Party case in general and Zhang Keqin's case in particular. With the revival of this, the more general suspicion of all formerly underground Party members was also revived. Effectively, the Cultural Revolution meant that all former Social Section operatives could easily fall prey to the charge of treason.

26 Nor was it simply in Beijing that police cadres were banished. Records from Guilin City Public Security Bureau also indicate banishment. The diary entry for that city police department indicates that between November 1968 and February 1969, three groups of police cadres, numbering something like four hundred officers, were sent out to various farms to undertake reform through labor (Guilin City 1995, 20). In 1969, the Ministry of Public Security only had forty cadres left. All the rest of them, I was told, had been packed off to the camp in Heilongjiang, which was by far the biggest (interview 1998).

27 I conducted a series of interviews with five senior police officers, all of whom had been sent to these camps and some of whom would come back to run the prison and police systems. All of them spoke of the harshness of the regime.

28   The records from Guilin city police prove telling. Up to four hundred police were sent down, but from 1970 through to 1980, only seventy-eight returned. In many of these provincial city programs, it seems, beatings and suicides took their toll. Indeed, there seems to have been an inverse relationship between crime and punishment. Wang Zhongfang (Luo Ruiqing's political secretary while he was in the Ministry of Public Security) told me of his relief at being imprisoned in the notorious Qingcheng prison in Beijing. When I asked if he would have preferred being sent out to camps with the others or left alone, his response was emphatic: "Are you kidding? I would have been torn apart by the Red Guards! I was happy to be in the prison. At least, that way, we had military protection" (Guilin City 1995, 20; interview 1993).

29   The idea of "one divides into two" first came to prominence in 1964. It was used against the former head of the Party school, Yang Xianzhen, who was said to have advocated "two divides into one." This was said to be heretical for it denied the class struggle and the uninterrupted nature of the revolution (see *Great Trial* 1968, 21–25). In public security matters, the idea would come to the fore in 1970 after the Fifteenth Public Security Work Meeting. This time, senior left-leaning police objected to its use. For example, the Shanghai City Public Security Bureau Military Control Committee head, Wang Weiguo, said in relation to public security work that "one divides into two! It's pretty hard to split that side which falls into counter-revolution into two!" Similarly, Zhu Quanlin, head of the Zhejiang Provincial Public Security Department Military Control Commission said, "I'm afraid that in relation to previous public security work, one can only talk of one dividing into one, not one dividing into two" (*Gong'an Jiianshi*).

30   On June 22, 1970, the military leadership in the ministry was both strengthened and simplified by the adoption of a program based on the old Yan'an slogan calling for less troops and simpler administration. On November 28, 1970, the Ministry of Public Security put these simplifications into operation. The entire ministry would be reorganized into one office and four groups. The office was for general administration while the four groups were for specialist work. These four groups were the political work group (*zhenggongzu*), the political protection group (*zhengbaozu*), the public security protection group (*zhibaozu*), and the pretrial interrogation and detention group (*yushenzu*). At the same time, there was also a leadership reshuffle. Wang Dongxing would step down from both the public security revolutionary committee and the core leadership group of the Ministry of Public Security (*gong'an hexin xiaozu*). With his resignation and the inclusion of new military members the new leadership core group membership consisted of Li Zhen, Yu San, Zeng Wei, Shi Yizhi, Zhao Dengcheng, Liu Junzhi, and Zhang Qirui, while the public security revolutionary committee now included Li Zhen, Yu San, Zeng Wei, Shi Yizhi, Zhao Dengcheng, and twenty-two others (confidential material 1988).

31   There were very few war criminals left in Chinese prisons because most had received amnesties. Up until the end of March 1966, six batches of (principally) Japanese war criminals had been released in general amnesties. This program more or less ceased during the Cultural Revolution, leaving 293 prisoners languishing in jail until March

1975. At that time, the seventh and last amnesty release program took place, and this led to the release of this final group (confidential material 1988).

32 In June, the Ministry of Public Security core group gave Zhou Enlai "A Report Requesting Instructions Concerning the 'Adjustment' [*tiaozheng*] to the Authorized Structure" that foreshadowed significant changes within the ministry. Of all the changes, the most important was the addition of two new specialist groups. These two new groups were the reform-through-labor work group and the (state) security protection group (confidential material 1988). The formation of the latter group, in particular, seems to have been at the behest of Mao, who was most concerned with activities on the "foreign front." That is to say, he feared an impending war with the Soviet Union and worried even more about China's preparedness.

33 The details of the Lin Biao plot to kill Mao are as scandalous as they are intriguing. Clearly out of favor by 1970, Lin is alleged to have hatched a plot to kill Mao, known as the "571 Engineering Project." In Chinese, the characters for 571 are pronounced *wuqiyi*, and this is a play on *wu*, which is short for *wuzhuang*, meaning "armed," and *qiyi* (for the numbers 71), which is a play on another word, pronounced in the same way but with slightly different tones, meaning "righteous uprising." The coup attempt, alleged to have been launched in September 1971, never really got off the ground. Lin, on the other hand, did. Boarding a plane in a vain attempt to flee to the Soviet Union he either crashed, was bombed, or was shot down (depending upon which account one believes). Neither Lin nor any of the plane's entourage survived. For a brief summary of the charges laid against the Lin Biao clique, see *Great Trial* 1981. Wu Faxian's daughter has recently written a book disputing the very existence of the plot (see Jin Qiu 1999). Teiwes and Sun similarly cast some doubt on this plot charge (1996, 39).

34 Indeed, the campaign to criticize Lin Biao and Confucius that dominated the political landscape in 1973–74 was said to be a continuation of the Cultural Revolution. See Hong Guangsi 1974.

35 Lenin makes the point that while the commune was a form of the dictatorship of the proletariat, it did not employ its forces with "*sufficient* vigor to suppress the resistance" (1964, 26:401). This lack of vigor in repressing opposition is repeated endlessly as a fundamental weakness of the commune. Indeed, one crucial aspect of its failure lay with its "excessive magnanimity." Thus "instead of destroying its enemies, it sought to exert moral influence over them" (1962, 13:476).

36 Fu Zhengyuan makes a similar point about the importance of Legalism to the Chinese communists. For Fu, Chinese Marxism-Leninism owes much to the Legalist school and, in fact, could be read as a variant on this theme. From the people's communes through to the system of household registration, he notes, Legalism prevailed, albeit in "Marxist-Leninist garb" (1996, 148). While one can accept much of Fu's argument, I would suggest that accompanying this unconscious acceptance of Legalism by the left was a conscious use of this school of thought in this campaign to promote a particular reading of the state, class struggle, and the reemergence of remnant forms. It was these things that came to authorize an "all-round dictatorship of the proletariat."

37   Indeed, Legalism would end up losing to Confucianism in the battle for control of the Chinese state (Luo Siding 1974, 67–73).

38   Army representatives within the public security structure, I was told, were far from numerous. A small number operated within the Ministry of Public Security, and they were called "army representatives." Every bureau within the ministry had one or two such representatives. They were, however, far more numerous in the number 13 bureau, which dealt with "special cases" and held the files on people such as Liu Shaoqi and Peng Dehuai (interview 1995).

39   The other items on the radicals' agenda included "how it came to pass that the bourgeoisie within the Party became embroiled in the counterrevolution." Yet another demanded that police account for the spread of slanderous materials around marketplaces which focused almost entirely upon the so-called last will and testament of Zhou Enlai. One of the last agenda items was to ascertain whether or not the police were, in fact, the appropriate vehicle through which these struggles should be waged. In particular, the radicals wanted to discuss what form this struggle would take, what group should be targeted, and what organization could be relied upon now that the Party itself had been infected with revisionist tendencies. The final point on the radicals' agenda was to insist that Party committees would still take the lead (confidential material 1977).

40   All specialist texts agree that crime statistics from this period need to be handled with great care, for they invariably underrepresented the problem. The extremely low crime figures for the first four years of the Cultural Revolution are said to result from a systemic breakdown. As one authoritative source puts it: "With regard to the veracity of the figures for the years 1966 through to 1970, some qualifications should be made. During the period of the so-called Cultural Revolution, the public security units were 'smashed'. . . [and] . . . the vast majority of statistical materials were lost or no statistics were collected or the figures that were collected were incomplete" (confidential material 1986). Nevertheless, with the prevalence of slogans such as "revolution is no crime, to rebel is justified," this high tide of crime was, in fact, greater than the previous two. See Yu Lei 1993, 43.

41   In 1970, there were said to be 230,040 common criminal cases investigated and only 107,181 solved (46.6 percent). In 1971, the situation was worse, with 323,623 cases opened and only 149,201 solved (46 percent). 1972 saw a slight improvement with 402,573 cases opened and 218,228 solved (54 percent), while 1973 witnessed a so-called high tide of crime with 535,829 cases opened and 340,641 solved (64 percent) (confidential material 1986).

42   In the Fengqiao district of Zhuji county between 1964 and 1967, only 11 people were arrested on social order disturbances and only about 30 criminal cases laid. In the period from 1967 until 1973, some 1,771 people were arrested, and this does not include the 742 cadres and 904 "four black category" people who had their houses searched and property confiscated, or the 2,881 people seized and struggled against, or the 510 injured in these struggles, or the 23 killed (PSHM 1994: 2 v32, 103).

5. The End of the (Mass) Line?

1 The "three represents" of Jiang Zemin highlight what the Party now stands for. According to Jiang Zemin, it has always represented the demands to develop the advanced productive capabilities of the Chinese nation, to represent the nation's advanced civilizational demands, and to represent the fundamental interests of the broad mass of the population. First raised in February 2000, this subsequently became Party policy after it was ratified by the Sixteenth Party Congress in November 2002.

2 It was at this time, too, that specialization was raised. This led to the Ministry of Rail, Transport, and Communications officially forming the railway police in January 1975 (Xu Xinyuan 1999, 93). Preparations for this announcement had begun in 1974. Initially, the force in 1974 had some 27,154 police and cadres and ran 863 police stations. Within ten years, it had grown to a force of 53,799 persons running 1,171 police stations (confidential material 1986). It was also at this time that the shelter and investigation centers (*shourong shencha*) made their reappearance, but this regime will be dealt with later in the chapter.

3 Even if one adopts the very broad definition of police used by Clifford Shearing (1992, 399), that is, as a force for the "preservation of the peace," one would still have some difficulties describing the pre-reform Chinese public security forces as a police force since they were designed to protect and promote the revolution, *not* the peace. Indeed, the pre-reform public security forces quite often proved a central force in the prosecution of Maoist-style political campaigns, making them, if anything, disrupters of the peace.

4 The parody comes from a word play. The character for money in Chinese is *qian* and is pronounced in exactly the same way as the character used for the word *forward* or *in front of*.

5 Police figures tell us why this would be the case. The growth of transient crime has become one of the major issues in contemporary policing in China. The problem first appeared in the eighties, when police discovered that crime committed by itinerants was coming to constitute a rising percentage of all crime. One study led by the Deputy Minister of Public Security, Yu Lei, examined the rising trend of itinerant crime throughout the eighties. Cases that involved the floating population constituted only about 15 percent of the total in 1985, but the number rose to 17 percent in 1987 and then 18 percent in 1988 (Yu Lei 1993, 172). While Yu Lei's study offers a general picture, it tends to disguise the nature of the problem which is demographically concentrated in the cities. As the police scholar Gu Xinhua has noted, the problem of "floating crime" becomes much more significant when one concentrates on market areas and large population concentrations (1990, 48). Hence if one closely examines key market areas and population concentrations, one discovers that the percentage of crime committed by itinerants rises dramatically. In the Shenzhen economic zone, for example, it was discovered that over 90 percent of all serious crime was perpetrated by the so-called three have-nots (*sanwu*) from the countryside. These three have-nots refer to those who have no long-term employment, no legal identification, and no long-term residency. While one may

claim that Shenzhen is a special case, Guangzhou is not. Yet in 1996, a study found that 85 percent of all arrests were of itinerants and, while this is unusually high, the general trend it suggests is evident in just about every city (He Qinglian 1998, 265). In 1996, a study in Shanghai found that itinerant crime had increased fifteen-fold in just thirteen years. Some 55.86 percent of cases concerned itinerants (Shanghai Policing Studies Group 1998, 17). In Beijing in 1994, police found that 46 percent of all arrests were of itinerants. Given that stability is needed in order to promote economic reform, transient and itinerant crime has become one of the key concerns of the police (He Qinglian 1998, 254, 255, 265).

6 There have been five high tides of crime in China since 1949. The first of these occurred shortly after the establishment of the PRC. In 1950, this tide reached its peak with 513,461 crime cases prosecuted. This meant about 93 crimes committed per 100,000 people. Serious cases numbered around 47,000, which meant they constituted 9.22 percent of all criminal cases. These crimes mainly involved counter-revolutionary sabotage and so-called remnant crimes such as drugs, prostitution, and the trade in human beings. The second high tide peaked in 1961. In that year, crime cases reached 420,000. These cases involved new types of crimes by new types of criminals. In the main, these were committed by young adults and juvenile offenders who were said to be a new type of criminal raised in the new society. The key characteristic of the first two high tides was that they dropped off sharply after they reached their respective peaks and countermeasures were undertaken. The third tide rose during the Cultural Revolution (May 1966–October 1976). It reached its peak in 1973. The next two high tides came during the reform period. The fourth emerged around the late 1970s and early 1980s, and peaked in 1981. In that year, over 890,000 criminal cases were logged, and the crime rate was estimated at about 89 per 100,000 people. The fifth wave began in the late 1980s but continued on into the 1990s. By 1991, the number of crime cases had reached 2,360,000, and the crime rate was said to be around 200 per 100,000 people. Unlike previous periods, the reform era was to witness only minor fluctuations in what, by Chinese standards, constitutes an inordinately high crime rate. For the fifth wave, the peak came between 1995 and the first quarter of 1996. For more information on these five waves, see Yu Lei 1993, 37–47. For an alternative view that only registers four waves (that is, it does not include the Cultural Revolution), see Wang Zhimin and Huang Jingping 1992, 48–49. For a close examination of the fifth wave, see Cao Feng, 1997, 14. The figures given here have all been rounded off. For more exact figures, see table 4.

7 Evidence of the degree of this social panic can be found in the text *Do You Feel Safe?* This text summarizes the results of a survey undertaken by the PSM between 1988 and 1989. Questioning some 15,000 people across 15 provinces and cities, 75 areas, 150 city districts, 75 counties, and 750 neighborhoods, this survey was the most comprehensive of its type ever undertaken. The results for the police were not good. While judgments about social order and personal security suggest that they were barely satisfactory (77.5 percent of people said social order was either just satisfactory or below par, while 58 percent of people said the same about their personal security), popular judgments about

sentencing claimed that it was too lenient (nearly 60 percent of people gave this answer). See *Do You Feel Safe?* 1991, 40, 46, 150–59, 250–59. It should be added, however, that despite a lack of significant improvements in the law-and-order situation in the nineties, more recent surveying witnessed something of a reduction in popular anxiety about crime. A follow-up survey in May–June 1991 discovered that while only 7.3 percent of the population felt safe, 43.7 percent felt "relatively safe" and a further 17.9 percent felt the situation was "average." "Average" and "below" for personal security, therefore, account for 48.4 percent of respondent answers, which amounts to a decrease of just under 10 percent. In terms of social order, the situation was perceived to be even better, with only 58.7 percent of the population feeling that the situation was average or below. See Ministry of Public Security Public Safety Research Group 1992, 58–64. There is little space to develop these points here, but for those interested in a more detailed articulation and analysis of these figures, see Dutton and Lee 1993, 319–22.

8   From 1978 onward, the Ministry of Public Security began opening professional police schools (that is, specialized secondary schools). These schools offered training programs for recruits who had graduated from high school. From 1978 through to 1987, there were eighty-three of these police schools built and something like 80,000 graduates were sent from these schools into the police force (Yu Lei 1992, 440–48). By November 1984, the Ministry of Public Security was closely attending to the issue of police training. At that time, it convened the National Public Security Educational Work Meeting, which suggested the need for a coordinated and national approach to the question. This resulted in a call for central-, provincial-, and regional-level governments to work toward creating a multileveled and diverse public security educational system offering intensive educational and training programs for police. At the same time, this meeting also drew up a six-year training program for police. As a result of these initiatives, it is said that police educational and training programs have undergone rapid development. From the early eighties on, police academies began to reappear and, by 1986, they were joined by five police cadre management academies. The academies offered two- to three-year courses that included a variety of legal, political, cultural, and professional subjects, as well as specialized police subjects such as public security, public order management, and crime investigation (*Outline of Public Security* 1997, 410). Higher education institutions run by the police also developed in this period. From 1978 through to 1987, three police universities (with four-year degree programs) and eleven institutions (with three-year degree programs) were established. These fourteen institutions had 10,979 students in 1987 (Yu Lei 1992, 448). The subjects offered in these degree programs included public security management, detective work, preliminary trial preparation, public order management, security guard work, public security political work, document examination, forensic medicine, crime photography, traffic management, household registration management, radio communication, television techniques, graphic communication, computer application, as well as some other specializations (Yu Lei 1992, 450). Some police universities have also established law programs (Yu Lei 1992, 453).

9   On the development of the koban pillbox system, see Hao Hongkui 1989, 38, and Wang Mian 1991, 37. On forensics, see Yu Lei 1992, 450, 453. On the creation of police patrols and the emergency 110 telephone number system, see Zhang Min 2000, 31–33.

10   On the issue of visceral and populist responses to crime, one Western observer goes so far as to suggest that the 1983 Severe Strike Campaign constituted an attempt on the part of the police to reassert their power in the "balance of awe" between police and offenders (Murray-Scot Tanner 2000, 93–125).

11   These cities being Beijing, Tianjin, Shanghai, Guangzhou, and Wuhan.

12   There are a range of accounts that claim to offer a behind-the-scenes look at why campaigning returned to policing. Most of these have been summarized in the work of Murray-Scot Tanner (1999, 85–86) who concludes that Deng Xiaoping gave the order to the newly installed Minister of Public Security, Liu Fuzhi. One well-placed informant I consulted offered yet another variant on this tale, suggesting that campaigns came up as a strategy during a discussion Liu was having with Deng about the social order situation in a number of areas in Guangdong province (interview, 1996).

13   The diversity of the various organs that called for this policy and were later included in it is indicative of the type of "comprehensiveness" being called for. The eight organs that petitioned the Party were the Ministry of Propaganda, the Ministry of Education, the Ministry of Culture, the Ministry of Public Security, the National Labor Bureau, the National Worker's Union, the Communist Party Youth League, and the National Women's Federation. See Wang Zhongfang 1989, 7.

14   Interestingly, this is a point not lost on Chinese legal scholars. They now celebrate Maine's thesis and argue that the story of the contract is the tale of modernization, freedom, autonomy, and equality (Albert Chen, 1996, 9–10).

15   Indeed, as Hazard (1969) notes, communist China began by following the Soviet idea of stability very closely, but, by 1957, it had veered toward the necessity of elasticity to ensure that the revolution did not die out. The Soviets were scathing in their criticism of this, and, according to Hazard, they quoted the Chinese press, which demanded that law "possess definite elasticity, and may be called an elastic measure" ("Ilychev Speech Indicts Chinese Social Sciences," qtd. in Hazard 1969, 99).

16   While an array of voices rejected this position (e.g., Tang Congyao 1980, 7–9), this view tended to predominate. For a recent summary of new debates in law including this one and the rule of law/rule of man debate, see He Qinhua 1991, 16–61.

17   Oestreich details the pre-history of modern contractualism by tracing the development within the church of the covenant of grace and, from there, through to the secularized forms of contract. His argument is that since Weber, this covenant of grace within Protestantism has largely been ignored as all eyes have turned instead to predestination. Yet for Oestreich, the recovery of this part of theology proves crucial for any understanding of more modern forms of contractual obligation in the process of secular state building (1982, 135–54).

18   *Oeconomy* means the "correct manner of managing individuals, goods and wealth within the family . . . and making it thrive" (Foucault 1979, 11).

19 Here, I am not trying to suggest that continental models and the English model of policing are the same. Rather, I am merely alluding to the fact that the process of professionalization was occasioned by similar sorts of pressures.

20 Liu Wenqi summed up this conservative position and offered a criticism of the Party in the process. He spoke for many within police ranks when he bemoaned the lack of class analysis and class focus in police work. In relation to class struggle, he said: "In any particular period, because we have refrained from using these types of concepts and methods to proceed in examining international and national questions, when we are faced with the development of an internal rebellion and chaos, we are not in a position to provide answers to the troubles that come about" (1990, 21). For their part, Yang Zhaomin and Wang Gongfan would write: "In recent years, we haven't paid enough attention to class struggle" (1990, 8).

21 Zweig et al. argue that the introduction of the contract began in 1982, but contracts were beginning to be introduced from around 1981. By 1982, as I shall go on to show, they would not only spread into other domains but also go deeper into the society. Indeed, as Zweig et al. show, by April 1985, the unified purchasing of grain that had been operative since the central plan came into existence in 1953 was replaced by a system of voluntary contracts between producers and the state. As Zweig et al. conclude, "The success of the current rural economic reforms depends upon whether contractual relations will facilitate rural China's transformation from a command economy to one based on an amalgam of indicative-planning and market mechanisms." See Zweig et al. 1987, 320.

22 The purposive contract in Weber is juxtaposed to the status contract in that the former is programmatically applied and temporally limited. For more details, see Weber 1978, 668–81; and Rosenfeld 1985, 810–14.

23 Articulated in 1979, these Four Cardinal Principles were the promotion of the socialist road, the dictatorship of the proletariat, the leadership of the Communist Party, and finally, Marxism-Leninism, Mao Zedong Thought.

24 Note, for example, the position taken by Wang Zhimin, Li Tianfu, and Huang Jingping in the pages of the key police journal *Public Security Studies*: "How is it possible to compare the situation today with that of yesteryear when modernization is now in full swing and when the scale, speed, and scope of change in society, politics, economics, and cultural systems is so great? Given that the situation with regard to law and order is the result of objective environmental factors, it seems hard to imagine the likelihood of a return to the 1950s. Under the influence of such evaluation criteria, public security organs undoubtedly neglected the actual conditions and were eager to achieve success by resorting to short-term measures, even when these ran contrary to their own interests" (1988, 6).

25 In one interview with one of China's leading experts on demographic policing, it was pointed out that since the end of the 1980s, population flows had stabilized at around 50 to 60 million people per day on the road in China. He added, however, that this figure would double if one were to include intraprovincial movement (interview 1994).

26 In 1979, there were 12,719 police stations throughout China. This number increased to 16,112 by 1980, and a large part of that rise came with the development of a more exten-

sive rural police station network. Something like 4,000 new police stations were established in rural areas in that year. Indeed, the growth of rural stations has been highly significant. At the beginning of reform in 1978, there were 5,276 rural police stations, 3,515 urban ones, and a total nationwide of 11,480. By 1983, after substantial investment in the police station system, there existed 25,434 rural stations, 4,357 urban ones, and 30,441 overall. Clearly some significant investment had taken place, but what is of particular interest here is the way funds were directed at the countryside, no doubt in part to prop up the ailing household registration system and slow the burgeoning rural crime rate (confidential material 1986).

27 As far as I can tell, the first document to put this system forward came in June 1981 and was entitled "The Central Committee of the Chinese Communist Party Approves the Minutes of the Central Committee's Politics and Law Committee Forum on Security in the Five Cities of Beijing, Tianjin, Shanghai, Guangzhou and Wuhan (June 14, 1981)" (qtd. in *Collection of Rules* 1992, 1–4).

28 Comprehensive management was a system devised to tie mass-line organs and formal policing agencies more closely together by building up a total security network that could prevent crime before it actually occurred (Wang Zhongfang 1989, 8–14; H. M. Tanner 1995, 297–99). Running counter to many of the reforms which disaggregated things, comprehensive management wed formal police agencies to mass-line organs, educational institutions, work unit security sections, and so on to build up a system of total control.

29 Social help and education, according to Shao Daosheng is "a means to mobilize sectors of society to educate youth who have committed minor offences in order to help them correct their mistakes and to encourage them to embark on a path of healthy development. It is neither an administrative sanction nor criminal punishment, but is a form of political and ideological education of youth. It is a necessary measure to maintain social order and bring about an improvement of the social environment. It is a new form of and a new invention in mass participation in the comprehensive treatment of youth crime." As he goes on to note, it is also used as a means to police newly released prisoners still on parole. Those charged with the task of helping and educating are the "people living and working with the young people who have committed minor offences," as well as locals with a high political consciousness such as cadres, model personalities, advanced workers, or colleagues, teachers, neighbors, schoolmates, relatives, and parents. Shao concludes that "because there are emotional ties between these people and the juvenile offenders, they are in the best position to understand what those young people think, what they do, and what they need. This contingent of educators is thus highly motivated and consists of progressive, honest, and upright people who are at the same time committed to youth education and are capable of undertaking this task." See Shao Daosheng 1987, 198.

30 For an example of one very well-developed set of regulations from Shanghai indicating the nature of the inducements and the way the system worked, see Bai and Ma 1990, 207–8.

31   In his speech to the National Politics and Law Work Meeting, Qiao Shi gives a good sum-
     mary of the way in which policing work at base levels would be reinvigorated by a system
     of contracts. He begins by outlining the third stage of the Severe Strike Campaign in
     1986. Redirecting this campaign onto the streets and toward transient crime, he high-
     lights the way in which base-level work can be strengthened: "Strengthening base-level
     organs and raising the fighting power of these organs is germane to the program. Only
     by doing this can the various measures implemented in these places truly be put into
     effect and the comprehensive management of social order ensured. This work involves
     building up all base-level party and government powers and bringing them into play so
     that they are of use in organizing the comprehensive management of social order. To
     do this, we need to advance and put into effect the security contract responsibility sys-
     tem [zhi'an chengbao zerenzhi] and the safety security responsibility system [anquan baowei
     zerenzhi], and this will give each security committee of the neighborhood committees
     and each mediation unit new life. We have already successfully put in place the security
     contract responsibility system in rural areas, and these have, on the whole, resolved the
     problem of financial remuneration for people involved in the [village] security commit-
     tee and mediation work. This, in turn, resolved the problem of inadequate recognition
     of their skills and inadequate linking of their work to rewards and penalties, which was
     all a part of the philosophy of eating from the big pot. Through this, the activism of these
     people can be brought into play, and this will speed up the process that is changing the
     face of public security. So this system has received a warm welcome from the broad body
     of the masses. . . . We have already implemented the safety security responsibility sys-
     tem within factories, mines, and enterprises. On the whole, this has meant that these
     economic contract responsibility systems (jingji chengbao zerenzhi) have strengthened the
     responsibilities of the entire cadre and worker body. In relation to security departments,
     cadres and workers are now much more active in matters of safety and production. On
     the basis of these sorts of experiences, we now need to summarize, generalize, and ex-
     tend these lessons to other areas" (qtd. in Collection of Rules 1992, 52–55).

32   Indeed, the use of fines to replace punishment had become such a widespread phenome-
     non by the end of the eighties that the phrase describing it—yifa daixing—had become
     a common colloquial expression.

33   Legislation did come to cover these institutions until 1985, but even then it was in the
     form of an internal notice from the supreme court and seven other relevant depart-
     ments. For an example of this legislation, see Dutton 1998, 125–29.

34   Fifties revivals to deal with renewed outbreaks of old crimes or misdemeanors are a con-
     stant feature of the Chinese justice system. Note, for example, that the reemergence of
     a Chinese drug problem has occasioned the revival of clinics modeled on the early fifties
     jieyansuo or anti-smoking clinics while the reappearance of large-scale transient crime,
     as has been noted, led to the revival of the shelter and investigation centers (shourong
     shencha) until their abolition, due to international pressure, in 1996.

35   The six evils are (a) prostitution; (b) manufacturing, selling, or spreading indecent ma-
     terials; (c) kidnapping and trading women or children; (d) planting, smoking, or dealing

in drugs; (e) gambling; and (f) using superstition to trick people. See *Collection of Rules* 1992, 150.

36   Similarly strict guidelines also came to dominate the treatment of gamblers. In terms of prostitution, the internal regulations promulgated during the six evils campaign of 1989 state that custodial sentences, not fines, should be used in the following situations:

> 1. Where the prostitute has already been dealt with in the past by the police (i.e., had prior convictions)
> 2. Where the crime was particularly severe (e.g., where the entire family had moved into a city or town to live off the proceeds)
> 3. Where it involved sex with foreigners
> 4. Where the case involved multiple counts of sex
> 5. Where the prostitute is actively soliciting customers

See *Collection of Rules* 1992, 146–49. Similar sorts of guidelines were also issued on gambling.

37   The other main reason given was also financial. High legal costs were held to be responsible for people avoiding legal remedies and dealing with matters privately (Wu Zhongfei and Chen Yuanxiao 2000: 27).

38   For more detailed regulations stipulating wages, subsidies, and bonuses in Shanghai, see "Shanghai Notice Offering an Opinion on the Increases in Financial Subsidies to Professional Cadres from the Neighborhood Committees" in Bai Yihua and Ma Xueli 1990, 207–8.

39   For a dramatic example of the "user pays" household registration experiments, see Dutton 1998, 99–102.

40   In 1987, the police reported favorably on voluntary schemes operative in both Wuhan and Chongqing which organized residents into groups of fifteen and rotated the responsibility between them. Such schemes resurrected an old Maoist method itself built on a very ancient (Legalist) base. For details of this system, see *A Basic Outline* 1987, 247.

41   The following information on informants is drawn from *A Basic Outline* 1987, 261–88 unless otherwise indicated.

42   This was made official in October 1984, when the Ministry of Public Security issued an internal document entitled "Temporary Regulations Concerning the Establishment of Public Security Eyes and Ears." For further details, see *A Basic Outline* 1987, 265–66.

43   The importance of the joint protection defense force, or lianfang, should not be underestimated. They were formed in the early sixties by the security committees of the neighborhood committees (zhibaohui), led by local governments and local public security forces, and populated with civil and military personnel and local cadres. They were designed as a local neighborhood security force. Currently boasting a cadre force of 2,500,000, they are estimated to have assisted police by discovering and cracking around 20 percent of crime cases. This, it is said, "helps reduce the problem of the shortage of police." It is their importance in this regard that has led to these groups also beginning to experiment with responsibility systems and the replacement of unpaid retirees with

salaried younger members. These younger members are often retrenched workers. For more details, see Zheng Yuhua and Cen Shengting 1992, 1–8.

44 This stands in stark contrast to the past. Previously, police would check and approve all appointments and ensure that these units were well staffed. Indeed, a quota of no less than 0.3 percent of total staff and workers were to be employed in these units in the pre-reform years. See Hu Yongming 1993, 58.

45 Internal protection units organized dossiers on (a) special cases (b) common criminal cases, (c) cases requiring supervision, (d) those under investigation, (e) serious incidents, (f) key projects, (g) criminal detention, (h) secret forces, and (i) any other general cases deemed worthy of attention. See *Internal Protection* (1991, 44) for further details.

46 In one well-publicized dispute between an enterprise and local peasants over land in 1988, the enterprise chief sent the enterprise police out to arrest a number of peasants and, as a result, other peasants descended upon the factory and caused considerable trouble at the factory gates (Zhou and Yang 1991, 49).

47 The use of police uniforms and identification badges by nonauthorized personnel is yet another problem produced by economic reform. See Zheng Yuhua and Cen Shengting 1992, 58; and Zhao Mingqiang and Yang Yuejin 1991, 58.

48 The number of police in Beijing varies between 30,000 and 40,000, according to the head of the bureau (interview 1998).

49 So derivative of the Ministry of Public Security are these forces that even the officer ranks within the security firms are based upon the organization of the police. All profits go back to the ministry, but in the case of the Beijing company, they are said, at this stage, to remain within the company to allow further expansion. Taxes are high, with a rate of 55 percent leveled on any profits earned (interview 1998).

Concluding Reflections

1 Pashukanis 1980, 355.

2 For an examination of Vyshinsky's Marxist theory and its strange amalgam of law and terror, see Sharlet and Beirne 1984, 153–77.

3 See, for example, Wu Daying's entry in the *Chinese Encyclopedia of Law* 1984, 448.

4 Nor is it just in relation to the rise of the CCP and Mao that the literature displays this tendency. Fred Teiwes and Warren Sun complain of similar tendencies in relation to works covering later periods of China's political history. They suggest that much of the Western literature on Chinese politics written in the late 1960s and 1970s "slavishly" followed a variant of the Chinese "two-line" struggle model and did so in everything but name. In place of the name "two lines" they would write of two lines in terms of personal disputes (Mao Zedong versus Liu Shaoqi) or in the language of the social sciences (revolutionary modernizer versus managerial modernizers). Irrespective of the "code" being used, however, the method was the same. See Teiwes with Sun 1999, 7.

REFERENCES

The Activities of the Chinese Communist Party's Special Agents: The Third Volume of Compilations of Chinese Communist Party Original Material. 1983. Liming Wenhua Gufen Gongsi, Taipei. 中共问题原始资料编辑委员会编《中共的特务活动（中共原始资料汇编之三）》，黎明文化事业股份公司。

Adorno, Theodor, and Max Horkheimer. 1979. *Dialectic of Enlightenment.* Trans. John Cumming, Verso, London.

Anderson, Benedict. 1983. *Imagined Communities: Reflections on the Origin and Spread of Nationalism.* Verso, London.

Apter, David, and Timothy Cheek. 1994. "Introduction: The Trial." In Dai Qing, *Wang Shiwei and "Wild Lillies": Rectification and Purges in the Chinese Communist Party, 1942–1944.* M. E. Sharpe, Armonk, N.Y., xvii–xxxi.

Apter, David, and Tony Saich. 1994. *Revolutionary Discourse in Mao's Republic.* Harvard University Press, Cambridge, MA.

Arendt, Hannah. 1958. *The Human Condition.* University of Chicago Press, Chicago.

Averill, Stephen C. 1995. "The Origin of the Futian Incident." In Tony Saich and Hans van de Ven, eds., *New Perspectives on the Chinese Communist Revolution.* M. E. Sharpe, Armonk, NY, 79–115.

Bai Yihua and Ma Xueli, eds. 1990. *A Handbook on Neighborhood Committee Work.* Chinese Society Press, Beijing. 白益华，马学理主编《居民委员会工作手册》，中国社会出版社。

Bakken, Børge. 2000. *The Exemplary Society: Human Improvement, Social Control, and the Dangers of Modernity in China.* Oxford University Press, Oxford.

Balakrishnan, Gopal. 2000. *The Enemy: An Intellectual Portrait of Carl Schmitt.* Verso, London.

Barghoorn, Frederick C. 1971. "The Security Police." In H. Gordon Skilling and Franklyn Griffiths, eds., *Interest Groups in Soviet Politics.* Princeton University Press, Princeton.

A Basic Outline of Grassroots Level Security. 1987. China People's Public Security University Press, Beijing. 《治安基层基础概论》，中国人民公安大学出版社。

Baum, Richard. 1969. "Revolution and Reaction in the Chinese Countryside: The Socialist Education Movement in Cultural Revolutionary Perspective." *China Quarterly,* no. 38:92–119.

Bennett, Gordon. 1976. *Yundong: Mass Campaigns in Chinese Communist Leadership*. University of California Press, Berkeley.

Benton, Gregor. 1992. *Mountain Fires: The Red Army's Three-Year War in South China, 1934–1938*. University of California Press, Berkeley.

Blecher, Marc. 1986. *China: Politics, Economics and Society*. Frances Pinter, London.

Böckenförde, Ernst-Wolfgang. 1998. "The Concept of the Political: A Key to Understanding Carl Schmitt's Constitutional Theory." In David Dyzenhaus, ed., *Law as Politics: Carl Schmitt's Critique of Liberalism*. Duke University Press, Durham, 37–55.

Brinkley, George. 1998. "Leninism: What It Was and What It Was Not." *Review of Politics* 60, no. 1:153–61.

Brugger, Bill. 1981a. *China*, vol. 1, *Liberation and Transformation, 1942–1962*. Croom Helm, London.

———. 1981b. *China*, vol. 2, *Radicalism to Revisionism, 1962–1979*. Croom Helm, London.

Byron, John, and Robert Pack. 1992. *The Claws of the Dragon: Kang Sheng; The Evil Genius behind Mao and His Legacy of Terror in People's China*. Simon and Schuster, New York.

The Campaign to Suppress Counter-Revolutionaries in the Period Immediately after the Founding of the PRC. 1992. Masses Press, Beijing. 《建国初期镇压反革命运动》，群众出版社。

Cao Boyi [Tsao Po-I]. 1969. *The Rise and Fall of the Chinese Soviet in Kiangsi (1931–1934)*. Institute of East Asian Studies, National Chengchi University, Taipei. 曹伯一《江西苏维埃之建立及其崩溃 (1931-1934)》，国立政治大学东亚研究所。

Cao Feng. 1997. *The Fifth High Tide: The Crime Problem in Contemporary China*, China Today Press, Beijing. 曹凤《第五次高峰-当代中国的犯罪问题》，今日中国出版社。

Cao Ying. 1996. "A Participant in the Yan'an Rectification Campaign and the Seventh Plenum." In Chinese Communist Party History Study Office, ed., *Chinese Communist Party Historical Materials*, vol. 58. Chinese Communist History Press, Beijing, 1–17. 曹瑛 "在延安参加整风运动和七大"，中共党史研究室《中共党史资料第58辑》，中共党史出版社。

Capital Red Guards (Shoudu Hongweibing). 1967. January 21. 《首都红卫兵》。

Carr, Edward Hallett, and R. W. Davies. 1969. *Foundations of a Planned Economy: 1926–1929*. Vol. 1. Macmillan, London.

CCA (Central Committee Archives), ed. 1990–92. *Selections of Documents from the Central Committee of the Chinese Communist Party*. Central Committee Party School Press, Beijing. 中央档案馆《中共中央文件选》，中共中央党校出版社。

CCPRET (Central Communist Party Research Editorial Team), ed. 1973. *A Compilation of Important Materials on the Cultural Revolution*. Chinese Communist Party Research Press, Taipei. 《中共文化大革命重要文件汇编》，《中共研究》杂志社。

Central Committee of CCP. 1978. "Communique of the Third Plenary Session of the Eleventh Central Committee of the Communist Party of China (Adopted on December 22, 1978)." *Peking Review* 21, no. 52: 6–16.

Chen, Albert H. Y. 1996. "The Developing Theory of Law and Market Economy in Contemporary China." In Wang Guiguo and Wei Zhenying, eds., *Legal Developments in China: Market Economy and Law*. Sweet and Maxwell Asia, Hong Kong, 3–20.

Chen Du and Gu Xinhua. 1988. "The Strategies of Developing Public Security Work in Coastal Areas." *Public Security Studies* 3, no. 3:28–34. 。陈度，顾新华"沿海外向型经济发展与公安发展战略"，《公安研究》。

Chen Lifu. 1994. *Reminiscences*. Zhengzhong Shuju, Taipei. 。陈立夫《成败之鉴》，正中书局。

Chen Yongfa [Chen Yung-fa]. 1990. *Yan'an Shadows*. Modern History Research Institute, Academia Sinica, Taipei. 陈永发《延安的阴影》，中央研究院近代史研究所。

Chen Yung-fa [Chen Yongfa]. 1995. "The Blooming Poppy under the Red Sun: The Yan'an Way and the Opium Trade." In Tony Saich and Peter van de Ven, eds., *New Perspectives on the Chinese Revolution*. M. E. Sharpe, Armonk, N.Y., 263–98.

Chesneaux, Jean. 1979. *China: The People's Republic, 1949–1976*. Trans. Paul Auster and Lydia Davis. Harvester Press, Hassocks, United Kingdom.

Chi Heng. 1974. "Persist with the Worldview of the Working Class." *New China Monthly*, no.1:40–42. 池恒"坚持无产阶级世界观"，《新华月报》。

Chinese Communist Party Educational Reference Materials. 1979. People's Press, Beijing. 《中共党史教学参考资料》，人民出版社。

Chinese Encyclopedia of Law. 1984. Chinese Encyclopedia Press, Beijing. 《中国法律百科全书》，中国百科全书出版社。

Ci Jiwei. 1994. *Dialectic of the Chinese Revolution: From Utopianism to Hedonism*. Stanford University Press, Stanford.

Claudin, Fernando. 1975. *The Communist Movement: From Comintern to Cominform*. Trans. Brian Pearce and Francis MacDonagh. Peregrine, Middlesex, United Kingdom.

Claudin-Urondo, Carmen. 1977. *Lenin and the Cultural Revolution*. Trans. Brian Pearce, Harvester Press, Hassocks, United Kingdom.

Clubb, O. Edmund. 1972. *Twentieth-Century China*. Columbia University Press, New York.

Cohen, Jerome. 1969. "The Chinese Communist Party and Judicial Independence 1949–1959." *Harvard Law Review* 82 (March): 967–1006.

A Collection of Rules, Regulations and Policies on the Comprehensive Handling of Social Order. 1992. Masses Press, Beijing. 《社会治安综合治理政策法规汇编》，群众出版社。

Collins, Hugh. 1986. *The Law of Contract*. Weidenfeld and Nicolson, London.

Compton, Boyd. 1952. *Mao's China: Party Reform Documents, 1942–44*, University of Washington Press, Seattle.

Confucius. *Confucian Analects, the Great Learning and the Doctrine of the Mean*. 1971. Trans. James Legge. Dover, New York.

A Concise Dictionary on Public Security. 1990. Masses Press, Beijing. 《简明公安词典》，群众出版社。

Conquest, Robert, ed. 1968. *The Soviet Police System*. Bodley Head, London.

A Course in the Uses of Protection Work. 1990. Police Officer Educational Publishing House, Beijing. 《保卫工作实用教程》，警官教育出版社。

Critchley, T. A. 1967. *A History of Police in England and Wales, 900–1966*. Constable, London.

Dai Qing. 1994. *Wang Shiwei and "Wild Lillies": Rectification and Purges in the Chinese Communist Party, 1942–1944*. M. E. Sharpe, Armonk, N.Y.

Dai Wendian. 1991a. *Developments and the Nine Point Policy in Counter-espionage Work*. People's University Press, Beijing. 戴文殿 《防奸工作九条方针及其发展》，中国人民大学出版社。

———, ed. 1991b. *Basic Theoretical Research on Chinese Public Security*. China People's Public Security University Press, Beijing. 戴文殿主编《公安基础理论研究》，公安大学出版社。

Dai Xiangqing et al. 1986. *A History of the Central Revolutionary Base Camp*. Shanghai People's Press, Shanghai. 戴向青等 《中央革命根据地史稿》，上海人民出版社。

Dai Xiangqing and Luo Huilan. 1994. *The A-B League and the Futian Incident*. Henan People's Publishing House, Kaifeng. 戴向青，罗慧兰《AB团与富田事变始末》，河南人民出版社。

Dedijer, Vladimir. 1953. *Tito Speaks: His Self Portrait and Struggle with Stalin*. Weidenfeld and Nicolson, London.

Derrida, Jacques. 1992. *Given Time 1, Counterfeit Money*. Trans. Peggy Kamuf, University of Chicago Press, Chicago.

Domes, Jürgen. 1976. *China after the Cultural Revolution: Politics between Two Party Congresses*. Trans. Annette Berg and David Goodman. C. Hurst, London.

Dorris, Carl. 1976. "Peasant Mobilization in North China and the Origins of Yenan Communism." *China Quarterly*, no. 68:697–719.

Do You Feel Safe? 1991. Public Security Research Unit. Masses Press, Beijing. 公安部公安研究小组《你感觉安全吗？》，群众出版社。

Dutton, Michael R. 1992. *Policing and Punishment in China: From Patriarchy to "the People."* Cambridge University Press, Melbourne.

———. 1995. "Dreaming of Better Times: Repetition with a Difference and Chinese Community Policing." *Positions* 3, no. 2: 418–49.

———. 1998. *Streetlife China*. Cambridge University Press, Cambridge.

Dutton, Michael, and Lee Tianfu. 1993. "Missing the Target? Policing Strategies in the Period of Economic Reform." *Crime and Delinquency* 39, no. 3:316–36.

Dutton, Michael, and Li Shaorong. 2002. "Seize the City: Policing in the Era of City Takeover (1945–1949)." *Berliner China-Hefte*, no. 22:48–67.

E-Yu-Wan [Editorial Committee]. 1989. *E-Yu-Wan Revolutionary Base Camp*. Vol. 4. Henan People's Publishing House, Zhenzhou. 鄂豫皖革命根据地编委会 《鄂豫皖革命根据地》，第4卷，河南人民出版社。

Faligot, Roger, and Kauffer, Remi. 1989. *The Chinese Secret Service*. Headline, London.

Fang E. 1974. "Consolidating the Proletarian Dictatorship and Researching the Struggle between Confucianism and Legalism." *New China Monthly*, no. 9, 85–89. 方锷"为巩固无产阶级专政而研究儒法斗争"，《新华月报》。

Feldmann, Allen. 1991. *Formations of Violence: The Narrative of the Body and Political Terror in Northern Ireland*. University of Chicago Press, Chicago.

Foucault, Michel. 1979. "Governmentality." *I&C*, no. 6:5–24.

Fujian Public Security Department. 1989. "Some Thoughts on an Investigation into the Underrecording of the Criminal Cases." In Yu Lei, ed., *Studies on Current Chinese Crime Problems*. China People's Public Security University Press, Beijing, 1:332–40. 福建公安厅"对立案不实问题的调查与思考", 俞雷主编《中国现阶段犯罪问题的研究论文集》第1集, 中国人民公安大学出版社。

Fu Zhengyuan. 1996. *China's Legalists: The Earliest Totalitarians and Their Art of Ruling*. M. E. Sharpe, Armonk, N.Y.

The Gansu Provincial Gazetteer, vol. 5, *The Public Security Gazette*. 1995. Gansu Cultural Press, Lanzhou. 《甘肃省志（第五卷）-公安志》, 甘肃文化出版社。

Gao Feng. 1988. "A Brief Discussion of the Reforms in Internal Protection Work." *Public Security Studies* 2, no. 2:17–21. 高峰"内保工作改革刍议",《公安研究》。

Gao Hua. 2000. *How Did the Sun Rise over Yan'an? A History of the Rectification Movement*. Chinese University of Hong Kong, Hong Kong. 高华《红太阳是怎样升起的：延安整风的来龙去脉》, 香港中文大学。

Gao Xianrui. 1990. "The Problems of Detention and Investigation and the Way Forward." *Public Security Studies* 11, no. 3:18–21. 高宪瑞"收容审查的问题和出路",《公安研究》。

Gao Xinmin and Zhang Shujun. 2000. *A Record of Rectification in Yan'an*. Zhejiang People's House, Hangzhou. 高新民, 张树军《延安整风实录》, 浙江人民出版社。

Ginsburgs, George, and Arthur Stahnke. 1968. "The People's Procuraturate in Communist China: The Institution Ascendant, 1954–1957." *China Quarterly*, no. 34:82–132.

Goldman, Merle. 1975. "China's Anti-Confucian Campaign, 1973–74." *China Quarterly*, no. 63:435–62.

Gong'an Jianshi [A Draft History of Public Security]. N.d. N.p. 《公安简史》。

Gong Xikui. 1998. "Household Registration and the Caste-Like Quality of Peasant Life." In Michael Dutton, ed., *Streetlife China*, Cambridge University Press, Cambridge, 81–84.

Gottfried, Paul Edward. 1990. *Carl Schmitt: Politics and Theory*. Greenwood, New York.

The Great Cultural Revolution in China. 1968. Compiled and edited by Asia Research Centre. Flesch, Sydney.

The Great Trial in Chinese History. 1981. New World Press, Beijing.

Griffin, Patricia. 1974. "Prison Management in Kiangxi and Yenan Periods." *China Quarterly*, no. 58:310–11.

———. 1976. *The Chinese Communist Treatment of Counterrevolutionaries*. Princeton University Press, Princeton.

Gu Xinhua. 1990. "The Mode of Economic Development in Suzhou and Changes in Rural Crime." *Public Security Studies* 13, no. 5:47–50. 顾新华"苏州经济发展方式与农村犯罪变化",《公安研究》。

Guilin City Public Security Bureau. 1995. *Gazetteer of the Public Security Bureau of Guilin City*. Guilin City Public Security Bureau, Guilin. 桂林市公安局编《桂林市公安志》, 桂林市公安局。

Guo Hualun [Warren Kuo]. 1969. *An Outline History of the Communist Party*. Vol. 2. ROC

International Relations Research Institute, Taipei. 郭华伦《中共史论》，中华民国国际关系研究所。

Guo Zhi. 1974. "A Brief Outline of the Most Important Restorationist Dangers in the Early Period of the Western Han." Study and Criticism, no. 11, 39–43. 郭志"试论西汉前期复辟的主要危险"，《学习与批判》。

Han Feng. 1993. "A Record of the Outlawing of the Sex Industry in Old Tianjin." In Ma Wei-gang, ed., The Prohibition on Prostitution and Drugs. Police Officer Educational Publishing House, Beijing, 40–71. 韩风"取缔旧天津娼业纪实"，引自马维纲编《禁娼禁毒》，警官教育出版社。

Handbook on Dossier Work. 1988. Dossier Press, Beijing.《档案工作手册》，档案出版社。

Hao Hongkui. 1989. "The Regulation of Comprehensive Countermeasures to Be Taken against Crime and the Changing Nature of Criminal Activity." Public Security Studies 8, no. 4:35–38. 郝宏奎"犯罪活动的时代性变化与犯罪总体对策的调整"，《公安研究》。

Harding, Neil. 1996. Leninism. Duke University Press, Durham.

Harrison, James Pinckney. 1972. The Long March to Power: A History of the Chinese Communist Party, 1921–72. Praeger, New York.

Hazard, John N. 1951. Soviet Legal Philosophy. Trans. Hugh W. Babb, Harvard University Press, Cambridge.

———. 1969. Communists and Their Law: A Search for the Common Core of the Legal Systems of the Marxian Socialist States. University of Chicago Press, Chicago.

Heinzig, Dieter. 1970. "Otto Braun and the Tsunyi Conference." China Quarterly, no. 42, 131–35.

Henriot, Christian. 1995. "'La Fermeture': The Abolition of Prostitution in Shanghai, 1949–1958." China Quarterly, no. 142: 467–86.

He Qinhua, ed. 1991. New Trends in Law Studies, Shanghai Social Science Press, Shanghai. 何勤华主编《当代中国法学新思潮》，上海社会科学出版社。

He Qinglian. 1998. The Traps of Modernization, Today's China Press, Beijing. 何清涟《现代化的陷阱》，今日中国出版社。

He Xinhan. 1998. "People of the Work Unit." In Michael Dutton, ed., Streetlife China. Cambridge University Press, Cambridge, 42–53.

Hershatter, Gail. 1997. Dangerous Pleasures: Prostitution and Modernity in Twentieth-Century Shanghai. University of California Press, Berkeley.

Hingley, Ronald. 1970. The Russian Secret Police: Muscovite, Imperial Russian, and Soviet Political Security Operations, 1565–1970. Hutchinson, London.

Hirst, Paul. 1999. "Carl Schmitt's Decisionism." In Chantal Mouffe, ed., The Challenge of Carl Schmitt. Verso, London, 7–17.

Hollier, Denis, ed. 1988. The College of Sociology (1937–39). Trans. Betsy Wing. University of Minnesota Press, Minneapolis.

Hong Guangsi. 1974. "Grasp Well the Class Struggle in the Ideological Sphere." New China Monthly 1:42–45. 洪广思"抓好意识形态领域的阶级斗争"，《新华月报》。

380 REFERENCES

Huang Jingping, Li Tianfu, and Wang Zhimin. 1988. "The Situation with Regard to Public Security Management." *Public Security Studies* 4, no. 4:6–7. 黄京平，李田夫，王智民"公安管理现状"，《公安研究》。

Huang Jinlin. 1988. "Going Beyond Party and Government, Blind Faith in 'Bi-Gong-Xin': Reflections on the Expansion of the Early Stages of the 1930s Campaign Against Counter-Revolutionaries." *Public Security Studies* 2, no. 2:74–78. 黄金林"盲从、逼供信、超党超政-三十年代初期肃反扩大化的反思"，《公安研究》。

Huang Yao. 1991. "A Short Account of Luo Ruiqing." Part 2. In Central Committee Office for Research into Party History, ed., *Materials on Party History*. Party History Publishing House, Beijing, 37:154–204. 黄瑶"罗瑞卿传略（下）"中共中央党史研究室编《中共党史资料第37辑》，中共党史出版社。

Huang Yao and Zhang Mingzhe. 1996. *Luo Ruiqing*. Contemporary China Press, Beijing. 黄瑶，张明哲《罗瑞卿传》，当代中国出版社。

Hu, Chi-hsi. 1974. "The Sexual Revolution in Kiangsi Soviet." *China Quarterly*, no. 59:477–90.

Hu Qiaomu. 1994. *Hu Qiaomu's Remembers Mao Zedong*. People's Press, Beijing. 胡乔木《胡乔木回忆毛泽东》，人民出版社。

Hu Yongming. 1993. "Economic Protection Work in the New Era Also Needs to Be Separated from Administrative and Enterprise Responsibilities." *Public Security Studies* 28, no. 2:58–61. 胡永明"新时期经保工作也要实行政企职责分开"，《公安研究》。

Hu Zhiguang, ed. 1986. *An Outline of the Study of Public Security Political Work*. People's University Press, Beijing. 胡之光《公安政工概论》，中国人民大学出版社。

Internal Protection Work Handbook. 1991. Public Security University, Beijing. 《内保工作手册》，公安大学出版社。

"An Investigation into a Number of Questions Regarding the Kidnapping and Selling of Women into Marriage and the Abduction of People in Jiaxiang County, Shandong Province." 1990. In Yu Lei, ed., *Studies on Current Chinese Crime Problems.* Vol. 2. China People's Public Security University, Beijing, 386–93. "关于山东嘉祥县拐卖人口犯罪与异地买婚违法问题的调查"，俞雷主编《中国现阶段犯罪问题的研究论文集》第二集，中国人民公安大学出版社。

Jin Qiu. 1999. *The Culture of Power: The Lin Biao Incident in the Cultural Revolution.* Stanford University Press, Stanford.

Kampen, Thomas. 2000. *Mao Zedong, Zhou Enlai, and the Evolution of the Chinese Communist Leadership.* Nordic Institute of Asian Studies (NIAS), Copenhagen.

Kane, Penny. 1987. *The Second Billion.* Penguin, Middlesex, United Kingdom.

Kang Li. 1974. "Confucius, Confucianism, and Propriety." *Study and Criticism*, no. 1:54–57. 康立"孔子，儒家和礼"，《学习与批判》。

Keith, Ronald C. 1991. "Chinese Politics and the New Theory of 'Rule of Law.'" *China Quarterly*, no. 125:109–18.

Knight, Nick. 1996. *Li Da and Marxist Philosophy in China.* Westview Press, Boulder, Colo.

———. Forthcoming. *From Qu Quibai to Mao Zedong: Marxist Philosophers and Philosophy in China, 1923–1945*.

Kong Lin and Zhang Weiguo. 1987. "The Contract System: Selected Laws for the Development of a Commodity Economy." *Law Science Monthly* 73, no. 12:5–7. 孔林, 张伟国"契约制度：发展商品经济的法律选择", 《法学》。

Ladany, Laszlo. 1992. *Law and Legality in China: The Testament of a China-Watcher*. Hirst, London.

Latour, Bruno. 1993. *We Have Never Been Modern*. Trans. Catherine Porter, Harvard University Press, Cambridge.

Law Yearbook. 1987–2001 (multi volumes). Law Yearbook Press, Beijing. 《法律年鉴》, 法律年鉴 出版社。

Lefort, Claude. 1986. *The Political Forms of Modern Society: Bureaucracy, Democracy, Totalitarianism.* Ed. John B. Thompson. Polity Press, Cambridge.

Leggett, George. 1981. *The Cheka: Lenin's Political Police*. Clarendon, Oxford.

Lenin, V. I. 1962, 1964, 1965, 1966. *Collected Works*. Progress Publishers, Moscow.

Liang Xiao. 1974. "Researching the Historical Experiences of the Confucian-Legalists Struggle." *New China Monthly*, no. 10:127–31. 梁效"研究儒法斗争的历史经验" 《新华月报》。

Liberation Daily, September 21–22. 《解放日报》。

Lichtheim, George. 1964. *Marxism: An Historical and Critical Study*. Routledge and Kegan Paul, London.

Lieberthal, Kenneth G. 1980. *Revolution and Tradition in Tientsin, 1949–1952*. Stanford University Press, Stanford.

Li Jinping. 1993. *Public Security Teaching Program on the Chinese Revolution*, Police Officer Educational Publishing House, Beijing. 黎津平《公安实用中国革命史教程》, 警官教育出版社。

Li Kangrui et al. 1989. "A Number of Issues Relating to Legislation on Detention and Investigation." *Public Security Studies* 6, no. 2:61–64. 李康瑞, 许德勇, 周荆南, 毛同坤 "收容审查立法的几个问题", 《公安研究》。

Li Runshan and Mao Dianliang. 1993. "A Record of the Closure of the Brothels of Beijing." In Ma Weigang, ed., *The Prohibition on Prostitution and Drugs*. Police Officer Educational Publishing House, Beijing, 72–93. 李润山, 毛殿良"北京市封闭妓院纪实", 引自马维纲编《禁娼禁毒》, 警官教育出版社。

Li Weihan. 1986. *Reminiscences and Research*. Vol. 1. CCP Party Materials Press, Beijing. 李维汉《回忆与研究》, 中国共产党党史资料出版社。

Li Wennan and Jin Lu. 1998. "Some Thoughts on the Reform of the Public Security Management System." *Public Security Studies* 59, no. 6: 25–27. 李文南, 金路"关于公安管理体制改革的思考", 《公安研究》。

Lin Qingshan. 1988. *An Unauthorized Biography of Kang Sheng*. Chinese Youth Press, Beijing. 林青山《康生外传》, 中国青年出版社。

Litten, Fredrick S. 1994. "The Noulens Affair." *China Quarterly*, no. 138:492–512.

Liu Chenggen. 1995. "Promote Community Developments, Control Serious Cases of

Repeat Offence." Paper presented at the International Conference on Education, Training, and Rehabilitation of Prisoners in Correctional Institutions, October, Chengdu, Sichuan, China.

Liu Enqi. 1989. "The Problem of the Contradictory Nature of Serious Crime." *Public Security Studies* 7, no. 3:2-7. 刘恩启"关于严重刑事犯罪的矛盾性质问题",《公安研究》。

Liu Wenqi. 1990. "It Is Necessary to Clear Up Confusion about the Theory of the People's Democratic Dictatorship." *Public Security Studies* 10, no. 2:20-24. 柳文启"人民民主专政理论上的混乱必须澄清",《公安研究》。

Liu Zaiping. 1989. "Examination of the Democratic Function of Public Security Units." *Public Security Studies* 7, no. 3:7-12. 刘在平"试论公安机关的民主职能兼论人民民主专政的对象",《公安研究》。

Lotta, Raymond, ed. 1978. *And Mao Makes 5: Mao Tsetung's Last Great Battle*. Banner Press, Chicago.

Lötveit, Trygve. 1979. *Chinese Communism, 1931–1934: Experience in Civil Government*. Curzon, London.

Lu Feng. 1998. "The Work Unit: A Unique Form of Social Organisation." In Michael Dutton, ed., *Streetlife China*. Cambridge University Press, Cambridge, 53–58.

Luedtke, Alf. 1989. *State and Police in Prussia, 1815–1850*. Cambridge University Press, Cambridge.

Luo Qingchang. 1995. "The Historical Lessons Drawn from the Framing of Pan Hannian." In Research Group on Party History of the Shanghai City Committee, ed., *Pan Hannian in Shanghai*. Shanghai People's Publishing House, Shanghai, 363–68. 罗青长"潘汉年冤案的历史教训", 中共上海市委党史研究社编《潘汉年在上海》, 上海人民出版社。

Luo Ruiqing. 1994. *On People's Public Security Work*. Masses Press, Beijing. 罗瑞卿《论人民公安工作》, 群众出版社。

Luo Siding. 1974. "On the Class Struggle between the Qin and the Han." *New China Monthly*, no. 8:67-73. 罗思鼎"论秦汉之际的阶级斗争",《新华月报》。

Ma Weigang, ed. 1993. *The Prohibition on Prostitution and Drugs*. Police Officer Educational Publishing House, Beijing. 马维纲编《禁娼禁毒》, 警官教育出版社。

MacFarquhar, Roderick. 1983. *The Origins of the Cultural Revolution*. Vol. 2. Columbia University Press, New York.

Maine, Henry Sumner. 1970. *Ancient Law: Its Connection with the Early History of Society and Its Relation to Modern Ideas*. Ed. Raymond Firth. P. Smith, Mass.

Mao Zedong. 1969, 1975, 1977. *Selected Works of Mao Tsetung*. Foreign Languages Press, Beijing.

———. 1974. *Miscellany of Mao Tse-tung Thought, 1949–1968*. Joint Publications Research Service, Arlington, Va.

———. 1984. *Mao Zedong Supplementary Collection*. Vol. 3. Ed. Mao Zedong Documents and Materials Research Association. Cangcang Publishing House, Tokyo.《毛泽东集补卷第三卷》, 毛泽东文献资料研究会, 苍苍社。

————. 1986. *The Writings of Mao Zedong, 1949–1976*. Ed. Michael Y. M. Kau and John K. Leung. M. E. Sharpe, Armonk, N.Y.

————. 1996. *Mao Zedong Collected Works*. Vol. 3. People's Press, Beijing. 《毛泽东文集》，人民出版社。

Martin, Brian G. 1996. *The Shanghai Green Gang: Politics and Organized Crime, 1919–1937*. University of California Press, Berkeley.

Marx, Karl. 1976. *Capital*. Vol. 1. Trans. Ben Fowkes, Penguin, Middlesex, United Kingdom.

Mauss, Marcel. 1990. *The Gift: The Form and Reason for Exchange in Archaic Societies*. Trans. W. D. Hall. Routledge, London.

McGowan, John. 1998. *Hannah Arendt: An Introduction*. University of Minnesota Press, Minneapolis.

McLane, Charles B. 1958. *Soviet Policy and the Chinese Communists 1931–1946*. Columbia University Press, New York.

Medvedev, Roy Aleksandrovich. 1971. *Let History Judge: The Origins and Consequences of Stalinism*. Trans. Colleen Taylor, Vintage, New York.

Meier, Heinrich. 1998. *The Lesson of Carl Schmitt: Four Chapters on the Distinction between Political Theology and Political Philosophy*. Trans. Marcus Brainard, University of Chicago Press, Chicago.

Meisner, Maurice. 1977. *Li Ta-chao and the Origins of Chinese Marxism*. Atheneum, New York.

————. 1986. *Mao's China and After: A History of the People's Republic*. Free Press, New York.

Melossi, Umberto. 1977. *Marx and the Third World*. Trans. Pat Ransford. Macmillan, London.

"Ministry of Public Security and the Ministry of Health Notice Concerning Prevention of Contagious Diseases Amongst Those Criminals Detained for Investigation (14/2/84)." 1985. In *Handbook on Preparatory Investigations and Watch House Work*. Masses Press, Beijing, 2:188–189. "公安部卫生部关于在押犯受审人员传染性疾病防治工作的通知"，《预审看守工作手册》（第二卷），群众出版社。

"Ministry of Public Security Notice Concerning the Utilization of Tight Control Procedures Over the Detention and Investigation Centers (31/7/1985)." *Handbook on Preparatory Investigations and Watch House Work*. Masses Press, Beijing, 3:229–31. 公安部关于严格控制使用收容审查手段的通知"，《预审看守工作手册》（第三卷），群众出版社。

Ministry of Public Security, Public Safety Research Group. 1992. "Our Nations Public Perception of Safety on the Rise: An Analysis of the Second Detailed Investigation into Public Perceptions of Safety." *Public Security Studies* 20, no. 6:58–64. 公安部"公众安全感指标研究与评价"课题科研小组"我国公众安全感水平有所提高-全国第二次公众安全感抽样调查情况分析"，《公安研究》。

Mouffe, Chantal, ed. 1999. *The Challenge of Carl Schmitt*. Verso. London.

National Bureau of Statistics of China. 1993. *China Population Statistics Yearbook*. China Statistics Press, Beijing. 国家统计局 《中国人口统计》，中国统计出版社。

Neumann, Franz. 1957. *The Democratic and the Authoritarian States: Essays in Political and Legal Theory*. Ed. Herbert Marcuse. Free Press, New York.

Ni Minle and Fang Lei. 1998. "A Discussion about the Legal Position and Future Development of Private Security Companies." *Public Security Studies* 57, no. 1:63–64. 倪敏乐, 方垒"论保安服务业的法律地位及未来发展",《公安研究》。

Nove, Alec. 1969. *An Economic History of the USSR.* Allen Lane, London.

"A Number of Special Characteristics of Criminal Cases in the Coastal Areas Before Economic Reform and the Open-Door Policy." 1989. In Yu Lei, ed., *Studies on Current Chinese Crime Problems.* China People's Public Security University, Beijing, 1:194–210. "改革开放前沿海地带刑事犯罪的若干特点", 俞雷主编《中国现阶段犯罪问题的研究论文集》第一集, 中国人民公安大学出版社。

Oestreich, Gerhard. 1982. *Neostoicism and the Early Modern State.* Ed. Brigitta Oestreich and H. G. Koenigsberger. Trans. David McLintock. Cambridge University Press, Cambridge.

Ogden, Suzanne. 1989. *China's Unresolved Issues: Politics, Development, and Culture.* Prentice Hall, Englewood Cliffs, N.J.

An Outline of Public Security History. 1997. Police Officer Educational Publishing House, Beijing. 《中国人民公安史稿》编写组《中国人民公安史稿》, 警官教育出版社。

Pashukanis, Evgeny B. 1978. *Law and Marxism: A General Theory.* Ed. Chris Arthur. Trans. Barbara Einthorn, Ink Books, London.

———. 1980. "State and Law under Socialism." In Piers Beirne and Robert Sharlet, eds., *Pashukanis: Selected Writing on Marxism and Law.* Academic Press, London, 346–61.

Provincial Gazetteer of Anhui. 1995. *Provincial Gazetteer of Anhui (Volume on Population).* Anhui People's Press, Hefei. 《安徽省志·人口志》, 安徽人民出版社。

PSHM (Public Security Historical Materials), 1987–1994. Ed. Public Security Historical Materials Collection Research Leadership Small Group Office. Unpublished material from the Ministry of Public Security. 公安部公安史资料征集研究领导小组办公室《公安史资料》。 [PSHM citations in the text indicate year, issue (if pertinent), volume number, page number.]

Questions and Answers on Public Security History. 1994. Ed. Ministry of Public Security, Public Security Historical Materials Collection Research Leadership Small Group Office, and the Police Science Society of China, Beijing. 公安部公安史资料征集研究领导小组办公室《公安史知识问答》, 群众出版社。

Raddock, David M. 1979. "Between Generations: Activist Chinese Youths in Pursuit of a Political Role in the San-fan and in the Cultural Revolution." *China Quarterly*, no. 79:511–28.

Rawlings, Philip. 1995. "The Idea of Policing: A History." *Policing and Society* 5, no. 2:129–49.

Red Guard Publication Supplement 1. 1980. Vol. 7. Center for Chinese Research Materials and Association of Research Libraries, Washington.

Reith, Charles. 1952. *The Blind Eye of History: A Study of the Origins of the Present Police Era.* Faber and Faber, London.

Research Materials on the Great Cultural Revolution. 1988. Vol. 1. Office for Party History, Development, and Political Works, China PLA National Defense University, Beijing.

中国人民解放军国防大学党史党建政工教研室《"文化大革命"研究资料》上册，中国国防大学。

Rice, Edward. 1972. *Mao's Way*. University of California Press, Berkeley.

Robinson, Joan. 1969. *The Cultural Revolution in China*. Pelican-Penguin, Middlesex, United Kingdom.

Rosenfeld, Michel. 1985. "Contract and Justice: The Relation between Classical Contract Law and Social Contract Theory." *Iowa Law Review* 70: 810–14.

Rue, John E. 1966. *Mao Tse-tung in Opposition: 1927–1935*. Stanford University Press, Stanford.

Saich, Tony. 1995. "Writing and Rewriting History? The Construction of the Maoist Resolution on Party History." In Tony Saich and Hans van de Ven, eds., *New Perspectives on the Chinese Communist Revolution*. M. E. Sharpe, Armonk, N.Y., 229–338.

Schmitt, Carl. 1985. *Political Theology: Four Chapters on the Concept of Sovereignty*. Trans. George Schwab, MIT Press, Cambridge.

———. 1996. *The Concept of the Political*, Trans. George Schwab, University of Chicago Press, Chicago.

Schram, Stuart, ed. 1974. *Mao Tse-tung Unrehearsed: Talks and Letters, 1956–71*. Penguin, Middlesex, United Kingdom.

Schram, Stuart R., and Nancy Jane Hodes, eds. 1994. *Mao's Road to Power: Revolutionary Writings, 1912–1949*. Vol. 2. M. E. Sharpe, Armonk, N.Y.

Schurmann, Franz. 1968. *Ideology and Organization in Communist China*. 2d. enl. ed. University of California Press, Berkeley.

Schurmann, Franz, and Orwell Schell, eds. 1967. *Communist China*. Penguin, Middlesex, United Kingdom.

Schwab, George. 1985. Introduction to Carl Schmitt, *Political Theology: Four Chapters on the Concept of Sovereignty*. MIT Press, Cambridge, i–xxvi.

Scobell, Andrew. 1990. "The Death Penalty in Post-Mao China." *China Quarterly*, no. 123:503–20.

Selden, Mark. 1972. *The Yenan Way in Revolutionary China*. Harvard University Press, Cambridge.

———. 1995. *China in Revolution: The Yenan Way Revisited*. M. E. Sharpe, Armonk, N.Y.

Seybolt, Peter J. 1986. "Terror and Conformity, Counterespionage Campaigns, Rectification, and Mass Movements, 1942–1943." *Modern China* 12, no. 1:39–73.

Shanghai Policing Studies Group. 1998. "Studies on Peasant Crimes in Large Cities." *Public Security Studies* 61, no. 5:17–20. 上海警察学会课题组"特大城市农民犯罪问题的研究"，《公安研究》。

Shao Daosheng. 1987. *Considerations on the Sociology of Youth Crime in China*. Social Science Literature Press, Beijing. 邵道生《中国青少年犯罪的社会学思考》，社会科学文献出版社。

Sharlet, Robert. 1977. "Stalinism and Soviet Legal Culture." In Robert C. Tucker, ed., *Stalinism: Essays in Historical Interpretation*. W. W. Norton, New York, 155–79.

Sharlet, Robert, and Piers Beirne. 1984. "In Search of Vyshinsky: The Paradox of Law and Terror." *International Journal of the Sociology of Law* 12, no. 21:153–77.

Shearing, Clifford D. 1992. "The Relation between Public and Private Policing." In Michael Tonry and Norval Morris, eds., *Modern Policing*. University of Chicago Press, Chicago, 399–434.

Shelley, Louise L. 1996. *Policing Soviet Society: The Evolution of State Control*. Routledge, London.

Shi Shanghui. 1974. "Hanfei: The Commander in Chief of the Anti-Confucian Forces in the Latter Part of the Warring States Period." *Study and Criticism*, no. 9:8–14. 史尚辉"韩非-战国末期的反孔主将",《学习与批判》。

Shi Zhe. 1992. *Peaks and Troughs: The Memories of Shi Zhe*. Red Flag Publishing House, Beijing. 师哲《峰与谷-师哲回忆录》, 红旗出版社。

SHMCBC (*Selected Historical Materials on the Central Base Camp*). 1983. Vols. 1–3. Ed. Jiangxi Archives and the Jiangxi Provincial Party School Research Office. Jiangxi People's Press, Nanchang. 江西省档案馆, 中共江西省委党校党史教研室编《中央革命根据地史料选编》上中下册, 江西人民出版社。

Sima Lu. 1981. *The Party History and Documents Relating to the Establishment of the Central Soviet*. Vol. 10. Zilian Publishing House, Hong Kong. 司马璐《中央苏维埃的成立中共党史暨文献选粹第十部》, 自联出版社。

Sklansky, David A. 1999. "The Private Police." UCLA *Law Review* 46, no. 4:1165–1287.

Snow, Edgar. 1977. *China's Long Revolution*. Penguin, London.

Song Haobo. 1994. "A Perspective on the Current Situation with Regard to Clients of Prostitutes." *Juvenile Crime Studies* 144, no. 6:2–5. 宋浩波"现阶段卖淫嫖娼现象透视",《中国青少年犯罪研究》。

Song Pingshun. 1989. "From the Political Chaos and the Counterrevolutionary Revolt, It Is Clear to See the Contemporary Class Struggle." *Public Security Studies*, no. 4:3–5. 宋平顺"从这场政治动乱, 反革命暴乱看当前的阶级斗争",《公安研究》。

Spitzer, Steven. 1987. "Security and Control in Capitalist Societies: The Fetishism of Security and the Secret Thereof." In John Lowman, Robert J. Menzies, and T. S. Palys, eds., *Transcarceration: Essays in the Sociology of Social Control*. Gower, Aldershot, United Kingdom, 41–58.

Stranahan, Patricia. 1998. *Underground: The Shanghai Communist Party and the Politics of Survival, 1927–1937*. Rowman and Littlefield, New York.

Strauss, Leo. 1996. "Notes on Carl Schmitt: the Concept of the Political." Trans. J. Harvey Lomax. In Carl Schmitt, *The Concept of the Political*. University of Chicago Press, Chicago, 83–107.

Stuchka, P. I. 1988. *Selected Writings on Soviet Law and Marxism*. Ed. Robert Sharlet, Peter B. Maggs, and Piers Beirne. M. E. Sharpe, N.Y.

Suleski, Ronald S. 1969. "The Fu-t'ien Incident, December 1930." In Ronald S. Suleski and Daniel H. Bays, eds., *Early Communist China: Two Studies*. University of Michigan, Center for Chinese Studies, Ann Arbor, 1–27.

A Summary History of the Chinese People's Police. 1989. Police Officers Educational Publishing House, Beijing. 《中国人民警察简史》, 警官教育出版社。

Sun Longji. 1986. *The "Deep Structure" of Chinese Culture*. Jixianshe, Taipei. 孙隆基《中国文化的'深层结构'》，集贤社。

Sun Tzu. 1988. *The Art of Strategy: A New Translation of Sun Tzu's Classic, "The Art of War."* Trans. R. L.Wing, Doubleday, New York.

Supplementary Edition: Important CCP Documents of the Great Proletarian Cultural Revolution. 1979. Institute for the Study of Chinese Communist Problems, Taipei. 《增订本：中共文化大革命重要文件汇编》，中共研究杂志社编印。

Tan Songqiu. 1990. "The Class Struggle in the Present Period in Our Country and a Number of Points to Know about the People's Democratic Dictatorship." *Public Security Studies* 10 no. 2:1–5. 谭松球"对我国现阶段的阶级斗争和人民民主专政问题的几点认识"，《公安研究》。

Tan Yuanheng. 1996. *Pan Hannian*. Gansu People's Publishing House, Lanzhou. 谭元亨《潘汉年》，甘肃人民出版社。

Tang Congyao. 1980. "Once Again on the Question of the Class Nature of Socialist Law." *Studies in Law*, no. 5:7–9. 唐琮瑶"再谈社会主义法的阶级性"，《法学研究》。

Tanner, H. M. 1995. "Policing, Punishment, and the Individual: Criminal Justice in China." *Journal of the American Bar Foundation* 20, no. 1:277–303.

———. 1999. *Strike Hard! Anti-Crime Campaigns and Chinese Criminal Justice, 1979–1985*. Cornell University East Asia Program, Ithaca, N.Y.

Tanner, Murray-Scot. 1999. "Ideological Struggle over Police Reform, 1988–1993." In Edwin A. Winckler, ed., *Transition from Communism in China: Institutional and Comparative Analysis*. Lynne Rienner, London, 111–28.

———. 2000. "State Coercion and the 'Balance of Awe': The 1983–1986 Stern Blows Anti-crime Campaign." *China Journal*, no. 44:93–125.

Tao Siju, ed. 1996. *Luo Ruiqing: New China's First Minister of Public Security*. Masses Press, Beijing. 陶驷驹主编《罗瑞卿：新中国第一任公安部长》，群众出版社。

Teiwes, Frederick C. 1979. *Politics and Purges in China: Rectification and the Decline of Party Norms, 1950–1965*. M. E. Sharpe, Armonk, N.Y.

———. 1990. *Politics at Mao's Court: Gao Gang and Party Factionalism in the Early 1950s*. M. E. Sharpe, Armonk, N.Y.

———. 2000. "Thomas Kampen, Mao Zedong, Zhou Enlai, and the Evolution of the Chinese Communist Leadership." Book review. *China Journal*, no. 44:242–44.

Teiwes, Frederick C., with Warren Sun. 1995. "From Leninist to a Charismatic Party: The CCP's Changing Leadership, 1937–1945." In Tony Saich and Hans van de Ven, eds., *New Perspectives on the Chinese Communist Revolution*. M. E. Sharpe, Armonk, N.Y., 339–87.

Teiwes, Frederick C., and Warren Sun. 1996. *The Tragedy of Lin Biao: Riding the Tiger During the Cultural Revolution, 1966–1971*. Crawford House, Bathurst, New South Wales.

Teiwes, Frederick C., with Warren Sun. 1999. *China's Road to Disaster: Mao, Central Planners, and the Provincial Leaders in the Unfolding of the Great Leap Forward, 1955–1959*. M. E. Sharpe, Armonk, N.Y.

Terrill, Ross. 1984. *The White-Boned Demon: A Biography of Madame Mao Zedong*. Heinemann, London.

Tonry, Michael, and Norval Morris, eds. 1992. *Modern Policing*. University of Chicago Press, Chicago.

Wakeman, Frederic, Jr. 1995. *Policing Shanghai, 1927–1937*. University of California Press, Berkeley.

Walder, Andrew, G. 1989. "Factory and Manager in an Era of Reform." *China Quarterly*, no. 118:242–64.

———. 2002. "Beijing Red Guard Factionalism: Social Interpretations Reconsidered." *Journal of Asian Studies* 61, no. 2: 437–71.

Wan Shengzi et al. 2000. "Issues about the Police Participating in Nonpolicing Activities." *Public Security Studies* 69, no. 1:21–24. 万生梓，李震宇，张财贵，张金存"关于公安民警参与非警务活动的调查"，《公安研究》。

Wang Jianhua. 1993. *The Iron Fist of Red Terror*. People's China Press, Beijing. 王建华《红色恐怖的铁拳》，人民中国出版社。

Wang Jianmin [Wang Chien-min]. 1965. *An Outline History of the Chinese Communist Party*, vol. 2, *The Jiangxi Period*. Hanjing Wenhua, Taipei. 王健民《中国共产党史稿第二编：江西时期》。汉津文化有限公司。

Wang Jinxiang. 1992. *Looking Back on Nine Years in Public Security in the North East*. Masses Press, Beijing. 汪金祥《东北公安九年回顾》，群众出版社。

Wang Mian. 1991. "A Discussion of the Social Nature of Public Security Work." *Public Security Studies* 16, no. 2:34–38. 王勉"试论公安工作的社会化"，《公安研究》。

Wang Qiuxia. 1994. "Mass Protection Work in the Revolutionary Base Areas in the Second Revolutionary Civil War." *Public Security Studies* 36, no. 2:58–61. 汪秋霞"'二战'时期根据地的群众保卫工作"，《公安研究》。

Wang Shoudao. 1983. *Collected Memories*. Hunan People's Publishing House, Changsha. 王首道《怀念集》，湖南人民出版社。

Wang Suyuan. 1991. "An Outline of the Shan-Gan-Ning Border Region's 'Rescue Campaign.'" In Central Committee Office for Research into Party History, ed., *Materials on Party History*. Party History Publishing House, Beijing, 37:205–33. 王素园"陕甘宁边区'抢救运动'始末"载中共中央党史研究室编《中共党史资料第37辑》，中共党史出版社。

Wang Zhimin. 1993. *An Outline Assessment of the Social Order Situation*. Masses Press, Beijing. 王智民《评价社会治安状况概论》，群众出版社。

Wang Zhimin and Huang Jingping. 1992. *Economic Development and Changes in Crime*. Chinese People's University Press, Beijing. 王智民，黄京平《经济发展与犯罪变化》，中国人民大学出版社。

Wang Zhimin, Huang Jingping, Lee Tianfu, and Zhao Xiaogang. 1988. "Considerations on Public Security Strategy Development along the Coast Areas." *Public Security Studies* 3, no. 3:18–28. 王智民，黄京平，李田夫，赵晓刚"沿海地区公安发展战略思考"，《公安研究》。

Wang Zhongfang. 1992. "Reviewing History: Comrade Wang Zhongfang Talks of the Suppression of the Counter-revolutionaries Campaign at the Beginning of the Fifties." In *The Campaign to Suppress Counter-revolutionaries in the Period Immediately after the Founding of the*

PRC. Masses Press, Beijing, 1–5. 王仲方《建国初期镇压反革命运动》，群众出版社。

Wang Zhongfang, ed. 1989. *Theory and Practice of Comprehensive Management of Public Order in China*. Masses Press, Beijing. 王仲方主编《中国社会治安综合治理的理论和实践》，群众出版社。

Weber, Max. 1978. *Economy and Society: An Outline of Interpretive Sociology*. Vol. 2. Ed. Guenther Roth and Claus Wittich. University of California Press, Berkeley.

Wu Buyun. 1980. "A Tentative Analysis of the Class Character and Objective Nature of Socialist Law." *Studies in Law*, no. 5:11–5. 武步云"试论社会主义法律的阶级性和客观性"，《法学研究》。

Wu Zhongfei and Chen Yuanxiao. 2000. "Enhancing Cost Control, Promoting Virtuous Development, and Improving the Public Security Organs' Capacity to Control Social Order." *Public Security Studies* 69, no. 1:27–30. 吴仲飞，陈远晓"加强成本控制，促进良性发展，提高公安机关驾驭社会治安的能力"，《公安研究》。

Wylie, Ray. 1980. *The Emergence of Maoism: Mao Tse-tung, Ch'en Po-ta, and the Search for Chinese Theory, 1935–1945*. Stanford University Press, Stanford.

Xu Enzeng [U. T. Hsu]. 1962. *The Invisible Conflict*. Dragonfly, Hong Kong.

Xu Hanmin. 1992. *Forty Years of People's Public Security*. Police Officer Educational Publishing House, Beijing. 徐汉民《人民治安40年》，警官教育出版社。

Xu Linxiang and Zhu Yu. 1996. *Biography of a General: Li Kenong*. Anhui People's Press, Hefei. 徐林祥，朱玉《传奇将军李克农》，安徽人民出版社。

Xu Xinyuan. 1999. "The Outline of Development of Public Security Organs and People's Police Organizations." *Public Security Studies* 65, no. 3:91–93. 许新源"我国公安机关和人民警察组织机构历史沿革"，《公安研究》。

Yahuda, M. 1972. "Kremlinology and the Chinese Strategic Debate, 1965–66." *China Quarterly*, no. 49:32–75.

Yang Dongping. 1994. *City Monsoon: Culture Differences between Shanghai and Beijing*. Oriental Press, Beijing. 。 杨东平"城市季风：北京和上海的文化精神"，东方出版社。

Yang Rongguo. 1974. "The Ideologies of the Pre-Qin Legalists and Confucianists Were Utterly Antithetical." *New China Monthly*, no. 8:62–67, 杨荣国"先秦儒法两家思想是根本对立的"，《新华月报》。

Yang Yonghua. 1992. *An Outline of the Legal System in the Shaan-Gan-Ning Border Region*. Vol. 3. Shaanxi People's Press, Xi'an. 杨永华《陕甘宁边区法制史稿》第三卷，陕西人民出版社。

Yang Zhaoming and Wang Gongfan. 1990. "Viewing the Current State of Class Struggle through the Period of Turmoil and Chaos." *Public Security Studies* 9, no. 1:8–11. 杨昭敏，王功藩"从动乱和暴乱透视当前的阶级斗争问题"，《公安研究》。

Ye Huaming. 1989. "An Exploration of the Socialization Model of Society's Public Order Management." *Public Security Studies* 7, no. 3:24–27. 叶华明"社会治安管理社会化模式的探索"，《公安研究》。

Ye Ming. 1998. "A Brief Discussion of New Developments in Basic Work within the Police Station in the New Situation." *Public Security Studies* 59, no. 3:65–67. 叶敏"浅谈新形势下派出所基础工作的新发展",《公安研究》。

Yichang Administrative Area Public Security Section Research Group. 1989. "Studies on the Problem of Underrecording Criminal Cases." In Yu Lei, ed., *Studies on Current Chinese Crime Problems*, vol. 1. China People's Public Security University Press, Beijing, 341–50. 宜昌地区行署公安处课题组"关于刑事案件立案不实问题的探讨", 公安部《中国现阶段犯罪问题的研究论文集》第一卷, 中国人民公安大学出版社。

Yick, Joseph K. S. 1995. *Making Urban Revolution in China: The CCP-GMD Struggle for Beiping-Tianjin, 1945–1949.* M. E. Sharpe, Armonk, N.Y.

Yin Qi. 1995. "The Pan Yang Case." In Research Group on Party History of the Shanghai City Committee, ed., *Pan Hannian in Shanghai.* Shanghai People's Publishing House, Shanghai, 369–86. 尹骐"'潘扬案件'始末", 中共上海市委党史研究社编《潘汉年在上海》, 上海人民出版社。

———. 1996. *A Biography of Pan Hannian.* China People's Public Security University, Beijing. 尹骐《潘汉年传》, 中国人民公安大学出版社。

Ying Hongbiao. 1996. "Criticism of the Reactionary Capitalist Line: The Rise of the Rebel Movement." In Liu Qingfeng, ed., *Cultural Revolution: Reality and Research.* Chinese University of Hong Kong, Hong Kong, 179–90. 印红标"批判资产阶级反动路线：造反运动的兴起", 刘青峰《文化大革命：史实与研究》, 中文大学出版社。

Young, Graham, and Dennis Woodward. 1978. "From Contradictions among the People to Class Struggle: The Theories of Uninterrupted Revolution and Continuous Revolution." *Asian Survey* 18, no. 9:912–33.

Yu Haibing. 1989. "The Problems Faced by Security Companies and Some Countermeasures." *Public Security Studies* 7, no. 3:28–30. 于海兵"保安服务面临的问题及对策",《公安研究》。

Yu Lei, ed. 1985. *An Introduction to the Study of Public Security.* China People's Public Security University Press, Beijing. 俞雷主编《公安学概论》, 中国人民公安大学出版社。

———. 1989. *Studies on Current Chinese Crime Problems.* Vol. 1. China People's Public Security University, Beijing. 俞雷主编《中国现阶段犯罪问题的研究论文集》第一卷, 中国人民公安大学出版社。

———. 1990. *Studies on Current Chinese Crime Problems.* Vol. 2. China People's Public Security University, Beijing. 俞雷主编《中国现阶段犯罪问题的研究论文集》第二卷, 中国人民公安大学出版社。

———. 1992. *Contemporary Chinese Public Security Work.* Contemporary China Publishing House, Beijing. 俞雷主编《当代中国的公安工作》, 当代中国出版社。

———. 1993. *Studies on Current Chinese Crime Problems: Summary Volume.* China People's Public Security University Press, Beijing. 俞雷主编《中国现阶段犯罪问题的研究论文集总卷》, 中国人民公安大学出版社。

Yu Shubin. 1992. "The Establishment and Development of Prisons in Revolutionary

Base Areas." In *Public Security Historical Materials*, vol. 26, ed. Public Security Historical Materials Collection Research Leadership Small Group Office. Unpublished material from the Ministry of Public Security, 105-12. 于树斌"革命根据地监所的建立与发展"《公安史资料》。

Zeng Fanzheng, ed. 1998. *Conflicts and Struggles During the Red Storm.* Vols. 1 and 2. Red Flag Press, Beijing. 曾繁正编《红色风波中的交锋与较量》，红旗出版社。

Zhai Ping. 1974. "Is the Struggle between Confucianism and Legalism 'Dog Eat Dog'?" *New China Monthly*, no. 8:47-49. 翟平"儒法斗争是'狗咬狗'吗？"《新华月报》。

Zhang Min. 2000. "A Brief Analysis of a Number of Issues to Be Considered When Formulating a Police Development Strategy." *Public Security Studies* 69, no. 1:31-33. 张民"浅析制定治安警务发展战略应当注意的几个问题"，《公安研究》。

Zhang Puxian. 1993. *An Introduction to Public Security Work.* Masses Press, Beijing. 张浦先《公安工作概论》，群众出版社。

Zhang Wenqing, ed. 1990. *A Dictionary of Chinese Policing.* Shenyang Publishing House, Shenyang. 张文清《中国警察辞典》，沈阳出版社。

Zhang Xibo and Han Yanlong. 1987. *A Legal History of the Chinese Revolution.* Vol. 1. Chinese Social Science Press, Beijing. 张希波，韩炎龙《中国革命法制史》，中国社会科学出版社。

Zhang Zhaoduan. 1993. "Some Strategic Thoughts on the Construction of Our Country's Police in the New Period." *Public Security Studies* 30, no. 4:25-29. 张兆端"关于我国新时期警察建设的战略思考"，《公安研究》。

Zhao Mingqiang and Yang Yuejin. 1991. Correspondence to *Public Security Studies* 15, no. 1:58. 赵明强，杨跃进《公安研究》。

Zhao Zhongtian. 1993. "A Partial Reminiscence of Public Security Cadre Work in the Taihang Area." In *Public Security Historical Materials*, vol. 30, ed. Public Security Historical Materials Collection Research Leadership Small Group Office. Unpublished material from the Ministry of Public Security, 202-7. 赵仲田"太行区公安局干部工作片断回忆" 公安部公安史资料征集研究领导小组办公室《公安史资料》。

Zheng Xuejia. 1976. *The Real Story of the Futian Incident.* Research Unit on Problems in International Communism, Taipei. 郑学稼《中共富田事变真相》，国际共产党问题研究室。

Zhen Yuegang and Guan Shuguang. 1993. *A Handbook on Public Security Internal Affairs.* Police Educational Publishing House, Beijing. 甄岳刚，管曙光《公安内勤工作手册》，警官教育出版社。

Zheng Yuhua and Cen Shengting, eds. 1992. *Joint Security Force Handbook.* Police Officer Education Publishing House, Beijing. 郑玉华，岑生挺编著《治安联防手册》，警官教育出版社。

Zhong Kan. 1982. *A Critical Biography of Kang Sheng.* Red Flag Press, Beijing. 仲侃《康生评传》，红旗出版社。

Zhou Changkang. 1994. "Theorizing Crime Control in the Fengqiao Community." *Research into Juvenile Crime* 141-42, no. 3-4:1-5. 周长康"论枫桥社区犯罪控制模式"，《青少年犯罪研究》。

Zhou Changyuan and Wang Yongzhe. 1999. "A Tentative Analysis of the Relationship between Crime and Inflation." *Public Security Studies* 64, no. 2:66–68. 周长源，王永哲"试论物价上涨与犯罪的关系"《公安研究》。

Zhou Enlai. 1981. *Selected Works of Zhou Enlai*. Vol. 1. Foreign Languages Press, Beijing.

Zhou Fengju. 1980. "Is Law Purely an Instrument in Class Struggle?" *Studies in Law*, no. 1:37–41. 周风举"法单纯是阶级斗争的工具吗？"，《法学研究》。

Zhou Rongzhao and Yang Ming. 1991. "A Brief Discussion of Profits, Losses, and Countermeasures Employed in the Enterprise Policing Structure." *Public Security Studies* 15, no. 1:49–50. 周容照，杨明"企事业公安机构的利弊及对策刍议"，《公安研究》。

Zhou Yongming. 1999. *Anti-drug Crusades in Twentieth-Century China: Nationalism, History, and State Building*. Rowan and Littlefield, Lanham, Md.

Zweig, David, et al. 1987. "Law, Contracts, and Economic Modernization: Lessons from the Recent Chinese Rural Reforms." *Stanford Journal of International Law* 23:319–64.

INDEX

Betrayal (continued)
purges, 36; and the Gao-Rao affair, 184;
and Jiang-xi style policing, 99–100; and
Kang Sheng, 121; overriding other con-
siderations, 36. See also "Enemy within";
Gao-Rao affair
Bi-gong-xin (forced confession), 14, 40–41,
82, 103; in anti-Trotskyite campaign,
103–104; banning, 126; Central Com-
mittee on, 74; in E-Yu-Wan base camp,
65; and Futian Incident, 46–48; and
Minxi base camp incident, 56; refusal to
commit, 119
"Big characters posters," 220
Bo Yibo, 88
Böckenförde, Ernst-Wolfgang, 201
Brothels, 151–152. See also Prostitution
Brugger, Bill, 166, 188, 190, 213, 218–219
Byron, John, 121

Cadres: banished, 229, 231; checking on,
73, 117–118, 123–124, 185, 191, 228–229
(see also Campaign to Check on Cadres);
and city takeovers, 110–113; importance
of "struggle" for, 6–7; in leadership
positions, 144; loyalty of, 203–204; in
police force, 144–145; in public security
committees, 286; "purity" of, 94; reading
of history, 8, 111; recall from banishment, 238; suspicions about, 34; training
of, 89–90, 102, 106–110, 127, 130
Campaign-style policing, 142–143, 259–260
Campaign to Check on Cadres (shengan
yundong), 73, 117, 120, 123
Campaign to Criticize Lin Biao and Confucius (pi Lin pi Kong yundong), 232,
235–236
Campaign to Eliminate Counter-
Revolutionaries (sufan), 33, 37–38, 52,
84, 131; "collective training" in, 209;
as excess, 70; interrogation techniques

of, 41; targeting of intellectuals, 65; in
Xiang-E'xi base camp, 59–60, 62. See
also Campaign to Suppress Counter-
Revolutionaries
Campaign to Learn from the People's
Liberation Army, 198
Campaign to seize power (duoquan yundong),
119, 224
Campaign to Study an All-Round Dictator-
ship of the Proletariat, 200, 235–236
Campaign to Study Lei Feng, 198, 217–218
Campaign to Suppress Counter-
Revolutionaries (zhenfan), 134–135, 141,
160–179; Mao's resolution to end, 172–
174; and reform, 168; Soviet advisors on,
163; targets of, 174. See also Campaign to
Eliminate Counter-Revolutionaries (sufan)
Campaign to Suppress Internal Counter-
Revolutionaries (neibu sufan yundong), 135,
174, 178–193, 203, 242–243
Campaigns: friend/enemy distinction in,
16; leadership in, 176; and legal system,
306–307; "professional," 187; as "too
Soviet," 179; transition in, 176. See also
specific campaigns (i.e., Campaign to
Eliminate Counter-Revolutionaries,
Three Antis Campaign, etc.)
Case-checking rectification campaign (xin
sanfan), 175
CCP. See Chinese Communist Party (CCP)
Cen Shengting, 291
Central Committee: on anti-Trotskyite campaign, 104; on bi-gong-xin, 74; and campaign against counter-revolutionaries,
158–159; on counter-espionage work,
124–125; and E-Yu-Wan base camp, 63;
eighth, 198, 213, 217; eleventh, 248; on
Futian Incident, 53; General Study Committee of, 114, 116; on Huxi Incident,
104–105; leadership in, 50; on Ministry
of Public Security, 193; on policing, 278;

on purges, 58; seventh, 169; sixth, 52, 72, 85; Social Section, 91–96; third, 50; on traitors, 102; on White Sparrow Garden Incident, 65

Central Social Section, 73, 91–96, 114, 290

Central Soviet government, 25, 42–54

Chaha'er, 171

Chants, political, 54–56

"Chats," with special agents, 40, 49

Cheek, Timothy, 115

Cheka, Chinese (Committees for the Elimination of Counter-Revolutionaries), 24, 38–42, 68

Chen, Albert, 264

Chen Du, 294

Chen Duxiu, 35, 68, 100–101

Chen Lida, 192

Chen Mingren, 150

Chen Pixian, 278

Chen Yi, 150, 181

Chen Yuanxiao, 283

Chen Yun, 104

Cheng Qian, 150

Chengqian bihou, zhibing jiuren ("Learn from past mistakes . . ."), 109

Chesneaux, Jean, 161

Chiang Kai-shek. *See* Jiang Jieshi (Chiang Kai-shek)

Children's Corps, 36–37

China Peasant Party, 186

Chinese Communist Party (CCP), 27; after Great Leap Forward, 211; birth of, 27; commitment to, 98–99, 130, 162–163; enemies of, 15–16, 30, 36 (*see also* Enemies; "Enemy within"); on errors of past, 68–69; established, 24, 25; and excess, 31–32, 315–316 (*see also* Excess); and fear of betrayal, 86; fleeing of, 24, 27–28; and friend/enemy distinction, 12, 29, 67, 129; histories of, 5–6; and internal protection system, 290; and the law,

201–202; "lenient" policy of, 125–126; and the mass-line, 14; membership in, 66, 106; moderation of, 141; moves to Yan'an, 72; national unity behind, 139–140; Nationalist Party campaign against, 74; peasants as "friends" of, 28; people's fear of, 65; and political intensity, 36–38, 252–253 (*see also* Intensity, political); response to purges, 8 (*see also* Purges); security organs of, 84–85 (*see also* Mass-line organs); and the Soviet Union, 213; takeover of cities, 110; and Trotskyism, 100. *See also* Central Committee

Chinese communists, purges of, 5–9, 27

Chinese language. *See* Language, Chinese

Chinese policing, history of, 20, 67–68. *See also* Policing

Chongqing, 171

Chuan-Shaan base camp, 37

Chujianbu (Elimination of Traitors Bureau), 87

Ci Jiwei, 6

"Circular Concerning the Prohibition of Opiates," 155–156

Cities: after economic reform, 296–297; "cleansing" of, 149–151; communist takeover of, 110–114

Class, language of, 304

Class background, 30–31, 46–47

Class enemies, 213–214

Class politics, 77

Class struggle, 235, 252, 304; and Cultural Revolution, 217, 224, 233; end of, 205; in Jiangxi base camp, 32, 78; Mao on, 201; questions of, 28; and revisionism, 216; in Soviet Union, 33–34

Class war, 129

Cleanup rates: for local police, 282; in 1970s, 238–239; for political cases, 206–207; using informants, 289. *See also* Arrests

matism of, 245, 254; rehabilitation of, 200, 239–240; "struggle" under, 252

Depoliticization, 251–252

Derrida, Jacques, 296

Detectives, and counterintelligence, 97–99

Detention powers, police, 275

Deviation, 68

Di Fei, 219

Dictatorship: all-round, 18, 200, 204, 233–238, 277; mass, 198, 227; policing as tool of, 269

Ding Ling, 115

"Directive on the Punishment of Counter-Revolutionaries," 167

"Directive on the Rectification Campaign," 190

"Directive to Suppress Counter-Revolutionary Activity," 170–171

Directives: on cleanups, 173–174; on counter-revolutionaries, 167, 170–171; "Double Ten," 134, 141, 167; on rectification, 190

Disciplinary power, 14–15, 107

Dog-beater brigades, 24

Dong Biwu, 142

Donggu, 48

"Don't execute a single one . . ." (slogan), 74, 127–128, 132

"Don't let one enemy agent through the net . . ." (slogan), 105, 131

"Don't let one spy from within escape . . ." (slogan), 131

"Don't miss one single enemy agent" (slogan), 102, 131

"Double Ten" directive, 134, 141, 167

Dousi pixie (struggle against self, criticize revisionism), 307

Drugs, campaign against, 134, 150–151, 155–161. See also Addicts, drug

Dual leadership system (tiaotiao kuaikuai), 279

Duan Dechang, 61

Duan Liangbi, 48–52

Duoquan yundong ("January storm"), 199, 224

Dutton, Michael, 137

E-Yu-Wan base camp, 116; A-B League in, 62–67; campaigns in, 25; influence of Soviets in, 33; purge in, 69; White Sparrow Garden Incident in, 13, 63–64

Earthquake, Tangshan, 241

Economic crimes, 19

Economic model, command, 163–164, 205

Economic policies, of Great Leap Forward, 196

Economic reform period, 262–265; activism in, 18; begins, 248; cities in, 296–297; counter-revolutionaries in, 270–271; crimes in, 256–258; and Deng Xiaoping, 262–263; and friend/enemy distinction, 300; household register system in, 289; intensity in, 314, 316; mass-line organs in, 261, 297; and mobility, 274; negative side effects from, 298–299; policing in, 255–256, 269–270; the political in, 12, 309; prostitution in, 280; protection units in, 291; rule of law in, 264–265, 298, 315

Economy: in Europe, 265–267; intensity unleashed on, 205–206; police work in defense of, 177–178, 239–240

Education: for police, 146–148; reform-through-education system, 189. See also Training

Eighth Route Army, 88–89, 103, 121

"Elements," suppression of, 170

Elimination campaigns, 83; in base camps, 33–36, 62–67; end of, 70; focus on traitors in, 72; and Great Leap Forward, 207–208; in Honghu area, 62; of Jiangxi period, 79 (see also Jiangxi period); mass-line, 73. See also specific

Luttidism, 267
Luxinan, 103–104

Ma Weigang, 151, 153, 156
Ma Xueli, 278, 284, 287
Macau, 140
Maine, Henry Sumner, 263, 309
Mangliu ("floating blind"), 256
Mao Dianliang, 152, 154
Mao Zedong: after Futian Incident, 52; ascent of, 81; attempts to assassinate, 150; on campaigns, 172–174; on checking cadres, 123, 125; on class struggle, 201, 235; and commitment politics, 315; on communes, 226, 233; and Cultural Revolution, 217, 221, 224, 228; death of, 200, 241; dictatorship of, 204–205; on enemies, 6–7, 15, 67; and excess, 66; and Futian Incident, 42–54; on Gao-Rao affair, 180–182; and Great Leap Forward, 219; on history as teacher, 6; and legal system, 202–203, 263–264, 304; on literature, 115; and Long March, 75; on loyalty, 94; and mass-line organs, 166, 195–196, 214; myth of, 76; *On New Democracy*, 73, 111; "Nine-Point Policy" of, 74, 125; "On Contradiction," 77, 81, 129; on policing, 139, 144; on public security work, 229–230; quotes of, 129; rebels opposing, 49–51; on rectification, 108, 114; "Resolution," 101; on sabotage, 183–184; and Schmitt, 303; *Selected Works*, 3, 311; and self-criticism, 307; slogans of, 74, 82, 132; on Soviet-style discipline, 190; thought of, 244; on "true art," 115; works of, 113; and the Yan'an spirit, 14; and Zhou Enlai, compared, 53–54
Maoism, 6, 110, 162
Marco Polo bridge incident, 72
Martyr, revolutionary, 7
Marx, Karl, 236, 267
Marxism, 111, 234, 252

Marxism-Leninism, 235–236
Mass democracy, 17, 224, 227, 233
Mass dictatorship, 198, 214–217, 227
Mass-line: elimination work, 73; end of, 247–300; in Great Leap Forward, 204–205; ideology, 139; and Party committees, 14
Mass-line organs: after economic reform, 261–262, 297, 299; for defense, 166–167; development of, 195–196; and leadership, 305; monetarization of, 283–288; vs expertise, 178
Mass-line policing: after Tian'anmen protests (1989), 271–272; commitment to, 19; and the contract, 272; learning from military, 244; and performance, 90; in war on drugs, 161; and work units, 165–166
"Mass surveillance and control" (*guanzhi*), 167–168, 175
Mauss, Marcel, 165
"May 30 Incident," 24
McGowan, John, 9
Medvedev, Roy Aleksandrovich, 33
Meier, Heinrich, 6–7, 307, 308
Meisner, Maurice, 231
Metaphors, rural, 137–138
Mimetic revolution, 253–254
Min Buying, 223
Minister of Public Security: deputy, 157, 183; Hua Guofeng as, 237; Luo Ruiqing as, 87, 134, 139; and rectification, 17; Xie Fuzhi as, 198
Ministry of Public Security, 135, 138–139, 143, 169; counter-revolutionaries in, 145–146; Great Leap Forward in, 198; leadership positions in, 144; leniency policy of, 160–161; and prisons, 168; "Public Security Six Points," 199; structure of, 193
Minxi base camp, 13, 25, 33, 53, 54–56
Mobility, 274, 298

Moderation, 79–80, 109, 113–117, 131, 141
Money, as motivator, 255–256
Monument to the People's Heroes, 240

Nanchang uprising, 24
Nanjing, 73, 112, 157, 159
Nationalist Party (Guomindang), 24; agents
of, 116, 180; attacks on base camps, 106–
107; campaign against CCP, 70, 74; "CC
faction," 97; and communist purges,
5; defection from, 29; defection to, 57;
disillusionment with, 35; encirclement
campaigns of, 25, 59–60; policing organs
of, 92–93; Reformist Faction of, 34–35,
58; and Shanghai massacre, 27; struggles
with, 6
Neibu sufan yundong (Campaign to Suppress
Internal Counter-Revolutionaries), 135,
174, 178–185, 203, 242–243
Networkers, 98–100
New China, 90
New Democracy, 132
Ni Minle, 294
Nie Rongzhen, 152
Nietzsche, Friedrich, 9
"Nine-Point Policy," 74, 125–126
Nixon, Richard, 200
"No one picked up others' things from the
road . . ." (lubushiyi, yebubihu), 256
Northern Bureau, 126–127
Northwest Political Protection Bureau, 72,
83, 84–85

Oestreich, Gerhard, 265
Ogden, Susanne, 161
"On Contradiction" (Mao Zedong), 15, 67,
77, 81, 129
On New Democracy (Mao Zedong), 73, 111
One Hundred Flowers campaign, 128,
190–191
110 emergency number, 249
"Open-door policy," 259

Opposing the Forced Extraction of Confessions,
Opposing Illegal Breaches of Discipline, 176
"Organizational Regulations of Resident
and Work Unit Security Committees,"
135

Pack, Robert, 121
Pan Hannian, 135, 150, 180, 182
Paris Commune, 225–226, 233
Pashukanis, Evgeny, 202, 300, 305–306,
308–310
Past, citing, 7–9, 68–69. See also History
Pastorlism, 110. See also Cities
Peasants, 28, 36–38, 43–45
Pell, Robert, 268
Peng Dehuai, 49–50, 91, 150, 211
Peng Zhen, 90, 104, 113, 170, 219
People's Armed Police, 145, 148–149
People's Daily (Renmin Ribao) (newspaper),
153, 163, 171, 264
People's Liberation Army, 113, 198, 211
People's Republic of China, 2, 134
Pi Lin pi Kong yundong (Campaign to Criticize
Lin Biao and Confucius), 232, 235–236
Pinyin system, 137. See also Language,
Chinese
PLA Daily, 218
Police / Policing: "best-practice," 279;
cadres, 8, 144–145, 228–229; campaign-
style, 142–143, 259–260; citing the past
in, 7–9; coercive administrative sanctions of, 188–189; in the countryside,
275; in Cultural Revolution, 220–222,
225, 231–232; and economic reform,
177, 178, 239–240, 269–270, 279; educating, 146–148; employing, 279–280;
enterprises requesting presence of, 292–
293; financial inducements for, 277–278,
283; financial pressure on, 281–282;
and Great Leap Forward, 205–213;
inadequacy of, 143–149; and informants,
288–290; Jiangxi-style, 99–100; local,

Three big transformations (*sanda gaizao*),
189
"Three mop-ups campaign" (*sanguang*
policy), 106
"Three represents" (Jiang Zemin), 250, 252
Tian'anmen Incident, 200, 238–242
Tian'anmen Square protests (1989), 20,
249, 271
Tianjin, 248
Tiaotiao kuaikuai (dual leadership system),
279
Tibet, 228
"Tight control within limits" (*yujin yuxian*),
153–155
Tongchuang Incident, 220–221
Torture, 14, 46. *See also* Bi-gong-xin (forced
confession)
"Total services," 165
"Toward a Dictatorship of Capitalist
Roaders" (Shi Yizhi), 237
Training, for cadres, 89–90, 106–113, 127
Traitors, elimination campaigns against,
72, 87, 102
Transient criminal activity (*liucuanfan*), 274
Trotsky, Leon, 35, 100–101
Trotskyism, 45, 100–102
Trotskyites, 80, 116
Two-line struggle, 195, 311–316

United Front: deterioration of, 94–96, 97,
131–132; end of, 27, 81; formation of,
24; growth of, 109; policing organs, 92–
93; policy, 80–81, 113, 130; second, 72;
United Frontism, 84, 305
United States, and Korean war, 140
Unity: national, behind CCP, 139–140;
political, 201–202; and threat of enemy,
307
USSR. *See* Soviet Union

Vagrants, campaign against, 150–151
Vyshinsky, Andrei Ianuaryevich, 306

Wan Shengzi, 280
Wang Dongxing, 121, 227
Wang Gongfan, 270, 271
Wang Hongming, 103–104
Wang Hongwen, 225–226, 241–242
Wang Jianhua, 5
Wang Jiaxiang, 52
Wang Jingwei, 180, 182
Wang Jinwei, 34, 73
Wang Jinxiang, 227–228
Wang Lianyou Incident, 221
Wang Ming: Bolshevik training of, 52, 58;
as Party leader, 25, 62, 68, 81
Wang Qiuxia, 37, 38
Wang Shiwei, 73, 80, 115
Wang Shuodao, 82, 83
Wang Suyuan, 121–122, 127–128
Wang Xuren, 103, 104
Wang Zhao, 227–228
Wang Zhongfang, 160, 162, 168, 260, 277
War of Austrian Succession, 266
"We don't fear heaven . . ." (slogan), 160
Weber, Max, 262–263, 273
Wei Dingyuan, 102–105
Western countries: police histories from,
8; policing strategies from, 18–19, 259,
300; security companies from, 294–295.
See also Europe
White Sparrow Garden Incident (*Baique-
yuan*), 13, 63–64
Wild Lilly (Wang Shiwei), 115
Women's Federation, 36–37
Women's Protection, Education and
Fostering Institutes (*Funü shengchan
jiaoyangyuan*), 152–153, 155, 280
Work units (*danwei*), 148, 164–165, 167, 208,
283
Wu Buyun, 264
Wu De, 121
Wu Faxian, 227
Wu Han, 218–219
Wu Zhongfei, 283

Wu Zhuozai, 54–55
Wufan. See Five Antis Campaign
Wuhan, 24, 112, 248, 277

Xia Xi, 58–59, 66
Xiafang (sent down to the countryside),
    205–206
Xi'an Incident, 72, 84
Xiang-E'xi base camp, 13; A-B League in,
    34–35; campaigns in, 25; dissolved,
    60–61; and Four High Tides of Repres-
    sion, 57–62; influence of Soviets in, 33;
    suspicion of cadres at, 34
Xiang Ming, 181
Xiang Ying, 50–52
Xie Fuzhi: calling on radicals, 198–199;
    banishment of, 229; and Cultural Revolu-
    tion, 228; as Minister of Public Security,
    211; and Public Security leadership
    purge, 219–220, 227; "Public Security Six
    Points," 224
Xie Hanchang, 47–48, 50
Xin sanfan (case-checking rectification
    campaign), 175
Xing Xiangsheng, 223
Xingdongtan (detectives), 98–99
Xu Hanmin, 272, 277–278
Xu Huanmin, 177
Xu Jinshen, 63–64
Xu Linxiang, 115–117, 123
Xu Zirong, 156, 183, 222, 227–228

Yan Xishan, 87–88
Yan'an: disciplinary power in, 15; limiting
    excess in, 71–132; and Long March, 76;
    Party HQ moves to, 72; raids in, 122
Yan'an model, 192
Yan'an period, 15, 70, 129; army during,
    244; defining, 78; enemies during, 79;
    excess in, 100; map of, 76; moderation
    in, 79–80, 109, 113–117, 131; political
    theater in, 90; radicalization of, 109–110;

revolutionary techniques of, 254; security
    work in, 79–80
Yan'an spirit, 14
Yang Dongping, 138
Yang Fan, 135, 180–181
Yang Guomao, 57
Yang Jie, 150
Yang Ming, 293
Yang Qiqing, 87, 139, 206, 227–228
Yang Zhaoming, 270, 271
Yao Wenyuan, 218, 225–226, 235, 241–242
Ye Huaming, 294
Ye Jianying, 113, 149–150
Ye Ming, 297
Yichang police, 283
Yigebusha, dadoubuzhua ("Don't execute a
    single one . . ."), 127–128
Yin Qi, 180–182
Ying Hongbiao, 221, 224
Yiqie xiangqiankan (socialism, forward march
    of), 256
Yu Lei, 141, 150, 167–168, 183, 211, 227, 229,
    238, 282–283
Yujin yuxian ("tight control within limits"),
    153–155

Zeng Fanzheng, 49, 52, 55, 58–59, 61, 218
Zhandoudui (combat battalions), 222–223
Zhang Chunqiao, 224–226, 235, 241–243
Zhang De, 62
Zhang Dingcheng, 56, 66
Zhang Guotao, 64–66, 69
Zhang Keqin, 120–121
Zhang Lie, 223
Zhang Min, 296–297
Zhang Mingzhe, 207, 217
Zhang Pinghua, 40
Zhang Shuyi, 264
Zhang Weiguo, 263
Zhang Xibo, 34, 38
Zhang Xihou, 57
Zhang Zuolin, 5

Michael Dutton is a reader in political science at the
University of Melbourne. He also has an appointment as a
professor of politics at Goldsmiths College, University of
London. He is the author of *Policing and Punishment in China:
From Patriarchy to "The People"* and *The Crisis of Marxism
in China*, and is the editor of *Streetlife China*.

Library of Congress Cataloging-in-Publication Data
Dutton, Michael Robert.
Policing Chinese politics : a history / Michael Dutton.
p. cm.— (Asia-Pacific)
Includes bibliographical references and index.
ISBN 0-8223-3477-1 (cloth : alk. paper) —
ISBN 0-8223-3489-5 (pbk. : alk. paper)
1. Internal security—China—History—20th century.
2. Political persecution—China—History—20th century.
3. Interpersonal relations—China—History—20th century.
4. China—Politics and government—20th century.
I. Title. II. Series.
HV6295.C5D88 2005   363.2'3—dc22
2004029838